廣東出土五代至清文物

Archaeological Finds from the Five Dynasties to the Qing Periods in Guangdong

廣東省博物館 • 香港中文大學文物館聯合主辦
Jointly presented by the Guangdong Provincial Museum and
the Art Gallery, The Chinese University of Hong Kong

香港中文大學文物館
一九八九年三月十八日至五月十四日
18th March to 14th May, 1989
the Art Gallery, The Chinese University of Hong Kong

鳴謝

文物館承本港熱心人士贈資成立出版基金，本圖錄得以出版印行，謹此致謝。

Acknowledgement

The publication of this catalogue was made possible by the Art Gallery Publication Revolving Fund.

廣東出土五代至清文物

出版：廣東省博物館
　　　香港中文大學文物館

國際統一書碼：962-7101-13-3

印刷：鮑思高印刷公司

一九八九年三月初版

版權所有・不得翻印

Archaeological Finds from the Five Dynasties to the Qing Periods in Guangdong

Copyright© 1989 by the Guangdong Provincial Museum and the Art Gallery, the Chinese University of Hong Kong.

All rights reserved.

ISBN 962-7101-13-3

Printed by Don Bosco Printing Co.

目錄
Contents

前言
Forewords ……………………………… 6

展品簡目
List of Exhibits ………………………… 10

年表、地圖
Chronology and Map …………………… 14

展品圖版
Colour plates …………………………… 17

展品說明
Entries of Exhibits ……………………… 49

廣東出土的五代至明清陶瓷（曾廣億）
Five Dynasties to Qing Ceramics Found in
　　Guangdong (Zeng Guangyi) ……… 139

廣東瓷器與國內外瓷窰的關係（楊少祥）
Guangdong Ceramics and Their Relationships
　　with Other Chinese and Foreign Wares
　　(Yang Shaoxiang) ………………… 169

淺析廣東古代陶罈（朱非素）
Studies on Ancient Pottery Urns of
　　Guangdong (Zhu Feisu) …………… 183

淺談南華寺木雕像座銘文（黃玉質）
On the Wooden Lohan Inscriptions Found in
　　Nanhua Temple (Huang Yuzhi) …… 194

潮州展品小識（饒宗頤）
Notes on Finds from Chaozhou
　　(Jao Tsung-i) ……………………… 199

主要參考書目
Selected Bibliography ………………… 203

前　言

　　廣東省博物館與香港中文大學文物館自一九八四年以來,以考古資料,按照歷史發展的順序,先後舉辦了《廣東出土先秦文物》、《廣東出土晉至唐文物》展覽,還有廣州市博物館亦與香港中文大學文物館舉辦的《穗港漢墓出土文物》展覽,這些展覽均受到各屆人士好評。這次再度合作,舉辦《廣東出土五代至清代文物》展覽,將為香港各屆人士全面了解廣東歷史發展的概貌提供方便。

　　五代,劉龑於公元917年在廣州稱帝,國號大越,次年改為漢,歷五十五年,史稱"南漢"。這一時期出土的文物不多。在廣州石馬村發現一座磚室墓,分前室、過道、主室三部分。出土的器物有瓷器、銅鐵器、漆器、石器和殘絲織物等,其中青釉瓷器造形美觀、釉色晶瑩,是這一時期青瓷中罕見的精品,另在陽春縣發現"乾亨重寶"石錢範(廣州也有發現"乾亨重寶"鉛錢及鐵花盆等)。據史料記載,我國歷史上以"乾亨"為年號的帝王有兩個,一是五代十國時期南漢高祖劉岩(917—925年),一是遼景宗耶律賢(979—983年)。遼統轄地域不包括廣東,因此,這個"乾亨"應是劉龑的年號。

　　宋元時期,廣東出土文物主要來自瓷窰和墓葬。宋代是我國瓷器發展史上的繁榮時期。廣東是古代對外貿易的重要門戶,有利於陶瓷業的發展。這時期的窰址分布全省各地,目前發現的窰址有幾百處之多。其中潮州筆架山,廣州西村、惠州、南海、海康、遂溪等沿海窰場成為廣東地區重要的陶瓷生產基地。南海縣官窰,主要生產彩繪青釉瓷器,是目前我省最早發現的釉下彩瓷器,為陶瓷裝飾技術開闢了新的途徑。海康發現的窰址分布在南渡河兩岸,瓷窰的產品主要是生活用具,瓷胎多為灰白,施青白或青黃釉,部分窰的瓷器印有蓮花、菊花等紋飾或彩繪赭紅色花紋。其中有十多座窰發現的彩繪瓷器,與過去海康縣發現宋元時期墓葬出土的器物相似。這次展出的瓷器是這一時期的精美作品。

　　宋代墓葬的結構除保留磚室外,出現了石槨、灰沙墓。隨葬品主要是瓷器,有的墓還有隨葬端硯,十二生肖俑等,以及圓雕和浮雕石質青龍、白虎、鳳、雞等器物。這時期的墓葬仍沿襲火葬習俗。出土的魂罐造形美觀,有仿亭、塔等建築形式,外表施釉,飾有蓮花紋、水波紋和附加堆紋。元代墓葬發現較少,僅在順德縣大良鎮發現一座雙棺男女合葬磚石結構墓,出土器物有陶罐、鐵剪、銀器和銅錢等器物。

　　明清時期的墓葬,比較注意墓外的裝飾,一般都設有半圓形拜堂,明代墓葬用石灰、沙加糯米飯等夯築,結構堅固緊密。隨葬品主要有絲織品,服裝、鞋襪、金飾品、石印章、筆墨、曲本和繪有花卉、山水、花鳥的扇面等器物。清代墓葬較為重要的是大埔縣吳六奇墓,該墓出土了有,傢具、俑、炊器、賭具、案、轎等陶塑模型。這些模型,形象地反映了吳六奇生前坐堂,出巡和內庭生活的情況。陶塑人物神態生動,造形逼真,是清代陶瓷工藝的精品。這一時期,由於海外貿易的拓展,陶瓷市場擴大,陶瓷業又得到恢復和發展。在明代中晚期,廣東瓷器大量輸出,在非洲、阿曼、新加坡、印尼等地均有發現廣東石灣、饒平九村、大埔窰場的產品。在清代除了日用瓷、建築瓷外,還出現工藝水平很高的藝術瓷。突出的有佛山石灣窰等。為了滿足海外貿易的需求,在饒平九村窰還出土有外商來樣定貨的樣品,這標誌着廣東陶瓷發展的新水平。

　　這次《廣東出土五代至清代文物》展覽的籌備工作,得到香港中文大學文物館鼎力支持,謹此表示深切的謝意。

廣東省博物館

Preface

Since 1984 the Guangdong Provincial Museum and the Art Gallery of the Chinese University of Hong Kong have launched a series of joint archaeological exhibitions devoted to the Pre-Qin and Jin to the Tang periods. With the Guangzhou Museum, the Art Gallery also mounted a highly successful exhibition of archaeological finds from Han tombs both in Guangzhou and Hong Kong. This present exhibition, "Archaeological Finds from the Five Dynasties to the Qing Periods in Guangdong" is another co-operative project along the same line and represents the final stage in this chronological study of the local culture and history of Guangdong.

In AD917 during the Five Dynasties period Liu Gong proclaimed himself emperor of the Dayue (after one year this was changed to Han) kingdom in Guangzhou. This regime, lasted for fifty-five years, is generally known as the Nanhan (Southern Han). Few cultural relics of this period were discovered in Guangdong. The only exception is a brick tomb in Shimacun, Guangzhou. The tomb was separated into front and main chambers, connected by a passage. Funerary objects unearthed range from fragmentary textile, ceramics, lacquerware to stone carvings and bronzes. The green glazed stoneware utensils are of exceptional quality. Apart from these, stone moulds for coins of the "*Qianheng*" reign were discovered in Yangchun county; lead "*Qianheng*" coins and iron flowers pots were also discovered in Guangzhou. "*Qianheng*" occurred twice in the history of China. One belonged to Liu Yan, Emperor Gaozu of the Southern Han (AD917 - 925) and the other was Yalu Xian, Emperor Jingzong of the Liao in northern China (AD979 -983). As the territory of Liao didn't reach Guangdong, therefore this "*Qianheng*" reign must be that of Liu Yan of Nanhan.

For the Song and Yuan periods the majority of the finds came from kiln and burial sites. The Song period was a most prosperous era in the history of Chinese ceramics and Guangdong, as an important doorway for overseas trade, provided an additional injection for the flourish of ceramic industry for export. Kiln sites of this period scattered all over the province. Those discovered so far amount to several hundreds, with important centres at Bijiashan, Chaozhou; Xicun, Guangzhou; Huizhou, Nanhai, Haikang and Suiqi, all situated along the coastal regions. The main products of the Nanhai Guanyao are green glazed ware with underglaze painting, the earliest occurrence of this innovative technique in Guangdong. The other major centre of underglaze painted wares is Haikang. The kiln remains are found along the banks of the Nandu River. The products are mainly daily utensils with a greyish body glazed in bluish white or yellowish green. The decorative techniques include underglaze painting and impressed designs of lotus and chrysanthemun. Brown painted wares were found in more than a dozen sites in Haikang and they are very similar to the ceramic finds unearthed in nearby Song and Yuan burials. The pieces selected for this exhibition are fine examples of this period.

In the Song period, apart from brick tombs, tombs built of stone or sandy mortar were also found in Guangdong. The main funerary objects were ceramics and in some tombs Duanqi inkslabs as well as stone carvings of the animals of the zodiac and the four quarters were also found. As in the Tang period the custom of cremation prevailed in the Song dynasty and very elaborate cremated ash containers were produced. Some of them were modeled after architectural structures, glazed and appliqued with relief bands of lotus flowers and wavy bands. Very few tombs of the Yuan period are found. The only example is the twin coffin burial in Daliangzhen, Shunde County. From this tomb pottery jars, iron scissors, silver ware and copper coins were unearthed.

For tombs of the Ming and Qing periods, more sophisticated above-ground structures were built. The most usual form is an arched altar and the tomb is normally made of lime, sand mixed with glutinous rice to form a hard mortar with rammed earth. Funerary objects range from textile, costumes, shoes and stockings, gold ornaments, to stone seals, brushes, inks, drama manuscripts and album leaves of paintings on fan. The most important tomb of the Qing period is that of Wu Liuqi in Dapu County. From that tomb three sets of pottery figurines were found, depicting the official as well as private lives of the early Qing elites. All of these figurines were finely modeled and realistically rendered.

As a result of the expansion of overseas trade, ceramic industry revived and flourished. Large quantities of porcelain and stoneware from Shiwan, Jiucun and Dapu were exported to Africa, Aman, Singapore and Indonesia. Products include not only daily utensils and architectural parts but also decorative items such as stoneware figures from the Shiwan kiln in Foshan. To cater for the taste of overseas buyers, some of the products were specially made according to foreign designs and samples. One such specimen, probably brought to Guangdong by foreign customers was found in the Jiucun kiln site in Raoping. This indicates a new and advance internal organization of the ceramic industry in Guangdong.

The preparation as well as the mounting of this present exhibition of "Archaeological Finds from the Five Dynasties to the Qing Periods in Guangdong" has been made possible with the support and co-operation of the Art Gallery, the Chinese University of Hong Kong. To all staff members of the Art Gallery we express our heartfelt thanks and appreciation.

Guangdong Provincial Museum.

前　言

　　《廣東出土五代至清文物》，由廣東省博物館及香港中文大學文物館聯合主辦。這次展覽標誌著本館與廣東省及廣州市文博機構合作分期介紹廣東歷代考古成果的一系列計劃的完成。連同曾經舉辦的《廣東出土先秦文物》、《穗港漢墓出土文物》和《廣東出土晉至唐文物》展覽，全面展現了從新石器時代至清代悠長歷史的文化遞邅之迹，為嶺南文化鈎劃出較為清晰的斷代輪廓，更實現了本館創辦以來致力發揚鄉梓文化的願望。欣幸之餘，銘感難忘的更是與粵方專家在學術交流合作上建立起來的深固友誼。

　　是次展覽的範圍，包括了五代南漢至清朝近千年的出土文物，乃從全省各地的遺址徵集所得，亦有來自窖藏和採集。在總數共一百一十二項的展品中，粵方提供一百項，以陶瓷為大宗，兼及金、銀、銅、鐵、鉛、玉、石、竹、木、水晶、玻璃、紙、布等質料。展品的造型和種類是歷次最豐富的，包括食具、水具、貯藏器、明器、葬具、建築構件、漁獵工具、銅鏡、錢幣、衣物、飾物、摺扇、文房、曲本，以至雕塑、書畫等，頗能反映各時期廣東的生活風俗、經濟生產、貿易交通和工藝水平。

　　一般而言，歷史時期愈後，由於傳世文物和史迹增多，考古發掘的重要性相應減低，尤以明清兩代為然。但對於僻處邊陲的地域來說，出土文物仍然有助於填補傳世文物的斷代空白，且能更鮮明地反映各時代的生活實況。清初高官吳六奇墓出土的大批陶俑和陶塑模型，即能生動地呈現吳六奇生前坐衙、出巡和內宅生活的場面，便是極佳的例子。

　　至於本地出土的港方展品，則來自赤鱲角深灣、沙洲、大嶼山稔樹灣、石壁、竹篙灣、糧船灣沙咀、佛堂門、東龍島、大埔、粉嶺等地，亦是以陶瓷為主。香港這一段時期的考古資料，雖不及史前時期的豐富，也能提供不少歷史證物。例如遺址中出土的瓷器與破片，當與海外貿易有關，而沙咀明代沉船的發現，其中出土的泰國及馬來半島的陶片，則具體地說明了華南與東南亞貿易的關係。

　　展覽的籌備工作，由兩館共同承擔。展覽專刊的出版，荷蒙廣東省博物館朱非素女士、黃玉質、曾廣億、楊少祥諸位先生，和我校中國文化研究所饒宗頤教授惠撰鴻文，使是次展覽更具學術價值。本館同寅則負責展品攝影及本刊的編印與英譯工作。

　　是次展覽荷蒙中國國家文物事業管理局、廣東省文化廳、廣東省博物館鼎力支持，香港新華通訊社協助聯絡，又承市政局香港博物館及香港古物古蹟辦事處惠借珍藏，以及中國文化研究所陳方正所長多方指導，謹此敬致謝忱。

高美慶
香港中文大學文物館

Foreword

The exhibition of *Archaeological Finds from the Five Dynasties to the Qing Periods in Guangdong*, jointly organized by the Guangdong Provincial Museum and the Art Gallery of the Chinese University of Hong Kong, marks the final phase of a long-term co-operative project to introduce to the people of Hong Kong the archaeology of Guangdong in a historical sequence. Together with three previous exhibitions devoted to earlier periods, the exhibition series traces the development of local history and culture in Guangdong from the Neolithic period to the Qing dynasty. They present visual documents of Lingnan culture and define more clearly its characteristics in each period. The completion of this exhibition project is indeed a joyous occasion, bringing us closer to our objective of studying and promoting Guangdong culture. But what moves us more greatly is the friendship with the experts in Guangdong that has developed as a result of years of academic exchanges and co-operation.

The present exhibition covers almost one thousand years of history, beginning with the regional kingdom of Southern Han in the Five Dynasties to the Qing period. All the exhibits contributed by the Guangdong Provincial Museum are gathered from archaeological sites in different regions of the province, supplemented by some items recovered from caches and archaeological surveys. Ceramics appear to dominate the scene, though other materials such as gold, silver, bronze, iron, lead, jade, stone, bamboo, wood, crystal, glass, paper and cotton are well represented. The types and forms of the exhibits are the most comprehensive so far, including food and water utensils, storage jars, funerary objects, architectural parts, tools, mirrors, coins, clothing, ornaments, fans, scholar's articles and dramatic script, in addition to sculpture, painting and calligraphy. Together they not only testify to the rich material culture of China since the tenth century, but also shed light on the daily life and customs in the Guangdong region, its economic production, trade, and transportation, as well as the achievement of its craftsmen.

Generally speaking, the importance of archaeological discoveries gradually diminishes in later historical periods, particularly in the Ming and Qing dynasties. This is because of the greater number of cultural relics and historical monuments from these periods surviving to this day. But for regions in the remote corners of the empire, archaeological finds are still useful in filling some of the gaps in the artifacts passed down from ancient times. Moreover, they are capable of projecting a more vivid image of the past. A very good example can be found in the pottery figurines and models excavated from the tomb of Wu Luiqi, a high official of the early Qing period, which group together to form scenes of *yamen*, procession and household life.

As for exhibits from Hong Kong, they are selected from archaeological finds from Shenwan of Chilajiao (Shum Wan, Chek Lap Kok), Shazhou (Sha Chau), Nianshuwan (Nim Shu Wan), Shibi (Shek Pik), Zhugaowan (Penny's Bay) of Dayushan (Lantau Island), Shazui of Liangchuanwan (Sha Tsui, High Island), Fotangmen (Joss House Bay), Donglong Fort (Tung Lung), Dapu (Taipo) and Fengling (Fanling). Ceramics are again the largest group. Though archaeological materials from the period covered by the present exhibition cannot be compared to those of the pre-historical periods, they nevertheless provide important data for the study of Hong Kong history. The excavated potteries and sherds tell us about the overseas trade engaged at that time, while the discovery of Thai and Malay pottery sherds, among Chinese wares of the sixteenth century, in a Ming wreck in Shazui gives concrete evidence for the trading links between South China and Southeast Asia.

The present exhibition is again a combined effort of the Guangdong Provincial Museum and the Art Gallery. The scholarly essays contributed by Mr. Huang Yuzhi, Mr. Zeng Guangyi, Ms. Zhu Feisu and Mr. Yang Shaoxiang of the Guangdong Provincial Museum and Professor Jao Tsung-i of this University bring to this monograph the latest research results of Guangdong archaeology. The Art Gallery staff is mainly responsible for photographing the exhibits and the publication of this monograph.

Without the support and co-operation of the Chinese Administrative Bureau of Museums and Archaeological Data, the Department of Culture of Guangdong Province and the Guangdong Provincial Museum, this project could not have been possible. We would also like to thank the Xinhua News Agency (Hong Kong Branch) for their assistance. To Hong Kong Museum of History of the Urban Council and the Antiquities and Monuments Office we offer a special vote of appreciation for the loan of the Hong Kong exhibits. Last but not least, we wish particularly to thank Dr. F.C. Chen, Director of the Institute of Chinese Studies, for his encouragement and guidance.

Mayching Kao
The Art Gallery
The Chinese University of Hong Kong

展品簡目

1	南漢　夾耳青瓷罐　廣州石馬村出土
2	南漢　六系青瓷罐　廣州石馬村出土
3	南漢　六系釉陶罐　廣州石馬村出土
4	南漢　六系陶罐　廣州石馬村出土
5	南漢　陶龍首構件　廣州石馬村出土
6	南漢　鐵花盆　廣州市出土
7	南漢　鉛錢　廣州市出土
8	南漢　石錢範　陽春縣出土
9	宋　菊花人物瓷罐　海康縣出土
10	宋　"桃花洞裏"瓷罐　海康縣出土
11	宋　"長命富貴"瓷罐　海康縣出土
12	宋　"彩繪軍持"、壺　南海縣出土
13	宋　"青瓷壺二件　海康縣出土
14	宋　點彩小碗　瓊海縣出土
15	宋　白瓷碗　崖縣出土
16	宋　青瓷碟、缽、碗　海康縣出土
17	宋　雙魚洗二件　西沙羣島,潮州市出土
18	宋　瓷盒　西沙羣島出土
19	宋　瓷瓶　西沙羣島出土
20	宋　荷花瓷枕　海康縣出土
21	宋　菊花蝴蝶瓷枕　海康縣出土
22	宋　詩詞瓷枕　海康縣出土
23	宋　彩繪瓷棺　海康縣出土
24	宋　青瓷罐　遂溪縣出土
25	宋　瓷罈　化州縣出土
26	宋　陶罈　東莞縣出土
27	宋　陶罈　珠海市出土
28	宋　陶罈　陽春縣出土
29	宋　彩繪陶瓶　佛山市出土
30	宋　陶爐　揭陽縣出土
31	宋　瓷盤、碗、壺　香港赤鱲角出土
32	宋　瓷片　香港沙洲出土
33	宋　陶生肖俑　海康縣出土
34	宋　城磚　海康縣出土
35	宋　瓦當　揭陽縣出土
36	宋　銀鋌　南雄縣出土
37	宋　銅錢　香港赤鱲角出土
38	宋　銀手鐲　東莞縣出土
39	宋　王大寶銅鏡　潮州市出生
40	宋　銅鏡　揭陽縣出土
41	宋　鐵投槍　順德縣出土
42	宋　鐵魚鏢　順德縣出土
43	宋　鐵鏃　順德縣出土
44	宋　琴式端硯　佛山市出土
45	宋　抄手端硯　高要縣出土
46	宋　石雕像　紫金縣出土
47	宋　木雕羅漢　曲江縣出土
48	元　彩繪瓷罐　海康縣出土
49	元　瓷罐　順德縣出土
50	元　青釉瓷罐　梅州市出土
51	元　瓷壺　遂溪縣出土
52	元　青瓷碗、碟　珠海市出土
53	元　青瓷大洗　潮州市出土
54	元　鐵魚鏢　順德縣出土
55	元　青釉高足杯　梅州市出土
56	宋/元　瓷片　香港稔樹灣出土
57	宋/元　青瓷片　香港石壁出土
58	元　雙耳瓷瓶　遂溪縣出土
59	元　醬釉瓷瓶　海康縣出土
60	元　三足爐　海康縣出土
61	元　彩繪枕　海康縣出土
62	元　彩繪陶瓶　深圳市出土
63	元　陶罈　揭陽縣出土
64	元　磚刻像　海康縣出土
65	元　銅鈔版　揭西縣出土
66	元　銅官印　南雄縣出土
67	明　彩繪瓷罐　海康縣出土
68	明　綠釉罐　中山市出土
69	明　刻花罐　中山市出土
70	明　綠釉罐　東莞縣出土
71	明　青瓷罐　大埔縣出土
72	明　青釉瓷碗　惠東縣出土
73	明　青瓷盤　化州縣出土
74	明　青瓷碗碟　大埔縣出土
75	明　青花碗碟　海康縣出土
76	明　瓷片　香港竹篙灣出土
77	明　蓋罐　香港石壁出土
78	十六世紀　陶片　香港沙咀出土
79	明　瓷騎牛人塑像　惠東縣出土
80	明　磚雕　陽春縣出土
81	明　墓誌銘　海康縣出土
82	明　修城磚　潮州市出土
83	明　金飾　普寧縣出土
84	明　銅鼓　揭陽縣出土
85	明　銅銃　高要縣出土
86	南明　鐵炮　香港佛堂出土
87	明　銅官印　揭陽縣出土
88	明　銅錠　西沙羣島出土
89A	明　銅錢　東沙羣島出土
89B	明　銅錢　西沙羣島出土
90	明　天王像　南雄縣出土
91	明　鐵香爐　揭陽縣出土

92	明	琵琶記抄本	揭陽縣出土
93	明	描金紙扇	大埔縣出土
94	明	百褶裙	揭西縣出土
95	清	青花罐	東莞縣出土
96	清	青花罐	開平縣出土
97	清	青花罐	西沙羣島出土
98	清	青花碗、碟、	汕頭市出土
99	清	青花杯	汕頭市出土
100	清	青花碗、碟、杯	大埔縣出土
101	清	瓷片	香港大埔出土
102	清	青花盤	大埔縣出土
103	清	和合二仙塑像	揭陽縣出土
104	清	陶坐衙模型	大埔縣出土
105	清	陶出巡模型	大埔縣出土
106	清	陶內庭生活模式	大埔縣出土
107	清	木官印	南澳縣出土
108	清	鐵鐘	香港粉嶺採集
109	清	彈丸、瓷片	香港東龍島出土
110	清	印章、印盒	陸豐縣出土
111	清	珠飾、玉環	潮州市出土
112	清	紙褶扇	潮州市出土

(除特別註明外,展品均由廣東省博物館借出)

LIST OF EXHIBITS

1. Covered jar with crossed handle, Southern Han, from Shimacun, Guangzhou.
2. Jar with looped handles, Southern Han, from Shimacun, Guangzhou.
3. Pottery jar with looped handles, Southern Han, from Shimacun, Guangzhou.
4. Pottery jar with looped handles, Southern Han, from Shimacun, Guangzhou.
5. Architectural part, Southern Han, from Shimacun, Guangzhou.
6. Iron flower pot, Southern Han, from Guangzhou City.
7. Lead cash coins, Southern Han, From Guangzhou City.
8. Stone moulds for coins, Southern Han, from Yangchun County.
9. Pot with brown painting, Song, from Haikang County.
10. Pot with brown painting, Song, from Haikang County.
11. Covered pot with brown painting, Song, from Haikang County.
12. Brown painted *kendi* and ewer, Northern Song, from Nanhai County.
13. Green glazed ewers, Southern Song, from Haikang County.
14. Small bowl with brown spots, Song, from Hainan Island.
15. Porcelain bowl, Song, from Hainan Island.
16. Green glazed dish and bowls, Southern Song, from Haikang County.
17. Celadon double-fish basins, Song, from Paracels and Chaozhou.
18. Covered porcelain box, Northern Song, from Paracels.
19. Green glazed bottle, Northern Song, from Paracels.
20. Pillow painted in brown, Song, from Haikang County.
21. Pillow painted in brown, Song, from Haikang County.
22. Pillow painted in brown, Song, from Haikang County.
23. Coffin painted in brown, Song, from Haikang County.
24. Porcelain weight in green glaze, Song, from Suiqi County.
25. Covered urn, Song, from Huazhou County.
26. Covered urn, Northern Song, from Dong'guan City.
27. Pottery urn, Song, from Zhuhai City.
28. Pottery urn, Song, from Yangchun County.
29. Brown painted vase, Song, from Foshan City.
30. Pottery basin, Song, from Jieyang County.
31. Dish, bowls and ewer, Song, from Chilajiao, Hong Kong.
32. Ceramic sherds, Song, from Shazhou, Hong Kong.
33. Pottery zodiac figures, Song, from Haikang County.
34. City wall bricks, Southern Song, from Haikang County.
35. Rooftile terminals, Song, from Jieyang County.
36. Silver ingots, Song, from Nanxiong County.
37. Copper coins, Song, from Chilajiao, Hong Kong.
38. Pair of silver bracelets, Northern Song, from Dong'guan City.
39. Bronze mirror, Southern Song, from Chaozhou City.
40. Two bronze mirrors, Song, from Jieyang County.
41. Iron spearheads, Song, from Shunde County.
42. Iron javelin heads for fishing, Song, from Shunde County.
43. Iron arrowheads, Song, from Shunde County.
44. Inkstone, Song, from Foshan City.
45. Inkstone, Song, from Gaoyao County.
46. Stone figures, Northern Song, from Zijin County.
47. Wooden *lohans*, Qingli, Northern Song, from Qujiang County.
48. Covered jar, Zhiyuan, Yuan, from Haikang County.
49. Covered jar, Zhizhen, Yuan, from Shunde County.
50. Green glazed jar, Yuan, from Meizhou City.
51. Stoneware ewer, Yuan, from Suiqi County.
52. Green glazed bowls and dishes, Yuan, from Zhuhai City.
53. Large celadon basin, Yuan, from Chaozhou.
54. Celadon basin, Yuan, from Jieyang County.
55. Celadon stemcups, Yuan, from Meizhou City.
56. Ceramic sherds, Song/Yuan, from Nianshuwan, Hong Kong.
57. Celadon sherds, Song/Yuan, from Shibi, Hong Kong.
58. Vase with twin handles, Yuan, from Suiqi County.
59. Brown glazed vase, Yuan, from Haikang County.
60. Tripod censer, Yuan, from Haikang County.
61. Painted pillow, Yuan, from Haikang County.
62. Painted vase, Yuan, from Shenzhen City.
63. Pottery urn, Yuan, from Jieyang County.
64. Inscribed tomb brick, Yuan, from Haikang County.
65. Bronze printing block, Yuan, from Jiexi County.
66. Bronze official seal, Zhiyuan, Yuan, from Nanxiong County.
67. Covered jar, Ming, from Haikang County.
68. Green glazed jar, Ming, from Zhongshan City.
69. Covered jar, Ming from Zhongshan City.
70. Green glazed jar, Ming, from Dong'guan County.
71. Celadon jar, Ming, from Dapu County.
72. Green glazed bowls, Ming, from Huidong County.
73. Celadon dishes, Ming, from Huazhou County.
74. Bowls and dishes, Ming, from Dapu County.
75. Blue and white bowl and dish, Ming, from Haikang County.
76. Ceramic sherds, Ming, from Penny's Bay, Hong Kong.
77. Covered jar, Ming, from Shibi, Hong Kong.
78. Ceramic sherds, 16th century, from High Island, Hong Kong.
79. Figurine on buffalo, Ming, from Huidong County.
80. Bricks, Ming, from Yangchun County.
81. Pottery tomb tablet, Wanli, Ming, from Haikang County.
82. City wall bricks, Ming, from Chaozhou City.
83. Gold ornaments, Ming, from Puning County.
84. Bronze drum, Ming, from Jieyang County.
85. Bronze gun, Ming, from Gaoyao County.

86 Iron cannon, Southern Ming, from Fotangmen, Hong Kong.
87 Bronze official seal, Chongzhen, Ming, from Jieyang County.
88 Copper ingot, Ming, from Paracels.
89 Copper cash coins, Ming, from Paracels and Dongsha Islands.
90 Iron Guardian figures, Wanli, Ming, from Nanxiong County.
91 Iron censer, Ming, from Jieyang County.
92 *Pipa ji* manuscript, Jiajing, Ming, from Jieyang County.
93 Folding fan, Wanli, Ming, from Dapu County.
94 Pleated skirt, Ming, from Jiexi County.
95 Covered jar, Qing, from Dong'guan County.
96 Covered jar, Qing, from Kaiping County.
97 Blue and white dish, Qing, from Paracels.
98 Blue and white dishes and bowl, Qing, from Shantao City.
99 Blue and white cups, Qing, from Shantao City.
100 Blue and white cups, dish and bowls, Qing, from Dapu County.
101 Ceramic specimens, Qing, from Dapu, Hong Kong.
102 Blue and white stem-dish, Qing, from Dapu County.
103 Pottery figurines, Qing, from Jieyang County.
104 Set of yamen figures, Kangxi, Qing, from Dapu County.
105 Pottery figurines, Kangxi, Qing, from Dapu County.
106 Pottery figurines, Kangxi, Qing, from Dapu County.
107 Wooden seal, Qing, from Nan'ao County.
108 Iron bell, Kangxi, Qing, from Fengling, Hong Kong.
109 Cannon balls and blue and white porcelain, Qing, from Donglong Fort, Hong Kong.
110 Stone seals and glass box, Qing, from Lufeng County.
111 Crystal necklace and jade bracelet, Guangxu, Qing, from Chaozhou City.
112 Folding fan, Guangxu, Qing, from Chaozhou City.

(Unless otherwise mentioned, exhibits are from the collection of the Guangdong Provincial Museum)

年代表
Chronology

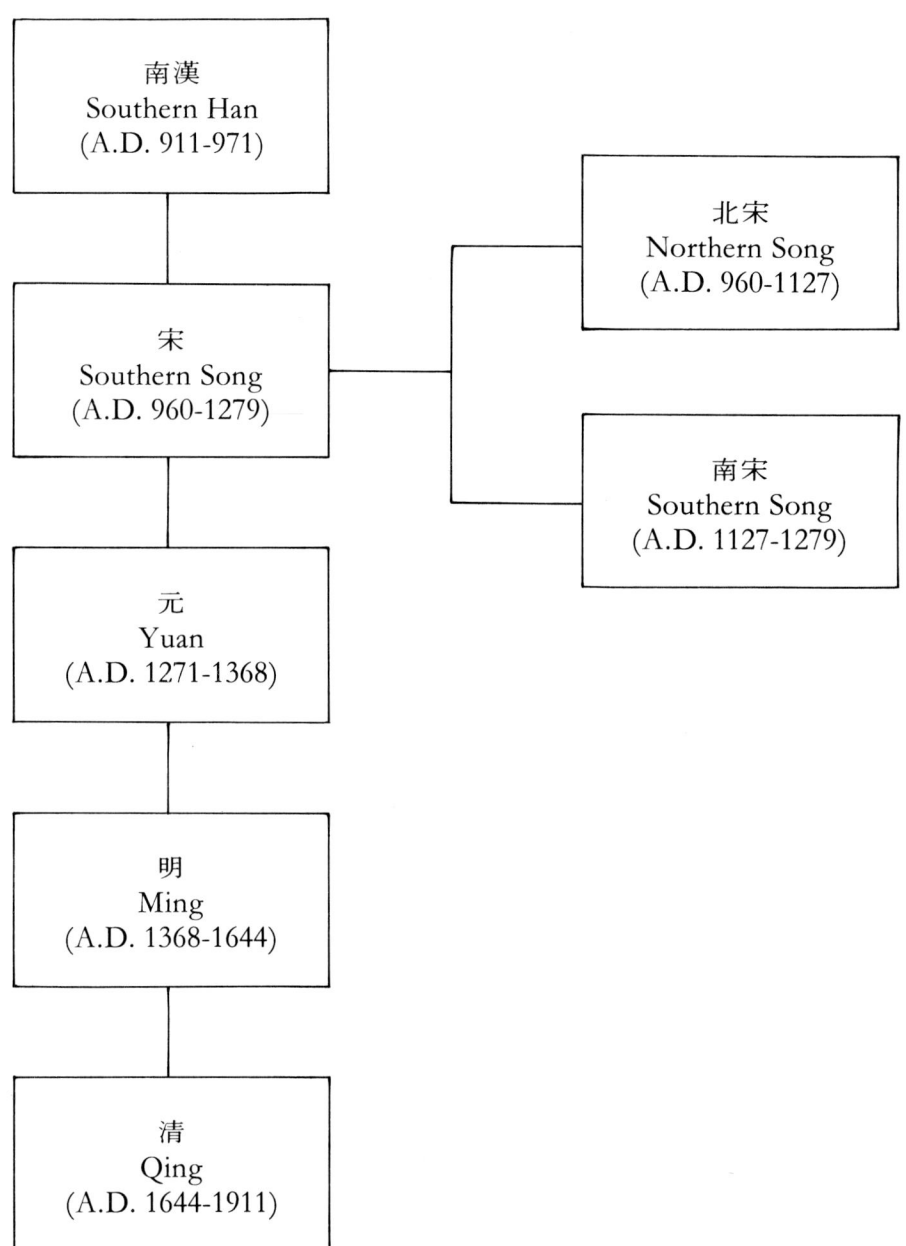

廣東五代至清墓葬窯址圖
Five Dynasties to Qing Tomb and Kiln Sites

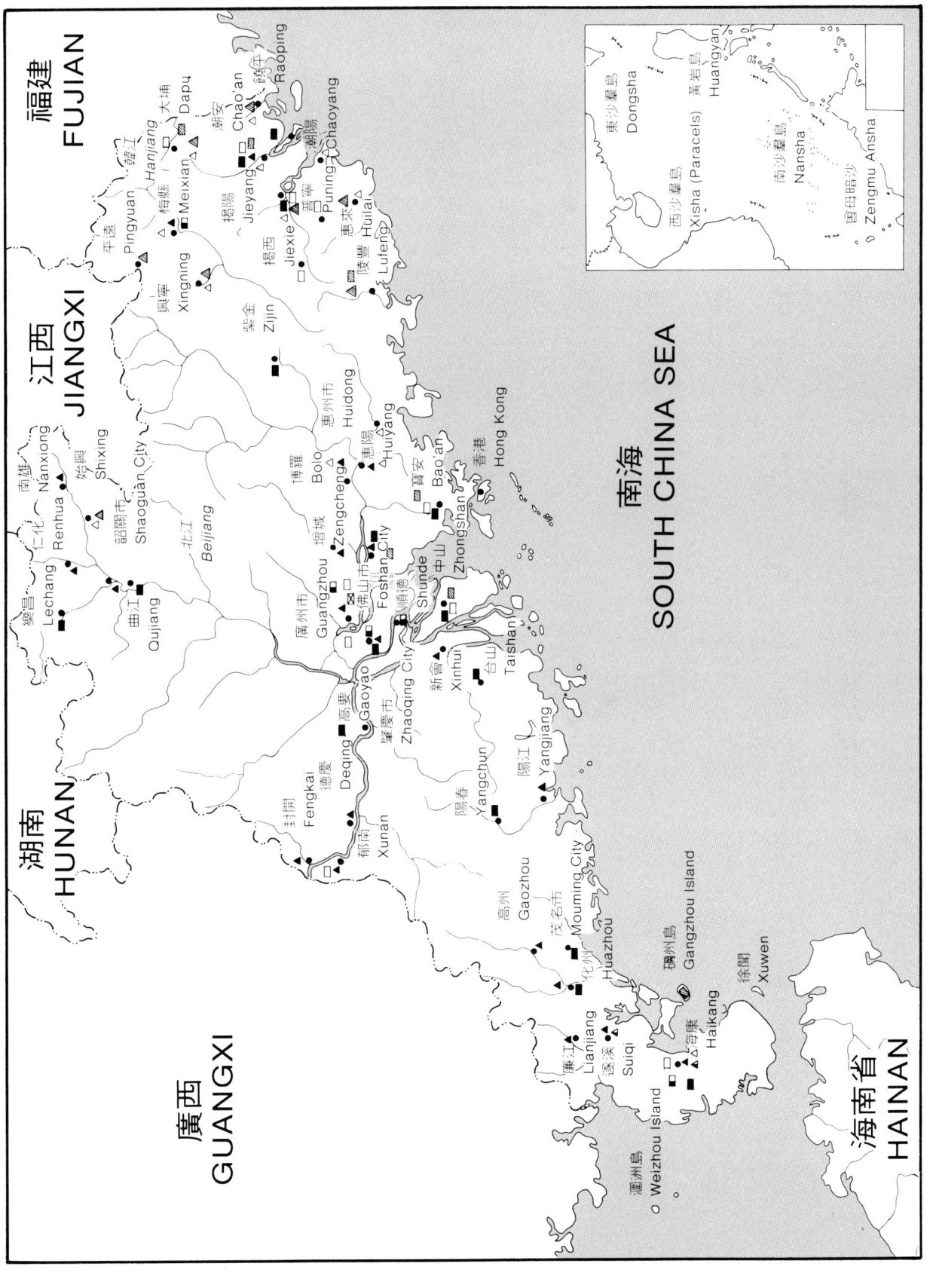

1
南漢 夾耳青瓷罐 廣州石馬村出土
Covered jar with crossed handle, Southern Han, from Shimacun, Guangzhou.

2
南漢 六系青瓷罐 廣州石馬村出土
Jar with looped handles, Southern Han, from Shimacun, Guangzhou.

3
南漢 六系釉陶罐 廣州石馬村出土
Pottery jar with looped handles, Southern Han, from Shimacun, Guangzhou.

4
南漢 六系陶罐 廣州石馬村出土
Pottery jar with looped handles, Southern Han, from Shimacun, guangzhou.

5
南漢 陶龍首構件 廣州石馬村出土
Architectural part, Southern Han, from Shimacun, Guangzhou.

6
南漢 鐵花盆 廣州市出土
Iron flower pot, Southern Han, from Guangzhou City.

7
南漢 鉛錢 廣州市出土
Lead cash coins, Southern Han, From Guangzhou City.

8
南漢 石錢範 陽春縣出土
Stone moulds for coins, Southern Han, from Yangchun County.

9
宋　菊花人物瓷罐　海康縣出土
Pot with brown painting, Song, from Haikang County.

10
宋　"桃花洞裏"瓷罐　海康縣出土
Pot with brown painting, Song, from Haikang County.

11
宋　"長命富貴"瓷罐　海康縣出土
Covered pot with brown painting, Song, from Haikang County.

12
宋 彩繪軍持、壺 南海縣出土
Brown painted *kendi* and ewer, Northern Song, from Nanhai County.

13
宋 青瓷壺二件 海康縣出土
Green glazed ewers, Southern Song, from Haikang County.

14
宋 點彩小碗 瓊海縣出土
Small bowl with brown spots, Song, from Hainan Island.

15
宋 白瓷碗 崖縣出土
Porcelain bowl, Song, from Hainan Island.

16
宋 青瓷碟、鉢、碗 海康縣出土
Green glazed dish and bowls, Southern Song, from Haikang County.

17
宋　雙魚洗二件　西沙羣島　潮州市出土
Celadon double-fish basins, Song, from Paracels and Chaozhou.

18
宋　瓷盒　西沙羣島出土
Covered porcelain box, Northern Song, from Paracels.

19
宋　瓷瓶　西沙羣島出土
Green glazed bottle, Northern Song, from Paracels.

20
宋　荷花瓷枕　海康縣出土
Pillow painted in brown, Song, from Haikang County.

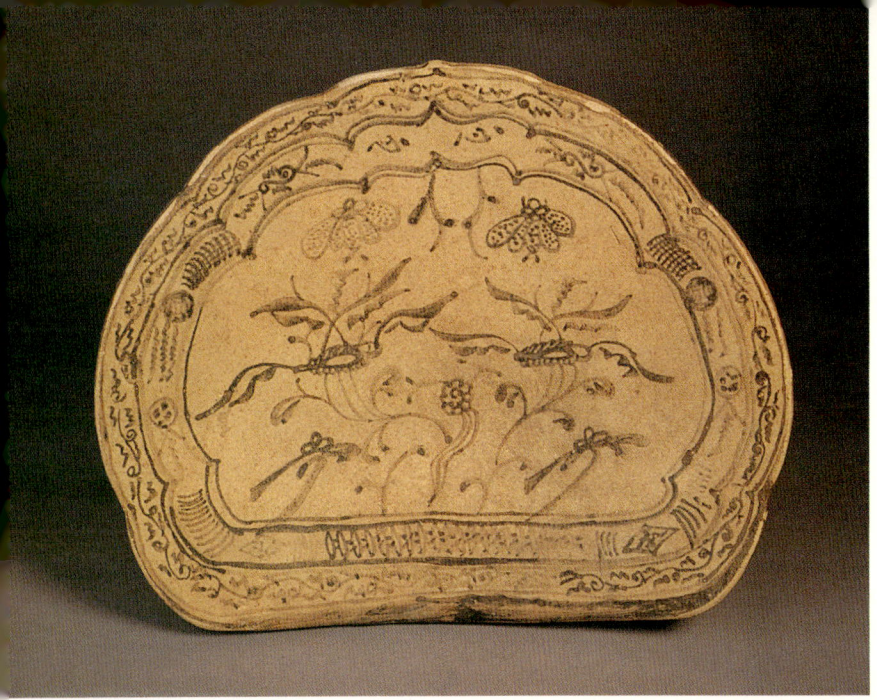

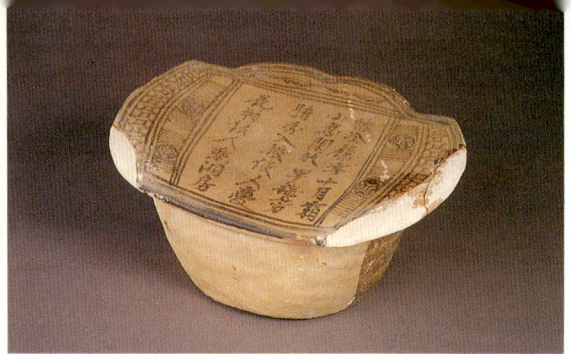

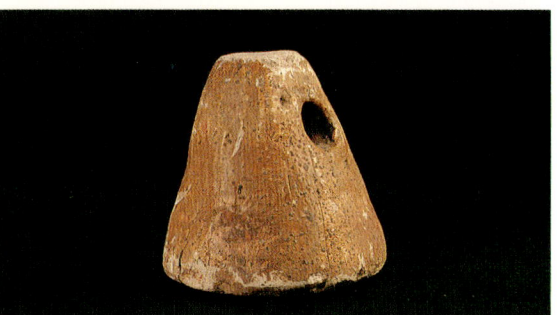

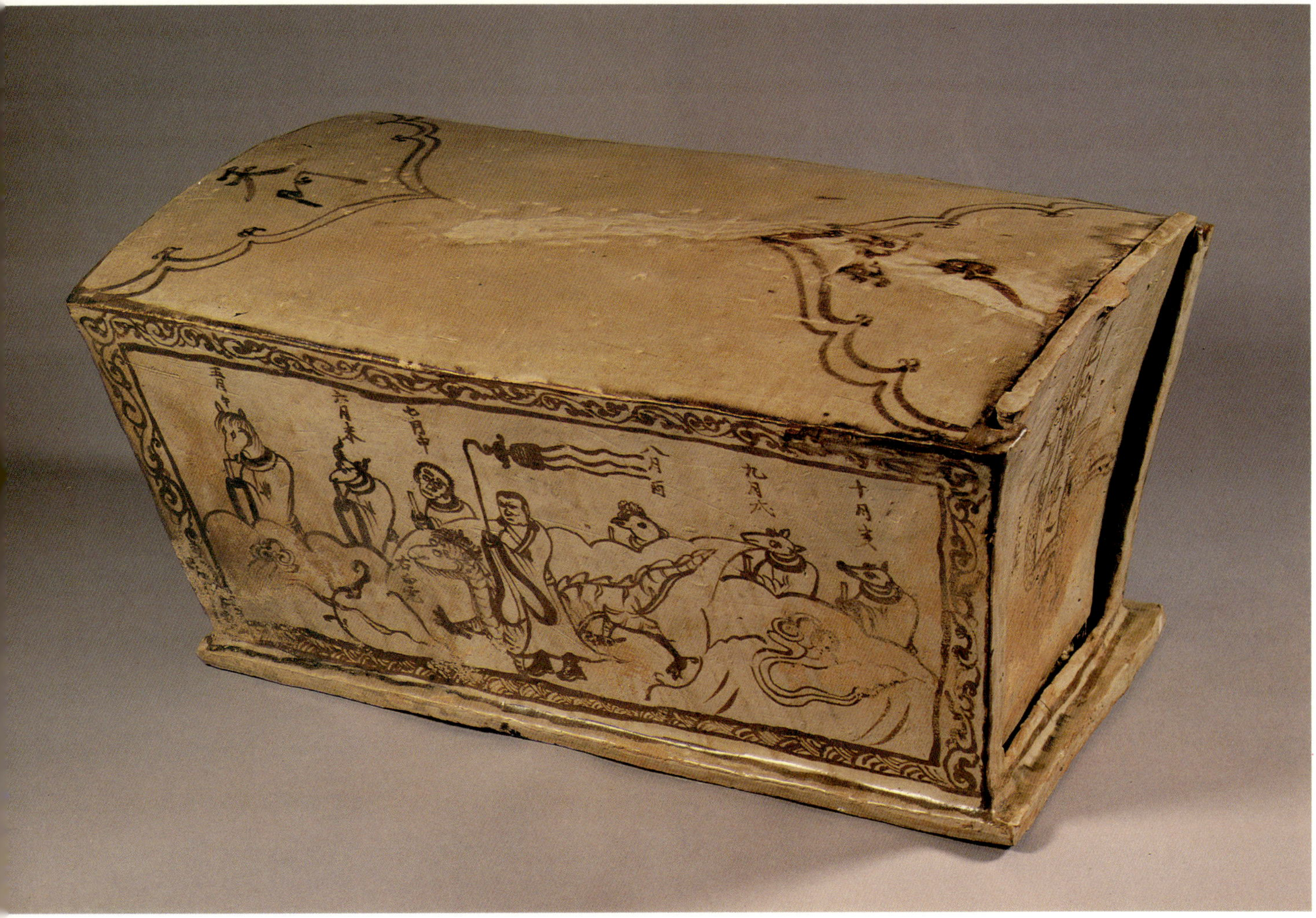

21
宋　菊花蝴蝶瓷枕　海康縣出土
Pillow painted in brown, Song, from Haikang County.

22
宋　詩詞瓷枕　海康縣出土
Pillow painted in brown, Song, from Haikang County.

23
宋　彩繪瓷棺　海康縣出土
Coffin painted in brown, Song, from Haikang County.

24
宋　青瓷權　遂溪縣出土
Porcelain weight in green glaze, Song, from Suiqi County.

21 | 22
24
23

25
宋　瓷罈　化州縣出土
Covered urn, Song, from Huazhou County.

26
宋　陶罈　東莞縣出土
Covered urn, Northern Song, from Dong'guan City.

27
宋　陶罈　珠海市出土
Pottery urn, Song, from Zhuhai City.

28
宋　陶罈　陽春縣出土
Pottery urn, Song, from Yangchun County.

29
宋 彩繪陶瓶 佛山市出土
Brown painted vase, Song, from Foshan City.

30
宋 陶爐 揭陽縣出土
Pottery basin, Song, from Jieyang County.

31
宋 瓷盤、碗、壺 香港赤臘角出土
Dish, bowls and ewer, Song, from Chilajiao, Hong Kong.

32
宋 瓷片 香港沙洲出土
Ceramic sherds, Song, from Shazhou, Hong Kong.

33

宋　陶生肖俑　海康縣出土
Pottery zodiac figures, Song, from Haikang County.

34

宋　城磚　海康縣出土
City wall bricks, Southern Song, from Haikang County.

35

宋　瓦當　揭陽縣出土
Rooftile terminals, Song, from Jieyang County.

36

宋　銀鋌　南雄縣出土
Silver ingots, Song, from Nanxiong County.

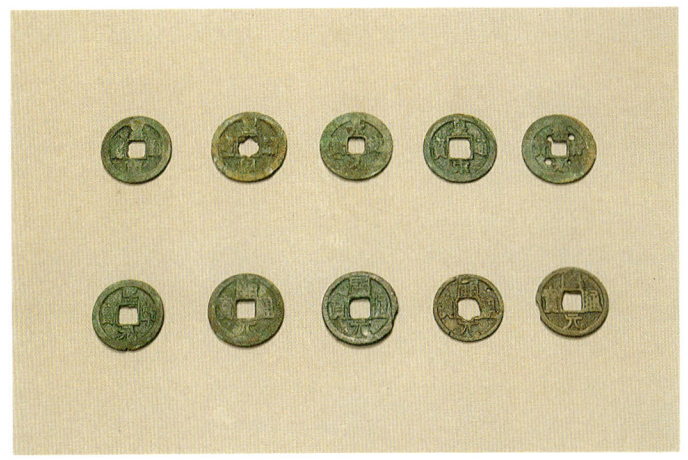

37
宋 銅錢 香港赤臘角出土
Copper coins, Song, from Chilajiao, Hong Kong.

38
宋 銀手鐲 東莞縣出土
Pair of silver bracelets, Northern Song, from Dong'guan City.

39
宋 王大寶銅鏡 潮州市出土
Bronze mirror, Southern Song, from Chaozhou City.

40
宋 銅鏡 揭陽縣出土
Two bronze mirrors, Song, from Jieyang County.

| 41 | 42 | 43 | 44 |
| | | | 45 |
| 46 |

41
宋 鐵投槍 順德縣出土
Iron spearheads, Song, from Shunde County.

42
宋 鐵魚鏢 順德縣出土
Iron javelin heads for fishing, Song, from Shunde County.

43
宋 鐵鏃 順德縣出土
Iron arrowheads, Song, from Shunde County.

44
宋 琴式端硯 佛山市出土
Inkstone, Song, from Foshan City.

45
宋 抄手端硯 高要縣出土
Inkstone, Song, from Gaoyao County.

46
宋 石雕像 紫金縣出土
Stone figures, Northern Song, from Jijin County.

47
宋　木雕羅漢　曲江縣出土
Wooden lohans, Qingli, Northern Song, from Qujiang County.

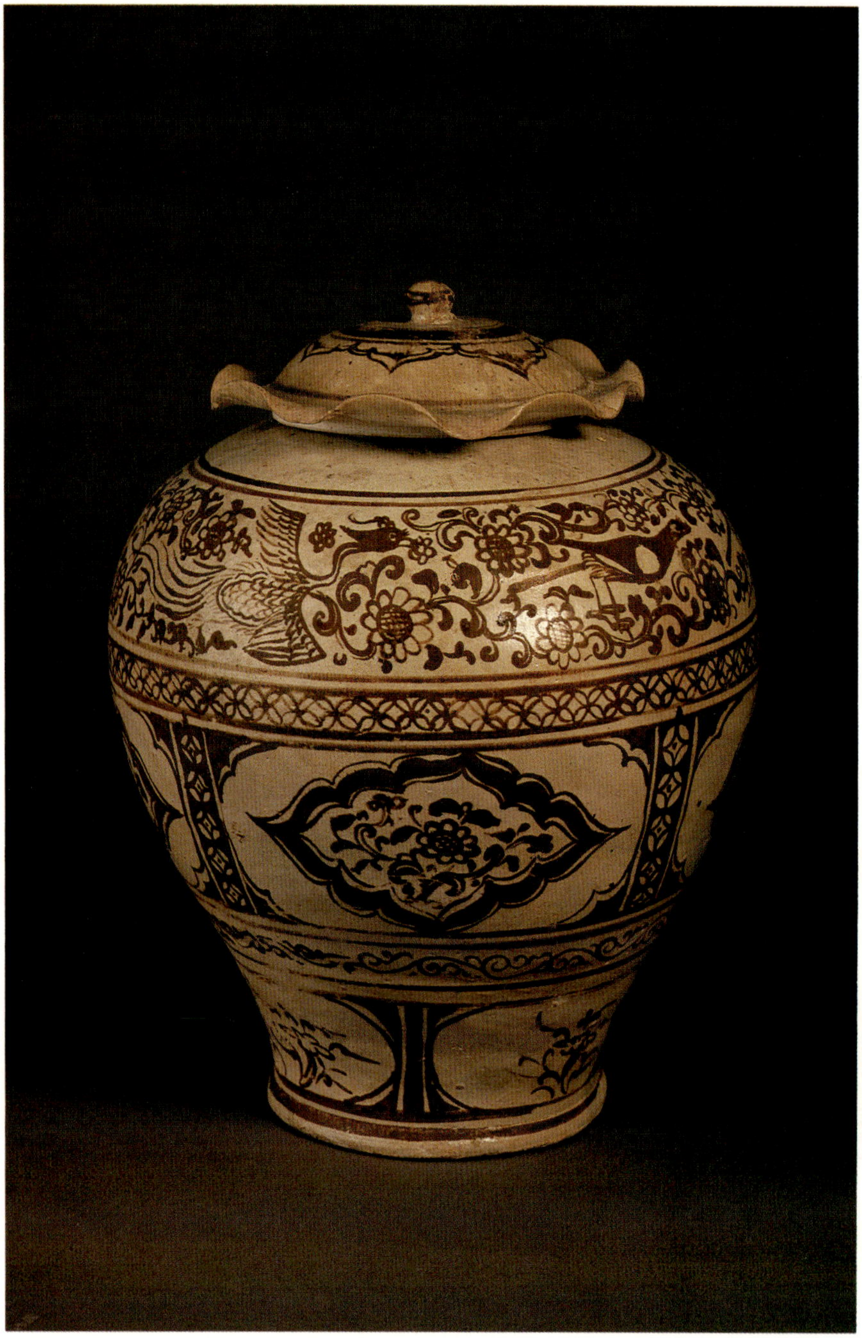

	50
48	49
	51

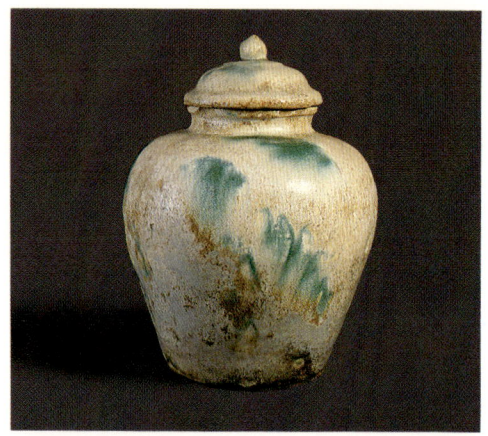

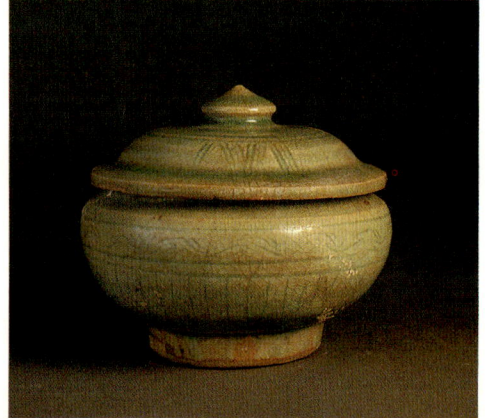

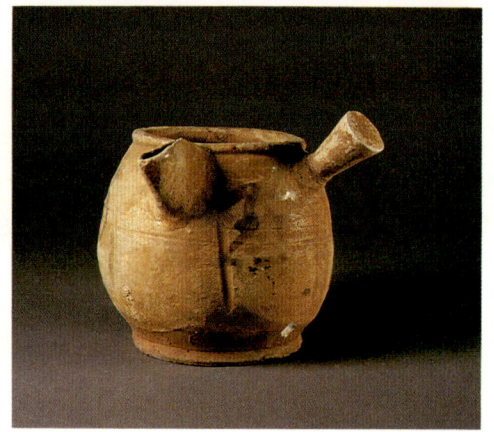

48

元　彩繪瓷罐　海康縣出土

Covered jar, Zhiyuan, Yuan, from Haikang County.

49

元　瓷罐　順德縣出土

Covered jar, Zhizhen, Yuan, from Shunde County.

50

元　青釉瓷罐　梅州市出土

Green glazed jar, Yuan, from Meizhou City.

51

元　瓷壺　遂溪縣出土

Stoneware ewer, Yuan, from Suiqi County.

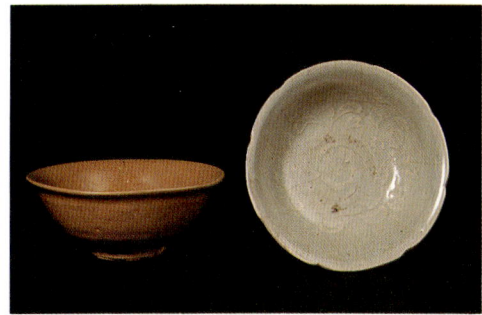

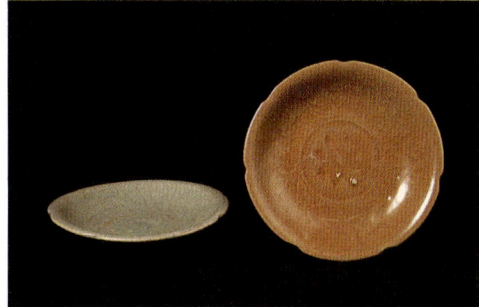

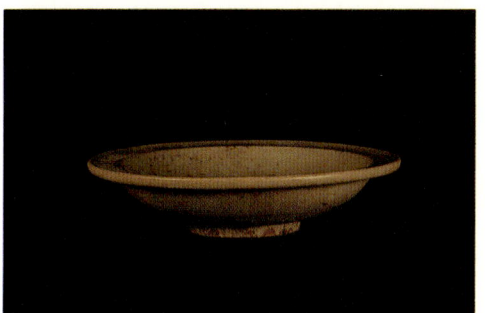

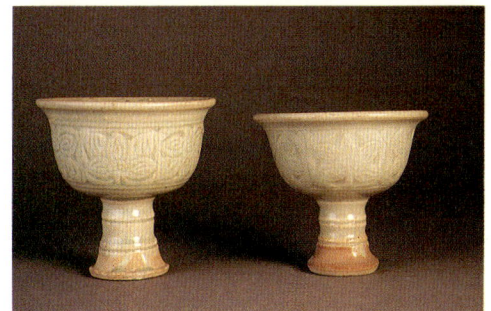

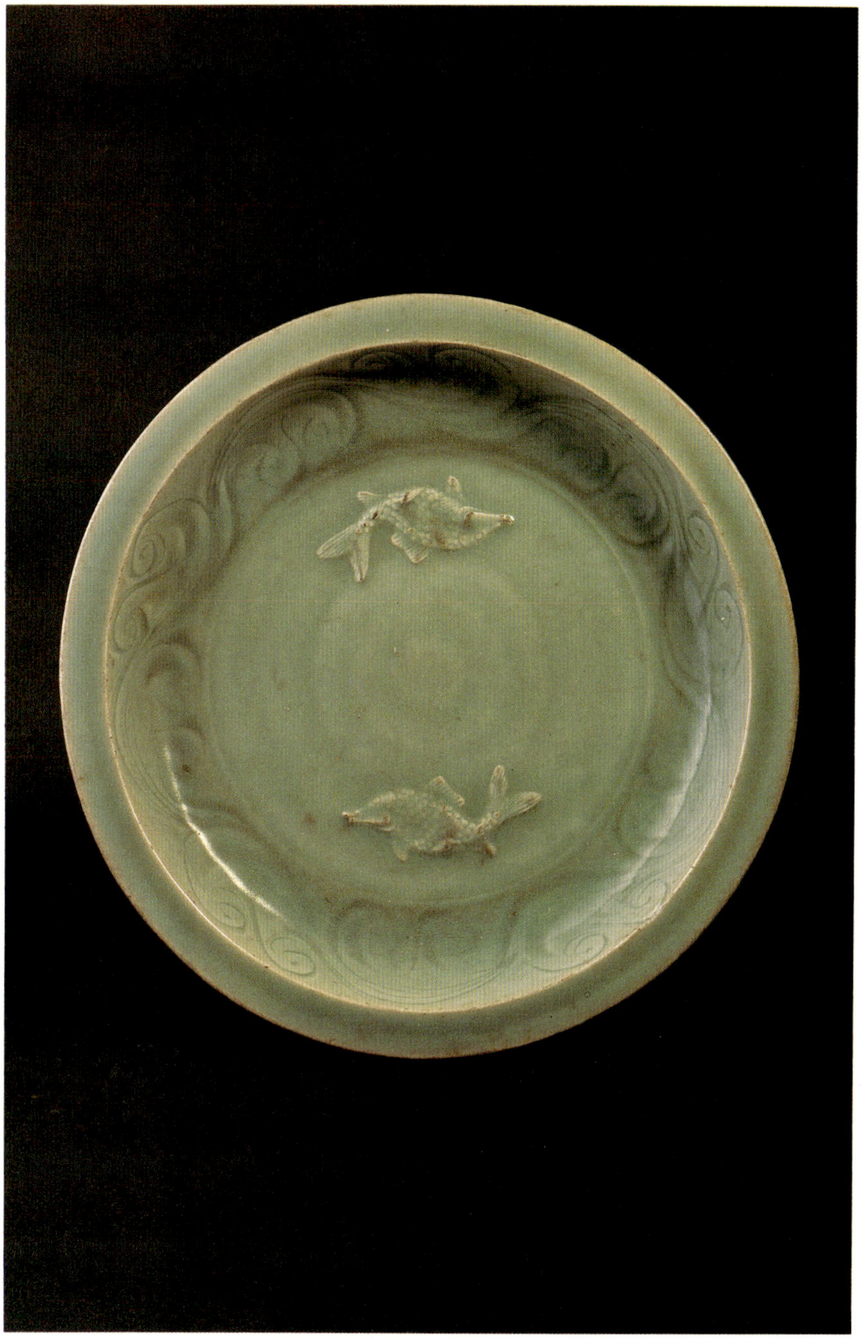

52
52
53
54
55

52

元　青瓷碗、碟　珠海市出土

Green glazed bowls and dishes, Yuan, from Zhuhai City.

53

元　青瓷大洗　潮州市出土

Large celadon basin, Yuan, from Chaozhou.

54

元　青瓷洗　揭陽縣出土

Celadon basin, Yuan, from Jieyang County.

55

元　青釉高足杯　梅州市出土

Celadon stemcups, Yuan, from Meizhou City.

56
宋/元　瓷片　香港稔樹灣出土
Ceramic sherds, Song/Yuan, from Nianshuwan, Hong Kong.

57
宋/元　青瓷片　香港石壁出土
Celadon sherds, Song/Yuan, from Shibi, Hong Kong.

58	59	60
	61	

58
元 雙耳瓷瓶 遂溪縣出土
Vase with twin handles, Yuan, from Suiqi County.

59
元 醬釉瓷瓶 海康縣出土
Brown glazed vase, Yuan, from Haikang County.

60
元 三足爐 海康縣出土
Tripod censer, Yuan, from Haikang County.

61
元 彩繪枕 海康縣出土
Painted pillow, Yuan, from Haikang County.

62
元　彩繪陶瓶　深圳市出土
Painted vase, Yuan, from Shenzhen City.

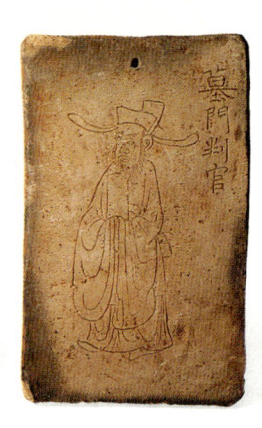

63
元 陶罈 揭陽縣出土
Pottery urn, Yuan, from Jieyang County.

64
元 磚刻像 海康縣出土
Inscribed tomb brick, Yuan, from Haikang County.

65
元 銅鈔版 揭西縣出土
Bronze printing block, Yuan, from Jiexi County.

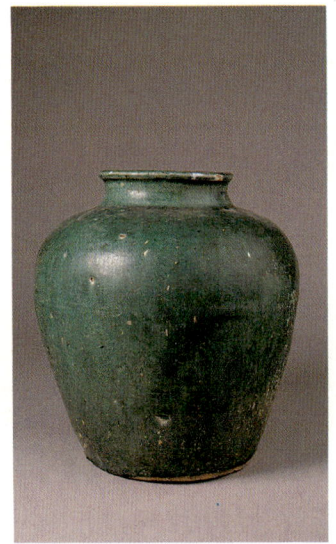

	66	67	
68	69	70	71

66
元 銅官印 南雄縣出土
Bronze official seal, Zhiyuan, Yuan, from Nanxiong County.

67
明 彩繪瓷罐 海康縣出土
Covered jar, Ming, from Haikang County.

68
明 綠釉罐 中山市出土
Green glazed jar, Ming, from Zhongshan City.

69
明 刻花罐 中山縣出土
Covered jar, Ming from Zhongshan City.

70
明 綠釉罐 東莞縣出土
Green glazed jar, Ming, from Dong'guan County.

71
明 青瓷罐 大埔縣出土
Celadon jar, Ming, from Dapu County.

72	74	
	73	75
76	77	

72
明　青釉瓷碗　惠東縣出土
Green glazed bowls, Ming, from Huidong County.

73
明　青瓷盤　化州縣出土
Celadon dishes, Ming, from Huazhou County.

74
明　青瓷碗碟　大埔縣出土
Bowls and dishes, Ming, from Dapu County.

75
明　青花碗碟　海康縣出土
Blue and white bowl and dish, Ming, from Haikang County.

76
明　瓷片　香港竹篙灣出土
Ceramic sherds, Ming, from Penny's Bay, Hong Kong.

77
明　蓋罐　香港石壁出土
Covered jar, Ming, from Shibi, Hong Kong.

78
十六世紀　陶片　香港沙咀出土
Ceramic sherds, 16th century, from High Island, Hong Kong.

79
明　瓷騎牛人塑像　惠東縣出土
Figurine on buffalo, Ming, from Huidong County.

80
明　磚雕　陽春縣出土
Bricks, Ming, from Yangchun County.

81
明 墓誌銘 海康縣出土
Pottery tomb tablet, Wanli, Ming, from Haikang County.

82
明 修城磚 潮州市出土
City wall bricks, Ming, from Chaozhou City.

83
明 金飾 普寧縣出土
Gold ornaments, Ming, from Puning County.

84
明 銅鼓 揭陽縣出土
Bronze drum, Ming, from Jieyang County.

85
明 銅銃 高要縣出土
Bronze gun, Ming, from Gaoyao County.

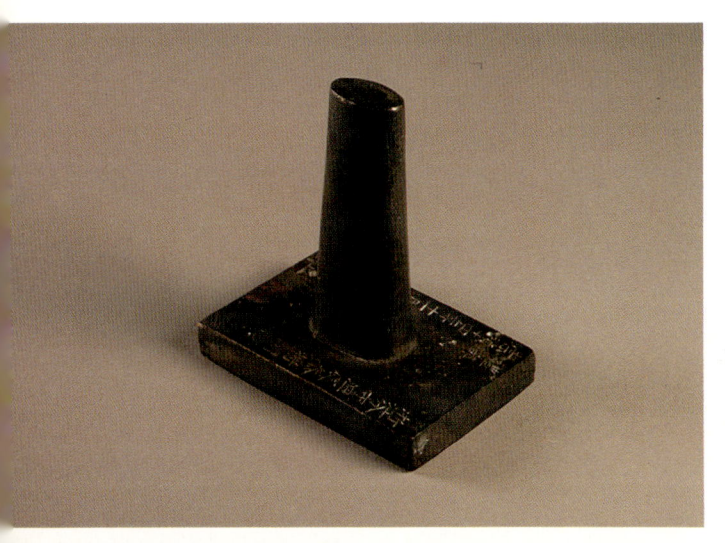

87
明　銅官印　揭陽縣出土
Bronze official seal, Chongzhen, Ming, from Jieyang County.

89A
明　銅錢　東沙羣島出土
Copper cash coins, Ming, from Paracels and Dongsha Island.

86
南明　鐵炮　香港佛堂門出土
Iron cannon, Southern Ming, from Fotangmen, Hong Kong.

88
明　銅錠　西沙羣島出土
Copper ingot, Ming, from Paracels.

89B
明　銅錢　西沙羣島出土
Copper cash coins, Ming, from Paracels.

90
明　天王像　南雄縣出土
Iron Guardian figures, Wanli, Ming, from Nanxiong County.

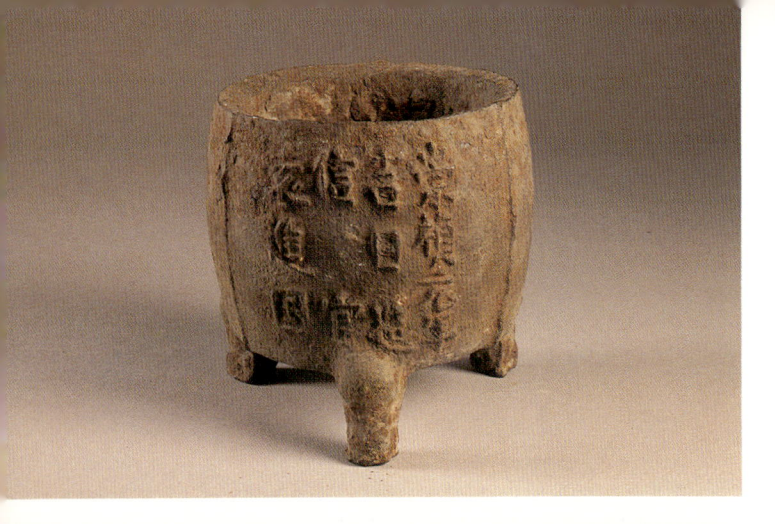

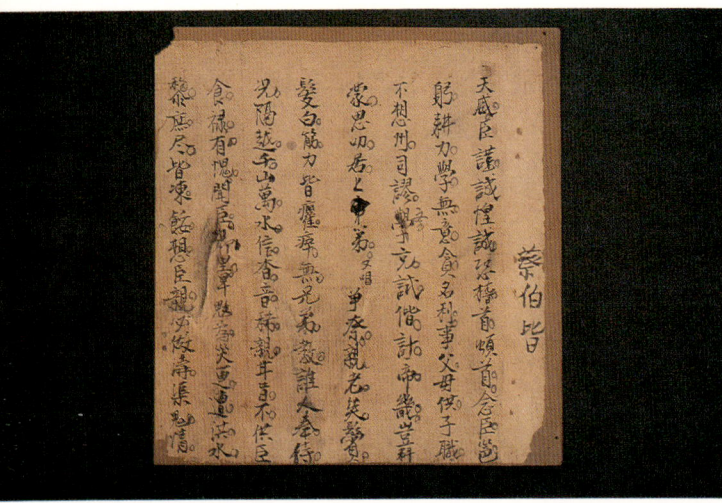

91
明　鐵香爐　揭陽縣出土
Iron censer, Ming, from Jieyang County.

92
明　琵琶記抄本　揭陽縣出土
Pipa ji manuscript, Jiajing, Ming, from Jieyang County.

93
明　描金紙扇　大埔縣出土
Folding fan, Wanli, Ming, from Dapu County.

94
明 百褶裙 揭西縣出土
Pleated skirt, Ming, from Jiexi County.

95
清 青花罐 東莞縣出土
Covered jar, Qing, from Dong'guan County.

96
清 青花罐 開平縣出土
Covered jar, Qing, from Kaiping County.

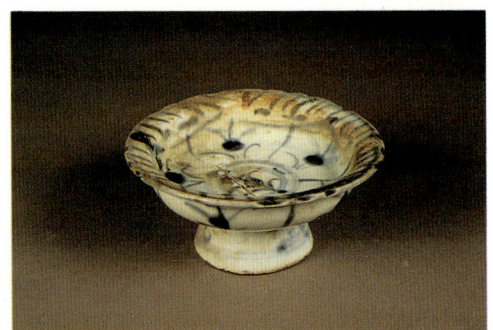

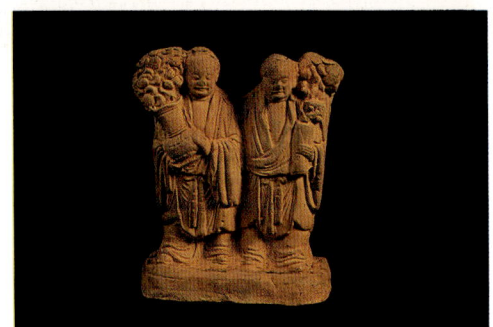

97	98
99	100
101	102
	103

97
清　青花盤　西沙羣島出土
Blue and white dish, Qing, from Paracels.

98
清　青花碗、碟　汕頭市出土
Blue and white dishes and bowl, Qing, from Shantao City.

99
清　青花杯　汕頭市出土
Blue and white cups, Qing, from Shantao City.

100
清　青花碗、碟、杯　大埔縣出土
Blue and white cups, dish and bowls, Qing, from Dapu County.

101
清　瓷片　香港大埔出土
Ceramic specimens, Qing, from Dapu, Hong Kong.

102
清　青花盤　大埔縣出土
Blue and white stem-dish, Qing, from Dapu County.

103
清　和合二仙塑像　揭陽縣出土
Pottery figurines, Qing, from Jieyang County.

104
清　陶坐衙模型　大埔縣出土
Set of yamen figures, Kangxi, Qing, from Dapu County.

105
清　陶出巡模型　大埔縣出土
Pottery figurines, Kangxi, Qing, from Dapu County.

106
清 陶內庭生活模型 大埔縣出土
Pottery figurines, Kangxi, Qing, from Dapu County.

107
清 木官印 南澳縣出土
Wooden seal, Qing, from Nan'ao County.

108
清 鐵鐘 香港粉嶺採集
Iron bell, Kangxi, Qing, from Fengling, Hong Kong.

109
清 彈丸、瓷片 香港東龍島出土
Cannon balls and blue and white porcelain, Qing, from Donglong Fort, Hong Kong.

110
清 印章 陸豐縣出土
Stone seals, Qing, from Lufeng County.

110
清 印盒 陸豐縣出土
Glass box, Qing, from Lufeng County.

111
清 珠飾、玉環 潮州市出土
Crystal necklace and jade bracelet, Guangxu, Qing, from Chaozhou City.

112
清 紙摺扇 潮州市出土
Folding fan, Guangxu, Qing, from Chaozhou City.

展品說明
Entries of Exhibits

1

夾耳青瓷罐

南漢(公元911—971年)
通高19.4、口徑7.3厘米
1954年廣州市東郊石馬村墓葬出土

淺黃胎。直口、圓唇、矮頸、廣肩、長身、弧壁、深腹、底內凹。肩部左右一對板耳，前後各一對夾耳。帶蓋，蓋有雙翼，翼中有橫孔與夾耳相對應，蓋翼放入夾耳中，可以木栓或縛以繩固定。兩板耳有孔，可繫繩便於提攜。

器裏外施青綠釉，呈冰裂紋。底露胎。

該墓出土的幾十件青瓷器，造型美觀，釉色晶瑩，反映出當時廣東陶瓷製作技術達到了相當高的水平。

該墓還出有"乾和十六年"的磚銘。據研究，此墓是南漢第三個皇帝劉晟的陵墓。劉晟是南漢高祖劉龔的第四子，卒於乾和十六年八月(公元958年)，年三十九，在位十六年，謚"文武光聖明孝皇帝"，廟號中宗，陵曰昭陵。

Covered jar with crossed handle

Southern Han (AD911-971)
Overall Height: 19.4, diameter: 7.3 cm
Excavated in 1954 from the Shimacun burial in eastern suburb, Guangzhou.

This globular jar has a buff body and the base is slightly concave. On the shoulders is a pair of pierced vertical handles alternating with another pair of double handles also likewisely pierced. The cover has a pair of diametric and pierced projections for fitting onto the double handles. A wooden peg or a piece of string would be used to fix the cover through the perforations.

The green glaze is crackled and stops short of the footrim. Several dozens of green glazed jars were discovered from this tomb. All of them were finely potted and glazed, reflecting the high workmanship of the Guangdong potter in this period.

An inscribed brick with a date corresponding to AD958 was also found in the tomb and according to recent research the deceased has been identified as Liu Cheng, the third emperor of the Southern Han state. Liu Cheng was the fourth son of Liu Gong, the founder of the state. He died in AD958 and was given a posthumous title, the " *Wenwu guangsheng mingxiao Emperor*". His reign title was "*Zhongzong*" and his tomb "*Zhaoling*".

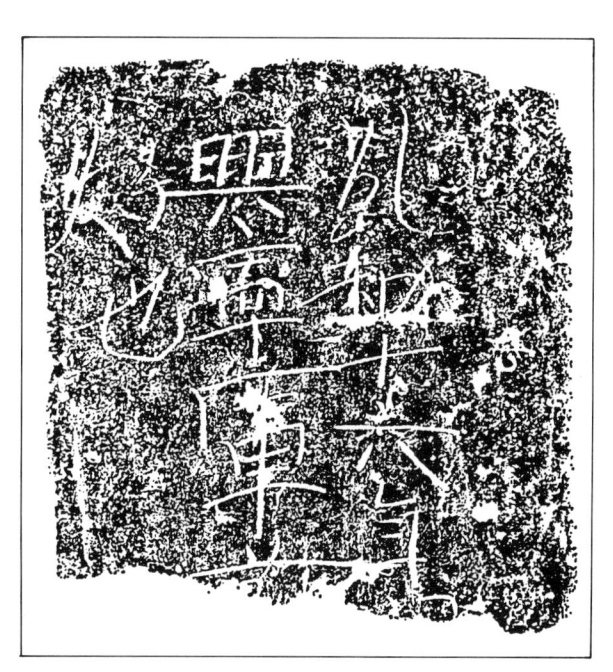

乾和十六年磚銘
Rubbing of the dated inscribed brick.

2

六系青瓷罐

南漢（公元911—971年）
通高18.6、口徑7.1厘米
1954年廣州市東郊石馬村墓葬出土

灰黃胎。帶蓋，蓋頂有圓形乳鈕。直口，圓唇，矮頸，廣肩，弧壁，深腹。底內凹。肩上六個橫耳。器內外施青綠釉，呈冰裂紋，底露胎。

Jar with six loop handles

Southern Han (AD911-971)
Overall Height: 18.6, diameter: 7.1 cm.
Excavated in 1954 from the Shimacun burial, eastern suburb, Guangzhou.

This covered jar has a buff body, the cover is topped with a mushroom shaped knob. The globular body has a short neck and the base is slightly concave. Six looped handles are luted on the shoulders. The green glaze is finely crackled and stops short of the footrim.

3

六系釉陶罐

南漢（公元911—971年）
高16.2、口徑9厘米
1954年廣州市東郊石馬村墓葬出土

灰褐胎。斂口，折沿，小肩，長身深腹，上腹六個橫耳，平底。上腹施醬黃釉，釉質薄，部分脫落。口、肩及下腹至底露胎。

Pottery jar with looped handles

Southern Han (AD911-971)
Height: 16.2, diameter: 9 cm.
Excavated in 1954 from the Shimacun burial, eastern suburb, Guangzhou.

This globular jar has a greyish brown body, with six looped handles on the shoulders and a flat base. The upper part of the body is coated with a dark brown glaze, much of which is now flaked off.

4

六系陶罐

南漢（公元911—971年）
高14、口徑6.6厘米
1954年廣州市東郊石馬村墓葬出土

灰褐胎。直口，平沿，矮頸，廣肩，肩部六個橫耳，深腹，平底。肩至上腹劃四組弦紋，每組兩周。腹部有輪旋紋。

這種陶罐該墓出土147件，其中有的罐內還保存有雞、魚的骨頭和蚶殼，說明這類陶器是用來盛放食物作隨葬用品的。

Pottery jar with looped handles

Southern Han (AD911-971)
Height: 14, diameter: 6.6 cm.
Excavated in 1654 from the Shimacun burial, eastern suburb, Guangzhou.

This globular jar has a greyish brown body, on the shoulders are six horizontal looped handles. The upper part of the body is decorated with a group of four double incised bands. Horizontal grooves, from the potter's wheel are clearly visible on the lower part of the body. A total of 147 similar jars were unearthed from the tomb, some of which still contained bones of chicken and fish, as well as clam shells, indicating that they were used as food containers for the burial.

5

陶龍首構件

南漢（公元911—971年）
通高20.7、通長35、寬17厘米
1976年廣州市東郊石馬村出土

灰褐胎。器作浮雕式龍首形。正面及兩側面塑出牙齒，卷鼻，圓眼，鬚角。綫條粗大，犬齒突出。

器身上端為凹槽形，下端為半圓拱，中空。平底。

這是一件建築物上的脊飾，使用這類藝術構件的應是具有相當規模的建築。這件器物出土於南漢皇帝劉晟墓的附近，推測可能是當時陵墓建築物上的構件。

Architectural part

Southern Han (AD911-971)
Overall height: 20.7, length: 35, width: 17 cm.
Excavated in 1976 from the Shimacun burial, eastern suburb, Guangzhou.

Made of Greyish brown clay, this piece of architectural remain is powerfully modelled on the front and two sides with the head of a dragon, with teeth, coiled nostril, round eyes, hair and horns. The interior is hollow with a U-shaped upper part and the lower part is rounded.

Judging from the size of this piece, it was probably part of the overground structure of the mausoleum of Liu Cheng, the emperor or Southern Han.

6

鐵花盆

南漢(公元911—971年)
通高29.7、口徑30.8厘米
五十年代廣州市出土

　　器身厚重。銹蝕。敞口，侈唇作花瓣形，斜內收深腹，平底，下有三矮足。有盆座，爲六角形，寬平沿，直腹較淺，平底，下有三個較寬的矮足。

　　器身兩側鑄有隸書銘文，一側爲"供奉芳華苑永用"；另一側爲"大有四年冬十一月甲申朔造"。"大有"爲南漢高祖皇帝劉龑的年號。《南漢書》載："大有四年冬十一月甲申朔，日有食之"。大有四年即公元931年。芳華苑位於廣州城西，是南漢王朝帝王與宮人宴遊的地方。清人《南漢春秋》中有它的記載。

Iron flower pot

Southern Han (AD911-970)
Overall height: 29.7, diameter: 30.8 cm.
Discovered in Guangzhou in the fifties.

　　This heavy vase is covered with a thick encrustation of iron rust. The body is facetted with a slightly trumpeted mouth. The base is flat and stands on three feet; the whole pot is then supported by a hexagonal basin.
　　On the two sides of the exterior are cast inscriptions. On one side, the inscription reads, "for eternal use in the Fanghua Garden", on the other side, "Made on the *jiashen*, first day of the 11th moon in the winter of the 4th year of the Dayou reign". According to the *Nanhan shu* (The Dynastic history of Southern Han), there was an eclipse of the sun on this day, and the 4th year Dayou corresponds to AD931. The Fanghua Garden was in the western part of the Guangzhou city and was an amusement park for the imperial household of the Southern Han state. There is a detailed record of this garden in the *Nan Han chunqiu* compiled in the Qing dynasty.

銘文拓片
Rubbing of the inscription.

7

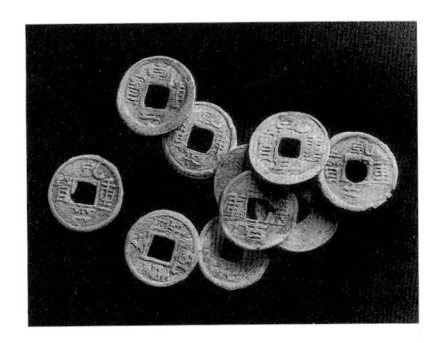

鉛錢

南漢(公元911—971年)
直徑2.4—2.6、方穿徑0.7—0.8厘米
五十年代廣州市出土

錢幣。外圓內方。或寬緣或窄緣,不規整,方穿亦大小不一。自上下右左鑄"乾亨重寶"四字,文字粗細不勻,歙斜不正,鑄工甚劣。背面無字。

自五十年代以來,廣州市內和市郊已出土乾亨重寶鉛錢達二千多斤。《南漢書》載:"鑄'乾亨重寶'鉛錢,十當銅錢一。大徑寸,重三銖九參,'寶'字傳形;小,徑九寸,重如銅錢"。乾和以後,又實行"城內用鉛,城外用銅,禁其出入,犯者抵死,俸祿非特恩不給銅錢"的規定。使劣幣泛濫,銅貴鉛賤,幣值極度混亂。這是南漢王朝搜刮民脂,窮奢揮霍的實證。

Lead cash coins

Southern Han (AD911-971)
Diameter: 2.4-2.6, width of perforation: 0.7-0.8 cm.
Discovered in Guangzhou in the fifties.

Cash coins with a circular edge and a square perforation in the centre. Both the edge and perforation are irregular and the characters were roughly cast. The inscription reads "*Qianheng chongbao*". There is no inscription on the reverse.

A great many similar coins of the same period have been discovered in Guangzhou since the fifties. According to the *Nanhan shu* two types of lead coins were minted and normally ten such coins would equivalent to one copper cash. After the Qianhe reign these lead coins were used only inside the city, outside which copper cash was circulated. Strict laws were enforced to forbid the flow of copper coins into the city, leading to a most chaotic currency policy as well as a sharp inflation of the value of copper coins.

8

石錢範

南漢(公元911—971年)
陽範長17.7、寬9.2、厚2厘米
陰範長19.1、寬10、厚3厘米
1982年陽春縣石望鄉小峒鐵屎徑村出土

砂質板岩。均作圓角長方形。陽範上有十個圜錢鑄模,分列兩行,左行下面三個圜錢鑄模已殘缺。錢文陰刻,上下左右順讀為"乾亨重寶",反文。有周廓,寬緣。陰範上有十二個圜錢鑄模,分列兩行,右行上面三個及左行第一個鑄模殘缺。範上端有一道較深的橫凹槽,為合範後注鉛液的入口處。主槽刻在兩行錢模中間,支槽較淺,聯接各錢模。

石範每個錢模的方穿正中,均留有細眼,是製範時以方穿正中為圓周中心,劃出錢形的使用痕迹。陽範四角各透穿一圓孔,陰範左邊上下兩角各透穿一圓孔,應是合範後固定錢範之用。

與錢範共存的遺物有青釉瓷器、鉛錠以及大量的廢棄爐渣,可見該地是鑄造鉛錢的處所。

"乾亨"為南漢皇帝劉龑王朝的年號(公元917—925年)。

Stone piece moulds for coins

Southern Han (AD911-971)
Obverse, length: 17.7, width: 9.2, thickness: 2 cm.
Reverse, length: 19.1, width: 19, thickness: 3 cm.
Excavated in 1982 in Xiaotong Tieshijingcun, Shiwang, Yangchun County.

Two rectangular slate moulds with corners slightly rounded off. The obverse mould is carved with ten coins arranged in two rows, with the lower three on the left chipped off. The inscription, in reverse reads "*Qianheng chongbao*", and is enclosed by a wide circular edge. On the reverse mould are twelve coins arranged in two rows with a horizontal pour channel on the top. The main channel divides the two row and individual coins are linked together with smaller channels (runners).

In the centre of each coin is a tiny pit, a result from the compass used to outline the coins. Registration of the moulds are secured by putting a piece of thread through the perforations on the corners of the moulds.

Cultural relics co-existed with the moulds include green glazed ware, lead ingots and a great deal of furnace debris, indicating that the site must have been a workshop for minting lead coins.

"*Qianheng*" was the reign period of the Southern Han emperor Liu Gong and corresponded to AD917-925.

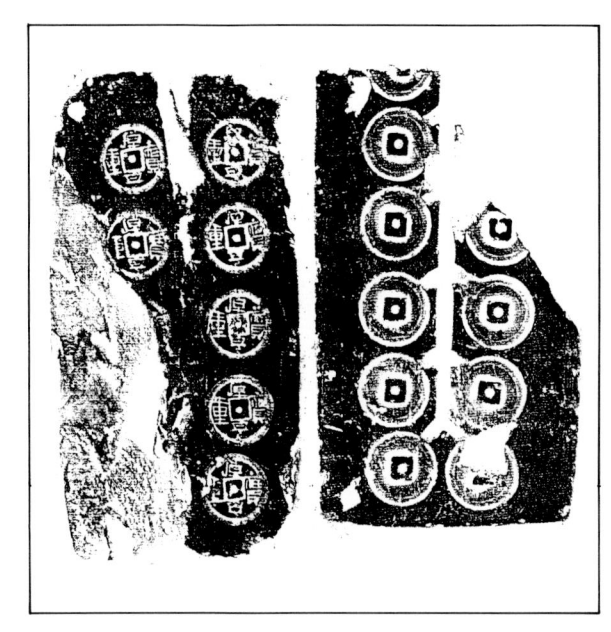

錢範拓片
Rubbings of the moulds.

9

菊花人物瓷罐

宋代（公元960—1279年）
高26、口徑11.5厘米
1976年海康縣雷城鎮縣醫院後坡墓葬出土
海康縣博物館藏品

敞口，短束頸，溜肩，肩下漸往內收，圓形大餅底，外壁施青白色釉，釉下用褐色彩繪畫化紋，肩上主要是裝飾帶狀紋飾，從上向下依次畫方格圓圈紋、纏枝卷草紋、錢紋各一周，腹部用六條一組的短直綫分爲八格，格內相間畫折枝菊花和仕女像，仕女頭上兩鬢梳髻，身穿交領花衫，下穿長裙，手捧一圓盤狀物，面形方正，體形豐滿，其中髮式與潮州筆架山窰出土的女俑髮式完全相同，罐腹下畫雙重蓮瓣紋。

Pot with underglaze brown painting

Song dynasty (AD960-1279)
Height: 26, diameter: 11.5 cm.
Excavated in 1976 from a burial on the back slope in the county hospital, Leichengzheng, Haikang County.
Collection of the Haikang County Museum.

This pot has a slightly collared neck, the exterior wall tapers towards the flat base. Underneath the bluish glaze are decorative motifs painted in iron brown; the shoulder with four bands of circles and crosses, classical scroll and interlocking cashes. The main band of decoration on the outside consists of eight rectangular panels of female figures alternating with chrysanthemum, each separated by six vertical stripes. The lady figure, with two buns on the hair, wearing a long skirt and a blouse is holding a round pan in her hands. The squarish face and plum body as well as the hair style are very similar to the ceramic lady figure unearthed in the Bijiashan kilnsite in Chaozhou. The lower part of the jar is painted with a band of hanging lotus petals in double outlines.

10

桃花洞裏瓷罐

宋代（公元960—1279年）
高22.2、口徑9厘米
1985年海康縣白沙鄉赤坡鋪墓葬出土
海康縣博物館藏品

　　敞口，短束頸，鼓腹，圓餅形厚餅底，肩上堅塑有四隻半環形耳，外壁施青灰色釉，釉下用褐彩繪畫花紋，其中肩部四耳之間畫複瓣蓮花紋，腹部上端畫兩周卷草紋，中間分為四格，每格內弧形開光，開光內相間畫折枝菊和寫"桃花洞裹"（裏）四字，腹下畫一周纏枝卷草紋和二周弦紋。

　　此罐為海康窰產品。海康窰址眾多，共發現六十多處，其中十多處有褐色彩繪瓷器生產，是廣東目前發現生產褐色彩繪瓷的主要產地。

Pot with underglaze painting

Song dynasty (AD960-1279)
Height: 22.2, diameter: 9 cm.
Excavated in 1985 from a burial in Chipopu, Baisha village, Haikang County.
Collection of the Haikang County Museum.

　　This ovoid jar has a flat base and on the shoulders are four vertical looped handles. The glaze has a bluish grey tinge, under which are decorations painted in iron brown. Between the handles are pendant lotus petals in double outlines. Below the two bands of classical scrolls is the main decoration of four oval panels of chrysanthemum sprays alternating with characters. "*Taohua dongli*" (Inside the Peach Spring Caves). This main band is then supported by a classical scroll and two bands near the foot.

　　This pot was very probably fired in the Haikang kiln complex. A total of more than 60 kiln sites have been located in Haikang, among which about a dozen fired underglaze brown painted wares, making Haikang an important centre of production of such type of painted wares in Guangdong.

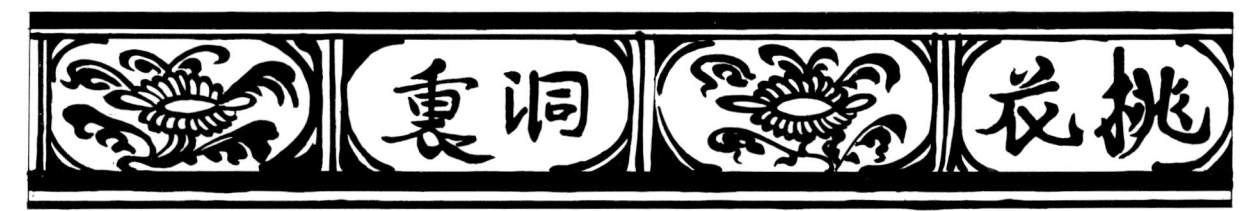

花紋展開圖。
Drawing of the iron brown designs.

11

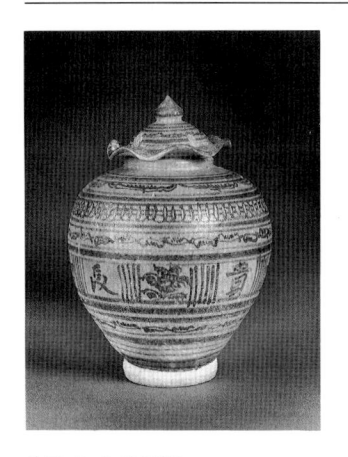

"長命富貴"罐

宋代（公元960—1279年）
通高28、口徑9厘米
1976年海康縣雷城鎮後坡墓葬出土
海康縣博物館藏品

罐直口，短頸，溜肩，鼓腹，餅形厚底，外壁施青灰色釉，釉下用褐彩繪畫花紋，其中肩部畫弦紋、重瓣蓮花紋和帶狀錢紋，腹部上部畫纏枝卷草紋，中部以六條為一組的短直綫分為八格，相間畫折枝菊花和書寫"長命富貴"四字；罐蓋作荷葉形，弧形頂，圓錐形鈕，蓋下有子口，外壁畫弦紋和一周纏枝卷草紋。

此罐為海康窰產品，它和海康發現的大多數褐色彩繪瓷罐一樣，是作為裝骨灰用的，可見宋、元時期海康地區火葬極為流行。

Covered pot with underglaze painting

Song dynasty (AD960-1279)
Overall height: 28, diameter: 9 cm.
Excavated in 1976 a burial on the back slope, Leichengzhen, Haikang County.
Collection of the Haikang County Museum.

This ovoid jar is topped with a lotus leaf shaped cover and the base is flat. The glaze has a greyish celadon tinge, under which is painted in iron brown with decorative motifs arranged in bands: classical scroll on the cover, double lotus petals, interlocking cashes and classical scrolls on the shoulders and the main band of "*Changming fugui*" characters alternating with chrysanthemum sprays in rectangular panels.

This jar was a product of the Haikang kiln. Like similarly brown painted ones, this was originally used as a container for holding cremated human bones for burial, which was a very common practice in Guangdong in the Song and Yuan dynasties.

花紋展開圖
Drawing of the designs.

12A

彩繪軍持

北宋（公元960—1127年）
高19.5、口徑9.1厘米
1987年南海縣和順鎮蓬涌村文頭嶺窰址出土

盤口，寬沿凸唇，長頸，鼓腹，直流，餅形大足，口至頸上部及腹下部施醬褐色釉，頸下部至腹中部不施釉，用褐色彩畫纏枝卷草紋。

Brown painted *kendi*

Northern Song (AD960-1127)
Height: 19.5, diameter: 9.1 cm.
Excavated in 1987 in the Wentouling kiln site, Fengchongcun, Heshunzhen, Nanhai County.

This *kendi* has a flanged and trumpeted mouth and a solid disc base. The mouth and the upper neck as well as the lower part of the body are glazed in dark brown, leaving the middle portion in biscuit, on which is painted in dark brown with a floral scroll.

12B

彩繪瓷壺

北宋（公元960—1127年）
高15.3、口徑8厘米
1987年南海縣和順鎮蓬涌村文頭嶺窰址出土

敞口，厚圓唇，筒形長頸漸向上收，鼓腹，矮餅底，前面有流，後面有弧形把，頸部和把飾褐色大點彩，腹部畫褐色纏枝卷草紋，施青灰色釉，釉不到底。

南海文頭嶺窰址範圍較大，彩繪瓷器除褐色彩繪外，還有醬黑色彩繪瓷器，是廣東北宋時期一處重要窰場。

Brown painted ewer

Northern Song (AD960-1127)
Height: 15.3, diameter: 8 cm.
Excavated in 1987 in the Wentouling kiln site, Fengchongcun, Heshunzhen, Nanhai County.

The globular body is topped by a cylindrical neck which slightly tapers towards the mouth. The glaze is in a greyish green colour and stops above the solid disc base. The neck is decorated with bold spots in brown and the body is painted with floral scrolls also in brown.

The Wentouling kiln site occupies a wide area. The characteristic feature of its products is underglaze painting in brown and black. It was an important ceramic centre in Northern Song Guangdong.

輔照一.
Supp. illustration 1

褐色彩繪瓷鼓、器蓋

北宋（公元960—1127年）
A（後）：鼓腰直徑7.2厘米
B（前）：器蓋直徑12.5高3.5厘米
1987年南海縣和順鎮蓬涌村文頭嶺窰出土

　　A：已殘缺，可看出鼓前後部分直徑較大，中間較長而直徑較小，形狀近似於長腰鼓，鼓外壁畫弦紋和纏枝卷草紋。
　　B：釉已脫落，直壁，平頂，頂上畫弦紋圈，圈內畫卷草紋。
　　瓷鼓，是古代樂器，現廣西一些少數民族還有使用。廣東除南海縣和順鎮文頭嶺窰有出土外，廣州西村窰也有發現，廣西永福宋窰中曾有較完整的出土。

Fragments of waist drum and cover

Northern Song (AD960-1127)
Drum, diameter: 7.2 cm
Cover, diameter: 12.5 cm, height: 3.5 cm.
Excavated in 1987 in the Wentouling kiln site, Fengchongcun, Heshunzhen, Nanhai County.

　　The drum fragments are of funnel shape, with a larger diameter at the two ends. The outside is painted in brown with floral scrolls separated by bands.
　　Most of the glaze on the flat cover has been flaked off, the top is painted with a floral spray enclosed by a circle.
　　Waist drums made of porcelain were very common in ancient China and is still used by some of the minority tribes in Guangxi. Similar drums were also discovered in the Xicun kiln site in Guangzhou and complete specimens have been unearthed in the Song kiln site in Yongfu, Guangxi province.

13A

青瓷壺（A）

南宋（公元1127—1279年）
高18、口徑6.8厘米
1986年海康縣紀家鎮公益村窰址出土

　　敞口，束頸，鼓腹，餅形厚底，長弧形流，無把，施青色釉，釉不到底。此壺無把的作法，與軍持相接近。

Green glazed ewer

Southern Song (AD1127 - 1279)
Height: 18, diameter: 6.8 cm.
Excavated in 1986 from a kiln site in Gongyicun, Jijiazhen, Haikang County.

　　In shape this ewer resembles a *kendi*; both are without handles. The spout in this specimen is curved in a 'S'-shaped profile. The yellowish green glaze stops near the flat disc base.

13B

青瓷壺（B）

南宋（公元1127—1279年）
高19.2、口徑7.2厘米
1986年海康縣紀家鎮公益村窯址出土

敞口，短束頸，最大徑在腹下部，厚餅底，弧形流前端有三角形決口，弧形把連接在壺頸部和腹部，施青灰色釉，開冰裂紋片。

海康公益窯位於公益村邊，窯爐結構為龍窯，殘長18.7，寬1.18至1.86米，窯爐經過重建，在窯壁外還發現有一早期窯壁，可見燒窯時間較長。遺物堆積極其豐富，厚3.14米，可分為八層，在第二層堆積中，出土有一枚金國"正隆元寶"（公元1156—1160）銅錢。

Green glazed ewer

Southern Song (AD1127-1279)
Height: 19.2, diameter: 7.2 cm.
Excavated in 1986 from a kiln site in Gongyicun, Jijiazhen, Haikang County.

The body is of pear shape and topped by a trumpet mouth, with a flat disc base. The tip of the spout has a triangular pour. A curved handle joins up the neck and the body. The green glaze has a greyish tinge and is crackled.

A fragmentary dragon kiln structure was discovered in this kiln site. The kiln measures 18.7 meters in length, and 1.18 to 1.86 in width. The kiln chamber had been rebuilt as an earlier wall was discovered outside the kiln debris, indicating that the kiln had been in operation for quite a long period. A rich deposit layer was also found in the site. A total of eight strata was discernible and in the second stratum a Jin dynasty *Zhenglong yuanbao* copper coin (AD1156-1160) was discovered.

14

點彩小碗

宋代（公元960—1279年）
高4．口徑12.1厘米
1982年海南島瓊海縣出土

敞口，弧壁，小底內凹；施青黃色釉，口沿上點有褐色斑彩，內底有四塊墊燒痕迹。

此碗出土於因地震沉沒的海底村落，為海康、遂溪或廉江縣窯產品，是當時雷州半島瓷器銷往海南地區的見證。

Small bowl with brown spots

Song dynasty (AD960-1279)
Height: 4, diameter: 12.1 cm.
Excavated in 1982 in Qionghai County, Hainan Island.

This small bowl stands on a slightly concave base. The interior has four spur marks from stack firing. Under the yellowish green glaze are brown spots.

This bowl was discovered in a submerged village site in the Hainan Island and was a product of Haikang, Suiqi or Lianjiang kilns, all located on the Leizhou Peninsular. This is an evidence of the trade of porcelain between Leizhou and Hainan in Song times.

15

白瓷碗

宋代(公元960—1279年)
高5.4、口徑11.8厘米
1979年海南島崖縣墓葬出土

撇口,壁微弧,圈足,內外壁施白釉。

宋代廣東瓷器常見的釉色為青白、青灰、青黃、醬褐等,施白釉瓷器較少。

Porcelain bowl

Song dynasty (AD960-1279)
Height: 5.4, diameter: 11.8 cm.
Excavated in 1979 from a burial in Yaxian, Hainan Island.

This bowl has a slightly everted rim and a high foot ring. Both inside and outside are glaze in white. The more common glaze colours found in Guangdong in the Song period are *qingbai*, greyish green, yellowish green, and brown. Pure white glaze as in this specimen is relatively rare.

16

青瓷、碟、缽、碗

南宋(公元1127—1279年)
A(左):碟高3.4、口徑15.4厘米
B(中):缽高9.7、口徑18.8厘米
C(右):碗高6.7、口徑16.3厘米
1986年海康縣紀家鎮公益村窰址出土

A:敞口,弧壁,圓餅形足內凹,內底寬平,中間印折枝牡丹花,四周有四個小泥塊墊燒痕迹,施青灰色釉。

B:口微斂,弧壁,圓餅形足內凹,外壁釉下用褐彩畫一周纏枝卷草紋,內底中間壓下一圓圈,邊上有四個墊燒痕迹。

C:敞口,弧壁,餅形實足內凹,內底印菊花一朵,並用褐彩寫一"飽"字,外壁中部寫一"福"字。

Green glazed dish and bowls

Southern Song (AD1127-1279)
Dish: (A) Height: 3.4, diameter: 15.4 cm.
Bowls: (B) Height: 9.7, diameter: 18.8 cm.
(C) Height: 6.7, diameter: 16.3 cm.
Excavated in 1986 from a kiln site in Gongyicun, Jijiazhen, Haikang County.

(A) The lid is everted and the solid base is slightly concave. The interior centre is impressed with a peony spray surrounded by four firing spur marks. The glaze is of greyish green colour.

(B) A round bulb bowl with slightly in-turned mouthrim and a solid concave base. The exterior is painted in iron brown with a classical scroll and the interior impressed with a circle in the centre, also surrounded by four firing spur marks.

(C) A small bowl with curved wall and everted lip, and a solid concave base. The interior is impressed with a chrysanthemum medallion, over which is written in underglaze iron brown a "*Bao*" (well fed) character. The exterior is also painted in brown with a "*Fu*" (blessing) character.

17

青瓷雙魚洗

宋代（公元960—1279年）
A（左、西沙）：高3.6、口徑12.8厘米
B（右、潮州）：高5.1、口徑22厘米
1975年西沙北礁、五十年代潮州東風橫沙堤遺址出土

二件洗造型相同，大小相異，作寬平折沿、弧壁、圈足，足下無釉，外壁飾一周蓮瓣紋，內底模印二條頭向相反，尾部上翹鯉魚，鯉魚形態生動，與青綠色釉相影交輝，如魚在碧水中游動。

這些青瓷洗，潮州出土的胎與龍泉瓷有一定的區別，過去潮州南郊宋窰曾有雙魚洗出土，有可能是潮州所生產。西沙北礁發現的，即是當時我國瓷器運銷國外的見證。

Celadon double-fish basins

Song dynasty (AD960-1279)
(A) Height: 3.6, diameter: 12.8 cm.
  Excavated in 1975 from the Northern Reef, Paracel Islands.
(B) Height: 5.1, diameter: 22 cm.
  Excavated in the fifties from Dongfeng Hengshati, Chaozhou.

The two basins are of similar form, with a flattened rim, the underside moulded with lotus petals in relief. The interior is sprigged with double carps swimming in opposite directions.

The green glazed basins unearthed in Chaozhou can be differentiated from those manufactured in Longquan, Zhenjiang by their bodies. In the fifties some of these basins were found in the southern suburbs of Chaozhou. They were probably local products. The specimens found in the Paracels were probably remains from the trade route to overseas countries.

18

瓷盒

北宋（公元960—1127年）
通高10.6、口徑9厘米
1975年西沙北礁礁盤出土

盒身和盒蓋高大致相等，呈瓜棱形，盒身子口較高，平底稍向內凹；盒蓋平頂無鈕，由於長期浸在海水中，釉已完全剝落。

這類瓷盒，在廣東省潮州窰、廣州西村窰都有大量生產，是當時外銷商品之一。

Covered porcelain box

Northern Song (AD960-1127)
Overall height: 10.6, diameter: 9 cm.
Excavated in 1975 from the Northern Reef, Paracel Islands.

The cover and the body of this box are of approximately the same height. The body is lobed and once glazed, but much of the glaze has eroded by the sea water.

A great many boxes of this type were produced both in the Chaozhou and Xicun kiln sites, and were popular export items in the Song period.

19

青瓷瓶

北宋（公元960—1127年）
高8.6、口徑3.4厘米
1974年西沙甘泉島唐宋遺址出土

瓶小口，唇外翻，細長頸上有三道凸弦紋，鼓腹，圈足，外壁施青白釉，是廣州西村窰產品。

甘泉島唐宋居住遺址，1974年和1975年二次共發掘80平方米，除了這件瓷瓶外，還出土有一批瓷碗、瓷盒、瓷缽、陶罐、鐵刀、鐵鑿等生產、生活用品，並發現有當時人們吃剩的鳥骨和螺殼，說明了早在唐宋時期，中國人民已在西沙羣島居住、勞動，生息。

Green glazed bottle

Northern Song (AD960-1127)
Height: 8.6, diameter: 3.4 cm.
Unearthed in 1974 from a Tang/Song settlement site on Ganquan Island, Paracels.

This small bottle has an outrolled lip and a cylindrical neck with grooved bands. The bluish glaze stops above the footring. This is a standard type from the Xicun kiln in Guangzhou.

During two excavations in 1974 and 1975, a total of 80 sq. m. were dug up in this Tang to Song settlement site on Ganquan Island. Among the finds are porcelain bowls, boxes, pottery pots, iron knives, chisels and other daily utensils as well as bones of birds and shells, indicating an early Chinese occupation on the island.

20

荷花瓷枕

宋代（公元960—1279年）
長27、寬25、前高8.9、後高15.1厘米
1983年海康縣雷城鎮蟹坡墓葬出土
海康縣博物館藏品

枕面作如意頭形，前低後高，中間下凹，平底，枕面花紋從邊端起，用褐彩向內依次畫三角形幾何圖案、纏枝卷草紋、和短水波紋，中間畫一朵盛放蓮花，枕面施青黃色釉，枕面下不施釉，前面寫有一"大"字，是海康窰產品。

Pillow painted in brown

Song dynasty (AD960-1279)
Length: 27, width: 25, height (front): 8.9, (rear): 15.1 cm.
Excavated in 1983 from a burial in Xiepo, Leichengchen, Haikang County.
Collection of the Haikang County Museum.

A cloud shaped pillow with a concave surface and a flat base. The main theme of decoration is a lotus spray surrounded by bands of wavy pattern, classical scroll and segmented waves. The top is covered with a yellowish green glaze and the lower part is unglazed. There is an underglaze character "*da*" (big) on the front of the underside. This is a product of the Haikang kiln.

21

菊花蝴蝶瓷枕

宋代（公元960—1279年）
長31.5、寬22.5、前高9、後高11.6厘米。
1984年海康縣雷城鎮蟹坡墓葬出土
海康縣博物館藏品

枕上大下小，枕面呈如意頭形，前低後高，兩邊翹起，中間下凹，枕底平，前面鏤有半月形孔，枕面從邊起向內依次用褐彩畫帶狀纏枝卷草紋、纏枝花草、短弧綫、方格、水波、錢紋組合紋，中間畫五朵盛放菊花和兩隻飛翔蝴蝶。應為海康窰產品。

瓷枕，早在唐代廣東窰場已有生產，出土物可見於唐代梅縣水車窰，生產的是圓角長方形枕，無紋飾。宋代海康生產的瓷枕，枕面作如意頭形或長方形，枕面用褐色釉繪菊花、荷花等紋飾，或寫詩句，比唐代枕更為實用美觀。

Pillow painted in brown

Song dynasty (AD960-1279)
Length: 31.5, width: 22.5, height (front): 9, (rear): 11.6 cm.
Excavated in 1984 from a burial in Xiepo, Leichengzhen, Haikang County.
Collection of the Haikang County Museum.

A cloud-shaped pillow with a concave top, supported by a flat base. There is a crescent opening in the front. The underglaze brown painted design consists of a garden scene with five chrysanthemum flowers in bloom with two flying butterflies above, all enclosed within bands of classic scroll, floral sprays, interlocking cash and cross-hatchings. Probably fired in the Haikang kiln.

Porcelain pillows were produced in Guangdong as early as in the Tang dynasty. Rectangular pillows with rounded off corners were discovered from the Tang Shuiche kiln site in Meixian, but none of them was decorated. The ones from Haikang are always painted in iron brown with chrysanthemum, lotus or poems, with a cloud-shaped or rectangular top, making them more practical and attractive than the Tang ones.

22

詩詞瓷枕

宋代（公元960—1279年）
長26.5、寬17.15、前高9、後高12.3厘米
1984年海康縣白沙鄉赤坡埔墓葬出土
海康縣博物館藏品

枕上大下小，枕面呈長方形，前低後高，中間稍下凹，左右兩邊用褐彩釉下畫二組錢紋和短弧綫、圓圈組合紋，後端畫纏枝卷草紋，枕中間寫有"枕冷襟寒十月霜，小窗閑放早梅芳。暗香入被侵人夢、花物依人樂洞房"詩句。

海康發現的彩繪瓷枕，多畫菊花或蓮花紋，寫詩句枕現僅此一件。

Pillow painted in brown

Song dynasty (AD960-1279)
Length: 26.5, width: 17.5, height (front): 9, (rear): 12.3 cm.
Excavated in 1984 from a burial in Chipopu, Baisha village, Haikang County.
Collection of the Haikang County Museum.

A rectangular pillow with slightly concave top and the supporting block tapers towards the flat base. Arched flanges attach to the main surface which is painted in underglaze brown with a four line poem, written in semi-cursive script and surrounded by panels of classic scroll, interlocking cash and cash with arcs.

Pillows painted with chrysanthemum or lotus flowers are common products of Haikang, but so far only this single specimen has been found with poetic inscriptions.

23

彩繪瓷棺

宋代（公元960—1279年）
長56、寬36、高28厘米
1976年海康縣雷城鎮上坡村M1合葬墓出土

出土時共二件，此件為女棺。棺呈長方形，弧形頂，前面有活動插板可開關，平底；頂前後兩端用褐色彩畫雙綫蓮瓣紋，前端蓮瓣內寫有"地戶"兩字，後端蓮瓣內寫有"天門"兩字；棺左右兩壁邊緣畫雙綫框，其中左壁框中間畫一持幡童子騎在青龍背上，青龍前面豎寫有"左青龍"二字，童子前面畫鼠、牛、虎生肖，後面畫兔、龍、蛇生肖，生肖均作人身獸頭，身穿長袍，持笏立於雲霧之中，每生肖像頂部分別寫有"十一月子"、"十二月丑"、"正月寅"、"二月卯"、"三月辰"、"四月巳"等生肖所屬月份；右壁框內中間畫一童子持幡騎於龍形虎背上，白虎前面有"右白虎"三字，童子前面畫馬、羊、猴生肖，後面畫雞、狗、豬生肖，生肖造形與左壁同，各生肖像頂部分別寫有"五月午"、"六月未""七月申"、"八月酉"、"九月戌"、"十月亥"等生肖所屬月份；棺前壁畫朱雀，旁邊寫有"前朱雀"三字，中間寫有"黃化姚孺人"六字；後壁畫玄武，旁邊寫有"後玄武"三字。

Coffin painted in iron brown

Song dynasty (AD960-1279)
Length: 56, width: 36, height: 28 cm.
Excavated in 1976 from the M1 twin-burial in Shangpocun, Leichengzhen, Haikang County.

Two such coffins were unearthed from the tomb, and this one belongs to the female. This rectangular coffin is arched on the top, the front has a detachable sliding plate. The top is decorated in the two ends with ogival panels in double lines, within which are "*tianmen*" and "*dihu*" (heavenly doorway and earthly household) inscriptions.

The decorations on the sides include animals of the four quarters and the zodiac, all with captions. On the two longer sides, the green dragon and white tiger were mounted by boys holding a banner leading the zodiac animals in the background.

彩繪花紋
Drawing of the designs.

24

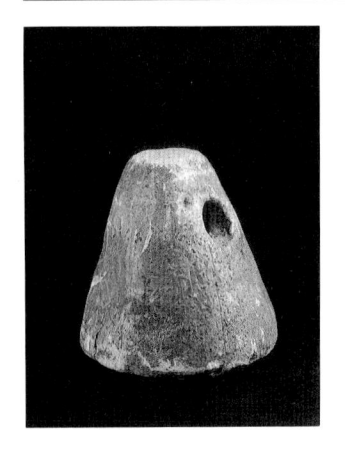

青瓷權

宋代（公元960—1279年）
高12、頂部直徑4.5、底部直徑12.5厘米
1983年遂溪縣下六鎮東港仔村窰出土
遂溪縣博物館藏品

權體作圓椎形，上小下大，頂及底平，上端橫穿一孔，施青黃釉。是我國古代衡器的附件之一。

Porcelain weight in green glaze

Song dynasty (AD960-1279)
Height: 12, diameter (top): 4.5, (base): 12.5 cm.
Excavated in 1983 from a kiln site in Donggangzaicun, Xialiuzhen, Suiqi County.
Collection of the Suiqi County Museum.

This conical shaped weight is flattened both on the top and base. The upper part is pierced across. The glaze is yellowish green in colour. Probably an accessory for a steelyard or a weighing instrument.

25

瓷罈

宋代（公元960—1279年）
通高23.3、口徑13.4厘米
1982年化州縣合江鎮天龍馬鞍嶺出土
化州縣博物館藏品

胎潔白。器壁較薄。直口，短頸，圓肩，長圓腹，矮圈足。帶蓋，子口，頂蓋爲鏤孔珠鈕。器身肩、腹各堆胎一周水波紋，肩上貼附一周菱形鏤空裝飾，高出於口沿。器施青白釉，釉質晶瑩，潤澤如玉。是廣東宋瓷中的精品。

Covered urn

Song dynasty (AD960-1279)
Overall height: 23.3, diameter: 13.4 cm.
Excavated in 1982 in Ma'anling, Tianlong, Hejiangzhen, Huazhou County.
Collection of the Huazhou County Museum.

The white paste is covered with a glossy and lustrious *qingbai* glaze. On the body and shoulder are two "pastry" bands in relief. On the upper band stands a vertical flange of two rows of perforated triangles. The cover is topped with a pierced bud-shaped knob. A fine piece of porcelain.

26

陶罈

北宋（公元960—1127年）
通高65、口徑10.6厘米
1972年東莞市篁村鎮白泥坑封德清墓出土
東莞市博物館藏品

灰黃色胎。施醬黃釉，施至足中部，釉質保存尚好。

器整體較高，分蓋身兩部分。器蓋分三層，一、二層貼附水波紋，上爲葫蘆形塔利式，縱貫四道塔脊。器身口小腹大，侈口，圓唇，矮頸，深腹內收。上腹堆貼三周水波紋，下腹堆貼二周水波紋，中腹刻劃二周水波紋。高圈足，足上部鏤四孔。肩部模貼二周造像，上一周爲四飛鳥與四獸相間，鳥呈站立狀，昂首，雙翅展開，長尾；獸呈坐式，半浮雕式塑出頭、毛髮及前後足。下一周爲十二個供養人，每三個爲一組，站立。這些造像均較粗糙。

出土時罈內殘存少量稻谷，說明此器是盛放谷物作隨葬品的。

該墓爲合葬墓。此器出於女棺室。據現存的咸豐十年（1860）重修墓碑載，這是宋大夫二世祖封德清與羅氏之合葬墓。封德清官至朝奉大夫，卒於宋政和（公元1111—1118）年間。

Covered urn

Northern Song (AD960-1127)
Overall height: 65, diameter: 10.6 cm.
Excavated in 1972 from the Feng Deqing tomb in Bainikangcun, Huangcunzhen, Dongguan City.
Collection of the Dongguan City Museum.

The greyish buff body is covered with a brown glaze which stops half way near the foot. The gourd shaped cover is applied with two "pastry" bands near the rim and four flanges leading to a stepped dome-knob. Similar "pastry" bands adorned the shoulders and the foot, separating two incised wavy bands along the lower half of the body. On the upper part of the shoulders are luted with rows of twelve figures, four crouching beasts and four birds in flight.

Remains of rice husks were found inside the urn, indicating that it was used as a cereal container for the burial.

The tomb was a twin-burial and this urn was discovered in the coffin chamber of the female. According to a stone tablet erected in 1860 in the late Xianfeng reign in the Qing dynasty this tomb belongs to Feng Deqing and his wife Lady Luo. Feng died in the Zhenghe reign (AD1111 - 1118) in the Song dynasty and had been a Grand Master for Court Service.

27

陶罈

宋代（公元960—1279年）
高35、口徑20.3厘米
1986年珠海市東岸沙丘出土
中山市博物館藏品

灰黃胎。帶蓋，蓋頂一乳鈕，蓋面堆貼兩周水波紋，從乳鈕放射性向四周堆貼兩組瓦脊紋，上面一組為八條，下面一組為十六條。器身斂口，平唇，圓肩，深腹，平底內凹。肩部一周堆貼水波紋，其上為十六條瓦脊紋，與蓋上的紋飾相對應。全器施醬黃釉，略有脫落。

用堆貼水波紋裝飾陶罈，是廣東宋代陶罈較流行的裝飾藝術。

Pottery urn

Song dynasty (AD960-1279)
Height: 35, diameter: 20.3 cm.
Excavated in 1986 from the sand terrace on the eastern bank, Zhuhai city.
Collection of the Zhuhai City Museum.

This covered urn has a greyish buff body covered by a flaky dark brown glaze. The dome-shaped cover and the shoulders are decorated with radial "rafter" bands in relief, eight on the top and sixteen on the lower part as well as on the shoulders, separated by similar horizontal bands.

Raised "rafter" bands are common decorations found on urns of the Song dynasty in Guangdong.

28

陶罈

宋代（公元960—1279年）
通高74、口徑10厘米
1983年陽春縣馬水鄉石菉汶埇墓葬出土
陽春縣博物館藏品

灰褐胎。施醬褐色釉，大部脫落。

分蓋身兩部分。蓋呈亭閣式，頂端兩層為亭閣，檐角上翹，飾以鏤空花窗，外圍以一周菱形鏤空裝飾。器身較高，斂口、圓唇，矮頸，廣肩，深腹，高圈足。肩部模貼兩周裝飾，靠裏一周較高，繞一周龍身，貼附兩龍尾及兩龍爪，龍身下一周供養人像，每個人像之間為長方形鏤孔；靠外一周為鏤空卷葉紋。腹堆貼四周水波紋及貼附纏枝花卉。足部有六個塔形鏤空。全器造型巧妙，工藝複雜。

Pottery urn

Song dynasty (AD960-1279)
Overall height: 74, diameter: 10 cm.
Excavated in 1983 from a burial in Shiluwenchong, Mashuixiang, Yangchun County.
Collection of the Yangchun County Museum.

The greyish buff body is covered by a flaky dark brown glaze. The high cover is in the form of a two tiered pavilion in openwork supported by a vertical band of interlocking cash, also in openwork. On the shoulders is a dragon in the round supported by votive figures and surrounded by another raised bands of classic scroll in openwork. The body is decorated with an applique band of lotus scroll and several raised scallop bands. The upper part of the foot stem is pierced with arch shaped openings.

This is a most elaborately decorated piece.

花紋展開圖
Drawing of the decoration.

29

彩繪陶瓶

宋代（公元960—1279年）
高31、口徑6.7厘米
1964年佛山市瀾石鎮鼔頸崗墓葬出土

　　灰白胎。直口，圓唇，口較小，矮頸，高身，廣肩，長深腹，底微凹。

　　肩腹繪鐵銹色圖案、花紋和人物。自上而下共六組，各組間以弦紋。第一、三、五組爲流綫組成的圖案;第二、六組爲纏枝花卉，底紋爲細密的直綫;第四組爲海浪紋和四個人物，底紋爲斜綫。四個人物均穿長袍，袒胸，戴頭巾飾，作坐姿，動作表情各不相同，依次爲:一、兩眼凝視，雙手捧

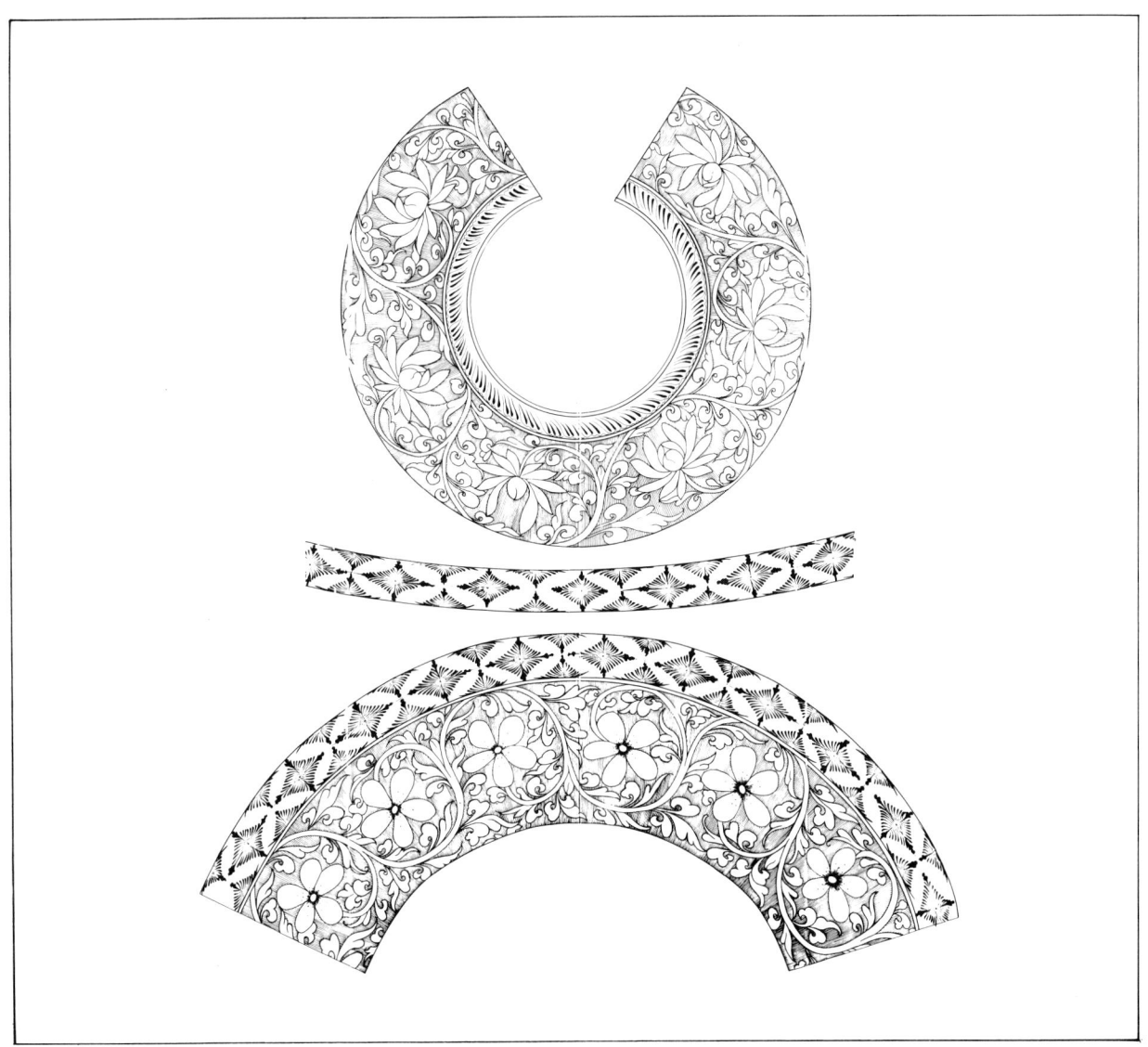

花紋展開圖
Drawing of the designs.

71

碗作待飲狀;二、手靠酒罎,作歇息狀,跟前置碗、盤;三、背靠酒罎,雙手扶地,作醉意矇矓狀,左倒置碗具;四、雙手拱放於右膝上,頭枕於右手臂,作醉臉酣睡狀,跟前置碗盤。這是對同一人物作四種形態的刻畫,表現了從喝酒開始,到醉酒後入睡的過程。人物形像生動自然,動態表情傳神逼真。線條簡單流暢,寥寥幾筆,將酒香人醉的情景描繪得維妙維肖。這是一件繪畫水平很高的藝術品。

Vase with brown painting

Song dynasty (AD960-1279)
Height: 31, diameter: 6.7 cm
Excavated in 1964 from a burial in Gusanggang, Lanshizhen, Foshan City.

A meiping vase with a greyish body and a slightly concave base. The decoration is painted in iron brown and arranged in six bands, with two floral bands on the shoulders and lower half of the body enclosing the main band, each separated by bands of rhomboids in oval panels. The floral scrolls are painted in outlines reserved on a hatched ground. The main decoration consists of a series of four drunken figures within ogival panels on a serpentine wave ground. The figures are meant to represent the same person engaged in drinking wine and are finely painted.

30

陶爐

宋代(公元960—1279年)
高8.1、口徑19厘米
1975年揭陽縣曲溪鎮港畔村隴頭園遺址出土
揭陽縣博物館藏品

直口,短頸,鼓腹,平底內凹,底下有三隻三角形獸面紋小足,不施釉,頸部和腹下端各飾有一周乳釘紋。

Pottery basin

Song dynasty (AD960-1279)
Height: 8.1, diameter: 19 cm.
Excavated in 1975 from the Longtouyuan site, Gangbancun, Ququzhen, Jieyang County.
Collection of the Jieyang County Museum.

A drum-shaped basin with a slightly concave base, stands on three triangular monster mask feet, unglazed. Two rolls of raised bosses adorn the upper and lower rims on the outside.

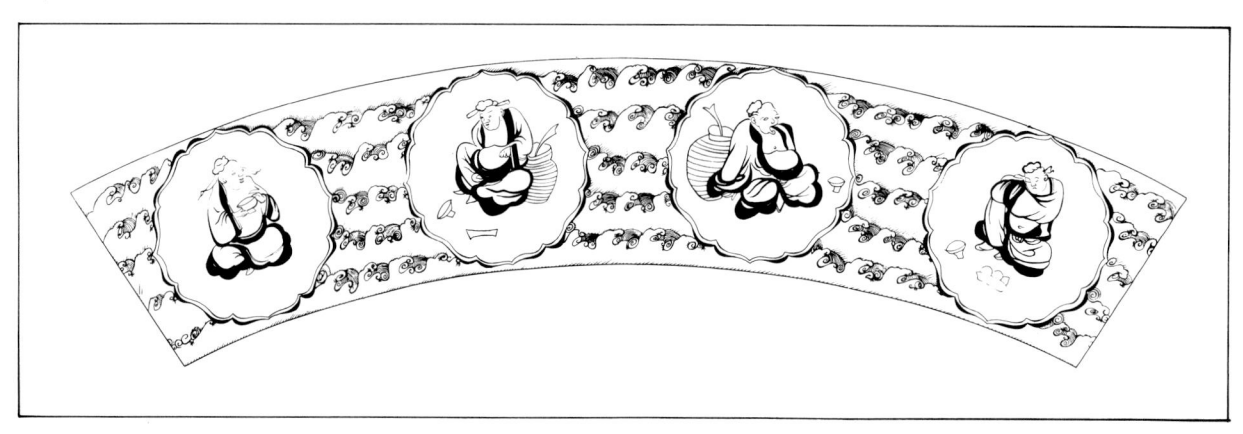

花紋展開圖。
Drawing of the designs.

31A

淺青釉碗

宋代(公元960-1279年)
口徑:13.3-17.5厘米
1979/80年香港赤鱲角深灣村出土
香港博物館中央考古資料庫藏品

深灣村位於大嶼山北部的赤鱲角島上,曾出土陶瓷器,並發現灰窰數座。圖中瓷碗為外銷常見器物;其中兩件為青黃釉,內壁篦劃及篦點花卉紋,同類型碗於福建沿海一帶多有生產,日本人稱之為「珠光青磁」。另外一件青白瓷碗,斜直壁,口沿外卷,應是廣州西村窰的產品。

Bowls

Song dynasty (AD960-1279)
Diameter: 13.3-17.5 cm.
Excavated in 1979/80 from Shenwancun, Chilajiao (Shum Wan Tsuen, Chek Lap Kok), Hong Kong.
Collection of the Central Archaeological Repository of the Hong Kong Museum of History.

A large number of ceramic artefacts and several lime kilns have been discovered on this small island site, at the north of Dayushan (Lantao), Hong Kong. These bowls were common item for export in the Song period. Two of them are glazed in olive green and decorated with incised floral sprays with details in "dotted combing", a characteristic of Fujian coastal kiln sites, while the other is in *qingbai* glaze and has a thickened rim, a feature of the Xicun kiln in Guangzhou.

31B

青白瓷盤、青釉注子

宋代(公元960-1279年)
徑:12.4-15.6厘米
1979/80年香港赤鱲角深灣村出土
香港博物館中央考古資料庫藏品

青釉注子,已殘,釉色及胎體應屬浙江越窰系產品。肩及腹部均刻劃繁縟花卉紋,並有模印花紋豎耳一對。此標本與青白瓷碗(展品31A)共出,同出者尚有北宋末期的銅錢(展品37),可作斷代依據。另外的一件瓷盤,牙黃釉呈開片,盤心劃折枝花卉紋,為廣州西村窰的典型產品。

Dish and ewer

Song dynasty (AD960-1279)
Diameter: 12.4-15.6 cm.
Excavated in 1979/80 from Shenwancun, Chilajiao, Hong Kong.
Collection of the Central Archaeological Repository of the Hong Kong Museum of History.

The fragmentary ewer, is of fine quality that one would attribute to Zhejiang. The body and shoulder are incised and combed with elaborate floral pattern within panels, and two moulded lugs are luted on the shoulder, alternating with the spout and handle. This specimen together with the above *qingbai* bowl were found together with a group of early 12th century Song coins (exhibit 37). The dish is glazed in a creamy, crackled glaze and incised in the centre with a floral spray. A typical product of the Xicun kiln.

32

瓷片

宋代（公元960-1279年）
長:10.8-23.4厘米
1975/76年香港沙洲出土
香港博物館中央考古資料庫藏品

沙洲位於香港西端，爲一「啞鈴」小島；自本世紀三十年代已爲考古學者所注意，屢經調查試掘，出土遺物有幾何印紋陶，磨光石器及宋元陶瓷等。圖內瓷片標本，均爲灰白胎，淺青或青黃釉，開片；其中大盤，折唇，中央以褐彩繪拆枝花卉；另青白小盤內刻菊瓣團花；俱是廣州西村窰的典型特色。當是外銷產品。

Ceramic sherds

Song dynasty (AD960-1279)
Length: 10.8-23.4 cm.
Excavated in 1975/76 from Shazhou (Sha Chau), Hong Kong.
Collection of the Central Archaeological Repository of the Hong Kong Museum of History.

Shazhou, located on the western limits of Hong Kong territory is an uninhabited dumb-bell island site known to local archaeologists since pre-war times. Large quantities of geometric pottery, polished stone artefacts and historic ceramics have been found. The specimens selected here are all glazed in pale green. The large bowl with a slightly flattened rim is painted in the centre with a large brown floral spray; and the small dish is incised with a floral medallion. All of them were probably fired in the Xicun kiln site in Guangzhou and were made for export.

33

陶生肖俑

宋代（公元960—1279年）
通高:約33—29厘米
1983年海康縣附城鄉榜山石狗坡墓葬出土
海康縣博物館藏品

灰白胎。陶質較軟。中空。爲十二生肖俑。已缺三件，僅存九件。人身獸冠。面部塑出眼、耳、口、鼻。身穿寬袍長袖，兩手拱於胸前。下爲圓形座，座中足尖露出。頭上冠飾爲各生肖屬相。其中七件（A—G）冠飾依次爲"鼠、猴、豬、鷄、牛、羊、犬，"人首後面各刻有一個地支，分別爲"子、申、亥、酉、丑、未、戌"。另二件（H、I）頭冠缺失，背後刻地支爲"午、辰"，推知頭冠爲"馬、龍"。缺失的三件爲"虎、兔、蛇"。

該墓出有"元符通寶"銅錢。

Pottery zodiac figures

Song dynasty (AD960-1279)
Overall height: c. 33-29 cm.
Excavated in 1983 from a burial in Shigoupo, Bangshan, Fuchenxiang, Haikang County.
Collection of the Haikang Museum.

Only nine of the original twelve figures of the zodiac are extant. All of them are made of greyish soft clay with a hollow central cavity and modelled in the form of a male figure with long sleeves, clasped hands, standing on a circular support. The zodiac animals are depicted on the headgear and the earthly stem characters are incised on the back. The headgears for two of the pieces are now missing.

Copper coins of the Yuanfu reign (AD1098-1103) were discovered from the tomb.

34

城磚

南宋(公元1127—1279年)
A:長29.2、寬18、厚4厘米
B:長31.5、寬18、厚3.6厘米
1985年海康縣城南門頭出土
海康縣博物館藏品

　　磚爲長方形。A,磚的一側長邊銘記"水陸巡檢監造",一側寬邊銘記"南匠韋細"。B,在磚的一個平面上銘記"紹興修城官磚"。銘記均係陽文。

　　"紹興"爲南宋高宗趙構的年號(公元1131—1162年)。清代《海康縣志》載:"紹興二十二年黃勛繼之,勛以土城不堅,改用城磚,明年南北城畢合,東西未成,勛又去。二十四年朝奉郎趙伯瓘畢前功"。可知城磚當爲紹興二十二年至二十四年間(公元1151—1162)所造。磚上銘記工匠姓名及監造官員,說明建造城池在當時至爲重要。

City wall bricks

Southern Dong (AD1127-1279)
(A) Length: 29.2, width: 18, thickness: 4 cm.
(B) Length: 31.5, width: 18, thickness: 3.6 cm.
Excavated in 1985 from Southern Gate, Haikang County.
Collection of the Haikang County Museum.

　　Both bricks are of rectangular shape and impressed with inscriptions: "Supervised by the Chief Military and Naval Inspector", "Southern artisan Wei Si", and "Official city wall construction brick of the Shaoxing reign".

　　"Shaoxing" was a reign title of the Southern Song emperor Zhao Gao and was from AD1131 to 1162. According to local gazetteer of the Haikang County, in the 22nd year of Shaoxing, Huang Xun a local magistrate initiated a construction project to replace the earthen wall with bricks. After one year the south and north walls were completed and Huang was transferred. In the next year (24th year Shaoxing) Zhao Bo succeeded the post and continued with the construction. Thus these bricks should be manufactured between the 22nd to the 24th year of Shaoxing (AD1151-1162).

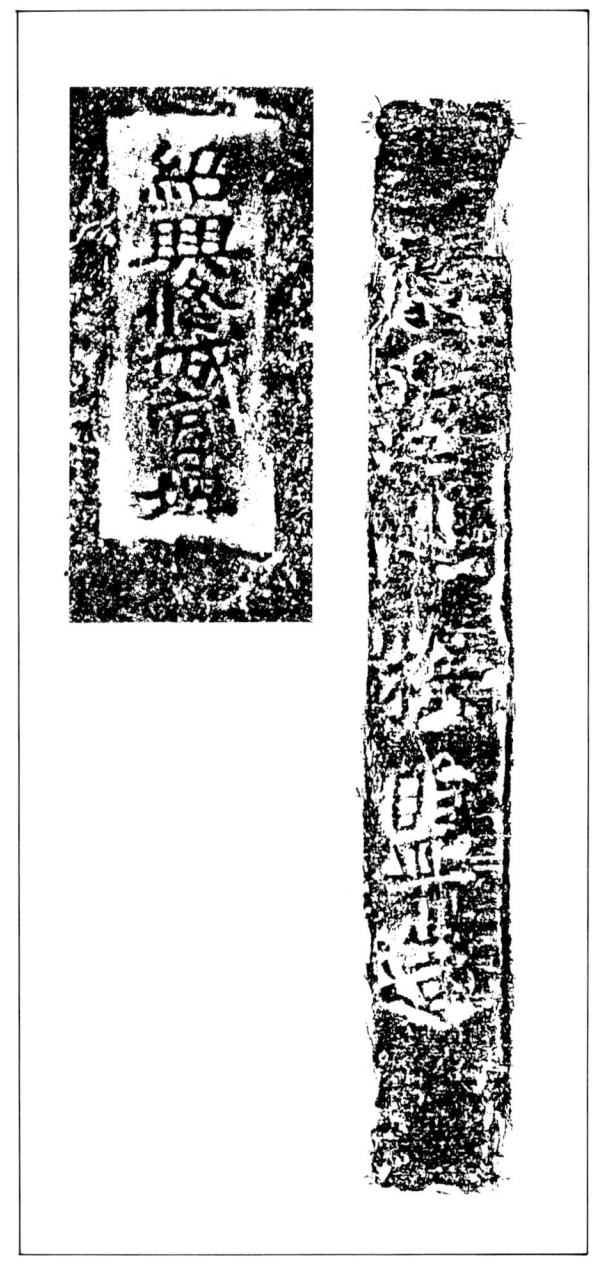

磚銘拓本
Rubbings of the inscriptions.

瓦當

宋代（公元960—1279年）
A（左）:長22、寬9厘米
B（中）:直徑10厘米
C（右）:直徑9.3厘米
1983年揭陽縣仙橋鎮、地都鎮、桂嶺鎮出土
揭陽縣博物館藏品

A:橢圓形，青灰色胎，正面邊緣印二周弦紋，弦紋之間飾凸點紋，中間印蓮花紋。

B:圓形，橙紅色胎，正面邊緣三道弦紋之間飾凸點紋，中間印蓮花紋。

C:圓形，橙紅色胎，正面邊緣和中間各有一道弦紋圈，圈內印短斜綫紋。

三種紋飾瓦當，均爲屋檐裝飾，宋代以圓形蓮花紋瓦當發現較多，橢圓形蓮花紋瓦當和圓形短斜綫紋瓦當較爲少見。

Rooftile terminals

Song dynasty (AD960-1279)
(A) Length: 22, width: 9 cm.
(B) Diameter: 10 cm.
(C) Diameter: 9.3 cm.
Excavated in 1983 from Xianqiazhen, Diduzhen and Guilingzhen, Jieyang County.
Collection of the Jieyang County Museum.

(From left to right)
(A) Oval shape, with greyish green paste, moulded with a lotus medallion in the centre and enclosed by raised bands and bosses.
(B) Circular shape, with reddish brown body, moulded with a central lotus medallion enclosed by three raised bands and two rolls of bosses.
(C) Circular shape, with reddish brown body, moulded with short slanting lines enclosed by raised bands.
All of them are eave tile decorations. (A) and (B) are rare types.

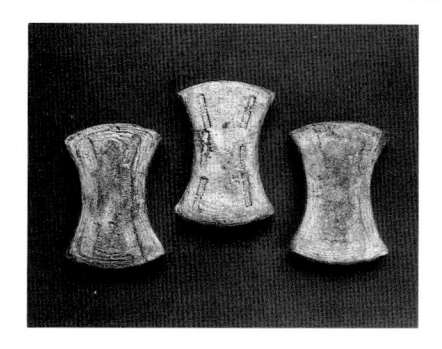

銀鋌

宋代（公元960—1279年）
長:8.8—9.1
厚:1.1—1.3厘米
重:409—438克
1979年南雄縣大塘鎮延村上井塘出土

器灰白色。兩端圓弧，中間束腰。器表鏨刻文字。

A:鋌面銘記，四角爲"霸北街東"，中右爲"蘇宅韓五郎"，中左爲"重拾貳兩半"。

B:四角爲"覇北街西"，中右爲"建康盧八郎"，中左爲"京銷銀"。"覇"字爲"霸"的異體字。

C:四角爲"覇北街東"，中右印文不清晰，中左爲"京銷鋌銀"。

這些銀鋌出土時共十七件，總重74649.3克。出土時分置於兩個陶罐內。

Silver ingots

Song dynasty (AD960-1279)
Length: 9.1-8.8, thickness: 1.1-1.3 cm,
Weight: 409-438 gm.
Excavated in 1979 from Shangjingtang, Zhenyancun, Datang, Nanxiong County.

These ingots are dumbbell shaped with curved ends. The greyish silvery surface is punched with inscription marks which read: "East Babei Street", "Han Wulang of the Su family", "Weight: twenty-four and half taels", "West Babei Street", "Lu Balang of Jiankang", "Capital expenditure silver", "East Babei Street", and "Capital expenditure silver ingot".

This hoard of silver were placed inside two earthenware jars and there are altogether 17 pieces weighing 7649 gms.

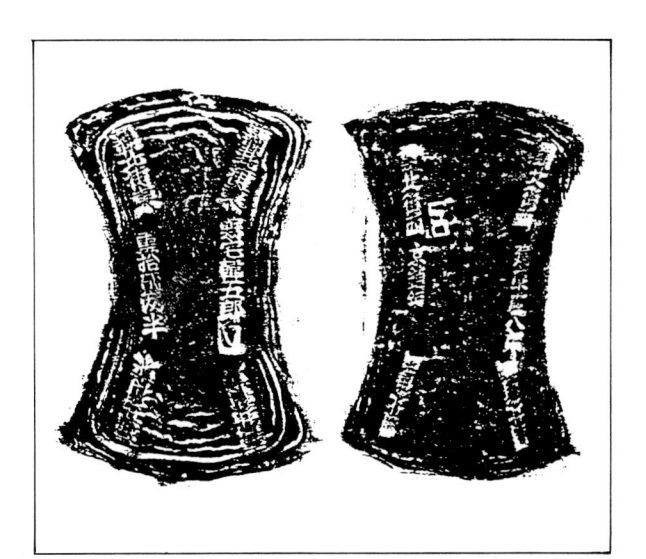

銀鋌銘文
Rubbings of the inscriptions.

37

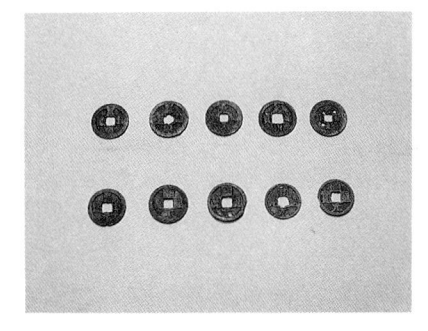

銅錢

宋代（公元960-1279年）
徑：約2.5厘米
1979/80年香港赤臘角深灣村出土
香港博物館中央考古資料庫藏品

深灣遺址出土銅錢不少，有早至漢代新莽時期的「貨泉」，亦有唐代的「開元通寶」錢；宋錢多枚，多屬北宋晚期，全出於墓葬C，計有：「皇宋通寶」、「景德通寶」、「祥符元寶」、「熙寧元寶」等。

戰後香港曾出土多次大批宋代銅錢，出土地點有大嶼山石壁，新田米埔和九龍宋皇台遺址等。

Copper coins

Song dynasty (AD960-1279)
Diameter: c 2.5 cm.
Excavated in 1979/80 from Shenwancun, Chilajiao, Hong Kong.
Collection of the Central Archaeological Repository of the Hong Kong Museum of History.

The majority of these coins, found in burial C of Shenwancun, belong to the late period of the Northern Song dynasty and can be dated to the beginning of the 12th century. From the site, some earlier coins, dating from the Wang Mang (after AD14) to the late Tang dynasty were also found. In the past decades a few hoards of Song coins have been discovered in Hong Kong; the most well known ones include those from Shibi (Shek Pik), Lantao Island, Mipu, Xintian (Mai Po, San Tin), and the "Travelling Palace Site" in Kowloon.

輔圖二：
摩崖刻石拓片

南宋咸淳十年（公元1274年）
高:124　闊:137厘米
原石於香港北佛堂
香港中文大學藏品

　　原石位於九龍半島東部北佛堂「大廟」後之山坡叢莽中；南宋度宗咸淳十年（公元1274年）甲戌官富鹽場主官嚴益彰撰書刻石。碑文刻於摩崖石上，石上四週有邊緣凸出，刻字面積磨平；全文一百零八字，九行，行十二字，字闊十厘米，行文簡練，書法近蘇體，莊重遒勁。碑文亦是研究香港本地史的珍貴文獻。

Supp. illustration 2
Rubbing of stone inscription

10th year Xianchun, Southern Song (AD1274)
Height: 124, width: 137 cm.
From Beifotang (Joss House Bay), Hong Kong.
Collection of the Art Gallery, the Chinese University of Hong Kong.

　　The original inscription is situated on a hillslope, behind the Tianhou Temple in Beifotang (Joss House Bay) in the eastern part of Kowloon, Hong Kong. The inscription was executed by the order of the salt officer, Yan Yizhang in the 10th year of Xianchun in the Southern Song dynasty (AD1374). The characters were carved on a large boulder with the surface polished. The text, consisting of 108 characters, is arranged in nine columns, and written in well proportioned standard script in the style of the Song calligraphist, Su Shi.

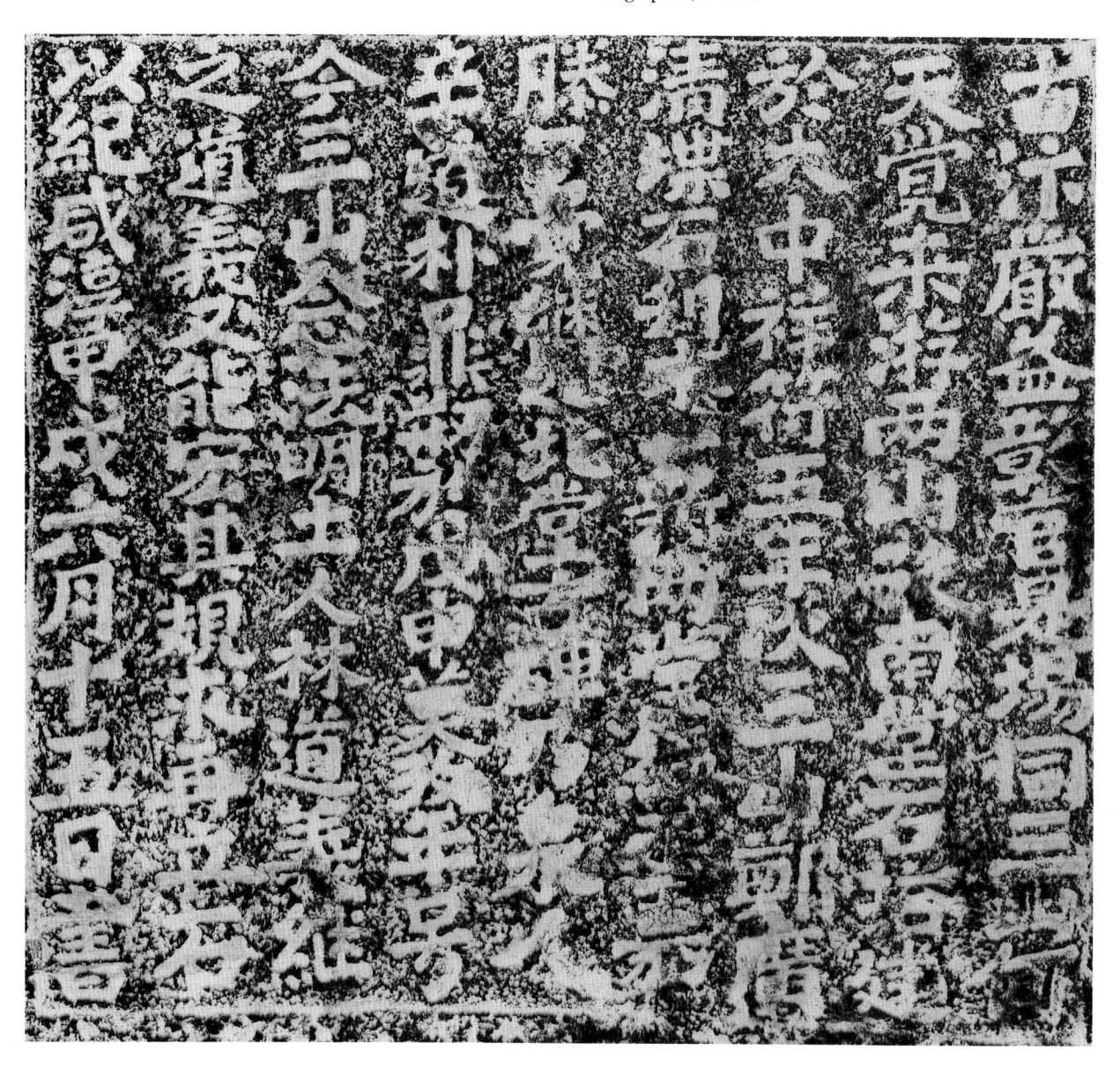

38

銀手鐲

北宋(公元960—1127年)
最大徑爲6—6.4厘米
1972年東莞市篁村鎮白泥坑封德清墓出土
東莞市博物館藏品

一對。灰色。橢圓形。器體作扭繩紋。有一開口,對口兩邊嵌刻鳳首紋。

此器出於女棺室,共存物還有銀釵、銅鏡等器。

Pair of silver bracelets

Northern Song (AD960-1127)
Largest diameter: 6-6.4 cm.
Excavated in 1972 from the tomb of Feng Deqing in Bainikang, Huangcunzhen, Dongguan City.
Collection of the Dongguan City Museum.

Greyish silver bracelet of oval form with an opening. The main body is twisted with the two ends flattened and chased with phoenix heads. This pair was found in the coffin of the female and associated finds included silver hairpins and bronze mirrors.

39

王大寶銅鏡

南宋(公元1127—1279年)
直徑14厘米
1973年潮州市歸湖鎮神前村王大寶墓出土

圓形,鏡面微弧,斜凸緣,半環形鈕已殘,鈕右邊鑄有"臨安府承父陸家眞煉銅照子"銘文。此鏡含錫量較高,鏡面呈白色,光可照人。

王大寶字元龜,海陽縣龜湖湯頭人,生於宋紹聖元年(公元1094),南宋建炎二年廷試第二,曾任南雄州敎授,連州知州,除國子司業兼崇政殿說書,直敷文閣,溫州知州、提點福建刑獄、提點廣東刑獄、禮部侍郞、兵部侍郞、禮部尚書等職。他不畏權貴,剛直不阿,力主抗金,終年七十七歲,死後葬於潮州市龜湖神前山。其墓佔地約四畝,前面有二米多高,刻有"宋禮部尚書大寶王公墓"石碑,墓兩邊排列有石翁仲,石獅、石羊、石馬、石笋、石望柱等石雕羣像,石雕綫條粗獷簡練,1962年曾被列爲廣東省重點文物保護單位。這件銅鏡是墓中出土的重要遺物。

Bronze mirror

Southern Song (AD1127-1279)
Diameter: 14 cm.
Excavated in 1973 from the tomb of Wang Dabao in Shenqiancun, Guihuzhen, Chaozhou city.

A circular mirror with a slightly convex surface and a bevelled edge. The loop handle is broken, on the right of which is a moulded shop mark of the Lu family of Lin'an. The tin content is very high making the surface patina silvery white and glossy.
Wang Dabao (AD1094-1171), a native of Chaozhou, attended the imperial examination in AD1128 and served various posts, including prefects of different districts, vice director of the departments of rites and military as well as the minister of the department of rites. Wang was noted as an honest and loyal official. He also proposed to resist the

Jin tartans from the north. Wang died at an age of 77 and was buried in Shanqianshan, Guihu in Chaozhou, his home town. The tomb occupies an area of four acres, the entrance of which is erected with a two metre high stone tablet bearing his title, flanked on the two sides with stone carvings of figures, animals and pillars. In 1962 the tomb was registered as a provincial important monument. This mirror is an important cultural relic from the site.

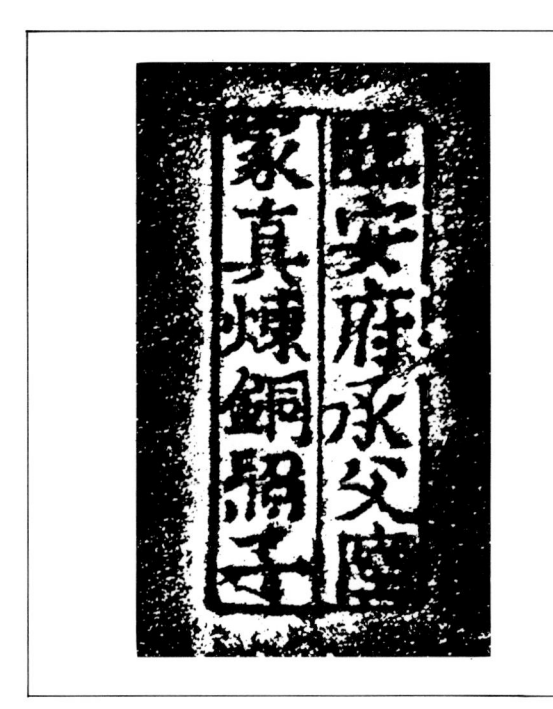

銘文
Rubbing of the shop mark.

40

銅鏡

宋代(公元960—1279年)
A:最大徑16、厚0.3cm
B:直徑6.2、厚0.2厘米
A:1976年揭陽縣東山鎮新河村黃岐山出土
B:1977年揭陽縣漁湖鎮雙溪嘴庵堂埔出土
揭陽縣博物館藏品

　　A:六出葵瓣形,鏡面平直。背面寬緣,橋型小鈕,方座,內飾海水及飛鳥紋,外區為四組雙龍纏體紋。體表有銅綠色銹斑。

　　B:體薄。器小。圓形。鏡面微弧。背面緣折起,鈕小而扁平,作花瓣形,圓座,內為六乳,外區為四乳,四乳之間為四組乳形紋,每組三乳點。外為一周弦紋及一周花蕊,近緣部為連弧紋。

Two bronze mirrors

Song dynasty (AD960-1279)
(A) Largest diameter: 16, thickness: 0.3 cm.
Excavated in 1976 from Huangqishan, Xinhecun, Dongshanzhen, Jieyang County.
(B) Diameter: 6.2, thickness: 0.2 cm.
Excavated in 1977 from Antangpu, Shuangqizui, Yuhuzhen, Jieyang County.
Collection of the Jieyang County Museum.

(A) A six bracket-lobed mirror with a flat surface, the back has a wide edge and a bridge-shaped central knob set on a square main field of birds in flight and waves, enclosed by intertwine dragons in pairs on the outer edge.

(B) A thin and small circular mirror with a slightly convex surface. The back has a raised edge and a small flat medallion knob set on a circular main field of four large bosses alternating with three smaller bosses. The outer band consists of convex arcs and slightly raised florets.

41

鐵投槍

宋代（公元960—1279年）
A：長9厘米
B：長12厘米
1973年順德縣杏壇鎮逢簡檸檬基出土

漁獵用具。略有銹蝕。

　A：單翼，有倒刺，器身較短，作圓筒形，前小後大，中空，近末端有一小孔。

　B：雙翼，前出銳鋒，有倒刺，器身較長，亦作圓筒形，前小後大，中空，內殘存木屑，近末端亦一小孔。

Iron spearheads

Song dynasty (AD960-1279)
Length: 9-12 cm.
Excavated in 1973 from Ningmengji, Fengjian, Xingtanzhen, Shunde County.

A fishing or hunting implement. Both are barbed with either one of two bladed points, now heavily rusted. The shaft is tubular, widening towards the end, which is perforated with a small hole. Traces of wood can still be found in one piece.

42

鐵魚鏢

宋代（公元960—1279年）
長12.4—13.4厘米
1973年順德縣杏壇鎮逢簡檸檬基出土

漁獵用具。略有銹蝕。前後均有鋒尖。器身作方形。A，前出雙翼，一翼有倒刺，後半段一側隆起一個弧形齒，便於綁繩；ＢＣ同一形制，前出單翼，有倒刺，後半段亦有弧形齒。

Iron javelin heads for fishing

Song dynasty (AD960-1279)
Length: 12.4-13.4 cm.
Excavated in 1973 from Ningmengji, Fengjian, Xingtanzhen, Shunde County.

Fishing or hunting implement, heavily rusted, with blades on both ends and a flat rectangular section. The front blade is always barbed and in one specimen it is twin-bladed. The end blade is longer and is for inserting into a wooden shaft secured with a piece of string.

43

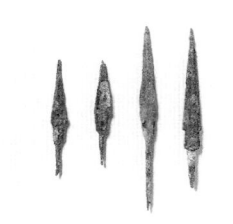

鐵鏃

宋代（公元960—1279年）
長 5—8.7厘米
1973年順德縣杏壇鎮逢簡檸檬基出土

漁獵用具。四件，大小不一，形製大致相同。略有銹蝕。器身窄長，銳鋒，隆脊，後端微出雙肩。圓鋌，末端較尖。

Iron arrowhead

Song dynasty (AD960-1279)
Length: 5-8.7 cm.
Excavated in 1973 from Ningmengji, Fengjian, Xingtanzhen, Shunde County.

Fishing or hunting implement. The four specimens are of different sizes, but all of similar shape with an elongated body, sharp blade, raised midrib and shouldered at the lower end near the cylindrical and pointed solid shaft.

44

琴式端硯

宋代（公元960—1279年）
長18.4、高2.6厘米
1964年佛山市瀾石鎮鼓顙崗墓葬出土

端石製作。石質略粗。灰黑色。硯面邊緣略有殘損。硯心中間有兩道殘損疤痕。器體作琴式，兩端圓弧形，一端略寬，一端略窄，器底四矮足。硯面一周窄緣。較窄的一端雕出對稱的弧綫圖案，較寬的一端雕出五個圓點和六個淺格。中部爲硯心，硯池爲一道半月形凹槽。

Inkstone

Song dynasty (AD960-1279)
Length: 18.4, height: 2.6 cm.
Excavated in 1964 from a burial in Gusanggang, Lanshizhen, Foshan City.

Made of Duanqi stone, this inkslab is fashioned in the shape of a Chinese zither supported by four low feet. The narrower end is carved with two symmetrical brackets and the other end with rolls of five dots and six squares. The central surface for grinding the ink is in oval form with a well for holding the liquid ink in the front. Chips along the edges as well as on the ink well.

45

抄手端硯

宋代（公元960—1279年）
長16.7、寬10、高5.8厘米
1973年高要縣連塘鎮蔡步廟嘴山墓葬出土

端石製作，石質細潤。灰黑色。硯面邊緣略有殘損。長方形。器身略高。硯面三個邊寬緣，一側有長形凹槽作硯池，另一側邊緣有一個直徑1.2cm的圓形眼，中心為金黃色，外周為紫色。底下為抄手。底部附飾七個長短不一的圓柱。抄手硯在當時較為流行。

高要古屬端州，是端石的產地。

Inkstone

Song dynasty (AD960-1279)
Length: 16.7, width: 10, height: 5.8 cm.
Excavated in 1973 from a burial in Cabumiaozuishan, Liantangzhen, Gaoyao County.

Made of purplish grey Duanqi stone, this inkslab is of the "*chaoshou*" type with a rectangular ink pool surrounded by wide borders on three sides. The underside is hollowed with seven columns of irregular size. On the top near one end is an "eye" of golden yellow colour surrounded by purplish irrescendence. This was a very popular form of inkstone in the Song period.

In Song times Gaoyao was under the jurisdiction of Duanzhou, the production centre of Duanqi stone.

46

石雕像

北宋（公元960—1127年）
高30—40厘米
1976年紫金縣城郊林田鄉高墩頂山墓葬出土

A：面形方正，頭戴圓冠，身穿敞領寬袖長袍，腰束寬帶下垂至足，足穿方頭靴，拱手持笏而立，生肖動物附加在冠頂上。出土時共有七件，除二俑頭部損壞不知所屬外，餘為牛、龍、鼠、猴、虎。

B：仰首戴冠，身穿圓領寬袖長袍，袖向後飄如風吹動，腰束寬帶下垂至足，足穿方頭靴，拱手胸前持笏而立，可能是仰天造像。

C：伏地俑，面頰肌肉豐滿，圓眼外凸，雙手握拳作跪伏狀，頭稍仰，身穿寬袖長袍，腰束帶，可能是伏聽造像。

這批石雕像，均用紅沙岩圓雕成，面形方正，服飾厚重，有着明顯的宋代作風。其中生肖俑以往墓葬發現以陶俑為多，表現方式亦以人身獸頭或人物抱一像生動物為多見，這次出土的石俑頭戴圓冠，身穿長袍，持笏而立，僅在冠頂上稍露出所屬生肖動物頭像，相似的廣東僅見於海康宋墓出土的陶生肖俑，這種作法，與過去發現的文使俑極相似，應是雕刻工匠在塑造文使俑基礎上，豐富起來的另一種生肖表現方式。同這批石雕出土的還有圓雕石狗、浮雕石龍、石虎、石鳳、石鷄、和陶罈、瓷碗等。

Stone figures

Northern Song (AD960-1127)
Height: 30-40 cm.
Excavated in 1976 from a burial in Gaodundingshan, Lintianxiang, Zijin County.

A group of seven sandstone figures, all wearing long robes with a square headgear, the feet resting on rectangular pedestals. Five of the pieces represent animals of the zodiac, which can be identified by the relief animal heads on the top of the hat. The other two, one looking up into sky and another crouching on the floor are attendants or worshipers.

This group of red sandstone figures are rendered in the typical Song style, with squarish faces and the clothings delineated in forceful but simple lines. The most unusual feature is the zodiac animals represented by animal heads on the hat. This differs considerably from the more common representation as seen in the exhibits earlier with the animals either in the form of a whole head fitted on human bodies or are held in the hands of the figures; and they are invariably made of pottery or stoneware. The only parallel example of this style are pottery figures from the Haikang kiln. Both of them were obviously developed from the funerary official figures since Tang times. Apart from these figures, stone carving of a dog in the round and relief carvings of dragon, tiger, phoenix and chicken as well as pottery urns and porcelains bowls were unearthed in this tomb.

47

木雕羅漢

北宋慶曆年(公元1041—1048年)
A:通高52.5厘米
B:通高53.5厘米
1963年曲江縣南華寺大雄寶殿佛藏內發現

A:身穿交領長衣,垂足半趺坐,右足踏座,左足平趺,頭向右傾,閉目微笑,右手屈至右膝托頤,左手按左腿,如在酣睡中悟道;實心座前面刻有"慶曆年閏正月廣州右第一廂第六界囡弟子譚一娘捨尊者曰□□南華禪寺永樂二十年□月曲江河西信官□□□重糚成化十七年正月弟子□道聰重糚飾"銘文。由此可知,此木雕羅漢在明永樂、成化年曾作過二次糚飾。

B:支腿半趺坐,正首,身穿交領寬袖衫,右手平伸放於右腿上,左臂繞左膝,執展開經卷,張口大笑如頓悟經中真諦。實心座,前面刻有"廣州第一廂第三界居住女弟子囡九娘抽捨淨財收贖羅漢一尊□韶州南華寺供養乞保平安慶曆七年二月日置"銘文。

這些木雕羅漢像,採用檀香木和柏木雕成,刀法簡練,人物形態生動,大部分座上有銘文,在現存宋代木雕中極罕見,不愧為宋代木雕藝術的珍品。在宋代,這批羅漢像共有500尊,後因火災被燒毀140尊,明代曾進行補刻,但雕刻風格與宋代木雕完全不同,比宋代木雕羅漢大為遜色。

Wooden lohans

Qingli reign, Northern Song (AD1041-1048)
Overall height: (A) 52.5, (B) 53.5 cm.
Discovered in 1963 from the interior of a buddha statute in the grand hall, Nanhua temple, Qujiang County.

(A) Wooden lohan seated in the posture of "royal ease", with one leg flexed, the other raised and the knee supporting the right arm. The head is tilted and rests on the right hand as if in meditation. The cubical pedestal carries an inscription in the front, that includes the donar, Tan Yiniang and the Qingli reign date. The inscription also mentions that redecoration had been done in the 20th year of Yongle (AD1422) and 17th year Chenghua (AD1481), both in the Ming dynasty.

(B) Wooden lohan also seated in "royal ease", but with both hands holding a sutra scroll resting on the right foot. The joyous facial expression seems to indicate that he has attained enlightenment from the sutra. The frontal inscription mentions the donar, Ci Jiuniang and a date (7th year, Qingli - AD1047).

This splendid group of lohans were carved with simple and bold strokes out of sandalwood and cypress wood. Most of them carry inscriptions on the base or pedestal. According to the records, a total of five hundred different ones were originally dedicated to the temple in Song times. Later, 140 of them were destroyed in a fire and replacements were made in the Ming dynasty. But none of these later replicas matches with the Song originals and they are much inferior in quality.

銘文拓本
Rubbings of the inscriptions.

48

彩繪瓷罐

元至元三年（公元1337年）
通高31.5、口徑19.9厘米
1957年海康縣墓葬出土

罐直口，短頸，腹下漸往內收縮，圓餅形平底，外壁施青白釉，釉下用褐彩繪畫五層紋飾，第一層是肩部的飛鳳、喜鵲、纏枝菊組合紋，纏枝菊環繞在飛鳳、喜鵲四周，密而不亂，是主要紋飾之一。第二層是腹上部的一周帶狀錢紋，用以與肩部紋飾相隔。第三層位於腹中部，用豎錢紋分為四格，每格內棱花形開光，內畫一朵花葉四飄，生氣勃勃的折枝菊，亦為主要紋飾之一。第四層是腹下部上端的帶狀卷草紋，為第三層和第五層花紋的相隔層；第五層位於腹下部，用短直綫分為四格，每格內橢圓形開光，畫筆法簡單草率的折枝菊花；罐蓋作荷葉形，圓柱形鈕，弧形頂，頂上畫弦紋和蓮瓣紋。

這件瓷罐是元代褐色彩繪瓷器中的珍品，顯示了廣東元代生產褐色彩繪瓷器更臻於成熟。與這件瓷罐同出土的還有一塊買地券，寫明墓主人是一縣丞，死於元至元三年。

Covered jar

3rd year Zhiyuan reign, Yuan dynasty (AD1337)
Overall height: 31.5, diameter: 19.9 cm.
Excavated in 1957 from a burial in Haikang County.

This globular jar has a short neck and the lower part of the body tapers slightly towards the disc base. Under the *qingbai* glaze is painted in iron brown with five bands of decoration. The main band on the shoulders consists of phoenixes and magpie admist chrysanthemun scrolls. The lower part of the body is decorated with four ogival panels of chrysanthemun sprays separated by interlocking cash borders. Below a classical scroll border the base is painted with four oval panels of sketchy floral sprays. The cover is in the shape of a lotus leaf and topped by a cylindrical knob surrounded by brown painted bands and lotus petals.

Both the painting and potting of this specimen are of very high quality. A tablet from the tomb indicates that the deceased was a county magistrate and died in the 3rd year of the Zhiyuan reign (AD1337).

花紋展開圖
Drawing of the decorative bands.

49

瓷罐

元至正二十六年（公元1366年）
通高36、口徑10厘米
1973年順德縣大良鎮西山崗墓葬出土
順德縣博物館藏品

罐敞口，短頸，圓溜肩，肩下漸往內收，平底，外壁施白釉和斑塊狀綠釉；蓋頂隆起，中間有圓錐形鈕，厚邊，蓋下有子口。

該墓墓碑上刻有"元至正二十六年李宣義及梁氏合葬墓"銘文。

Covered jar

26th year Zhizhen reign, Yuan dynasty (AD1366)
Overall height: 36, diameter: 10 cm.
Excavated in 1973 from a burial in Xishangang, Dalaingzhen, Shunde County.
Collection of the Shunde County Museum.

The lower part of this jar tapers towards the flat base. The white glaze is mottled with green splashes. The cover has a conical knob and a thick flattened rim, under which is a flange for fitting onto the mouth of the body.

According to the tomb tablet, the deceased were Li Xuanyi and his wife Md. Liang and the tomb can be dated to the 26th year of the Zhizhen reign (AD1366).

50

青釉瓷罐

元代（公元1271—1368年）
通高9.2、口徑10.3厘米
1983年梅州市畬坑鎮出土

罐厚重，敞口，短頸，鼓腹，圈足，施青灰色釉，釉層較厚，外壁肩下劃弦紋一周，腹上部刻一周卷草紋，中部劃二周弦紋，下部刻劃斜綫紋；罐蓋弧形頂，寬邊，頂中間有圓錐形鈕，蓋下有子口，外壁刻劃二組連瓣紋。

Green glazed jar

Yuan dynasty (AD1271-1368)
Overall height: 9.2, diameter: 10.3 cm.
Excavated in 1983 in Yukengzhen, Meizhou City.

This heavily potted jar is covered with a thick greyish green glaze and stands on a footring. The lightly incised decoration consists of classical scrolls and vertical strips separated by horizontal lines. The domed cover has a conical knob and a flattened rim as well as a flange for fitting onto the mouth, and two groups of incised lotus petals.

51

瓷壺

元代（公元1271—1368年）
高12.8、口徑10.3厘米
1979年遂溪縣楊甘鎮下山井村窰址採集

直口，圓唇，最大徑在腹下部，平底，釉已剝落，腹部壓直凹槽，劃有兩道弦紋，並寫有"金玉滿堂"四字。

該壺與雙耳瓷瓶（展品58）同一地點出土，其年代亦當相距不遠。

Stoneware ewer

Yuan dynasty (AD1271-1368)
Height: 12.8, diameter: 10.3 cm.
Collected in 1979 from the Xiashanjingcun kiln site, Yang'ganzhen, Suiqi County.

This ewer has a globular body and a wide mouth with a thickened lid. The base is flat and most of the glaze has been flaked off. The lobed body is incised with two horizontal lines and written in brown with four characters, "*Jinyu mantang*" (gold and jade fill the hall).

This ewer was found together with the vase with twin handles (exhibit 58) and they should be of the same date.

52

青瓷碗

元代（公元1271—1368年）
A（左）：碗高6.5、口徑16.5厘米
B（右）：碗高6.5、口徑16.5厘米
1969年珠海市蚊洲島沙灘出土

A：胎質厚重，敞口，弧壁，圈足，足底壁向內削斜，內壁印纏枝花卉，施青黃色釉。

B：胎厚重，花瓣形口，弧壁，圈足，外口沿下劃有四道弦紋，外壁豎劃直綫紋，內壁印折枝花卉，內底印一朵圓形花，施淡青色釉。

珠海市蚊洲島出土的這批瓷器，胎骨厚重，內壁多模印花卉圖案，釉層較厚而使印花表面不甚明顯是其特徵，其中碗的造型與江西撫州元代合葬墓出土的碗基本相同，內壁印折枝菊花、蓮花圖案的作法在陝西銅川黃堡窰第三期金元文化層中也有發現。這批瓷器共出土二百多件，出土時發現有腐朽了的草木灰痕，說明當時這些瓷器是用草包裝的，從瓷器埋於沙灘和蚊洲島位於廣州至東南亞各地的必經之路看，這些瓷器應是當時的外銷商品。

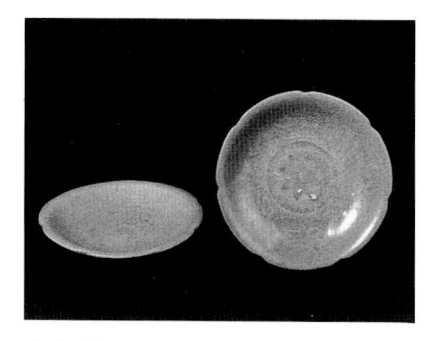

青瓷碟

元代（公元1271—1368年）
A（左）：高3.3、口徑15.6厘米
B（右）：高3.7、口徑16.1厘米
1969年珠海市蚊洲島沙灘出土

A:胎骨厚重,花瓣形口,淺弧壁,圈足,外口沿下劃弦紋,外壁豎劃短直綫紋,施淡青色釉,釉開冰裂紋片。

B:胎厚重,花瓣形口,淺弧壁,圈足,內底旋一圓圈,圈內印花朵,內壁印折枝花,施青黃色釉,由於釉層較厚,花紋不甚明顯。

Green glazed bowls and dishes

Yuan dynasty (AD1271-1368)
Bowls: height: 6.5, diameter: 16.5 cm.
Dishes: height: 3.3-3.7, diameter: 15.6-16.1 cm.
Excavated in 1969 in a beach in Wenzhou Island, Zhuhai city.

Both bowls and dishes are heavily potted and the foot roughly cut. On the interior are moulded with floral designs in relief. These specimens are part of a hoard of ceramics found in Wenzhou Island. They are characterized by a thick body, indistinct moulded decoration under a thick yellowish green glaze. The form of the bowls are very similar to the ones found in a Yuan tomb in Wuzhou, Jiangxi and the impressed designs of chrysanthemun sprays and lotus can be found on Yaozhou wares of the Jin to Yuan periods in Huangbaozhen, Tongchuan, Shaanxi. Thus it is very safe to date this hoard to the Yuan dynasty.

A total of more than two hundred items made up this hoard. During excavation it was observed that the pieces were surrounded by traces of disintegrated straw ash. It has been a common practice to tie ceramic pieces in bundles and wrapped in straws or reeds for transportation. This hoard was very probably packed in this way and as Wenzhou Island is on the trade route between Guangzhou and Southeast Asia, these items must have been ceramic commodities for export.

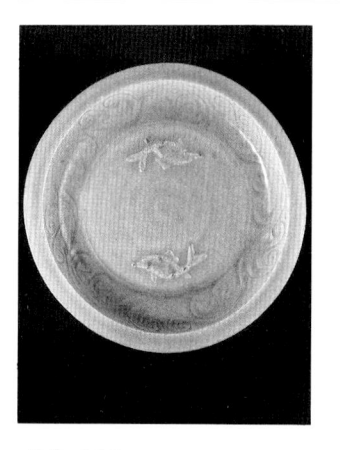

53

青瓷大洗

元代(公元1271—1368年)
高7.2、口徑37.8厘米
五十年代潮州東風橫沙堤遺址出土

施淡青釉,寬平折沿,弧壁,圈足,足壁向內斜,洗外壁壓印蓮花瓣紋,內壁刻波浪紋,內底模印兩條鯉魚,鯉魚尖頭,身上有鱗,背上有鰭,如魚在波浪中游戲,達到了極高的藝術水平。

Large celadon basin

Yuan dynasty (AD1271-1368)
Height: 7.2, diameter: 37.8 cm.
Excavated in the fifties from the Dongfeng Hengshati site, Chaozhou.

This basin, with a wide flattened rim is covered with a pale green celadon glaze. The footring is bevelled on the outside. The underside is moulded with relief petals and the inside cavetto is incised with classical scroll. The centre sprigged with two carps swimming in opposite directions. The carps are lively rendered with scales and fins.

54

青瓷盤

元代（公元1271—1368年）
高4.2、口徑18.4厘米
1976年揭陽縣東山鎮新蘇村鄭厝場出土
揭陽縣博物館藏品

盤口，弧壁、圈足，素面無紋，施青白釉，釉層較厚。

Celadon basin

Yuan dynasty (AD1271-1368)
Height: 4.2, diameter: 18.4 cm.
Excavated in 1976 in Zhengcuochang, Xinsucun, Dongshanzhen, Jieyang County.
Collection of the Jieyang County Museum.

Basin with flattened rim, curved well, a footring and undecorated. The light green glaze is thick and opaque.

55

青釉高足杯

元代（公元1271—1368年）
A（左）:高11、口徑11.3厘米
B（右）:高9.9、口徑10.9厘米
1983年梅州市畲坑鎮墓葬出土

A:胎骨厚重，壁微弧、喇叭形實足，足近底部外撇，中間有二道弦紋，外壁刻有八朵折枝花卉，施青灰色釉。

B:胎、造型和花紋與A件相同，不同的是足底壁向內削斜，杯內底旋有二道弦紋圈。

Celadon stemcups

Yuan dynasty (AD1271-1368)
Height: 9.9-11, diameter: 10.9-11.3 cm.
Excavated in 1983 from a burial in Yukengzhen, Meizhou city.

Two stemcups of similar form, heavily potted and supported by a solid flaring stem with twin ribs. One of the piece is bevelled near the footrim. The cup is incised with eight floral sprays on the exterior.

56

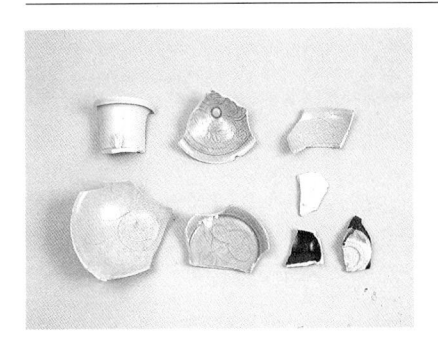

瓷片

宋/元，十二至十四世紀
長:6.5-15厘米
1978年香港大嶼山稔樹灣採集
香港博物館中央考古資料庫藏品

　　此八種瓷片標本均為宋元時期外銷瓷的常見品種。醬釉茶盌殘片，近似廣州西村窰產品；大缸殘片，米紅色胎，釉已剝落，殘存清晰的戳印花卉紋，是廣東南海奇石窰的特點。其餘青釉瓷片似是閩，浙兩省產品；福建青瓷，胎質較粗，釉呈青黃色調，另外篦點和篦劃花紋，是其特色。

　　稔樹灣出土的瓷片，年代應為北宋至元代，約十二至十四世紀，並與當時的海外貿易有關連。

Ceramic sherds

Song to Yuan dynasties, 12th to 14th centuries.
Length: 6.5-15 cm.
Collected in 1978 from Nianshuwan, Dayushan (Nim Shu Wan, Lantao Island), Hong Kong.
Collection of the Central Archaeological Repository of the Hong Kong Museum of History.

　　These eight sherds probably come from different provincial kiln sites. The two dark brown sherds of a tea bowl resemble those produced in Xicun, Guangzhou, while the buff sherd of a "Martaban" jar, with impressed leavy design is of a typical group commonly attributed to the Qishi kiln site, not far away from Shiwan, Foshan City, Guangdong. The other celadon sherds come from Zhejiang and Fujian, with the latter ones glazed in olive green and decorated with combings or "dotted combing" on a coarse body.

　　By comparison with specimens of known date, these specimens from Nianshuwan probably date from the Northern Song to the Yuan periods (12th to 14th centuries), and undoubtedly all of them were related with the massive export trade between Guangzhou and overseas countries.

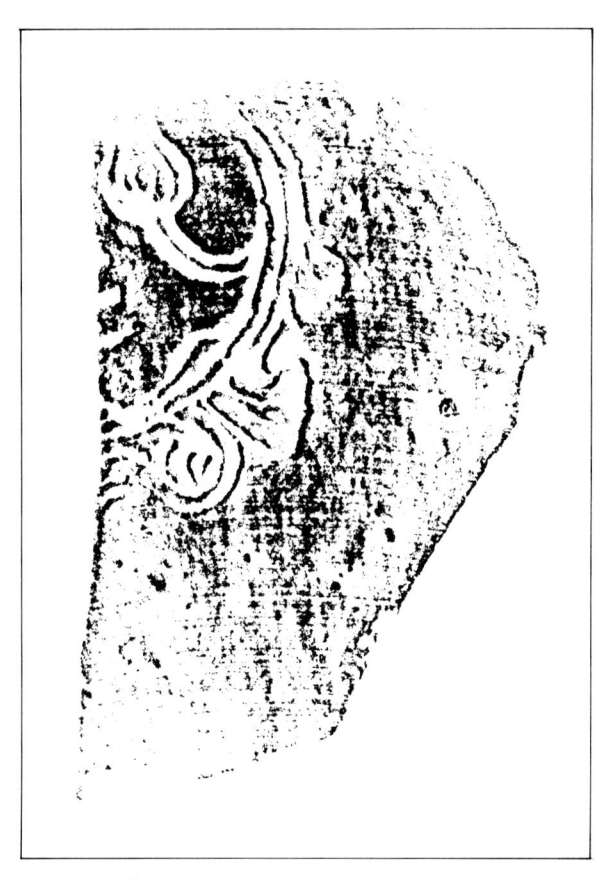

戳印花紋拓片
Rubbing of motif on sherd.

57

青瓷片

宋至元，公元十三至十四世紀
長/徑：4.9-9.7厘米
1962年香港大嶼山石壁出土
香港博物館中央考古資料庫藏品

六十年代初期，大嶼山興建石壁水塘，出土了大量青瓷及宋代銅錢。青瓷器胎質細膩，潔白，釉色粉青，釉層較厚，少開片；裝飾技法有印、貼、堆花等；花紋有團花，雙魚和纏枝花卉。器足或口沿露胎部份，經二次氧化成磚紅色。綜合以上特徵，此批青瓷器質量較閩、粵產品為優，應屬浙江龍泉窯系。

石壁出土青瓷的品種，亦見於韓國木浦新安十四世紀前期沉船遺物中，故其年代相近，應為南宋末至元代產品。

Celadon sherds

Song to Yuan dynasties, 13th to 14th centuries.
Length/diameter: 4.9-9.7 cm.
Collected in 1962 from Shibi, Dayushan (Shek Pik, Lantao Island), Hong Kong.
Collection of the Central Archaeological Repository of the Hong Kong Museum of History.

These celadon specimens together with a large number of coins were found in the early sixties during the construction of the Shek Pik Reservoir. They are of a very high quality, with a high fired off white body and covered with a thick, opaque sea green glaze, that one often associates with the typical products of Longquan, Zhejiang. The decorative technique includes sprigging and moulding of floral medallions, floral scrolls and double fish. The unglazed parts, such as footrims, appear in reddish brown, due to secondary oxidation, a hallmark of all Longquan products.

Nearly all the sherds can be compared to the celadons found in the Sinan shipwreck in Korea, which can be dated to the first half of the 14th century.

58

雙耳瓷瓶

元代（公元1271—1368年）
高54，口徑8厘米
1979年遂溪縣楊甘鎮下山井村窯址出土

花瓣形口，長頸，溜肩，底殘，外口沿下劃有弦紋五周，頸上有一對"S"形耳，肩上有一周凸弦紋，施醬褐色釉。

此處窯場範圍較大，從下山井村西邊連至薄寮村東面，面積近4500平方米，窯具往往刻有銘文，過去就曾發現有"張告用"銘文壓錘，和"大德九年"（公元1305年）銘文碗模。

Vase with twin handles

Yuan dynasty (AD1271-1368)
Height: 54, diameter: 8 cm.
Excavated in 1979 from the Xiashanjingcun kiln site, Yang'ganzhen, Suiqi County.

A tall vase with a cylindrical neck ended with a foliated mouth. Below the rim are five incised bands and a pair of "S" shaped ears are luted onto the lower part of the neck near the shoulders. The overall glaze is of a dark brown colour. The base is fragmentary.

This kiln site occupies a vase area of about 4500 square metres spreading from the west of Xiashanjingcun to the east of Boliaocun. Very often inscriptions are found on the kiln furnitures. Two of such inscriptions have been found. One is a pottery stamp with a "*Zhang Gaoyong*" mark and the other is a pottery mould for bowls with an inscribed date corresponding to AD1305.

59

醬釉瓷瓶

元代（公元1271—1368年）
高13.5、口徑4.4厘米
1986年海康縣紀家鎮公益鄉窰出土。

敞口，束頸，鼓腹、喇叭形實足，頸上有一對"S"形耳，肩上和腹下部各有凸弦紋一周，施醬黑色釉。這類"S"形耳瓷瓶，在元代較爲常見。

Brown glazed vase

Yuan dynasty (AD1271-1368)
Height: 13.5, diameter: 4.4 cm.
Excavated in 1986 from the Gongyixiang kiln site, Jijiazhen, Haikang County.

The globular body is suppported by a solid trumpet foot and topped by a flaring cylindrical neck with a pair of "S" shaped handles. On the shoulders and near the foot are raised bands. The overall glaze is of a dark brown colour. The "S" shaped handle is a very characteristic feature of Yuan ceramics.

60

三足爐

元代（公元1271—1368年）
高5.1、口徑12.6厘米
1986年海康縣紀家鎮公益村採集

敞口，束頸，鼓腹，平底，底下有三只獸蹄足，兩邊腹部連着口沿有一對板形耳，造形較爲美觀。

此爐的採集地點距公益村窰址約700米，是一塊鄰近小溪的狹長平坦坡地，在長200米、寬30米範圍內，地表散布着許多殘瓷片，可能是當時堆放待運貨物場地或碼頭。這裏的小溪流約五華里與覃後溪相通，覃後溪清代尚可通航，是海康主要河流——南渡河上游的一條支流，當時紀家鎮公益村附近窰場的產品，可能就是從這裏經水路通覃後溪和南渡河外運的。

Tripod censer

Yuan dynasty (AD1271-1368)
Height: 5.1, diameter: 12.6 cm.
Collected in 1986 from Gongyicun, Jijiazhen, Haikang County.

The globular body is topped by a restricted neck and an up-turned lid attached to two vertical flat handles, and stands on three cabriole feet.
This specimen was collected in a flat river slope about 700 metres from the Gongyicun kiln site. Scattered around the slope, within an area of 200 × 30 metres are numerous potsherd, indicating that the location was probably a depot or pier for the finished products to other places. A nearby river joins with Tanhouqi, which was navigable in Qing times, and the latter was an upper branch of the Nandu River, the main drainage in Haikang region. Therefore, the products of the kiln complexes in this area must have been transported to other regions through this river network.

61

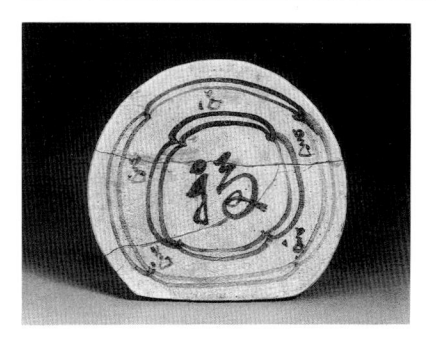

彩繪瓷枕

元代（公元1271—1368年）
枕面長23、寬21厘米
1986年海康縣楊家鎮土壙窰址出土

枕底已殘缺，枕面中間微凹，前沿平直，左右和後沿呈弧形，施青黃色釉，枕面釉下用褐彩繪二層雙綫弧形圈，兩圈之間草書五個小"花"字，中間寫一個大"福"字。

海康楊家鎮土壙鄉地處南渡河畔，古代水絡暢通，窰址成羣，1986年在土壙壚發掘了一條龍窰，長25.4米，寬1.82至2米，遺物主要是青釉瓷器，彩繪瓷器較少。

Painted pillow

Yuan dynasty (AD1271-1368)
Length: 23, width: 21 cm.
Excavated in 1986 from the Tukuang kiln site, Yangjiazhen, Haikang County.

The lower portion of this pillow is missing and the bean shaped top is slightly concave in the centre. Under the yellowish green glaze are painted in brown with a large *ruyi* panel with a "*fu*" (blessing) character enclosed by double band within which are five "*hua*" (flower) characters.

The Tukuang kiln site is located on the river bank of Nanduhe. In ancient times this was served by excellent river network and a great many ancient kiln sites have been located. In 1986 a dragon kiln was excavated in this site. This kiln is 25.4 metres long and 1.82 to 2 metres wide and the main products are celadon wares, painted pieces are rare.

62

彩繪陶瓶

元代（公元1271—1368年）
高37.6、口徑7厘米
1981年深圳市南頭後海出土
深圳市博物館藏品

器灰黃胎。敞口、直頸、廣肩、長身、深腹、圈足。肩部兩側各有雙橫耳，與耳垂直方向的圈足上各有兩孔，便於穿繩提攜。

頸部及圈足下部均為一周褐色彩。器身用褐彩描繪花紋圖案，自肩至圈足共五組花紋：一、四組為蓮瓣紋、二、五組為卷葉紋，三組為前後兩朵盛開的牡丹花，枝葉舒展，旁邊配以龜背錦紋相襯。

此器造型美觀，花紋精細別緻，圖案層次勻稱有序，有很強的藝術感。

Painted vase

Yuan dynasty (AD1271-1368)
Height: 37.6, diameter at mouth: 7 cm.
Excavated in 1981 in Haohai, Nantao, Shenzhen City.
Collection of the Shenzhen City Museum.

A *meiping* vase with a greyish buff body, two pairs of horizontal looped handles on the shoulder, and two corresponding holes on the footring for the insertion of a string for carrying. The decorative motifs are arranged in bands between solid brown bands around the neck and the foot. The painted bands include lotus petals, classical scrolls, and ogival panels of peony sprays reserved on a diaper ground. Both the drawing and potting are of refined workmanship.

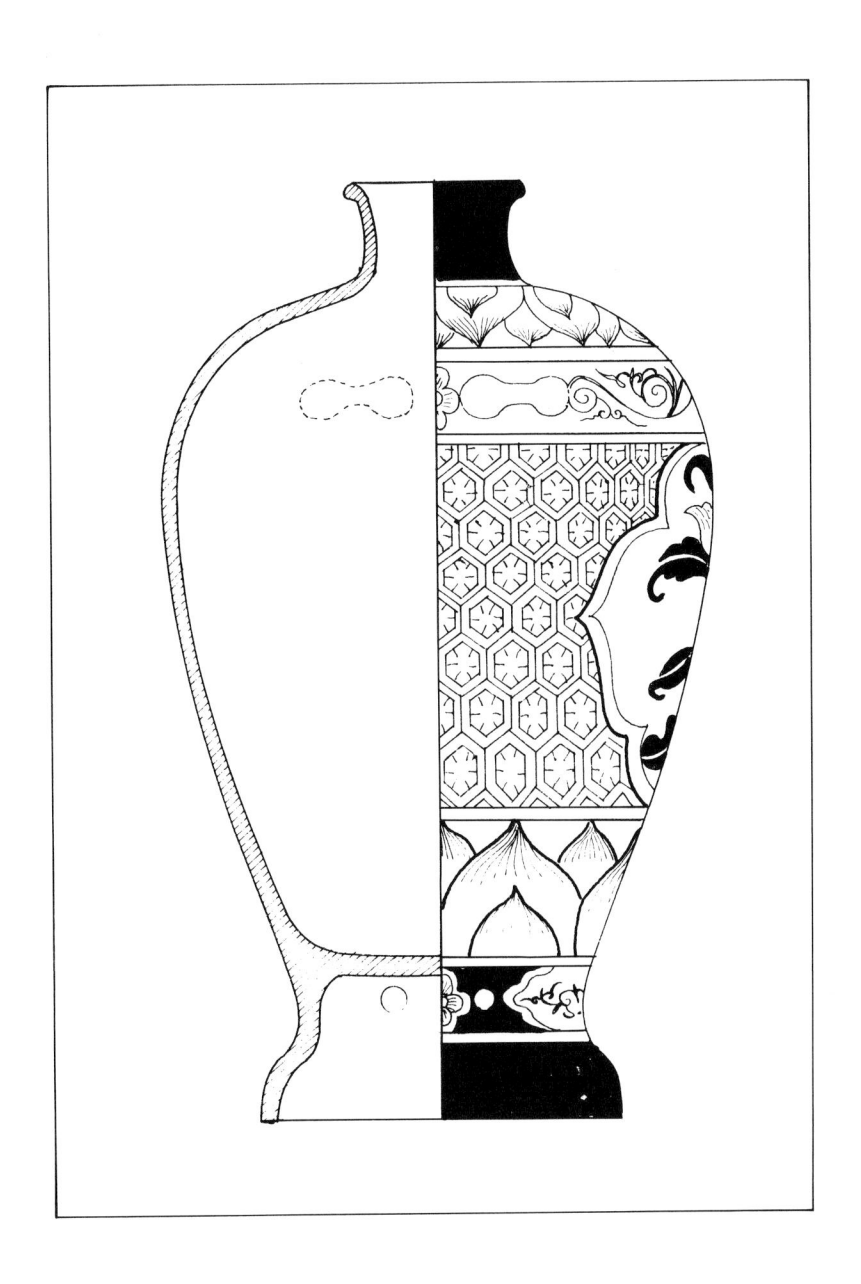

花紋展開圖
Drawing of the designs.

63

陶罈

元代（公元1271—1368年）
高43、口徑14.2厘米
1976年揭陽縣新亨鎮碩和石交椅山出土
揭陽縣博物館藏品

葬具。灰胎。帶蓋。蓋頂中央為一朵蓮花瓣形鈕。蓋面彩繪三組卷草紋，蓋肩部彩繪兩朵卷雲紋，均為赫褐色彩。

器身直口，矮頸，溜肩，深腹，腹較寬大，平底微凹。

器身貼塑造像較多，部分還殘留有褐色彩繪。近底部為蓮花瓣座，座上正中為長方形門框，門楣為半圓拱，上繪一朵桃花，枝葉向兩側伸展。門內刻劃出兩扇門扉及門環耳。門兩側貼塑兩尊守門武士俑，戎裝站立，手持器械。左右兩邊分別貼塑一龍一虎，龍身劃鱗櫛，虎身彩繪虎皮。有足。均作騰雲狀，其上各有一組六尊生肖屬相人俑，共十二尊，站立於祥雲之上，身穿衣袍，雙手持笏，頭冠上塑十二生肖，惜部分缺殘。

此器造型奇特，貼塑造像豐富多彩，工藝複雜，是一件反映當時民間風俗的陶瓷工藝品。

出土時，內置經火燒的骨殖。同類器物，在廣東廉江縣及雲南滇西元明火葬墓中也有發現。江西、福建出土的元代瓷瓶，器身上亦常見堆塑龍虎。

Pottery urn

Yuan dynasty (AD1271-1368)
Height: 43, diameter: 14.2 cm.
Excavated in 1976 from Jiaoyishan, Shiheshi, Xinhengzhen, Jieyang County.
Collection of the Jieyang County Museum.

A covered funerary jar with a grey body. The cover is topped by a lotus bud shaped knob and painted with three groups of classical scrolls on the surface and along the edge. The globular body stands on a relief lotus petal pedestal and the flat base is slightly concave. On one side is modelled with a doorway flanked by two warrior guardians and topped by an arch of peach spray. On the two sides of the door are a dragon and tiger in high relief each carrying six figures representing the animals of the zodiac. All the relief appliques are highlighted with brown painting. The form of this jar is unique.

Cremated bone was found inside the jar and similar pieces were also discovered in Lianjiang, Guangdong and Tianxi, Yunan. The tiger and dragon relief designs are common decorative motifs found on porcelain urns of the Yuan dynasty found in Jiangxi and Fujian provinces.

花紋展開圖
Drawing of the relief designs.

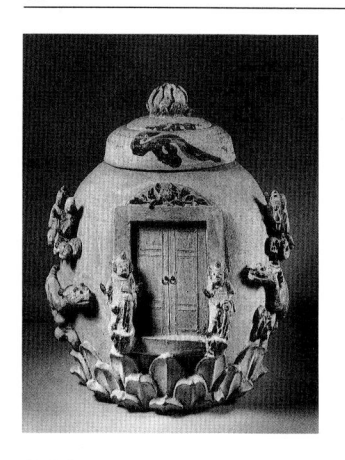

64

磚刻像

元代（公元1271—1368年）
長23、寬12.5、厚2厘米
1976年海康縣東里鎮淡水鄉墓葬出土
海康縣博物館藏品

A：生肖刻像，豎刻，人物面形方正，頭上戴冠，外穿敞領寬袖長袍，內穿長裙蓋足，雙手拱於胸前持笏而立，其中左邊一件冠頂上刻鼠頭，旁邊有一"子"字，中間一件冠頂上刻馬頭，旁邊有一"午"字，右邊一件冠頂上刻羊頭，旁邊有一"未"字。

B：左屈客、右屈客刻像，人物頭戴曲翅幞頭，內穿交領衫，外穿緊袖長袍，腰束帶，足穿鞋，兩手相握拱手胸前，其中左屈客（左）身、頭向右側、手左拱，右邊豎刻"左屈客"三字；右屈客（右）身、頭左側、手右拱，左邊豎刻有"右屈客"三字。這兩個屈客像，服飾等均與東叫、西應刻像不同，可能是身份較高的家奴。

C：西應刻像（左），頭戴裹巾，束髻，內穿交領衫，外穿緊袖圓領長袍，腰束帶，腳穿長褲，足穿鞋，雙手握一棒狀物舉至腹部，左邊有"西應"二字。此像與東叫成一對，為家奴刻像。

D：墓門判官刻像（右），立刻像，頭戴官冕，連鬚，身穿寬袖長袍，腰束帶，足穿靴，雙手拱於胸前，右邊豎刻有"墓門判官"四字。此像為墓門官吏，與《大漢厚陵秘葬經》所記天子陵墓中的閽門使、皇門使之類相似。

E：伏屍刻像，像橫刻，裸體，頭仰起，結圓髻，一手前伸，一手屈放於胸前，腰束帶，二腳向後直伸作臥伏狀，上面豎刻有"伏屍"二字。此為鬼奴刻像，漢代買地券中常有"如地中伏有屍骸者，男為奴，女為婢""田中若有屍死，男即為奴，女即當為婢，皆為□□趨走給使"等記載。

這批磚刻像，磚上端均有一小圓孔便於懸掛，出土時放在磚石合構墓室四周，共三十餘件，部分已散失，現存29件，內容有生肖像、青龍、豬雀、玄武、勾陳、地軸、金雞、玉犬、墓門判官、張堅固、覆聽、蒿里父老、左屈客、右屈客、東叫西應、喚婢、川山、伏屍和持笏人物坐像等。

Inscribed tomb bricks

Yuan dynasty (AD1271-1368)
Length: 23, width: 12.5, thickness: 2 cm.
Excavated in 1976 from a burial in Danshui Village, Donglizhen, Haikang County.
Collection of the Haikang County Museum.

This group of tomb brick are all rectangular slabs with a small perforation on the top, probably for hanging inside the tomb chamber. During the excavation they were found scattered around in the tomb interior of brick and stone structure. There should be more than 30 pieces, but some of them had lost and only 29 are preserved. Each brick is incised with a human figure in the centre accompanied by inscribed captions in standard script. The figures are meant to represent the animals of the zodiac and the four quarters, officials of the underground world, attendants and slaves.

The pieces selected for this exhibition are:

(A) Three animals of the zodiac: rat (*zi*), horse (*wu*), and ram (*wei*).
(B) Two attendants: servants of the right and left.
(C) Household slave of the west.
(D) Tomb gate administrative assistant.
(E) Lying corpse ("ghost slave").

砖刻拓片
Rubbings of the bricks.

65

銅鈔版

元代（公元1271—1368年）
長26.5、寬20、厚1厘米、重2.75千克
1975年揭西縣五雲鎮羅洛村老廍塘出土

灰黑色。中間有銹蝕殘損孔。這是印製紙鈔的錢版。平面為長方形，鑄銘陽紋及反體陽文，文字均作楷體。上端自左至右橫銘"至元通行寶鈔"；左右角各有一紋飾。下為一周鳳鳥花卉紋，中間鑄銘文字，分為上下兩個部分，上部中央為"貳貫"兩個大字，其下各一串銅錢紋；左右各有一行八思巴文，八思巴文之下，右邊為"字號"，左邊為"字料"（？）。下部共有十一行豎文，中央為"偽造者處死"，字體略大，其下兩行小字：首告者賞銀伍定仍給犯人家產。左邊五行小字："尚書省奏准印造至元寶鈔宣課差發內並行收受不限年月諸路通行寶鈔庫子攢司印造庫子攢司"。右邊四行小字："至元年月日寶鈔庫使副印造庫使副尚書省提舉司"。

中國使用紙幣始於北宋，元代發行紙幣較多。至元寶鈔為至元二十四年（公元1287）所發行。元末濫發紙幣，鈔幣幾乎等於廢紙。

至元寶鈔銅版在河北省也有發現。

Bronze printing block

Yuan dynasty (AD1271-1368)
Length: 26.5, width: 20, thickness: 1 cm, weight: 2.75 Kg.
Found in 1975 from Laomatang, Luolecun, Wuyunzhen, Jiexi County.

A bronze block for printing paper currency with a blackish surface patina and in some areas there are pit holes from wear and tear as well as rusting. The printing surface is rectangular, with characters in standard script. The enclosing border is made up of phoenixes admist floral scrolls. Above this border is a narrow rectangle, containing the title: *Zhiyuan tongxing baochao* (Precious paper currency of the Zhiyuan reign), flanked by two flaming pearls. The central region is divided into four portions; the upper part with a square in the middle, within which are two strings of cash, flanked on the two sides with Pagspa scripts. The lower portion consists of entirely inscriptions of the issuing department, reign date, titles of responsible officials and warnings.

Paper currency was first used in China in the Northern Song period but it was in the Yuan that paper notes gained their popularity. The "*Zhiyuan tongxing baochao*" was issued in the 24th year of the Zhiyuan reign (AD1287), but soon afterwards, due to inflation and reckless issuance, its value depreciated immensely.

Similar blocks of the same reign was also discovered in Hebei.

鈔版印本
Ink impression of the block.

66

銅官印

元・至元十五年（公元1279年）
邊長8.4、厚1.9、通高8厘米
1963年南雄縣出土

印體扁方形，上有扁形長執把。印面寬緣，內篆刻八思巴文字，分列三行，每行三字，順讀為"南雄州路總管府之印"。背面左右兩邊各刻一行草書漢字，右邊一行為"南雄州路總管府之印"。左邊一行為"至元十五年七月"。

宋至元初，南雄設州，至元十五年改州為路，設南雄路總管府。元代至元年號有二個，「後至元」共六年，故此印應為「前至元」（公元1279年）元世祖忽必列時代遺物。

Bronze official seal

Zhiyuan, Yuan dynasty (AD1279)
Length: 8.4, thickness: 1.9, overall height: 8 cm.
Unearthed in 1963 in Nanhsiong County.

A square seal with a rectangular grip. The seal characters in Pagspa script, arranged in three rows, read "Seal of the Nanhsiong Prefecture Route Command". Identical inscription, but in Chinese, was incised on the right edge of the top surface, and on the left edge was inscribed with a row of Chinese, "Seventh month of the 15th year of Zhiyuan" (AD1279).

In the Song and early Yuan periods Nanhsiong was administrated as a prefecture, but in the 15th year of the Zhiyuan reign the name prefecture was changed to "route". There were two Zhiyuan reigns in the Yuan dynasty, but the latter one only lasted six years. Therefore the reign date inscribed on the seal should belong to the former "Zhiyuan" and corresponded to AD1279 when Kublai Khan was the emperor.

印文
Vermilion impression.

67

彩繪瓷罐

明代(公元1368—1644年)
通高12、口徑7.6厘米
1983年海康縣雷城鎮蟹坡墓葬出土
海康縣博物館藏品

灰白色胎,直口,圓唇,鼓腹,圓餅形厚底,肩上堅塑有四隻半環形耳,外壁施青白色釉,釉下用褐色彩繪畫花紋。其中肩上各耳之間畫短纏枝卷草紋,腹部弦文,內畫帶狀卷草紋;蓋作碗形,弧壁,頂上有圓餅形鈕,外壁施青白釉,蓋內不施釉,無子口。

此罐出土時有明"洪武通寶"銅錢共存,器型明顯比宋元瓷器縮小,花紋裝飾風格雖與海康宋元時期瓷器相同,但趨向簡單,是海康明代窯場的產品。

Covered jar

Ming dynasty (AD1368-1644)
Overall height: 12, diameter at mouth: 7.6 cm.
Excavated in 1983 from a burial in Xiepo, Leichengzhen, Haikang County.
Collection of the Haikang Museum.

A globular jar with a solid disc base and a cover in the form of a bowl, the shoulders with four looped handles. The cover is in the form of a bowl, with *qingbai* glaze on the outside only, the base is also solid. The jar is cover by a *qingbai* glaze, under which is painted in brown with a band of classical scroll and abstract scrolls between the handles on the shoulder.

This jar was found together with Ming coins of the "Hongwu" reign. The decoration, though very similar in style to the Song and Yuan ones, is much simplified and the form is smaller than the earlier ones. A typical product of the Haikang kiln of the Ming dynasty.

68

綠釉陶罐

明代(公元1368—1644年)
通高55、口徑7.3厘米
1985年中山市石岐城區蓮花峯墓葬出土
中山博物館藏品

胎呈淺橙紅色,斂口,寬沿,鼓腹,平底內凹,肩上印有三重菊瓣紋;罐蓋弧形頂,無邊,下有子口,頂中間有花瓣形圓鈕,外壁印有二重蓮瓣紋,罐和蓋均施綠釉,肩部最下層菊瓣和蓋上層菊瓣施黃釉。

這類陶罐也有罐和蓋施黃釉的,如果罐施黃釉,則罐下層菊瓣和蓋頂菊瓣施綠彩,釉藥均是溫度較低的鉛釉。

Green glazed jar

Ming dynasty (AD1368-1644)
Overall height: 55, diameter at mouth: 7.3 cm.
Excavated in 1985 from a burial in Lianhuafeng, Shiqi, Zhongshan City.
Collection of the Zhongshan Museum.

The body is of reddish brown colour, and the flat base is slightly concave. The domed cover is topped by a round knob of floral medallion shape and surrounded by two rolls of chrysanthemun petals glazed in green and yellow. The shoulders of the body are moulded with three bands of similar petals with the outer band glazed in yellow, all the rest together with the body are in green.

The overall glaze is of the low-fired lead glaze type. In some other examples the main colour is in yellow but two of the petal bands as in this specimen are glazed in green instead.

69

印花罐

明代（公元1368—1644年）
通高31.5、口徑12.4厘米
六十年代中山市出土

敞口，短束頸，最大徑在肩部，肩下漸往內收，平底，腹部四開光，內模印陽紋花卉樹木和動物圖案，罐口沿、頸、腹部開光之間和樹葉施綠釉，開光地施白釉，邊沿和樹幹施醬釉；蓋頂高隆，中間有圓錐形鈕，下有子口，外壁模印如意蓮瓣紋，蓋表面施綠釉，鈕施藍釉。

從此罐的胎質和裝飾手法看，應是佛山窰的產品。

Covered jar

Ming Dynasty (AD1368-1644)
Overall height: 31.5, mouth diameter: 12.4 cm.
Found in Zhongshan City in the sixties.

A covered stoneware jar with a flat base and moulded decoration. The body is decorated with garden scenes on a white ground within *ruyi* panels. Outside the panels are glazed in mottle green and the edges as well as the designs are highlighted in brown. The cover, with *ruyi* panels and a blue conical knob is in green glaze.

Both the paste and decorative technique are typical of the Foshan kiln complex.

70

綠釉罐

明代（公元1368—1644年）
高21.3、口徑10厘米
1987年東莞縣皇村鎮石鼓鄉採集

陶胎，敞口，厚圓唇，短頸，圓溜肩，肩下漸往內收，平底，外壁施綠色釉，內壁不施釉。

Green glazed jar

Ming dynasty (AD1368-1644)
Height: 21.3, mouth diameter: 10 cm.
Collected in 1987 from Shigu Village, Huangcunzhen, Dong'guan County.

A globular earthenware jar, with a thickened mouthrim and a flat base. The outside is glazed in green and the inside is unglazed.

71

青瓷罐

明代（公元1368—1644年）
通高8.7、口徑7.3厘米
1985年大埔縣高陂鎮青碗窰窰址出土

瓷胎潔白，罐直口，圓唇，鼓腹，圈足；蓋弧頂寬邊，頂中間有圓柱形高鈕，蓋下有子口，施青白釉。

青碗窰窰址位於有瓷土近山溪的墓山之中，距高陂鎮約5公里，沒有水路與高陂鎮相通，當時瓷器產品應是用人工挑至高陂鎮運銷外地的。

Celadon jar

Ming dynasty (AD1368-1644)
Overall height: 8.7, mouth diameter: 7.3 cm.
Excavated in 1985 from Qingwanyao kiln site, Gaopozhen, Dapu County.

A compressed round jar with a wide mouth and footring. The cover has a flattened edge and a cylindrical knob. The glaze is pale green.

The Qingwanyao kiln site is situated in a mountainous area about five kilometres from Gaopozhen. Porcelain clay was available from local mines and the mountain streams provide water for the refining of the raw material. But there is no river network connecting the site and Gaopo. So the finished products must have been transported to other places by land.

輔照三
Supp. illustration 3

青花瓷罐

明代（公元1368—1644年）
通高16—17厘米
口徑7.2—7.8厘米
1988年東莞市篁村羅亨信墓出土

AB器身的形製、花紋均相同，器蓋則有別。器身直口，短頸，圓肩，深腹，下部微束，平底。肩部一周蓮瓣紋，腹部爲纏枝蓮花紋，下腹一周雲頭紋。每組花紋又間以弦紋。器蓋，A蓋頂乳鈕較大，蓋面一周菊瓣紋及二周弦紋；B蓋頂乳鈕略小，蓋面一周雲頭紋。

Pair of blue and white jars

Ming dynasty (AD1368-1644)
Overall height: 16-17, mouth diameter: 7.2-7.8 cm.
Excavated in 1988 from the Luo Hengxin tomb in Huangcun, Dong'guan City

A pair of *guan*-shaped miniature jars of similar form and design. The decorative motifs consist of a lotus petal band on the shoulders, below which is a lotus scroll and around the foot is a band of trifoils. The two covers are different, one has a larger knob and decorated with chrysanthemun petals, while the other is painted with trifoils.

72

青釉瓷碗

明代（公元1368—1644年）
A:高6.7、口徑14.8厘米
B:高6、口徑14.8厘米
1960年惠東縣新菴鄉三村窰址出土

胎較厚，均作敞口，圓唇，深腹，矮圈足。施釉，底露胎。腹部印刻蓮瓣紋。

A:腹較深，內底凹下，中心微隆。腹壁花紋略顯。施青黃釉，呈冰裂狀。內外壁均可見胎眼。

B:腹略淺，內底心微隆。腹壁花紋清晰。近口沿處兩周弦紋。施青綠釉。

新菴窰燒造的瓷器，形製較爲粗重。釉色以青釉爲主，仿燒龍泉窰的產品。部分器物釉色晶瑩如玉，達到較高的水平。新菴瓷窰數量多，分布廣，均系饅頭窰。

Green glazed bowls

Ming dynasty (AD1368-1644)
(A) Height: 6.7, diameter: 14.8 cm.
(B) Height: 6, diameter: 14.8 cm.
Excavated in 1960 from the Sancun kiln site in Xin'an Village, Huidong County.

Both bowls are thickly potted with rounded wall and low foot, which is unglazed. The underside incised and impressed with lotus petals. Specimen (A) is deeper and the glaze is crackled with a yellowish tinge. Large pit holes appear on both the interior and exterior. Specimen (B) is shallower and incised with a more distinct and wider lotus petal bands. The glaze is sea green.

The products of the Xin'an kiln are dominated by coarse celadon wares, imitating the Longquan prototypes. Some of the pieces are finely glazed. A great many kiln structures have been located and all of them are of the "bread loaf" (bee-hive) type.

73

青瓷盤

明代（公元1368—1644年）
高6、口徑25.5—29厘米
1982年化州縣平定鎮積田鄉龍眼村窖藏出土
化州縣博物館藏品

二件瓷盤造形相同，胎質厚重潔白，盤口，淺弧壁，圈足，內壁模印成花瓣形，內底印一朵折枝花，釉色晶瑩潤澤，釉層較厚，其中(A)施青綠色釉，(B)施青灰色釉。

Celadon dishes

Ming dynasty (AD1368-1644)
Height: 6, diameter: 25.5-29 cm.
Found in 1982 from a hoard in Longyancun, Jitianxiang, Pingdingzhen, Huazhou County.
Collection of the Huazhou County Museum.

Two celadon dishes of similar form, with a thick white stoneware body, flatten rim, shallow well and ringed foot. The cavetto is impressed into petal shape with the interior centre stamped with a floral spray. The thick glaze is lustrous and glossy. One is greyish green while the other is bluish green.

74

青白瓷碗、碟

明代（公元1368—1644年）
碗：高4.5—6、口徑14.4—15.3厘米
碟：高2.4—2.6、口徑12—13厘米
1985年大埔縣高陂鎮青碗窯窯址出土

A：碗壁較深，敞口，唇稍向外侈，弧壁，矮圈足，施青白色全釉

B：碗壁較淺，敞口，矮圈足，內外壁施青白釉，內底微向上凸，不施釉。

C、D：兩件造形大致相同，敞口，淺壁，圈足矮扁，內外壁施青白釉，內底微向上凸，不施釉。

青碗窯窯址是大埔縣發現最早的瓷窯，瓷器保留有某些元代作風，時代可至明代早期，碟內底微上凸，不施釉是其最大的特點。

Bowls and dishes

Ming dynasty (AD1368-1644)
Bowl: height: 4.5-6, diameter: 14.4-15.3 cm.
Dish: height: 2.4-2.6, diameter: 11-13 cm.
Excavated in 1985 from the Qingwanyao kiln site, Gaopozhen, Dapu County.

(A) A deep bowl with a slightly flared lip, low ringed foot and glazed all over with a *qingbai* glaze.
(B) Shallow bowl with wide mouth, low foot, *qingbai* glaze. The unglaze interior centre is slightly convex.
(C,D) Two dishes of similar form with shallow foot and *qingbai* glaze. The interior centre is slightly convex and unglazed.

The Qingwanyao kiln was the earliest kiln complex discovered in Dapu County. Some of the products still exhibit Yuan style. But the majority can be dated to the early part of the Ming dynasty, with a common feature of unglazed and convex interior.

75

青花碗、碟

明代（公元1368—1644年）
碗：高7.6，口徑14.3厘米
碟：高4、口徑21厘米
1984年海康縣南興鎮外園村窖藏出土
海康縣博物館藏品

碗：撇口，直壁，壁下近足處呈弧形，圈足，青花藍中帶灰，內口沿下畫"回"形紋，內底畫雙綫弦紋圈，圈內畫折枝花卉；外壁中部畫山峯、樹木、折枝菊組合紋，近足處畫有三周弦紋。

碟：薄胎，花瓣形撇口，弧壁，臥圈足，青花藍中帶灰，內沿畫三角形幾何圖案，內壁模印成花瓣形，內底邊緣畫帶狀裝飾花紋，中間畫金剛寶杵紋，外壁上下端畫雙綫弦紋圈，中間繪纏枝菊花。

這類碗碟，不是廣東窯場的產品，與江西民窯瓷器較接近，年代約在明代中葉。

Blue and white bowl and dish

Ming dynasty (AD1368-1644)
Bowl: height: 7.6, diameter: 14.3 cm.
Dish: height: 4, diameter: 21 cm.
Found in 1984 from a hoard in Weiyuancun, Nanxingzhen, Haikang County.
Collection of the the Haikang County Museum.

The bowl has a slightly everted lip and a footring. The blue has a greyish tone. The interior is decorated with an angular meander band along the mouthrim and a floral branch in the centre enclosed by a double circle. The outside is painted with a landscape scene enclosed by plain borders. The dish is thinly potted and has a foliated flattened rim, and the cavetto is moulded with lobings. The blue pigment also has a greyish tinge. The interior is painted with a double vajra in the centre enclosed by a formalized leave band, and the mouthrim is a segmented triangular band. The underside has a chrysanthemun scroll between double bands.

These two specimens are probably products from the provincial kilns in Jiangxi and can be dated stylistically to the middle Ming period.

76

瓷片

明代（公元1368—1644年）
長:10.5-20厘米
1986年香港大嶼山竹篙灣出土
香港古物古蹟辦事處藏品

香港大嶼山東北角的竹篙灣，自1975年起，出土了不少青花瓷和其他種類的五彩，單色釉瓷器。圖中青釉碗，外壁刻劃菊瓣紋，為典型廣東明代仿龍泉青瓷的產品，其主要生產地區有惠陽等地。青花瓷片則應產自江西景德鎮附近之民窰，紋飾有夔龍紋，十字金剛忤及斷續纏枝花等，都是明代中期，成化至正德期間的民窰青花風格。

明代十六世紀初，海運暢通，陶瓷器大量外銷。此外佛郎機（葡萄牙）人亦於正德年間在香港地區屯駐，進行貿易活動，竹篙灣瓷器，或與此有關連。

Ceramic sherds

Ming dynasty (AD1368-1644)
Length: 10.5-20 cm.
Excavated in 1986 from Zhugaowan, Dayushan (Penny's Bay, Lantao), Hong Kong.
Collection of the Antiquities and Monuments Office, Hong Kong.

Zhugaowan, better known as Penny's Bay lies on the northeastern tip of the Lantao Island. Since 1975 a great mass of blue and white porcelain as well as other types of ceramic wares have been found from this site. The celadon bowl with chrysanthemun petals on the exterior belongs to the group of Guangdong celadons as represented by the Huiyang kiln site. The other three blue and white sherds were probably from non-official kilns in the vicinity of Jingdezhen and can be dated to the turn of the 15th/16th century. The most characteristic features of this group is a foliated dragon (makara) and "interrupted" lotus scrolls as seen on these specimens.

The ceramic finds, as well as the Zhugaowan site itself must have a close relationship with the massive junk trade in South China in the middle Ming. This also coincided with the increasing Sino-Portuguese trading activities in Hong Kong in the first quarter of the 16th century.

77

蓋罐

明代（公元1368-1644年）
罐高:24,碗口徑:14厘米
1968/69年香港大嶼山石壁出土
香港中文大學文物館

此蓋罐原為一對，出土於大嶼山石壁圍村西面之山坡上。陶罐為灰黃胎，質輕，外有褐色陶衣，現已大部分脫落。以青花碗為蓋，該碗圓弧壁，外繪蕉葉紋，內心有折枝荷花;年代應為明中葉弘治、正德年間。

同類型的蓋罐在廣州、佛山和深圳地區多有發現，是骨灰罎或隨葬盛器。

Covered urn

Ming dynasty (AD1368-1644)
Urn: height: 24, bowl: diameter: 14 cm.
Discovered in 1968/69 from Shibi, Dayushan, Hong Kong.
Art Gallery, the Chinese University of Hong Kong.

A pair of such earthenware jars with identical blue and white bowls as covers were discovered on a sloping hillside west of the Shibi village. The jar has a porous buff-coloured body with a degrading brown coating on the exterior. The bowl is conical and decorated on the outside with plantain leaves, on the inside with a lotus flower within a circle in the centre. Both the potting and decoration of the bowl point to the turn of the 15th century.

Very similar urns and bowls have been found in Guangzhou, Foshan and Shenzhen. They were used as containers for cremated ash or burial goods.

78

陶片

約十六世紀
長:8.5-12.8厘米
1974年香港糧船灣洲沙咀出土
香港博物館中央考古資料庫藏品

香港萬宜水庫興建期間,曾於沙咀發現古代木船一艘,艙內及殘骸之週圍出土大量陶瓷碎片。圖中標本為其中之一部分,共出者還有明代中葉的青花瓷及單色釉器。其中器蓋,邊沿翹起,中部陷下,有蓮子形鈕,為暹羅南部陶器。其他的印紋陶片,花紋有編織紋、貝紋等,應是泰國南部及馬來半島所產的歷史時期印紋陶,即所謂"葆馬來"型,以拍印紋為主;直至現在於雲南及東南亞,尚有製作,斷代至為困難。

Pottery sherds

circa 16th century
Length: 8.5-12.8 cm.
Excavated in 1974 from Shazui, Liangchuanwan (Sha Tsui, High Island), Hong Kong.
Collection of the Central Archaeological Repository of the Hong Kong Museum of History.

These earthenware sherds were found together with typical 16th century Chinese blue and whites, and monochrome wares from a wreck in Shazui during the construction of the High Island Water Scheme Reservoir. These sherds represent a generic group of protohistoric earthenware (better known as "Bau-Malay") popular in southern Thailand and Malay Peninsula. The vessel cover with a sunken centre and a conical knob is a very characteristic feature of Thai ceramics and the impressed "conch-shell" and basketry designs on the sherds are also a distinct hallmark of this group of "Bau-Malay" pottery. The associated Chinese wares provide a 16th century date for the whole group.

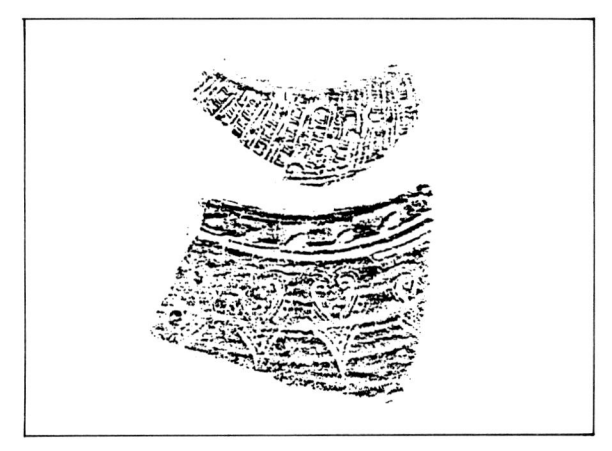

陶片拓片
Rubbings of designs.

79

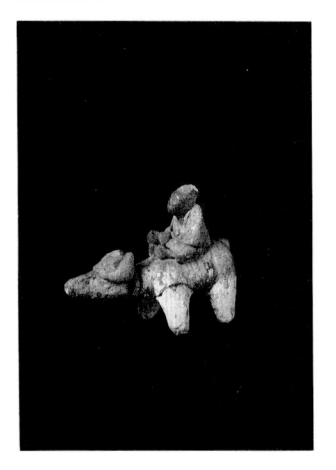

瓷騎牛人塑像

明代（公元1368—1644年）
通長7.3、通高5.2厘米
1955年惠東縣新菴鄉白馬山窰址出土

器較小。施黃釉。白胎。牛長身，四足站立，頭向前伸，吻部前突，雙角向上內彎，長尾，貼於右後腿上。牛背上一枚人盤足而坐，臉部向上昂起，雙目向上仰望，頭髮殘損，身穿衣袍，雙手交錯於膝上。

此塑像造型生動別緻，人物表情悠閒自得，富有田園風韻，十分寫意。

Figurine on buffalo

Ming dynasty (AD1368-1644)
Overall length: 7.3, height: 5.2 cm.
Excavated in 1955 from the Baimashan kiln site, Xin'anxiang, Huidong County.

A miniature with a white body and glazed in yellow. The buffalo stands on four feet, with twin curved horns and a tail between the hind feet. The figure seated on the back of the animal with feet crossed and the head raised, and dressed in a long robe. An exceptionally lively piece of miniature.

80

磚雕

明代（公元1368—1644年）
長34.5—35.5、寬16—16.5、厚7—7.2厘米
1985年陽春縣合水鎮平北鄉墓葬出土
陽春縣博物館藏品

側面均印斜角長方形框，框內雕刻一隻行走中的麒麟，人物趕奔馬及盛放的折枝花。

三件磚雕同出一墓，是鑲在墓室內壁作裝飾用的。磚青灰色，雕刻刀法簡練粗獷，圖案生動活潑，達到一定的藝術水平。

Bricks

Ming dynasty (AD1368-1644)
Length: 34.5-35.5, width: 16-16.5, thickness: 7-7.2 cm.
Excavated in 1985 from a burial in Pingbeixiang, Heshuizhen, Yangchun County.
Collection of the Yangchun County Museum.

Rectangular bricks moulded on one side with a rectangular panel with rounded corners, within which are qilin, galloping horse and figure and floral spray. These three bricks came from the same tomb. The side with decoration faces the tomb chamber. They are all greyish and the designs are boldly and fluently depicted.

81

墓誌銘

明萬曆二十六年(公元1598年)
長28、寬20、厚5厘米
1983年海康縣雷城鎮上坡村墓葬出土
海康縣博物館藏品

　　用長方形紅磚銘刻,磚面經磨平,四面刻有方綫框,框內刻有"徐末生江西南昌府靖安縣人生萬曆廿一年癸巳歲閏十一月初三卯時因父文溪升任海康學隨任居三年甫四歲以痘疹卒於廿六年戊戌歲正月初二子時擇本月十一未時卜葬西湖塘亭後山書此以志不朽萬曆二十六年戊戌歲正月吉日旦海康縣學諭父徐肯搖立"銘文。

Pottery tomb tablet

26th year Wanli, Ming dynasty (AD1598)
Length: 28, width: 20, thickness: 5 cm.
Excavated in 1983 from a burial in Shanpocun, Leichengzhen, Haikang County.
Collection of the Haikang County Museum.

A reddish brown earthenware tablet of rectangular shape. The surface had been polished and inscribed within a rectangular frame. The inscription mentions that the deceased was a boy named Xu Weisheng. Xu was born in the 21st year of Wanli (AD1593) and was a native of Jingan County, Nanchang Fu, Jiangxi. He came with his father to Haikang and died of measles on the second day of the first moon in the 26th year Wanli (AD1598). The burial took place in the same month.

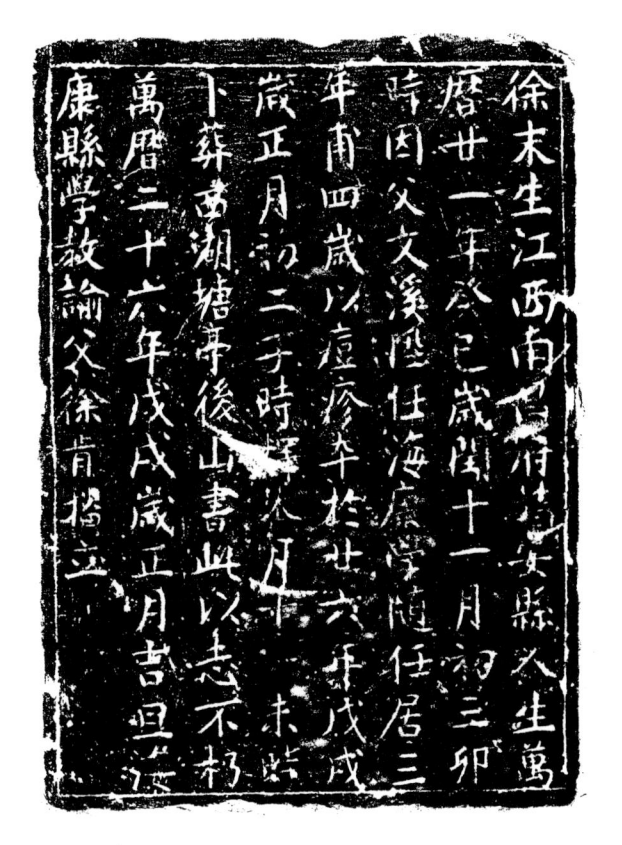

墓誌拓本
Rubbing of the inscription.

修城磚

明代（公元1368—1644年）
A（左）：長41.7、寬20.8、厚11.5厘米
B（右）：殘長36、寬15、厚12厘米
1982年潮州市韓江兩岸磚窯出土
潮州市博物館藏品

A：完好，磚青灰色，厚重，呈長方形，側面印有"饒平縣造"銘紋。

B：已殘，胎青灰色，厚重，側面印有"海陽縣造"銘紋。

這些城磚，與潮州市政府附近圍牆上發現的印有"海陽縣造一"、"潮陽縣造二"、"海陽縣造"、"饒平縣造"、"潮州衛前所造磚"等城磚完全相同，是明代洪武年潮州築城或後來修城時燒製的，燒製窯址在韓江兩岸歸湖，楓溪鎮境內，範圍長達數里，窯爐密集，有的相距僅三米，為饅頭形窯爐。這些窯址和出土的修城磚，說明了當時潮州府修築城牆的城磚，是府屬各縣共同承擔的，各燒造部門在韓江兩岸設窯，應是水路運輸方便之故。

City wall bricks

Ming dynasty (AD1368-1644)
(A): length: 41.7, width: 20.8, thickness: 11.5 cm.
(B): remaining length: 36, width: 15, thickness: 12 cm.
Excavated in 1982 from brick kilns along the banks of Hanjiang, Chaozhou City.
Collection of the Chaozhou Museum.

Thick and heavy brick with greyish body, on one side impressed with inscriptions (A) "Made by Raoping County", (B) "Made by Haiyang County".

These bricks are identical to the ones unearthed from the wall near the Chaozhou municipal government building. All of them were stamped with nearby county names, and were fired either in the Hongwu reign for the building of the city wall, or in later Ming reigns for the repair of the wall. They were all fired along the banks of Hanjiang in Guihu and Fengqizhen. The kiln complex occupied an area of several miles. Some of them were only three metres apart. The kiln structure was of the standard beehive type. The specimens found in the city wall and from the kiln site indicate that the bricks were contributed by both the provincial as well as county governments. They were all made in Hanjiang, which provided easy river transportation to the Chaozhou city.

磚銘拓本
Rubbings.

83

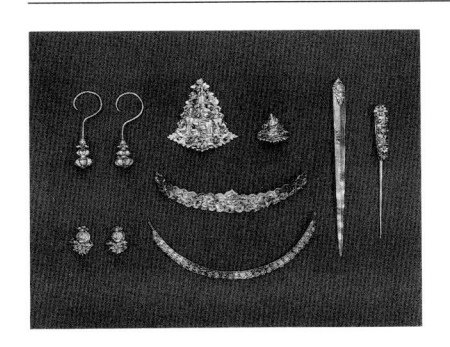

金飾

明代（公元1368—1644年）
長:2.2—13.7厘米
六十年代普寧縣墓葬出土

　　A 耳環:上部作圓綫形勾狀實體,下部呈葫蘆形,葫蘆頸部刻成垂葉狀,葫蘆身作瓜棱形。

　　B 帽飾:三角形透雕,上端刻觀音像,觀音頭戴冠,身穿敞胸長衣,一手舉至胸前,一手屈肘前伸,手指下垂至膝,裸足,一足下垂,一足平趺,安坐於座上,座下左右兩邊各站立一童子,童子身穿寬袖長衣,腳踏蓮花,一個雙手合"十",一個手捧一物,人物周圍雕花卉彩帶,上下左右四邊各鑲有一顆紅寶石。

　　C 冠飾:薄體,呈三角形,上面透雕一個老人,交腿端坐於蓮座上,老人長頭、長鬚,身穿交領長衫,一手撫膝,一手執一物件,四周雕刻花卉。

　　D 金釵:扁錐形薄體,中間起棱,斷面呈三角形,釵頭正面雕花卉,從釵頭至釵中部兩邊刻直綫陽紋,中部中間刻有纏枝花卉,釵下段無紋飾。

　　E 花金釵:上段扁平形,相間浮雕牡丹飛鳳紋,是先做好釵後鑲到釵頭上的,下段圓錐形,無紋飾。

　　F 髮箍:弧形薄體,邊雕成花瓣形、中間相間刻牡丹飛鳳紋。

　　G 冠飾:二件造形相同,上部作花形,下部作瓜形,瓜上伏着一隻小老鼠。

　　H 髮箍:弧形薄體,上邊刻成花瓣形,下邊刻成鋸齒形,中間浮刻有29朵細花,背面中間橫穿有一扁金條。

Gold ornaments

Ming dynasty (AD1368-1644)
Length: 2.2-13.7 cm.
Excavated in the sixties from a burial in Puning County.

　　A: Earrings: Lobed gourd shape with slender solid hooks.
　　B: Hat ornament: Triangular shape, with a Guanyin in the centre flanked by two children, inlaid with four ruby stones at the four corners.
　　C: Hat ornament for woman: Small triangular shape, thin gold foil with an old man in relief, seated with crossed legs on a lotus pedestal.
　　D: Hairpin: Of triangular cross-section, the end chased with a floral pattern.
　　E: Hairpin: Of cylindrical shape, the end flattened and decorated with phoenixes alternating with peony flowers.
　　F: Hairband: Arched foil, chased with phoenixes and peony flowers.
　　G: Hat ornament for woman: A pair, of melon shape, topped by a bundle of flowers and a squirrel.
　　H: Hairband: Arched foil, with bracket edges, front chased with flowers, back reinforced by a flat golden bar.

金飾線圖
Line drawings.

84

銅鼓

明代（公元1368—1644年）
通高11、鼓面徑15.3厘米
1955年揭陽縣雲路鎮軍田老虎陂水庫墓葬出土

器較小。鼓面邊緣塑兩對立蛙，其中一對爲疊踞，一大一小，頭向一致。立蛙均作順時針排列。鼓面中心無紋飾，中部兩周雲雷紋，外一周爲花卉紋。寬緣，器身亞腰形，中空，足外撇。腰部一對寬環耳，耳表面飾幾何紋。器身從上而下有三組花紋，第一組爲雲雷紋，第二組爲花卉紋，第三組爲蕉葉形紋。

這件銅鼓與流行於西南少數民族地區的古代銅鼓不相同，後者爲實用器，前者爲模仿後者的模型器，不僅器體大大縮小，花紋也截然不同。

Bronze drum

Ming dynasty (AD1368-1644)
Overall height: 11, diameter: 15.3 cm.
Excavated in 1955 from a burial in the Laohupo reservoir, Juntian, Yunluzhen, Jieyang County.

A small drum topped on the flat surface with two pairs of frogs; one of the pair carries a cub on its back; all arranged in a clockwise direction. The surface is decorated with two angular meander bands in the centre and a floral band near the edge. The body is concave and fitted with two vertical handles with geometric patterns, and cast with bands of angular meander, floral design and plantain leaves.

This is a miniature version of the large bronze drums popular in the minority tribes in Southeast China.

85

銅銃

明代（公元1368—1644年）
長36.2、口徑4厘米
1978年高要縣蜆崗鎮闌柯山陸崗出土

銃爲長身，上鑄圓箍五個。藥室在後半段，凸起呈橢圓形。藥室後端有一直徑0.3厘米的圓形小孔，供插入引火綫用。銃身前段鑄一"勝"字，草書。同時出土的共有八支銅銃，三支鐵銃。

蜆崗距肇慶僅二十公里，明洪武初，肇慶設立守禦千戶所，洪武二十二年（公元1389）改肇慶衞。蜆崗發現的銅鐵銃，與當時所處的軍事地理位置應有密切的關係。

Bronze gun

Ming dynasty (AD1368-1644)
Length: 36.2, mouth diameter: 4 cm.
Excavated in 1978 in Lugang, Lankeshan, Xiangang, Gaoyao County.

Cast bronze gun with a tubular barrel with five ribs. The explosion chamber is oval and is near the rear end, with a small hole for the insertion of a fuse or slow match. The front portion of the barrel is cast with a "*sheng*" (victory) character in cursive script. From this site a total of eight bronze and three iron guns were found.

The Xiangang site is about 20 kilometres from Zhaoqing city. In early Hongwu reign an Independent Battalion was set up in Xiangang, and in the 22nd year of the same reign (AD1389), the Battalion was reorganized and renamed Zhaoqing Guard. These guns must have been part of the weapons used by the garrisons stationed in this site.

86

鐵炮

南明永曆四年，(公元1650年)
長:179.5,徑(前端):22,(口):6.8厘米
1956年出土於香港佛堂門海灣
香港博物館藏品

中國鑄造火炮歷史較早，世界上現存最早的標本是元至順三年(公元1332年)鑄造的銅火炮。明代正德末年開始注意吸收歐洲鑄炮技術，引進葡萄牙的佛郎機炮；萬曆年間，荷蘭火炮又傳入中國。此標本於香港佛堂門海(大廟灣)撈出，以鐵鑄成，筒體前弇後豐，外有凸圈多道，中部有雙耳軸，爲安置炮架之用；炮身銘文七行：「督理東海都督府，掛定海將軍印系(?)。欽命總督兩廣部院杜造。廣東總鎭宮保byte范。督造參將蕭利仁。管局都司何興祥。永曆四年六月日，重五百斤」。據已故羅香林教授的考訂，銘中的「杜氏」爲杜永和，「范氏」爲范承恩，均曾一度效忠南明宗室，抗拒清軍。

Iron cannon

Southern Ming, AD1650
Length: 179.5, diameter (front): 22, (mouth): 6.8 cm.
Found in 1956 from Fotangmen (Joss House Bay), Hong Kong.
Collection of the Hong Kong Museum of History.

Long before the arrival of Europeans, cannons were cast in China. The earliest extant example, and very probably the oldest in the world is one cast in the Yuan dynasty, datable to AD1332. Later in the middle Ming, the Chinese cannon was modified after the Frankish culverin from Portugal as well as Dutch cannons. This specimen, dredged up from the Fotangmen Bay during the expansion of the Hong Kong Airport is one of these Chinese copies of the Frankish prototype. The barrel is ribbed, with two swivelling trunnions in the middle, on the top of which is cast with seven lines of inscriptions. The names of Du, Fan and Xiao Liren, all loyal officials to the surviving members of the imperial Ming family appeared in the inscription, together with a reign date, 4th year Yongli, corresponding to AD1650.

87

銅官印

明代(公元1368—1644年)
通高10、印長9.2、寬6.1、厚1.3厘米
1979年揭陽縣漁湖鎮榕江東寨村河邊沙灘出土
揭陽縣博物館藏品

器身厚重。印面有細小的沙眼。印面長方形，背上有橢圓形執把。印面一周寬緣，內篆體陽刻反文，分列兩行，每行五字，順讀爲"浙江分守溫處參將關防"。印的背面有刻字，楷書，右邊一行爲"浙江分守溫處參將關防"，左邊二行爲"崇禎十四年十一月　日"、"禮部　造"。印的右側面刻"崇字三千七百九十五號"。

Bronze official seal

Ming, 14th year Chongzhen (AD1641)
Overall height: 10, length: 9.2, width: 6.1, thickness: 1.3 cm.
Excavated in 1979 from a riverbank in Dongzaicun, Yongjiang, Yuhuzhen, Jieyang County.
Collection of the Jieyang County Museum.

A heavy seal with numerous pit holes from the casting. The rectangular seal surface is topped with a cylindrical grip of oval section. The inscription, enclosed within a wide border is arranged in two rows and reads, "Seal of the Assistant Commander in charge of the Branch Office of Wenzhou and Chuzhou, Zhejiang". The top is incised with three rows of inscriptions, which include the title, a serial number, and a reign date corresponding to AD1641 by the Department of Rites that produced this seal.

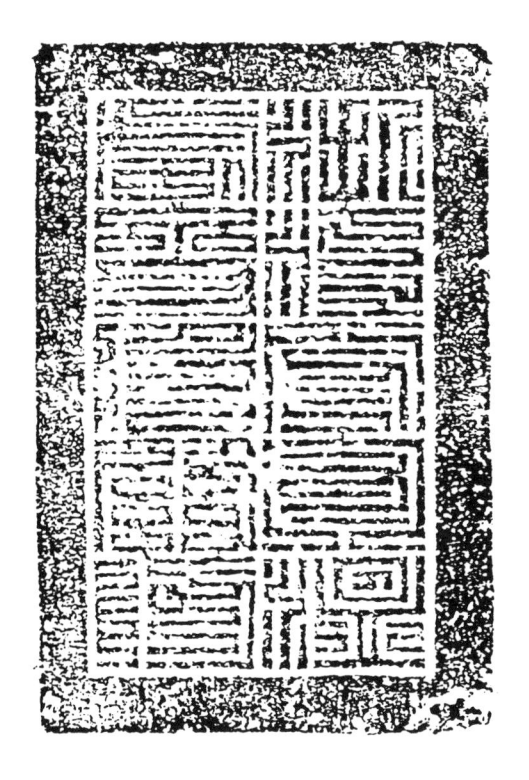

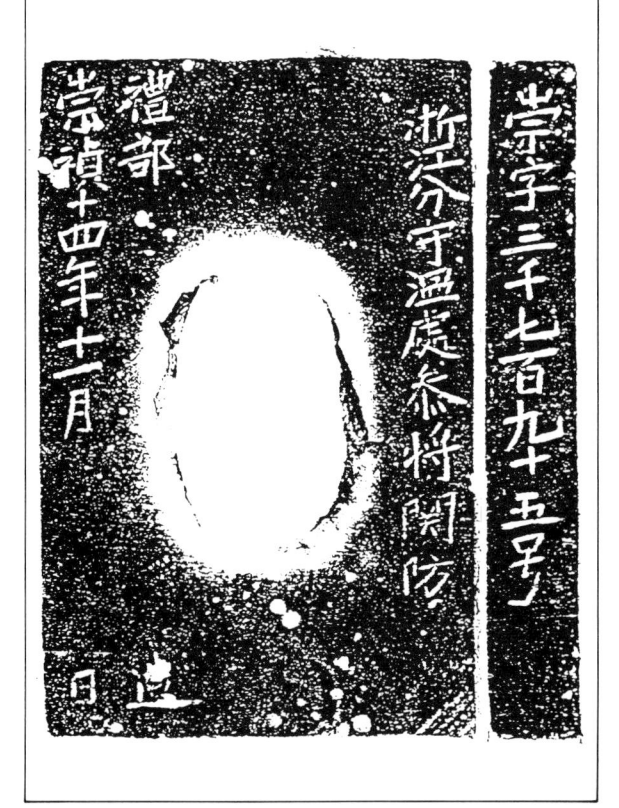

印文及邊款
Ink impression of the seal characters and rubbing of the inscriptions.

88

銅錠

明代（公元1368—1644年）
A（左）：長24.5、寬13.2、厚2厘米
B（右）：長18.5、寬9.7、厚2.2厘米
1974年、1975年西沙羣島北礁出土

　　由銅液灌鑄成形，呈長方形，底平，面稍呈弧形。
　　這類銅錠在西沙北礁共出土三十多塊，七十多公斤，出土地點與銅錢地點相同，應是同一船運銷國外的貨物。

Copper ingots

Ming dynasty (AD1368-1644)
(A) Length: 24.5, width: 13.2, thickness: 2 cm.
(B) Length: 18.5, width: 9.7, thickness: 2.2 cm.
Excavated in 1974, 1975 from the Northern Reef in the Paracel Islands.

Cast, rectangular ingot with a flat base and slightly rounded top.
A total of more than thirty similar ingots were found in this site, weighing some seventy kilograms. From the same site a massive quantity of copper coins were also found. All of them were probably commodities related with the export trade.

89A

銅錢

明代（公元1368—1644年）
洪武通寶　直徑3厘米
永樂通寶　直徑2.5厘米
1974年和1975年西沙羣島北礁東北角礁盤出土

　　錢圓形，中間有方孔。共發現四百多公斤，由於長期浸泡在海水中，有些錢幣已和珊瑚石膠結在一起，但銹蝕並不嚴重，大多數錢幣文字清晰可讀，膠結在珊瑚石中的成串銅錢，部分錢孔中還留有穿錢細繩。銅錢最早的是王莽時期的"大泉五十"最晚的是明代"永樂通寶"。其中"永樂通寶"錢輪廓整齊，文字清晰，全是新幣，似是沒有在民間流通使用過，而從倉庫直接上船出海的，如此多的新幣運往國外，可能與鄭和下西洋船隊有關。

Copper cash coins

Ming dynasty (AD1368-1644)
Hongwu coin, diameter: 3 cm.
Yongle coin, diameter: 2.5 cm.
Excavated in 1974 to 1975 from the Northeastern corner, Northern Reef, Paracel Islands.

　　Copper cash coins with a round edge and a square perforation. More than four hundred kilograms were discovered. Due to prolong burial in sea water, some of the coins become mixed with coral, but still in string form, with a portion of the original string still intact. The earliest coin in the hoard is "*Daquan wushi*" of the Wang Meng reign (AD8-23), and the latest is "*Yongle tongbao*" of the early Ming dynasty (AD1403-1424). The latter variety, seems to be newly minted and never circulated, as the characters are still sharp and distinct. This hoard was probably related with the Zheng He expedition.

89B

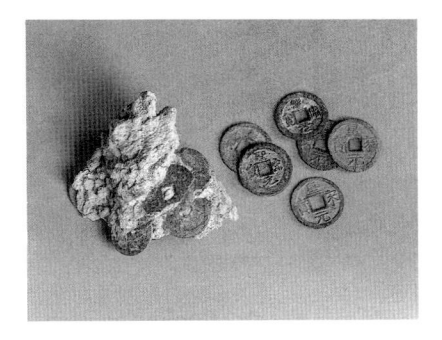

銅錢

明代（公元1368—1644年）
直徑3厘米
1936年東沙羣島礁盤出土

　　東沙羣島主要包括東沙島、南衛灘、北衛灘等島嶼。銅錢是1936年東沙島氣象台工作人員在島外水深2米的礁盤上發現的，總數約300多枚，由於長期浸於海水中，部分銅錢已和珊瑚石交結在一起，表面留有一層較厚的銅綠銹迹。這些銅錢字體有楷書，行書，篆書多種，最早的是唐代的"開元通寶"，最晚的是明代"永樂通寶"，其中以明代銅錢爲最多。這些銅錢，應是我國明代一艘遠航商船不幸遇難遺留下來的。

Copper cash coins

Ming dynasty (AD1368-1644)
Diameter: 3 cm.
Excavated in 1936 from the reef in Dongsha Islands.

　　These coins, a total of more than three hundred pieces were discovered by meteorological workers on the Dongsha Island in 1936. The site was a reef about two metres below sea level. Some of the coins have been overgrown with coral and badly rusted with green copper oxide. The characters vary from standard script to seal and semi-cursive script, and date from the Kaiyuan reign (Tang dynasty, AD713-741) in the earliest to Yongle (AD1403-1424) in the Ming dynasty, but the majority are Ming coins. Probably remains of a shipwreck.

90

鐵天王像

明萬曆年（公元1573—1620年）
A:北天王像、通高92厘米
B:西天王像　殘高74厘米
1980年南雄縣全安鎮三機塔基出土

A:臉正視,眼圓睜,嘴帶笑,頭戴佛冠,身穿盔甲,腳穿長靴,腰束帶,飄帶從頭部繞手下垂至足,右手叉腰,左手屈舉,雙足成八字形站立於須彌座上,像背後開有方形孔,孔兩邊刻有銘文,因時間久遠,刻文較淺,文字已無法認全,其中右邊銘文是"北方天王□合□",下邊有一"靜"字,左邊銘文是"□□丙申□□"。座前左邊還刻有"信官譚本庶"等銘文。

B:座已殘缺,造形穿戴與北天王同,只是手勢相反,即左手叉腰,右手屈舉,背後方孔右邊刻有"西方天王□□□",左邊刻有"萬□丙申冬立"銘文。

天王像出土時共四尊,放置於塔基底下四個石洞中,每洞各放一個,同出土的還有六條鐵鑄蜈蚣,可能是用於奠基托塔用的。鐵像中"萬□丙申冬立"銘文,說明了鐵像鑄於明萬曆二十四年,即公元1596年。

Iron guardian figures

Wanli, Ming dynasty (AD1573-1620)
Remaining height: 74-92 cm.
Excavated in 1980 from the foundation of the Sanji Pagoda in Quan'anzhen, Nanxiong County.

A pair of cast iron guardian figures (heavenly kings), wearing armour and standing on an open pedestal, with one arm bent and another raised. Inscriptions, partly illegible are found on the stand. One line contains a date corresponding to the 24th year of Wanli (AD1596).

A total of four similar guardian figures were unearthed from the site, and they were placed inside stone niches in the four corners, together with six iron centipedes.

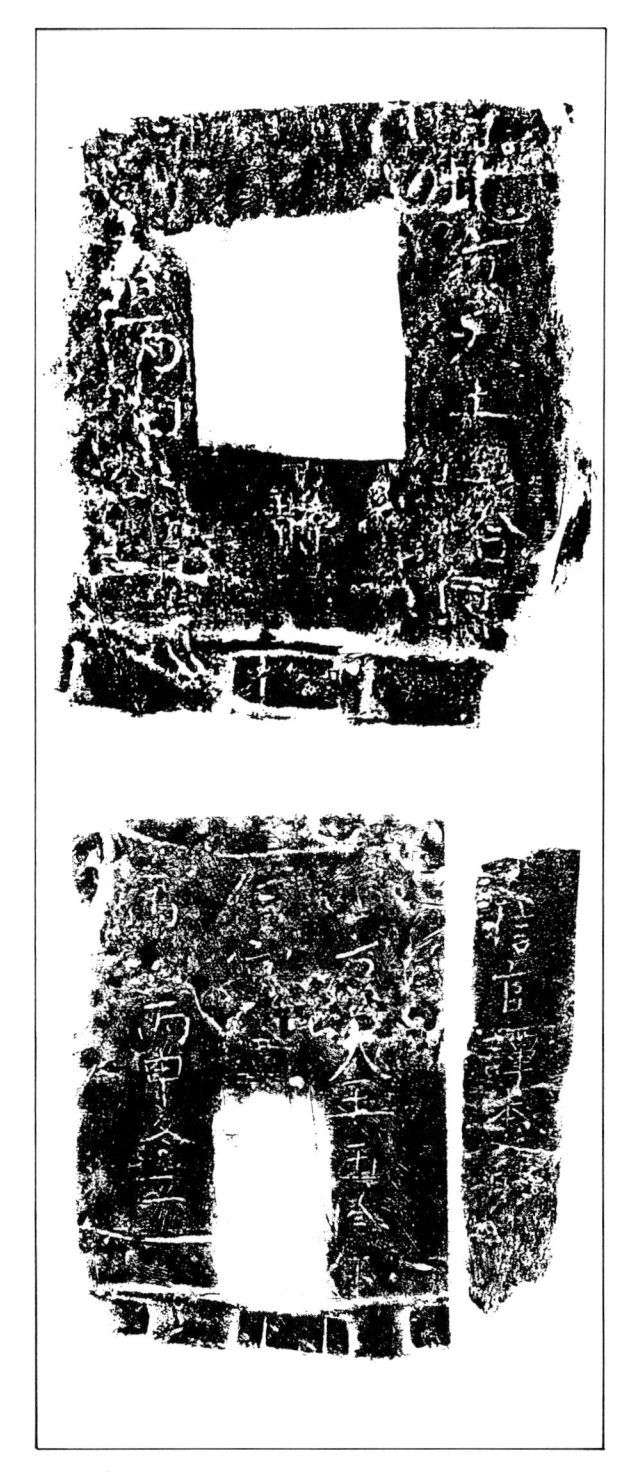

銘文拓本
Rubbing of inscription.

91

鐵香爐

明代（公元1368—1644年）
高10.4、口徑9.6厘米
1964年揭陽縣出土

　　器身厚重，略有銹蝕。口較寬大，斂口，侈唇，弧壁收深腹，平底，三條蹄形實足，底有一個不透穿的圓眼。

　　器表鑄有陽銘，自右而左；分列四行，共十二字："崇禎元年　吉日造　信官　袁進國"。崇禎元年即公元1628年，是明毅宗朱由檢的年號。

Iron censer

Ming dynasty (AD1368-1644)
Height: 10.4, diameter: 9.6 cm.
Excavated in 1964 in Jieyang County.

　　Heavy and thick tripod censer, with a cylindrical body, slightly bulbous body and a flat base, stands on three cabriole feet. The base has a sunken hole.

　　There is a four line inscription in relief on the exterior, that contains the name of the donor, Yuan Jinguo and a reign date, "1st year Chongzhen", which corresponds to AD1628.

銘文拓本
Rubbing of inscription.

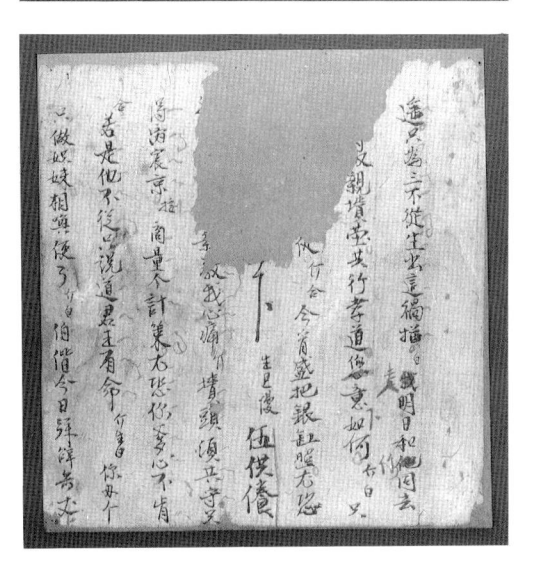

琵琶記抄本

明嘉靖年（公元1522—1566年）
長23.6、寬22.7厘米
1958年揭陽縣漁湖鎮百寨村明墓出土

　　蔡伯皆亦名琵琶記，出土共二本，用棉紙抄寫，紙捻裝釘，一本是總綱，一本是小生使用的己本，抄本內曲文和元末明初高明（則誠）的《琵琶記》相同處甚多，多採用中原音韻，但賓白略有不同，本中每段唱詞均註有曲牌名，唱詞旁註有演奏及打板符號，書腦部分寫有蔡伯皆三字，並有嘉靖年款記，表明了抄本應是藝人使用的自抄本。抄寫時間在明嘉靖年間。從出土抄本墓葬碑上刻有"明□黃州袁公妣江□陳氏墓"銘文，和黃州明代屬湖廣推測，抄本主人可能是流寓廣東的藝人，死後葬於揭陽。

Manuscript

Jiajing, Ming dynasty (AD1522-1566)
Length: 23.6, width: 22.7 cm.
Excavated in 1958 from a Ming tomb in Baizaicun, Yuhuzhen, Jieyang County.

　　These are manuscript pages of the well known drama *Pipa ji* (Story of the lute). The pages were bound together by paper thread into two volumes, one of which was the main plot while the other is the portion to be used by the hero. The text is very similar to the published version by Gao Ming in the 14th century, and still retains most of the Central China tones. In this version the lyrics were annotated with notes and signs for the musicians. "Cai Bojie" appears on some of the pages and there is a Jiajing date.
　　The tomb tablet bears the name of a certain Mrs. Wong (Madame Chen) of Huangzhou of the Ming dynasty. In the Ming period both Hunan and Guangdong were under the jurisdiction of Huangzhou. The deceased, an actress, was probably from other provinces and died in Guangdong.

93

描金紙扇

明萬曆十年（公元1582年）
扇面長46、寬17, 竹骨長28.3厘米
六十年代大埔縣黃展夫婦合葬墓出土

二十四竹骨，貫扇釘子及栓釘帽子用銅製造，扇面用金色描網狀棱格紋，扇竹骨塗黑漆地，兩邊竹骨繪金色花卉和棱格圖案，內竹骨一面四周繪金色方格紋，中間如意頭形開光，用紅、黑彩繪魁星像，另一面上端繪帶狀金色花卉圖案，兩邊及下端繪金色方格紋和紅、黑色彩折枝花卉，中間寫魁星贊，分二十八行一百六十五字，全文如下："魁星贊燦乎紫微垣之傍爲星之魁書乎進士第一之堂爲字之魁捷乎庚午之秋爲解之魁佔乎辛未之春爲省之魁齊美乎丙辰之狀元爲天下之大魁□魁之義得魁之趣文明之魁車載斗量不可勝計爾酒旣青爾淆旣馨維吾魁其光賁其炳靈引領臺仙下翠微雲開相逐步相隨桃花已透三春限月桂高攀第一枝闈苑應無先去馬杏圓惟有後吟詩男兒志須如此金榜題名四海知一包杏花紅十里狀元歸去馬如飛"。

黃展是大埔湖寮人，生於明正德十年，嘉靖三十五年考取進士，曾授浙江長興縣知縣，因防倭及治匪有功，擢南京戶部主事；出守贛州，後進階中憲大夫，擢福建按察副使，後又改廣西參議，後因贛庫失盜被牽連降爲衢州知府，萬曆十年死於大埔縣。其墓前殘留有石馬和石牌坊，牌坊上刻有"明嘉靖賜進士中憲大夫閩粵按察副使前南京戶部郎中黃公曁初敕封安人加封恭丘氏塋"銘文。

Folding fan

10th year Wanli, Ming (AD1582)
Fan surface, length: 46, width: 17, frame, length: 28.3 cm.
Excavated in the sixties from the tomb of the Huang Yi couple in Dapu County.

A folding fan, with bamboo frame and twenty-four folds. The ribs are held together by a brass rivet. The main fan surface is painted in ink on gold-flecked paper with net designs. The ribs are painted with black lacquer, on which are gold painted floral designs, panels containing flowers, *kuixing* and related inscriptions.

The deceased, Huang Yi, a native of Huliao, Dapu, was born in the 10th year Zhengde (AD1515) and passed the *Jinshi* degree in 35th year Jiajing (AD1556). He served various posts, including the Magistrate of Changxing County, Zhejiang, Secretary of the Census Bureau in Nanjing, Grand Master Exemplar, Surveillance Vice Commissioner of Fujian and Assistant Transmission Commissioner of Guangxi. But later Huang was involved in a theft in the Ganzhou storehouse and was demoted to the Prefect of Quzhou and died in Dapu in the 10th year of Wanli (AD1582). A stone shrine with a pair of stone horses still flank his tomb.

94

百褶裙

明代（公元1368—1644年）
裙頭55、裙長100、寬50厘米
1975年揭西縣東園鎭白虎埕村後背山墓葬出土

　　白棉布人工縫製而成。
　　此裙出自磚和灰沙合構的夫婦合葬墓,墓碑尤存,正面碑首中間刻一"明"字,碑首下左邊刻"考戶山魯公"右邊刻"妣魏人趙氏"銘文。

Pleated skirt

Ming dynasty (AD1368-1644)
Waist length: 5, skirt length: 100, width: 50 cm.
Excavated in 1975 from a burial in Houbaishan, Baihuchengcun, Dongyuanzhen, Jiexi County.

　　A hand knitted skirt of cotton cloth.
　　This skirt came from a brick tomb of a couple. The tomb tablet indicates that the deceased was a Mr. Lu and his wife Madame Zhao, both of the Ming dynasty.

輔照四
Supp. illustration 4

墨

明代（公元1368—1644年）
直徑11.7、厚1.2厘米、重165克
1988年東莞市篁村羅亨信墓出土

　　圓餅形。正面邊緣凸起,近緣處一周凸弦紋。中間一個複綫長方框,內有四行陽文,從右至左,順讀爲"玄之又玄　龍光射天　一輪明月　萬杵油烟"。框外左右各一行陽文小字,右邊爲"鳳陽□城",左邊爲"趙永興造"。框外下邊爲二行桃形花紋,上邊爲傘蓋形紋。背面邊緣亦凸起,內爲浮雕式畫面,下端爲海水,上有一馬作奔騰狀,頭向後張口作嘶叫狀。左右爲山峯,右邊山上一棵參天大樹,左上方有祥雲,雲彩上一個彎月。
　　羅亨信爲東莞人,官至左副都御史,後告老還鄉,卒於明天順元年（公元1457年）,享年八十一歲。明史中有關於他的記載。

Ink cake

Ming dynasty (AD1368-1644)
Diameter: 11.7, thickness: 1.2 cm, weight: 165 gm.
Excavated in 1988 from the tomb of Luo Hengxin in Huangcun, Dong'guan City.

　　A circular ink cake, the front with a double grooved edge, and a rectangular frame in the centre, within which is a four line inscription. This frame is flanked on the two sides with shopmarks, on the top a lotus leaf, and on the bottom two rows of peaches. The reverse is a landscape scene with a rhinoceros gazing at the moon.
　　The deceased, Luo Hengxin, a native of Dong'guan was a retired official and died in the 1st year of Tianshun (AD1457) at an age of 81. There is a short biography of him in the *Mingshi* (Dynastic History of the Ming).

95

青花罐

清代（公元1644—1911年）
通高40.5、口徑13.2厘米
1984年東莞縣大朗鎮松山鄉墓葬出土

瓷胎潔白細膩，罐身較直，直口短頸，最大徑在肩部，腹下稍向內收，至底部微向外撇，平底；青花發色鮮艷，頸部畫一周纏枝蓮花紋，肩至腹部畫四個如意形框，框內畫折枝牡丹，近底部一周弦紋上畫有三組蓮瓣紋；罐蓋隆起，斜邊，下有子口，外壁畫如意形框和折枝牡丹紋，蓋頂和蓋邊畫雙綫弦紋，頂部中間塑有一隻蹲伏獅子作鈕。

Covered jar

Qing dynasty (1644-1911)
Overall height: 40.5, mouth diameter: 13.2 cm.
Excavated in 1984 from a burial in Songshanxiang, Dalangzhen, Dong'-guan County.

A porcelain jar painted in bright underglaze blue. The body is bulbous at the shoulder and tapers towards the slightly flared flat base. The neck is decorated with a lotus scroll, the shoulders and body with four *ruyi* panels, within which are peony sprays, all reserved against a solid blue ground. Three groups of half lotus petals adorn the base. The dome-shaped cover is toped by a crouching lion and painted with peony sprays in *ruyi* panels.

96

青花大罐

清咸豐年（公元1851—1861年）
通高66、口徑22厘米
1962年開平縣赤坎鎮三聯村墓葬出土

罐直口，短頸漸向上收窄，最大徑在肩部，肩下漸往內收，至近底部處稍向外撇，平底、青花髮色較鮮，頸部畫火焰紋，肩和腹部畫雲紋，火焰紋和雙龍戲珠圖案，腹下部畫海浪紋；蓋隆起，中間雙綫弦紋圈內有圓錐形鈕，蓋壁畫雲紋和火焰紋，蓋邊畫海水紋，蓋下有子口，內壁鏨有"皇清二十三世祖國學生恭顯關公淑配勞氏安人世居駝駄巨村生於乾隆己亥年四月二十七日寅時終於咸豐甲寅年四月二十七日寅時享壽七十六歲自葬之後房房叢福代代榮昌"銘文。

Covered jar

Hianfeng, Qing (AD1851-1861)
Overall height: 66, mouth diameter: 22 cm.
Excavated in 1962 from a burial in Sanliancun, Chikanzhen, Kaiping County.

A covered baluster vase with bright underglaze blue decoration. The main motif on the outside is twin dragons chasing a flaming pearl admist clouds, above a band of serpentine waves around the base and below two plain line borders and flames around the neck. The cover is dome shape, topped by a conical knob and painted with clouds, flames and segmented waves. One the underside of the cover is a long incised inscription arranged in a coiled circle. The inscription mentions that the dead was Madame Lao, who was born on the 27th day, 4th moon, 44th year of Qianlong (AD1779) and died on the 27th day, 4th moon, 4th year Xianfeng (AD1854) at an age of 76.

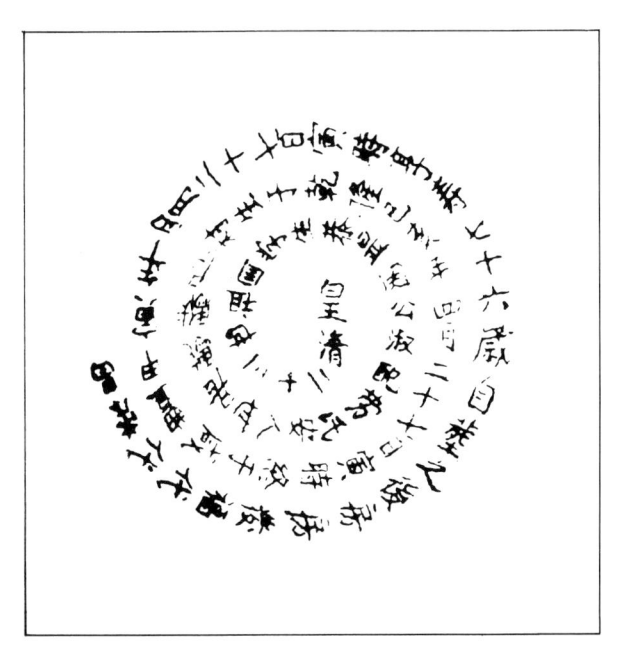

蓋銘
Cover inscription.

97

青花盤

清康熙至雍正時期(公元1662—1735年)
高3.9、口徑30厘米
1984年西沙金銀島西北角出土

敞口,弧壁,圈足,青花色澤明亮,夾有深色冰裂紋,盤內沿畫雙綫弦紋圈,內壁畫三條游動夔龍,內底雙綫弦紋圈內畫團狀夔龍,外壁畫三枝稀疏竹葉。

Blue and white dish

Kangxi to Yongzhen, Qing (AD1662-1735)
Height: 3.9, diameter: 30 cm.
Excavated in 1984 from the northwestern corner, Jinyin Island, Paracels.

Blue and white dish with a curved well, painted in the centre with a *kui*-dragon within double circles and three similar dragons on the cavetto. The underside is decorated with three bamboo branches.

During excavation, three such dishes were found stacking up, without any sign of erosion from the sea water. Probably remains from a residential site.

123

青花碟、碗

清代（公元1644—1911年）
A（左）：碟高4、口徑11.5厘米
B（中）：碟高4.3、口徑13厘米
C（右）：碗高6.3、口徑12.3厘米
1971年汕頭市郊金沙農機廠前面沙丘出土

A：胎骨潔白，敞口，弧壁，圈足，青花藍中微帶白，口沿下畫雙綫弦紋，內底畫獅子戲綉球圖案，足外壁畫單綫弦紋圈，足底豎寫"大明成化年制"楷書款。

B：胎骨潔白，敞口，弧壁，圈足，內外口沿下及內壁、內底畫雙綫弦紋，內底弦紋圈內繪有三朵纏枝菊花，外壁畫有三組點彩，足壁畫弦紋，無款。

C：胎細膩潔白，敞口，弧壁，圈足，青花藍中微帶灰，內外口沿、內壁、和足壁畫雙綫弦紋，外壁花紋分爲三組，每組上端寫一"囍"字，"囍"字下面繪有簡單花卉相托，二"囍"字之間上端畫"卍"紋，下端畫葵斗紋，內底畫雙綫方框，柜內豎寫"大明成化年制"款。

清代，汕頭市是廣東與國內外各地貿易的重要港口之一，當時潮州府所屬的大埔，饒平縣是廣東青花瓷器的重要產區，瓷器多通過汕頭港外運，這些瓷器埋藏在沙丘中，同出土的還有碗、碟、杯、罐、器蓋等六十多件瓷器，很可能是大埔饒平等地運往汕頭的外銷商品，後因故埋藏於沙丘中。瓷器的年代，過去曾認爲是明代產品，1982年我們在饒平建饒窰址中，採集到一件瓷碗，碗內底畫方框，框內寫有"大清成化年制"款，這個款顯然是窰工的偶然誤寫，反映了這種瓷器應是清代仿明成化年產品。

Blue and white dishes and bowl

Qing dynasty (AD1644-1911)
From left to right
A: height: 4, diameter: 11.5 cm.
B: height: 4.3, diameter: 13 cm.
C: height: 6.3, diameter: 12.3 cm.
Excavated in 1971 from a sandbar in front of the Jinsha Factory for Farming Implements, suburb, Shantao City.

A: Porcelain dish with a slightly everted lip, a round well and a footring. The underglaze blue has a pale tone. The interior painted with a Buddhist lion with brocaded ball, the base with a six character "Chenghua" mark in standard script.

B: Porcelain dish of similar form, interior painted with three chrysanthemun flowers, underside with three groups of blue dots and a double ring on the base.

C: Porcelain bowl with everted lip and a footring. The blue has a greyish tinge. The outside painted with three "*xi*" (happiness) characters supported by a floral spray, alternating with the *swastika* sign. Interior with a "Chenghua" mark within a double square, and a double circle on the cavetto.

Shantao (better known as Swatow) has been an important seaport in the Qing dynasty, serving the major ceramic production centres, such as Dapu and Raoping in the Chaozhou Prefecture. These ceramic pieces were from a hoard in the sandbar. A total of some sixty pieces were discovered, including bowls, dishes, cups, plates, jars and covers. They were very probably products from either Dapu or Raoping for export to overseas countries. Some of the specimens have been dated to the Ming period, but in 1982 a bowl with a wrongly written "*Da Qing Chenghua Nian Zhi*" mark was found in the Jianrao kiln site in Raoping. This supports a Qing date for the whole group.

99

青花杯

清代（公元1644—1911年）
A（左）：高3.7、口徑5.7厘米
B（右）：高5、口徑9厘米
1971年汕頭市郊金沙農機廠沙丘出土。

　　A：胎薄質白，撇口，壁向上外張不大，圈足大小與杯底相同，青花藍中帶灰，外沿下和足壁畫雙綫弦紋，外壁畫山水花卉、漁舟人物和飛雁。
　　B：胎與A件同，敞口，圈足，壁斜直，青花藍帶灰，外壁對稱畫二株蘭草，蘭草之間畫簡單的蝴蝶紋，足底畫單綫弦紋圈，圈內寫有楷書"大明成化年制款"。
　　這些杯與同出土的碗、碟一樣，同是清代仿明成化年瓷器。

Blue and white cups

Qing dynasty (AD1644-1911)
Height: 3.7-5, diameter: 5.7-9 cm.
Excavated in 1971 from a sandbar in the Jinsha Factory, suburb, Shantao City.

　　A: Porcelain cup with an everted lip and a sunken base. The blue has a greyish tinge. The outside decorated with a landscape scene between double lines.
　　B: Larger cup, with a conical wall. The blue also has a greyish tinge. The outside painted with two orchids alternating with butterflies. The base has a six character "Chenghua" mark within a circle.
　　As with the previous item (exhibit 98), these are imitation "Chenghua" pieces of the Qing dynasty.

100A

青花碗

清代（公元1644—1911年）
A（左）：高5、口徑12厘米
B（中）：高6.3、口徑12厘米
C（右）：高4.6、口徑12厘米
1984年大埔縣光德鎮泮溪井攔面，窰地窰址採集

　　A：敞口，壁斜直，圈足，外壁行書"老泉一日家宴命兒女作冷香語東坡曰泉在石中流出冷風從花裏過未香小妹曰叫月子規喉舌冷宿花蝴蝶夢魂香老泉曰爾兒不若也"詩句。
　　B：撇口，直壁，圈足，外壁對稱畫二朶葵斗紋。
　　C：敞口，壁斜直，圈足，外壁畫壽桃，並寫有一"壽"字。

Blue and white bowls

Qing dynasty (AD1644-1911)
Height: 4.6-6.3, diameter: 12 cm.
Collected in 1984 from the Jinglanmian and Yaodi kiln sites, Banxi, Guangdezhen, Dapu County.

　　A: Porcelain bowl, outside painted with a long poetic inscription.
　　B: Bowl painted with two floral sprays on the outside.
　　C: Conical bowl, painted with peaches of immortality and "*shou*" (longevity) character.

100B

青花杯、碟

清代（公元1644—1911年）
A（左）：杯高5、口徑8厘米
B（中）：碟高2.5、口徑12.8厘米
C（右）：杯高4.4、口徑8.5厘米
1984年大埔縣光德鎮泮溪井攔面、桃園鎮茅坪坑窰址採集。

A：敞口，壁微弧，圈足，足底可見有墊燒沙痕，外口沿下畫弦紋一周，外壁畫石榴蝴蝶圖案。

B：敞口，淺弧壁，矮圈足，內底畫雙綫弦紋圈，圈內畫花草紋，時代約在清代末期。

C：口外撇，壁斜直，圈足，外口沿下畫一道弦紋，外壁畫菊花蝴蝶紋。

大埔青花瓷器窰址，以光德、桃園二鎮發現最多，達數十座，年代以光德鎮窰址較早，桃園鎮窰址稍晚。

Blue and white cups and dish

Qing dynasty (AD1644-1911)
Cups: height: 4.4-5, diameter: 8-8.5 cm.
Dish: height: 2.5, diameter: 12.8 cm.
Collected in 1984 from the Banxi Jinglanmian and Maopingkeng Kiln sites in Guangdezhen and Taoyuanzhen, Dapu County.

From left to right:
A: Round cup with sandy adhesions on the base. Outside with pomegranate and butterflies painted in underglaze blue.
B: Late Qing piece, inside with a floral branch within a double circle.
C: Cup with everted lip and a footring. Outside painted with butterflies and pomegranates.

The kiln sites for producing blue and white wares in Dapu are found mainly in Guangdezhen and Taoyuanzhen. There were several dozens of them, and those located in Guangde were earlier.

101

瓷片

清代（公元1644-1911年）
長：7.5-25.5厘米
約七十年代於香港大埔碗窰遺址採集
香港博物館中央考古資料庫及
香港中文大學文物館藏品

大埔碗窰窰址位於香港新界東部，「碗寮」一名，見載於康熙版《新安縣志》，可見於明末，已有燒窰，唯現今所見窰址堆積，年代均屬清代晚期。以青花盤、碗為主要產品，青料泛灰，有印花，繪花兩種，大部份產品與廣東梅縣大埔青花相類。（見展品100號）

碗窰堆積中有大量窰具及廢件，匣缽有三式，圓墊餅多種，亦發現了陶車的瓷軸承和頂碗等。

Ceramic sherds

Qing dynasty (AD1644-1911)
Length: 7.5-25.5 cm.
Collected in the early seventies from Dapu Wanyao (Wun Yiu, Taipo), Hong Kong.
Collection of the Art Gallery, the Chinese University of Hong Kong and the Central Archaeological Repository of the Hong Kong Museum of History.

Wanyao (Wun Yiu) is a small village near Dapu (Tai Po) Market in the eastern part of the New Territories, Hong Kong. According to local gazetteer, there was already a primitive form of ceramic industry in Wanyao in the late Ming period, but all of the surface finds from this site are of late Qing date. The underglaze blue design in all the specimens has a greyish tone, and the forms as well as the decorative motives bear a close resemblance to the products made in the kiln sites further inland in Guangdong, especially in Dapu, Meixian County (Exhibit 100). Two types of blue and white decorative techniques were employed by the Dapu potter, namely painting and block printing, as illustrated by the specimens selected here.

A great many kiln furniture and wasters have been found from the kiln site, including three types of saggars and setters of different sizes as well as porcelain bearings for the potter's wheel.

102

青花盤

清代（公元1644—1911年）
高4.9、口徑11.2厘米
1984年大埔縣光德鎮澄坑庵格子窰址採集。

花瓣形折沿，內底寬平，淺弧壁，喇叭形高圈足，青花藍中帶灰，口沿上畫短斜綫紋，內底邊分爲五格，每格內畫一朵葵斗紋，中間畫雙綫弦紋圈，圈內畫單枝葵斗紋。

庵格子窰址除生產盤外，還生產杯等瓷器，瓷器花紋多畫葵斗紋，同類盤在饒平縣老窰坷窰址中曾有發現，時代大致在清代晚期。

Blue and white stem-dish

Qing dynasty (AD1644-1911)
Height: 4.9, diameter: 11.2cm.
Collected in 1984 from the An'gezi kiln site in Chengkeng, Guangdezhen, Dapu County.

The dish has a flattened and foliated rim, and supported by a trumpet foot. The blue has a greyish tinge. The interior centre is painted with floral sprays in five panels and the flattened rim with segments.

The An'gezi kiln site specialized in producing cups and stem-dishes. The most characteristic design is a floral spray that resembles sunflower. Similar dishes were also made in Laoyaoke kiln in Raoping, and both sites can be dated to the later period in the Qing dynasty.

103

和合二仙塑像

清代（公元1644—1911年）
通高7.7厘米
1985年揭陽縣新亨鎮溢溪鄉松柏坑出土
揭陽縣博物館藏品

陶質，器形較小，胎呈紅色，塑像並排站立在長方形座上，人像正首，身穿敞胸長衣，腿穿長褲，腰束帶，足穿鞋，不施釉，左邊人物臉較長，雙手斜捧鼓腹長頸花瓶，瓶內插滿花卉，右邊人物臉稍圓，右手抱長筒形瓶，瓶內插有靈芝等花草，身後露出芭蕉等植物。

Pottery figurines

Qing dynasty (AD1644-1911)
Excavated in 1985 from Songbokeng, Yiqixiang, Xinhengzhen, Jieyang County.
Collection of the Jieyang County Museum.

Unglazed, reddish brown earthenware miniature figurine of the "*hehe*"-twins standing on a rectangular pedestal. Both of them are wearing a long robe with a waist belt and holding a flower vase in their hands. On the back are banana trees.

104

陶坐衙模型器

清·康熙六年（公元1667年）
俑通高:19—20厘米
1962年大埔縣湖寮鎮吳六奇墓出土

　　明器。灰陶。出於殉葬箱中箱。包括有陶俑十六件，其中巡捕俑四件，衙役俑十二件。衙門器具六件。

　　陶俑均塗紅硃彩，多有脫落。人物神態各異、表情多猙獰可怖。這是封建時代官衙場面的真實反映。

　　吳六奇，廣東豐順縣人，官至掛印總兵官，左都督，卒於清康熙四年(1665年)，終年59歲，死後誥贈榮祿大夫少師太子太師。墓中出土康熙皇帝諭祭碑文的墓志。

Set of yamen figures

6th year Kangxi, Qing (AD1667)
Overall height: 19-20 cm.
Excavated in 1962 from the tomb of Wu Liuqi in Huliaozhen, Dapu County.

　　Grey earthenware funerary objects, all found in the middle chamber of the tomb. There are twelve *yamen* runners and four patrol guards as well as six miniature pieces of furniture of the *yamen*. The figures are realistically rendered and with details highlighted in red.
　　Wu Liuqi a native of Fengshun County, Guangdong, was an early Qing military official. He died in the fourth year of Kangxi (AD1665) at an age of 59 and was conferred posthumous titles of Grand Master for Glorious Happiness, Junior Preceptor, and Grand Preceptor of the Heir Apparent. An imperial stone tablet bestowed by the Kangxi Emperor was also found from the tomb.

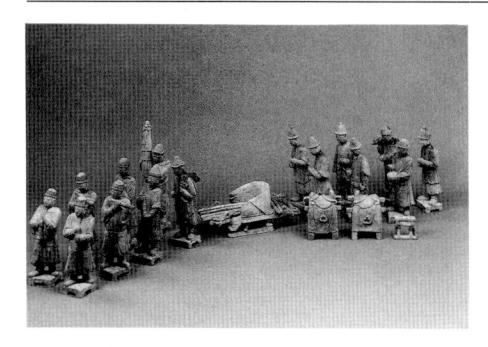

105

陶出巡模型器

清·康熙六年（公元1667年）
俑通高:19—20厘米
1962年大埔縣湖寮鎮吳六奇墓出土

　　明器。出於殉葬箱中箱，包括有陶俑十五件。其中儀仗俑八件。侍俑七件。另有器具四件。

　　陶俑器表塗紅硃彩，但多有脫落。人物動態多樣，表情肅穆威嚴，是封建時代有較高地位和身份的官員出巡場景的生動寫照。

Pottery figurines

6th year Kangxi, Qing (AD1667)
Height: 19-20 cm.
Excavated in 1962 from the tomb of Wu Liuqi in Huliaozhen, Dapu County.

　　Found in the middle chamber of the tomb, these figurines represent the official procession, with eight musicians and guards of honour, seven attendants and four pieces of furniture. Some of the figures were painted in red, but most of the pigment has flaked off. A vivid illustration of the official procession of high officials of the Qing regime.

106

陶內庭生活模型器

清·康熙六年（公元1667年）
俑通高:19—20厘米
1962年大埔縣湖寮鎮吳六奇墓出土

明器。灰陶。出於殉葬箱的右邊箱。包括有陶俑九件和寢床、倉、衣箱、方桌、椅以及其他臥房用具。這是封建時代上層貴族日常生活的一個縮影，從一個側面反映了墓主人生前過着窮奢極欲的生活。

Pottery figurines

6th year Kangxi, Qing (AD1667)
Height: 19.5 cm.
Excavated in 1962 from the tomb of Wu Liuqi in Huliaozhen, Dapu County.

Found in the right chamber of the tomb, these figurines as the previous groups are of grey earthenware and depict the household life of the Qing dynasty. Apart from nine female attendants, there are beds, table, chairs, cabinets and everyday utensils.

輔照五.
吳六奇墓誌銘

清康熙六年（公元1667年）
高130、寬62厘米
大埔縣吳六奇墓附屬文物

碑石長方形，弧形頂，邊緣刻單陰綫框，碑首兩邊刻龍紋，中間長方形雙綫框內刻"諭祭"兩字;碑首下銘文分爲三格，其中第一格四周刻龍紋，第二格和第三格之間有二條陰橫直綫紋相隔。碑文有篆書和楷書二種字體，內容主要是序述吳六奇生平事迹和其家庭情況。

Supp. illustration 5
Rubbing of epitaph

6th year Kangxi, Qing (AD1667)
Height: 130, width: 62 cm.
From the tomb of Wu Liuqi in Huliaozhen, Dapu County.

This epitaph stone from the tomb of Wu Liuqi is of rectangular shape, topped by a semicircular imperial eulogy written by the Kangxi emperor. The upper part is divided into three sections, with the eulogy and title surrounded by incised dragons. The third section, written in seal script contains the official titles bestowed to Wu. The main text, written in standard script records the military expedition that Wu Liuqi took part, as well as his life and family.

墓誌拓片
Rubbing of epitaph

107

木官印

清代（公元1644—1911年）
長10.1、寬9.9、高1.6厘米、重100克
南澳縣雲澳鎮港仔底灘塗出土，1982年徵集
南澳縣海防史博物館藏品

扁方形。印面一周寬緣。篆刻漢、滿、蒙三種文字，反體陽文。印文爲："鎮守福建台灣總兵官印"。

南澳爲粵東海島，西南距汕頭市二十四浬，東距福建省東山島二十浬，東北距台灣島一百六十浬。自明萬曆四年至民國三年間（公元1578—1913年），南澳爲福建、廣東兩省共管。

這件官印的發現，說明當時南澳與福建、台灣在軍事上有着不尋常的關係。

Wooden seal

Qing dynasty (AD1644-1911)
Length: 10.1, width: 9.9, height: 1.6 cm., weight: 100 gm.
Found in Yun'aozhen, Nan'ao County, collected in 1982.

Square seal of the Regional Military Commander of Taiwan, Fujian, with inscriptions in Chinese, Mongolian and Manchurian.

Nan'ao is an island in eastern Guangdong, very near to both Fujian and Taiwan. From the 4th year Wanli (AD1578) to the 3rd year Republic (AD1913) it had been under the joint jurisdiction of Fujian and Guangdong. The discovery of this seal indicates the strategical position of Nan'an as well as its military relationship with Taiwan and Fujian.

印文
Seal impression.

108

鐵鐘

清康熙四十年,（公元1701年）
通高:63.5, 口徑:51厘米
六十年代於粉嶺龍躍頭收集
香港博物館藏品

厚重鐵鐘,圓形,口沿外移,鐘頂中空,上有「蒲牢」形鈕。器壁上下各鑄弦紋兩道,有長方形框,內「風調雨順」、「國泰民安」八字,另有長銘:「簕竻圍信女鄧門林氏,因男信庠鄧士美往省應試,虔誠在大慈大悲觀世音菩薩殿前拜許洪鐘一口,重壹百餘觔……時康熙四十年歲在辛巳孟春吉旦建置」款後有秋葉款及「隆盛爐造」,對比香港其他鐵器款識,「隆盛爐」爲佛山鑄鐵店,香港地區所見鐵器,多爲其店舖所鑄造。

Iron temple bell

Kangxi, Qing dynasty (AD1701)
Overall height: 63.5, mouth diameter: 51 cm.
Collected in the sixties from Longyuetou, Fengling (Lung Yuek Tau, Fanling), Hong Kong.
Collection of the Hong Kong Museum of History.

A heavy temple bell topped by a monster knob. The side cast with a long votive inscription with a date corresponding to AD1701, flanked by two panels of auspicious phrases and floral design in raised lines; all within two double lines.

A shopmark at the end of inscription indicates that the bell was cast in Foshan, Guangdong.

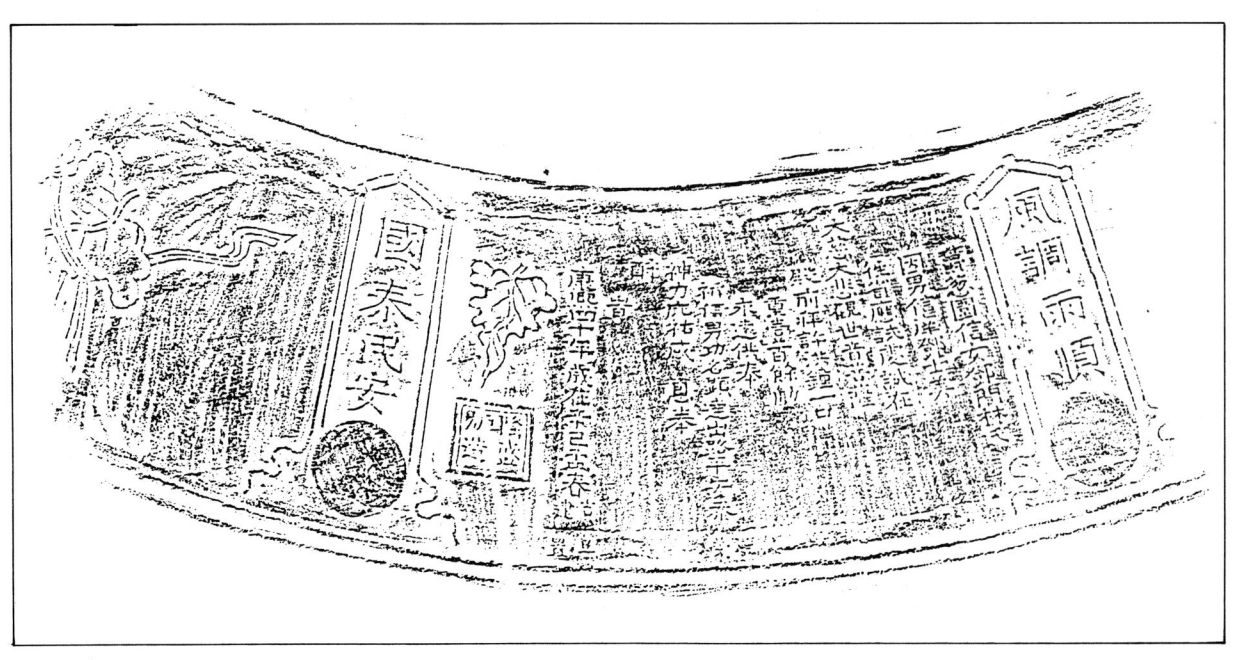

銘文拓片
Rubbing

109

鐵彈丸及瓷片

清代（公元1644-1911年）
彈丸徑:7.5-2.1;瓷片長:7.2-15.6厘米
1981-84年香港東龍炮台出土
香港古物古蹟辦事處藏品

東龍洲炮台，始建於清初康熙年間，其地勢險要，扼守佛堂門海峽，爲商船經港入粤之必經要道。然該島僻遠，補給不易，遂於嘉慶十五年（1810年）廢置，原有屯兵移駐九龍。爲配合修繕工程，考古工作者曾於炮台內部進行發掘，出土有陶瓷器、金屬器物、魚獸骨及貝殼等。圖示其中小部分，彈丸爲鐵鑄，實心；青花瓷片兩款，應爲十八世紀盛清江西景德鎭所燒製；青釉盤，亦是江西產品，底有「嘉慶年製」青花方章款。

Iron cannon balls and ceramic sherds

Qing dynasty (AD1644-1911)
Balls: diameter 7.5-2.1, sherds: length 7.2-15.6 cm.
Excavated in 1981/84 from the Donglong fort, (Tung Lung), Hong Kong.
Collection of the Antiquities and Monuments Office, Hong Kong.

The Donglu Fort, built in the early Qing period, is located at the strategic point overlooking the narrow Fotangmen passage through which trading junks sailed into the Hong Kong region on their way to Guangzhou. The Fort was evacuated in the Jiaqing period in early 19th century with the garrison and arms moved to Kowloon. These iron cannon balls and porcelain specimens were probably part of the supplies belonging to the garrison stationed there. The two blue and white sherds are typical types of the 18th century and the green glazed dish, a product from Jingdezhen, Jiangxi, has a blue and white Jiaqing (AD1796-1821) seal mark on the base.

110A

石印章

清代（公元1644—1911年）
高3.2—7.3厘米
1975年陸豐縣大安鎭華田小學墓葬出土

青田石質，大小共35枚，從印款上可分爲方形、長方形、橢圓形三種，部分印頂上圓雕或浮雕有植物、麒麟、或伏蟬。

從章款中可知墓主人名黃廷林，同章一起出土的還有茶壺、墨盤、印盒、陶罐、筆筒等器物。

章文如下：

1. 濟時　2. 黃廷霖印　3. 濟時　4. 波瀾揮灑墨華香　5. 廷霖之印　6. 用齋　7. 用齋　8. 黃廷霖印　9. 護封　10. 心向友朋開　11. 廷霖　12. 廷霖　13. □養聖賢心　14. 澤蒼　15. 廷霖　16. 濟時　17. 廷霖　18. 槀封　19. 用齋　20. 用齋　21. 用齋　22. 廷霖　23. 廷霖　24. 濟時　25. 用齋　26. 澤蒼　27. 一片冰心　28. 濟時　29. 霖　30. 廷霖　31. 廷　32. 三栖草聖傳　33. 澤蒼　34. 引鵝　35. 用齋

Stone seals

Qing dynasty (AD1644-1911)
Height: 3.2-7.3 cm.
Excavated in 1975 from a burial in the Huatian Primary School, Dayaozhen, Lufeng County.

Thirty-five soapstone seals of square, rectangular or oval shapes, some of which topped by animals, plants or cicada. The owner of these seals was Huang Tinglin, alias Jishi. Co-existing objects include teapots, inkwell, seal vermilion box, earthenware pot and brush pot.

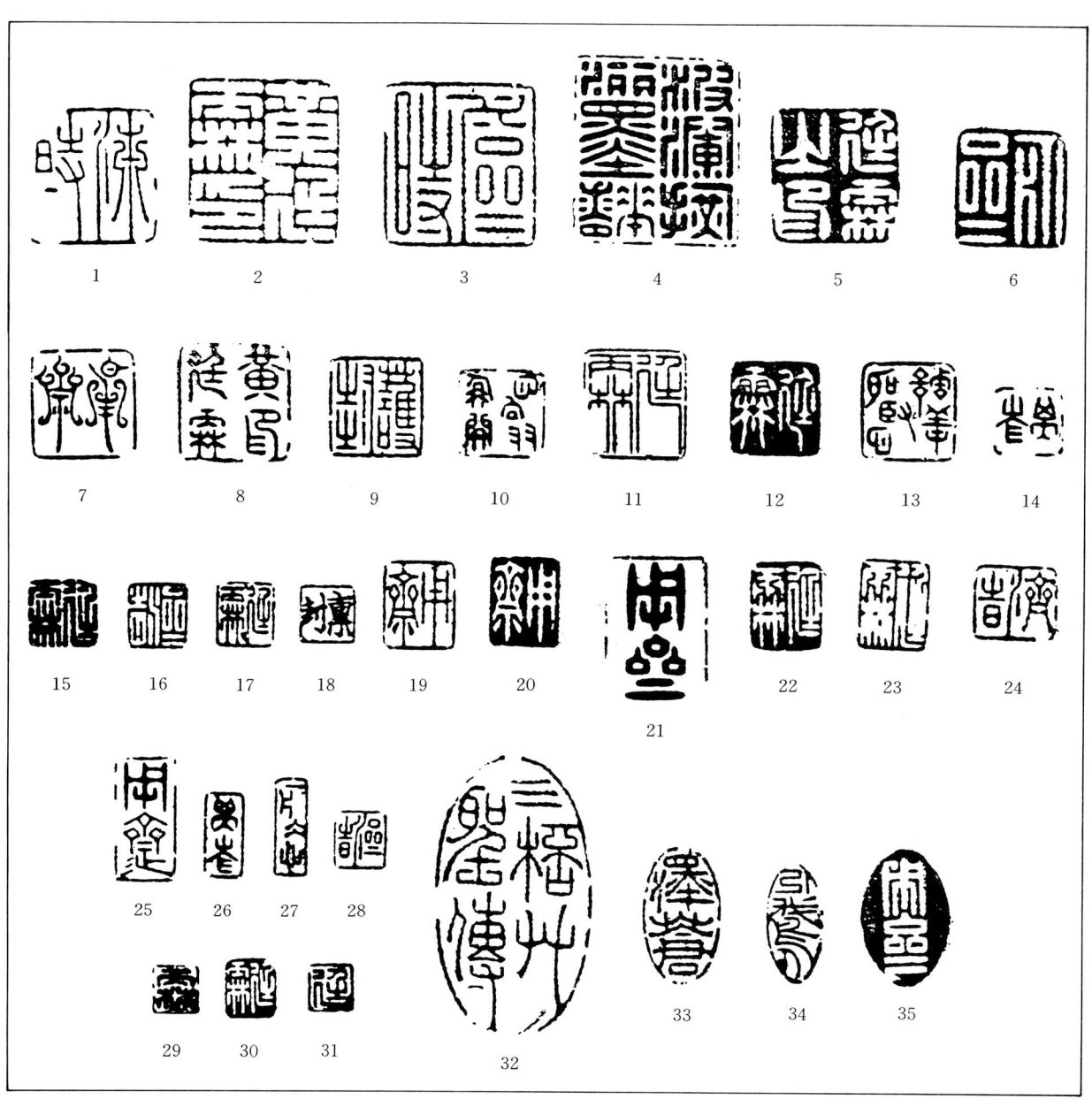

印文鈐本
Seal impressions.

110B

玻璃印盒

清代（公元1644—1911年）
通高3.2、邊長7.2厘米
1975年陸豐縣大安鎮華田小學墓葬出土

盒方形透明，直壁，平底，盒心圓形下凹，上有子口，盒底下四角各有一隻方形小矮足；蓋平頂，直壁，蓋心內凹。

Glass covered box

Qing dynasty (AD1644-1911)
Overall height: 3.2, width: 7.2 cm.
Excavated in 1975 from a burial in the Huatian Primary School, Dayaozhen, Lufeng County.

Transparent square box for holding seal vermilion, with sunken circular well and groove for the cover, and four feet on the corners.

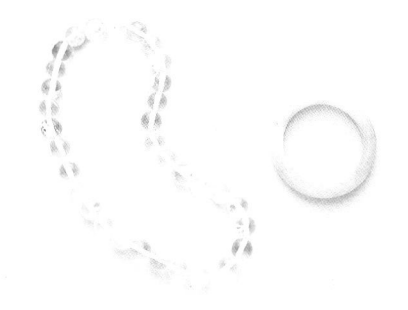

111

珠飾、玉環

清光緒十一年（公元1885年）
A（左）：珠飾，直徑1.4厘米
B（右）：玉環，外徑7.2、內徑5.5厚1厘米
1985年潮州市西北鳳山朱以鑒夫婦合葬墓出土

A：珠飾為水晶質，圓形，白色透明，中間有小圓孔穿繩，共33粒。出土時掛在男屍頸上。

B：玉環圓形，外壁呈弧狀，內壁較平直，玉色白裏透綠，出土時掛在女屍手骨上。

朱以鑒字寶珊，澄海縣人，世居郡城，曾任通奉大夫，江西南康、九江，福建澄州、漳州、延平等地知府，卒於光緒十一年七月二十八日。夫人鄭氏爲海陽縣鄭德彬通奉次女，死時先葬於城東烏石鄉黃田山，後遷至鳳山與夫合葬。發掘開棺時，朱以鑒屍體大部分保存完好，頭戴朝帽，身穿朝服，頸掛朝珠，腰系白色料佩，右手執摺扇。鄭氏夫人骨骸排列整齊，頭髮插有銀方簪，兩手腕骨上各戴有一隻玉環。

Crystal necklace and jade bracelet

11th year Guangxu, Qing (AD1885)
Beads: diameter: 1.4cm.
Bracelet: diameter (ext): 7.2, (int): 5.5, thickness: 1 cm.
Excavated in 1985 from the Zhu Yijian couple tomb in Fengshan, Chaozhou City.

The necklace is made up of thirty-three round, transparent rock crystal beads, pierced and held together by a piece of string; found on the neck of the male. The jade bracelet has a curved outer wall and straight inner wall. The white jade has a trace of green. Found in the arm of the female skeleton.

Zhu Yijian, *zi* Baoshan was a native of Chenghai County, but his ancestors had lived in Chaozhou for many generations. Zhu served a number of official posts, including the Grand Master for Thorough Service, and Prefects of Nankang and Jiujiang, Jiangxi; Chenghai, Zhangzhou and Yanping, Fujian. He died on the 28th day, 7th moon, 11th year Guangxu (AD1885). His wife, Madame Zheng was the second daughter of Zheng Debin of Haiyang County, and died earlier than Zhu. She was first buried in Huangtianshan, Niaoshixiang, east of Chaozhou, and was later buried together with Zhu in Fengshan.

During excavation, the corpse of Zhu was still largely intact, wearing a court hat and dressed in formal court costume, with a court necklace, white pendant and a folding fan in his right hand. His wife's skeleton was arranged in neat order, with a silver hairpin, and wearing jade bracelets in both hands.

112

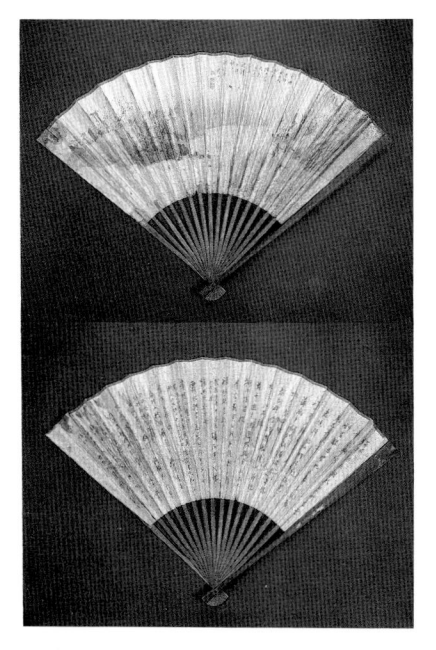

紙摺扇

清代（公元1644—1911年）
扇面長62、寬18.2，扇骨長32厘米
1985年潮州市城東黃石山朱以鑒夫婦合葬墓出土

十六竹骨，扇面淺絳色，一面撒金點，寫詩四首，部分文字已難於辨認，詩後有"作時壬午梅雨初□□研生□以呈寶珊世伯大人□□覽誨正世侄陸錫康謹誌"題款，另一面畫山水人物，上端有"寶珊老伯世大人授至湖口客次為□一是□□贈行即請鈞正陸錫康又誌"題款。

此扇作者陸錫康，字壽門，吳縣人；為潘祖蔭之舅氏。工書法，亦擅花卉、翎毛。

Folding fan

Qing dynasty (AD1644-1911)
Fan: length: 62, width: 18.2, rib: length: 31 cm.
Excavated in 1985 from the Zhu Yijian couple tomb, Huangshishan, east of Chaozhou City.

This fan has sixteen bamboo ribs, the paper was pale brown with gold flecks. On one side is a landscape scene, while on the other are four poems in semi-cursive script, both with dedication inscriptions and signatures of Lu Sikang.

Lu Sikang, *zi* Shoumeng, was a native of Suzhou, and brother-in-law of the late Qing scholar official Pan Zuyin (AD1830-1890). Lu was an accomplished calligraphist as well as a painter of flowers and birds.

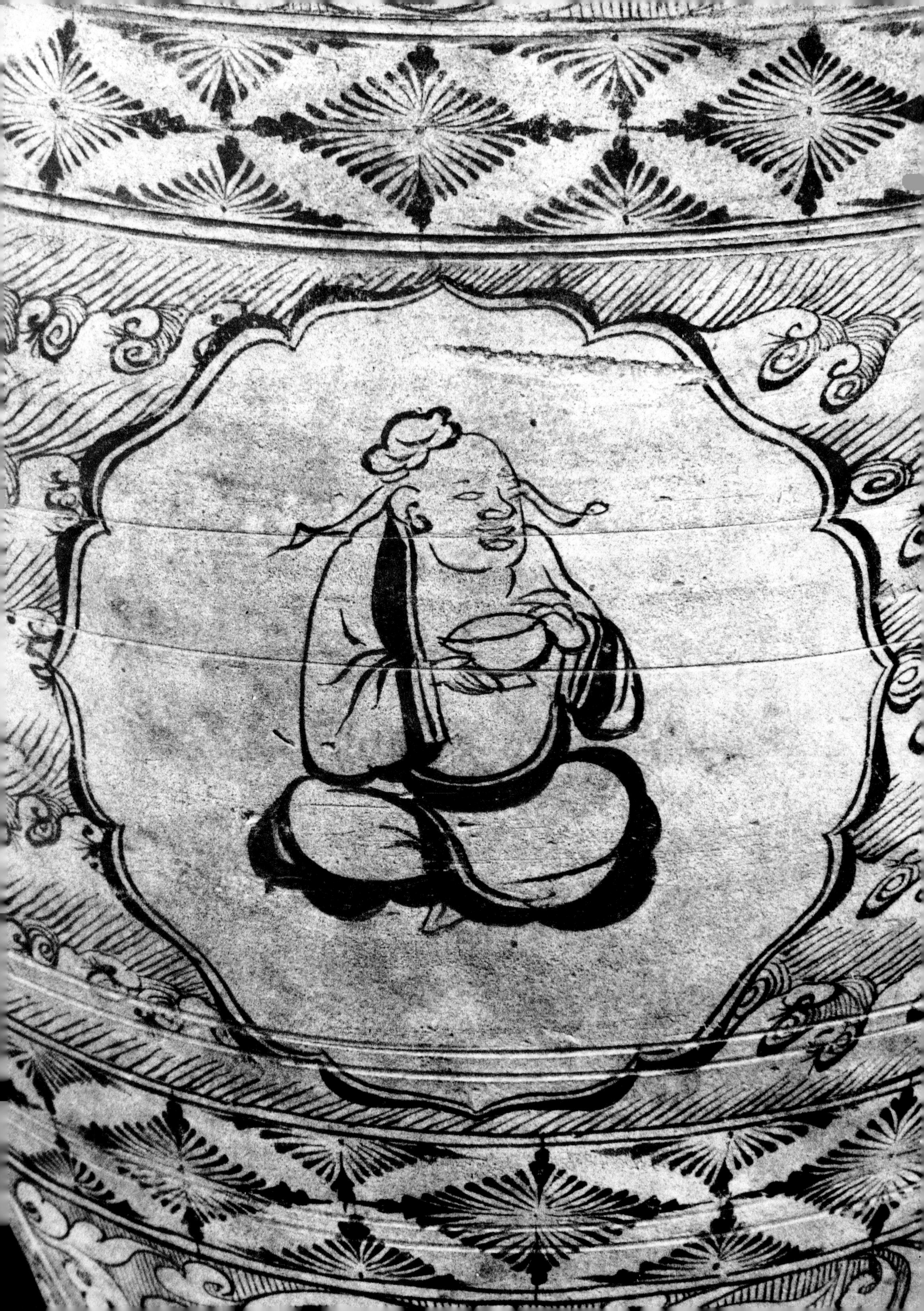

廣東出土的五代至明清陶瓷

曾廣億

　　五代十國時期，是唐末地方割據勢力的延續，當時廣東屬南漢國①，從劉龑割據立國（公元911年）起，至劉鋹大寶十四年（公元971年）降宋止，前後四個皇帝統治了廣東六十年。南漢在中國歷史發展中，不過是短暫的一瞬，這一時期的遺址至今尚未發現，出土的陶瓷數量不多，僅見番禺石馬村南漢劉晟墓和增城五代墓中有所出土。北宋是廣東陶瓷發展的鼎盛時期，燒瓷技術有着巨大的進步，它與當時社會經濟的發展，北方人口（包括陶工）的大量南遷，陶瓷器的大量對外輸出和陶瓷業對窰爐的不斷改革，都是分不開的。據多次文物複查所知，宋窰分佈範圍很廣，截至1986年底統計，宋代瓷窰全省共發現600多處，數量最多，元代瓷窰則僅見34處，明清瓷窰增至520處。宋至明清的墓葬發現上千座，通過正式發掘清理的數量不多。1957年及1972年陵水縣發現300多件窖藏宋代外銷瓷，1978年該縣海灘發現一處範圍很大的唐宋外銷瓷遺物地點，1969年及1971年又在珠海蚊洲島和汕頭海灘出土近300件元、明兩代的外銷瓷。1974年與1955年廣東省考古工作人員又先後兩次到西沙羣島進行考察，採集了大批古外銷瓷標本，1980年又考察了海南島瓊山海底陸陷沉海的明代地震遺址，亦獲得不少古陶瓷標本。此外，對廣州、潮州、惠州、佛山、海康、惠陽等宋代和明代窰址進行過發掘。上述考古材料大部分已分別發表過簡報或專著，本文主要是依據調查發掘資料按時代的先後順序，並按窰址、墓葬及外銷瓷遺物地點出土器物逐項作綜合性的或重點的描述介紹，對古陶瓷涉及到的某些問題，亦適當加以扼要論述，不妥之處，請批評指正。

一、廣東五代墓葬出土的陶瓷

　　廣東五代墓葬通過正式發掘的只有兩座，出土了195件陶瓷器，有一定的代表性，茲分述如下。

1．廣州番禺石馬村南漢墓出土的陶瓷

　　1954年廣東省文物管理委員會在廣州番禺石馬村清理了一座"乾和十六年"（公元958年）南漢第三個皇帝劉晟的昭陵②，該墓是磚室墓，主室有多處盜洞，已受嚴重破壞，出土的隨葬品中尚存完整的瓷器三十三件，陶瓷一百五十四件（另有一大批陶瓷已被擊毀，僅存碎片）瓷器僅見罐類，有青釉夾耳罐、青釉四耳大罐、青釉四耳小罐、青釉六耳蓋罐、黃釉六耳罐和黃釉四耳罐。青釉夾耳罐斜肩歛足，帶蓋，肩前後附圓孔板耳，左右各附夾耳一對，蓋有兩翼，夾耳與蓋翼各有圓孔，加蓋後夾耳與蓋翼可貫穿木塞或綁繩，使提挈時蓋不至跳動與丟失。同時穿綁一側後，罐蓋可自由開關（展品1）。這種造型設計周到的夾耳罐，極為罕見，近年來長沙窰雖然發現有相類似的陶器，但很粗糙，遠不及這裏的精美。青釉四耳罐與六耳罐（展品2）胎質細膩，火候很高，裏外均有一層晶瑩的青釉，遍體有小開片紋，但也有個別不開片的，胎釉的顏色和燒製方法與夾耳罐基本相同。黃釉罐，凸唇滑肩，鼓腹平底，最大徑在器腹中部，器壁滿布輪旋弦紋，器身大半截施釉，下端露胎，釉色部分已剝落。陶器器形有六耳罐、大缸、碗、雀四類。其中六耳罐一百四十七件，數量最多，胎呈灰色不施釉，口唇微向外卷，斜肩平底，最大徑在器上腹，肩附六耳，器外壁滿佈輪旋凹弦紋（展品3，4）。大缸和陶雀均殘破，原貌不明。陶碗僅見一件，質堅細而薄。此外，1976年在石馬村南漢墓葬附近，採集一件陶龍首建築構件，兩側略呈長方形，橫剖面近似正方形，空心，側面雕塑龍首，露口吐舌，突眼竪耳，鬚往後翹起，翹唇卷鼻（展品5）。"龍"是封建權威的象徵，皇帝以"真龍天子"自居，皇帝穿的長袍及居住的皇宮等均採用龍的裝飾。因此，這件龍首構件，很可能是臨時停放劉晟靈柩建築物上的一種瓦脊裝飾，是否如此？還有待進一步的考證。

　　上述青釉四耳罐、六耳罐和夾耳罐，製作精細，造形美觀，釉色晶瑩，是同時期青瓷中罕見的精品，無疑是廣東陶瓷藝人在生產實踐和科學實驗進程中，所獲得的一項重要成果，這批瓷器的出土，成為廣東地區五代瓷器斷代的重要依據，其中青瓷六耳罐和夾耳罐已先後收入《全國基本建設工程中出土文物展覽圖錄》（1955年）和《故宮博物院藏瓷選集》（1962年文物出版社出版），作為南方地區五代青瓷的代表作品。

　　皇陵陪葬的陶瓷一般都是精品，南漢還有三個皇帝，一個是劉玢，在位不及一年，即被其弟劉晟所殺，有無建陵未見文獻記載。劉鋹（後主）降宋，封南越王，其陵墓在韶州治北六里的獅子崗（未發掘）。劉龑的康陵早在明代崇禎九年秋已被發現，《番禺縣志》卷二十四記載頗詳（清〈郝玉麟《廣東通志》記載此事為崇禎十五年），該墓的磚室建築至今尚存，但未發掘，相信兩陵亦有不少精美瓷器，以後有條件，需要發掘時，即可見分曉。

2．增城五代墓出土的陶瓷

　　1972年6月廣東省博物館與增城縣文化館合作，在增

城附城鎮基建工地發掘了一座五代磚室墓,出土陶瓷器十一件,其中有唐代晚期的白瓷碗一件,四耳罐一件,五代的青釉碗一件,瓣口印花碟六件,燈盞一件,葫蘆形執壺一件。晚唐的白釉瓷碗,白胎,敞口凸唇,玉璧足,素面,製作精細,係河北曲陽定窯產品(圖1)。晚唐四耳陶罐,直口短頸,矮身平底,外壁施大半截釉,已脫盡(圖2)。據馮先銘先生說"可能是廣東的產品",窯口待考。五代青釉碗,釉色青中泛灰,敞口斜腹平底微凹,器內底遺留有二十三個支釘痕跡,內外壁均施釉,外底露胎,無紋飾(圖3)。廣東窯址未發現過這類碗形,窯口待考。五代菱形六瓣口印花碟,敞口淺身,斜壁平底,內底呈六角形,施淡黃褐釉,外壁下端與外底露胎,釉色部分已脫落,內底印花有兩種,均係凸綫紋,隱約可見。一種是內底印雙層仰蓮花紋一朵,花朵之外有雙綫六角形及雙綫菱形六瓣紋作邊框(圖4)。另一種是內底印折枝花卉,邊框與前者相同(圖5)。這六件印花碟均為湖南長沙銅官窯產品。盞,係燃點豆油的燈盞,外表似小碟,口微斂,淺身平底,內底近口沿處貼附一小圓紐,燈芯由紐部圓孔穿過,能固定位置不會擺動。器表施醬黃釉,脫落很甚,係五代長沙銅官窯產品(圖6)。葫蘆形執壺,其特點是器身加蓋為葫蘆形,揭去器蓋為喇叭口壺,肩下垂(即"美人肩"),橢圓腹圈足,最大徑在器腹中部,肩部附一彎長流,另一側貼附束帶形提手曲柄,蓋作空心半圓形,蓋頂為乳狀紐,蓋邊加附一小環紐,可穿小繩與曲柄相綁,使用時壺蓋不會失落。器蓋與器表彩繪綠色與醬黃色條紋、斑塊等圖案,均為釉下彩,其上及空隙中還有一層薄薄的透明色白釉,從器形及釉色觀察,此係長沙銅官窯產品無疑(圖7)。這件葫蘆形執壺,過去在展場中,長期以來定為"唐代",實屬偏早。理由是長沙銅官窯的時代,從已發表的材料來看,最遲興起於八世紀前期,或稍早一些,盛於九世紀中期,而衰於十世紀初期。該器形以壺類最多,壺大致分為三個發展階段,長沙窯的早期壺類屬第一階段,其造型是盤口長頸,兩耳,平底,演變為一個帶把手的瓶壺,但沒有流,而流部只有象徵性的乳狀器嘴,這類壺初唐墓中常見。第二階段是盤口壺,出現了八角形短嘴,這種短嘴是長沙窯瓷壺的基本特徵(這類壺書有"大中九年"(公元855年)題記,其時代當為唐宣宗時期。)這類壺逐漸演變為壺嘴略長,嘴下繪有飛雁戲水的圖形,屬於釉下彩繪畫。同時口形變成了大喇叭狀,瓜稜形腹,該類壺屬於繪畫與書法為裝飾的瓷壺的全盛時期,其相對年代大致相當於唐代中晚期。其演變情況是,一支向小喇叭口壺發展,另一支向直筒形小口壺演變。第三階段,壺的基本造型與喇叭口壺大致

相似,但肩部下垂,下腹稍大,似膽瓶,此壺亦稱"美人肩"壺,在唐末五代之際最為流行(同時期的壺造型多樣,如瓜形壺、鷄嘴壺等),此外有一種壺發展成彎長嘴帶蓋葫蘆形執壺,這類壺五代較為流行,在長沙五代墓中亦有出土④。增城墓出土的葫蘆形執壺,即屬此類,其年代亦應屬五代無疑。銅官窯面積大,產量多,工藝精,銷路廣,在國內長沙、西安、洛陽、邗江、鎮江、無錫、武昌、安徽、江西、福建、廣西、廣東等地的一些唐、五代墓中以及揚州、寧波遺址中和海南西沙羣島均有出土。此外,該窯產品當時亦大量外銷,據目前所知,在伊朗、伊拉克、日本、朝鮮、巴基斯坦、印尼、菲律賓、泰國、斯里蘭卡等國家也有出土⑤,可見銅官窯瓷器是當年國內外暢銷的產品。

二、廣東出土的宋代瓷器

1. 宋窯出土的瓷器

據普查所知,宋窯分佈範圍很廣,在梅縣、興寧、潮州、揭陽、澄海、惠陽、惠州、博羅、龍川、紫金、東莞、深圳、韶關、始興、南雄、仁化、樂昌、乳源、廣州、番禺、佛山、南海、三水、肇慶、德慶、郁南、新會、陽春、陽江、恩平、茂名、化州、高州、信宜、湛江、吳川、海康、廉江、遂溪、萬寧、東方、陵水等四十多個縣市均有發現,共600多處。瓷器的釉色歸納起來有青釉、青褐釉、青白釉、白釉、黑釉、醬黃釉、醬褐釉、黃褐釉、綠釉、窯變釉等。其中青釉和黑釉是廣東宋窯中常見的釉色。這裏主要是依據調查發掘材料⑥,對出土的比較有代表性的宋瓷進行分類綜合論述。

宋窯燒製的陶瓷器,有生活用具、文房用具、樂器、玩具、紡織工具、捕魚工具、炊具、葬具、製瓷工具、窯具和美術瓷等。歸納起來器形有碗、碟、盤、執壺、杯、茶盞、盞托、瓶、罐、盆、洗、瓷枕、軍持、腰鼓、吹雀、唾盂、香爐、熏爐、雀杯、粉盒、燈、燈盞、燈托、燭插、缽、硯、水注、水盂、净瓶、筆架、人像、佛像、武士、葫蘆、獅子、狗、馬、騎馬人、獸頭、彈丸、吹雀、紡輪、網墜、沙煲、爐篂、陶罎以及釉缽、擂杵、瓷臼、碾槽、碾輪、瓷權、漏斗、碗碟印花模、佛像印模、花瓣印模、壓錘、軸頂帽、盪箍、匣缽、渣餅、墊環、測溫標等。

碗出數量最多,種類也最多,有敞口、斂口、撇口、直口、瓣口、凸唇、卷唇、折唇、圓唇、青唇(青唇醬黑釉或醬褐釉身)之分,碗底有高圈足、矮圈足、大圈足、小圈足、臥足、平底之別,碗身亦有大小深淺之異。碗的裝飾有刻花、印花、剔花、刻劃印花組合、彩繪、點彩、刻花印花點彩組合等

七大類,如細分約有三、四十種之多。此外還有文字碗。其中青唇黑釉碗、青唇醬褐釉碗及瓣口碗,僅見於廣州西村窰、惠州窰、潮州窰和南雄窰燒製,一般均係碎片,完整器不易檢得。刻花碗一般均係青釉或青白釉,影青釉、白釉、黃釉和白陶衣的均有,但數量不多,其主要特點是在碗內外壁均刻劃紋飾,但也有不少只在碗內或只在碗外刻劃紋飾的。花紋題材種類,有纏枝菊花、團菊、菊瓣、蓮瓣、牡丹花、折枝花、蕉葉、卷草、草葉、斜綫紋、魚鱗紋、直綫紋、斜方格紋、卷草箆梳組合、直綫箆梳紋、弦紋卷草箆梳組合、弦紋花瓣組合、弦紋牡丹箆梳組合等。刻花一般都綫條流暢,顯得深淺均勻,熟練自然(圖8-10)。印花碗主要是在碗內底模印蓮花紋、菊花紋或水草紋等或在內壁模印纏枝花卉。這類碗惠州窰、仁化南宋窰和梅縣南宋窰(上述未標明南宋的均係北宋,下同)燒製的較爲精美。惠州窰的是在碗內中心印團菊一朵,內壁模印六朵纏枝菊花環壁對稱,空隙處加上枝葉分佈全身,連成一圈,卻不會顯得過於繁密,看起來花葉紛披,互相呼應,俯仰有緻,十分雅潔(圖11)。這類碗與廣州西村窰的菊花碗有所不同,其特點是菊花較多,外壁不刻劃紋飾,而與耀州窰菊花碗則基本相同⑦。仁化南宋窰的是在碗內中心印雙魚水草圖案,印紋一般都很深,綫條清晰。梅縣南宋窰的是在碗內模印雙鳳比翼紋,空隙處襯托花卉圖案。亦有碗內底模印雙魚水草的,紋飾精緻,佈局嚴謹,其特點是全部瓷碗均係芒口,覆燒而成。鳳凰紋飾的瓷器,在廣東宋窰中至今僅見梅縣窰有所燒製。宋代定窰、景德鎮窰和吉州窰的碗、盤、盞、盆等器物上,亦有這類紋飾。剔花碗,係在碗外壁雕剔仰蓮花瓣一周,有一定的立體感,這類碗形不多,僅見潮州窰和西村窰燒製。刻劃印花組合紋,僅見於惠州窰和廣州西村窰。惠州窰碗係在坯胎未乾時,口沿削出六處小缺口,然後修磨成六瓣口,碗外壁接近口沿處刻菊瓣紋一周,內壁刻弦紋,卷草紋,間加箆梳紋,內底模印蓮花紋(圖12)。另一種是口沿不飾瓣口形,內壁刻劃纏枝花卉,中央模印團菊一朵。此外,有不少大碗外壁刻劃斜行直綫紋或刻弦紋一周,碗內模印纏枝菊花紋。廣州西村窰碗係在碗內中心印團菊一朵,內壁印纏枝仰菊三朵,空隙處加填菊葉,外壁刻條形菊瓣紋(圖13)。彩繪碗,主要是用鐵銹色、醬黑色或紅褐色彩料在碗內彩繪折枝牡丹一朵或彩繪折枝菊花一朵。或在內壁彩繪兩道弦紋,外壁繪卷草紋一周,一般均係釉下彩,釉上彩的也有,但數量極少。其中有些在坯胎上彩繪後尚未施表層的白釉即入窰焙燒,其顏色較淺。南海等窰口均有這類產品。點彩碗,主要是用鐵銹色釉料點於青釉或青白釉碗唇或近碗邊沿,均係點於釉下,一般均係點一圈,疏密不一。廉江、遂溪、海康、廣州等窰口均有這類產品。彩繪和點彩裝飾,在廣東新石器時代晚期的陶器上和西周窰出土的陶瓷上,以及晉墓出土的青釉器中均有這類裝飾,可見這類紋飾淵源久遠。文字碗有書寫、刻寫、戳印三種。書寫的主要是用醬黑色釉料在碗內中心書寫"干□□""四月□□""酒",寫後經過入窰焙燒。亦有在碗外足底墨寫"彭"、"杜司"、"林且"等文字,這種墨寫姓名的可能是窰工自己的碗,是使用時才寫上去的。刻寫的是坯胎未乾時在碗內中心刻"大"、"五"、"十"、"田"、"唐"、"因"、"在"、"記"、"于"、"個"、"才"、"米"、"福"、"壽"等單個文字和吉祥語。戳印的也是在坯未乾時在碗內中心戳印方形或斧形印歎,內有"福"、"安祖"、"口記"等文字(其中有些印款文字難以辨認)。刻花印花點彩組合碗,青釉、青白釉、青黃釉均有,這類碗型較大,器身較淺,一般均係展唇撇口,口徑約30至40厘米左右,過去有人把它稱作"盆"、"缽"、"盤"、"碗"的均有。因其器形是屬淺身碗型,故筆者把它列爲碗類。其特點主要是在器內底刻弦紋一圈,內刻獸頭鸚鵡咀魚鱗身鳳尾圖案,空隙處模印雙綫圓圈紋或雙綫魚鱗紋,內壁刻纏枝指甲紋六組(每組均呈橢圓形指甲邊),內加箆梳紋,或刻劃纏枝花卉,然後在刻劃和模印紋飾上再加赭黑色點彩,形成刻、印、彩組合紋飾,這類作品係廣州西村窰產品,數量不多,殊爲難得,其中完整器香港中文大學文物館和北京故宮博物院均有收藏,由於外銷原因,前者是菲律賓出土,後者是洛辛(LOCSIN)先生及夫人的贈品也可能是菲律賓出土。

碟,出土數量僅次於碗,有侈口、菱口、敞口、六折口、撇口折邊、瓣口、淡灰釉口(淡灰釉口、青褐釉身)、卷唇等,一般均淺身圈足。平底或圓餅足的也有,但數量不多。碟的裝飾有刻花、印花、彩繪、點彩四類。刻花碟釉色有青釉、影青釉、醬黃釉、醬褐釉、白釉五種,其中青釉數量較多,其主要特點是在碟心刻雙綫弦紋和雙綫十字紋,內壁刻七蕉葉紋並加箆梳紋。或內壁刻卷草、牡丹花、水波紋、四瓣花紋。或雙綫花瓣紋,或卷草與箆紋組合,或刻蕉葉紋(有一、二、三、四綫之分)或內底只刻團菊一朵。或碟內刻折枝牡丹、葉間加填箆紋;或碟心刻折枝菊花,內壁刻雙綫菊瓣;或內刻花草,外刻菊瓣;或外壁刻大小雙層六至七花瓣紋,花心飾乳點紋,有些花間填箆紋。其中瓣口碟內外壁均刻花,外壁一般均係刻斜條菊瓣紋,內壁刻花變化也很大,有蝶心刻菊花,周壁刻雙綫菊瓣紋的。有蝶心刻草葉紋,周壁刻連弧五瓣或六瓣紋的。有碟心刻牡丹花,周壁刻五至七瓣紋

141

的,其間再填篦紋。有碟心刻雙綫或四綫花瓣紋,周壁刻五至六瓣紋的。或器底刻弦紋一道,其周壁刻六格直綫紋。刻花碟紋飾較多變化較大(圖14-27),如細分約有三十多種。印花碟釉色有青釉、青白釉兩種。其特點是在碟內模印兩朵纏枝菊花,菊葉佈滿內壁,外壁刻劃斜行菊花瓣一周。或只在碟內模印蓮花紋或模印交枝菊花三朵。或在碟內模印雙魚和水草圖案。或模印雙鳳比翼紋,空隙處襯托花卉圖案。或在碟內接近口沿處印回紋環碟一周,其下印菊花瓣一道,器內底印雙翼展翅的飛鳳與花卉圖案,印紋很深,綫條清晰(雙魚紋和飛鳳紋碟僅見於仁化和梅縣南宋窰出土)。彩繪碟釉色有青釉,黃釉兩種,青釉數量較多。其特點是在碟內底繪兩道弦紋,在邊沿繪桂花彩帶或卷草彩帶一周。或在碟內彩繪菊花、卷草或蘭草,亦有在碟內彩繪牡丹和竹葉的。或只在碟內繪釉上彩菊花紋,畫面均係隨筆揮毫,筆趣橫生。這類碟僅見海康窰、廣州西村窰、廉江窰有所燒製。點彩碟釉色僅見青釉一種,主要點在碟的口沿,一般均係點一圈,或點在刻有或印有蓮花紋的碟內,點數後有統一規定,疏密不一。

盤,器身比碟稍深,一般均圈足,有敞口、八瓣口、十瓣口、六折口、展唇、凸唇的,有撇口折腰,圈足向外傾斜或圈足外削成棱形的,亦有足沿內外均翻卷成圓邊的。此外,還有圓餅足的,但數量極少。盤的裝飾有刻花、印花、彩繪、刻劃印花組合、刻劃彩繪組合、刻劃點彩組合六類。刻花盤青釉、青白釉、白釉、黃釉、黑釉均有。紋飾主要刻在盤內,有盤心刻弦紋一圈,圈內刻牡丹花一朵,內壁刻折枝牡丹六朵連成一周。或盤心與周壁均刻纏枝菊花紋,或用指甲狀弧綫紋勾勒出花朵外廓,內填刻篦齒紋。或內底輪旋弦紋一圈,圈內刻卷草紋間加篦紋,內壁刻長條弧綫紋一周。或盤心刻弦紋,內刻花卉,周壁刻蕉葉紋(有單綫雙綫、三綫、四綫或五綫蕉葉之分),間加直綫條紋作為蕉葉的間隔,不加直綫條紋的也有,但數量較少。亦有盤內刻弦紋與三花瓣紋組合的。或內底飾輪旋紋一道,內壁刻雙綫花瓣紋。或單獨刻卷草紋,或刻蓮瓣紋。印花盤,青釉,盤內模印菊花瓣,環壁一周。彩繪盤有青釉和醬黃釉兩種,其主要特點是在內層彩繪折枝菊花一朵,或在盤內只彩繪菊葉紋。一般均為釉下彩,釉上彩的也有,但數量較少。刻劃印花盤,青釉,內壁模印纏枝菊花,外壁刻劃花瓣紋。刻劃彩繪盤,青釉,內壁刻劃花草紋,內底彩繪牡丹枝葉紋。或內壁彩繪兩朵折枝菊花紋,周壁刻劃纏枝花卉。刻花點彩盤,青釉,盤內刻纏枝花卉,間加彩,點數不一,多者二、三十點,少者僅一、二點。

執壺,釉色有青釉、青白釉、醬褐釉、醬黃釉、青褐釉、黑釉和白釉七種。青釉執壺有直口微敞,折肩,瓜棱腹,平底的有喇叭口卷唇,細長頸,圓肩,瓜棱腹,圈足的。有敞口或撇口卷唇,長頸,頸上端貼附鳳首。圓腹圈足的。有侈口唇微外卷,長筒頸、長圓腹,圈足的。有侈口短頸,圓腹,矮圈足或平底的。有盤口短頸,圓腹,圈足的。青白釉執壺,有喇叭口卷唇,短頸圓肩,魚形身,橢圓形平底的,有喇叭口卷唇,細長頸,折肩,瓜棱腹,圈足的。有撇口短頸,瓜棱腹,底微凹的。醬褐釉執壺,直口短頸,瓜棱腹,圈足,或敞口圓肩,矮身平底。或直口,長圓筒頸扁圓腹,圈足,醬黃釉執壺,喇叭口,長頸,瓜棱腹,圈足。青褐釉執壺,直口卷唇,長頸,瓜棱腹,圈足。黑釉執壺,有喇叭口,或盤口,瓜棱腹,圈足的。有撇口長頸,圓腹或橢圓腹,圈足的。白釉執壺,斂口凸唇,瓜棱腹或圓腹,圈足或平足的均有。這些執壺從外形來看,有瓜棱壺、蒜頭壺、盤口壺、長頭壺、短頸壺、喇叭壺、球形壺、鳳頭壺、鯉魚壺等。其共同特點是肩部貼附有彎曲細長流(有極少數的是直短流),另一側貼附扁形、扁圓形或圓條形提手曲柄。有些壺在曲柄之上往往貼附有一個綁蓋用的小耳。亦有個別壺是三耳的。其中瓜棱壺是廣東宋窰中常見的產品(瓜棱有壓印和刻劃兩種)。鳳頭壺始燒於唐代初年,它是吸收了波斯金銀器的造形特色,又融合中國傳統的製瓷工藝而燒製出來的一種外銷瓷,北宋時期潮州筆架山窰和廣州西村窰曾有仿製,但其壺腹用刻劃紋飾(上部刻劃牡丹,下部刻劃仰蓮花瓣),代替了唐代複雜的印花堆貼紋飾,這種器形宋以後已經消失,不再燒製。鯉魚壺則僅見於潮州窰,它亦是受北方唐代鯉魚壺的影響演變發展而來的,其造形與唐代的有所不同。從殘片搭配復原來看,壺身與魚頭、眼、鰓、鰭、鱗、尾全部均是模印而成,壺口從魚咀伸出作喇叭形,壺的底座化作魚尾形,平底,在口沿與肩部貼附咀柄,造型新穎,風格獨特,表現了宋代潮州藝人的卓越技巧。這類壺菲律賓曾有出土,星加坡國家博物館和日本東京私人均有收藏,造型完整[9]。

杯,釉色有青釉、青白釉、黃釉、白釉、醬褐釉、青褐釉六種。青釉杯直口淺腹或深腹,圈足。或直口圓腹,圜底高圈足。或敞口深腹,高喇叭足。或六花瓣口,矮身矮圈足。或六至八花瓣口,深腹高喇叭足。或敞口斜直身,棕淺底假圈足,外腹刻仰蓮花瓣一周,上下各刻弦紋一道。青白釉杯直口,深腹,圜底喇叭足。或口微斂,淺腹平底。或斂口深腹喇叭足。在接近口沿處飾弦紋一道,其下刻直綫條紋環壁一周,釉層較厚隱約可見或侈口鼓腹,淺身喇叭足,外壁刻葉脈狀紋一道,足部刻短條紋一周。或敞口深腹,喇叭足,薄胎，外壁刻劃密排細綫紋。黃釉杯口微斂，深腹喇叭足。或口微斂，淺腹平底。或直口淺腹圈足。白釉杯歛口，深腹喇叭足，足底外沿凸邊，外壁刻劃直綫篦梳紋，並刻弦紋兩道。醬褐釉杯，直口深腹喇叭足，或圈足，外壁接近口沿處刻弦紋一周。青褐釉杯，敞口斜直身，挖淺底假圈足，外壁刻弦紋五道，近口沿處與器腹點醬褐色釉彩兩層。或器外壁刻雙綫仰蓮瓣紋一周，上下加刻凹弦紋四道，近口沿處加飾醬褐釉點彩五點。

茶盞，釉色有青釉、青白釉、黃釉、醬黑釉、白釉、綠釉六種。器形有歛口凸唇，折邊斜腹小圈足的。有歛口或敞口深腹小圈足的。有敞口唇微外撇或直唇斜直腹，圈足的。有敞口圓卷唇或歛口，內圓底，或瓣口（有九至十一瓣口之分），均小圈足。紋飾有刻花和刻劃印花組合兩類。青釉刻花盞，內壁刻卷草紋，草葉紋間加篦紋，外壁刻菊瓣紋。青白釉盞內刻繪枝菊花，或內刻卷草紋。或內刻菊瓣、草葉間加篦梳紋。或盞心刻一團菊，周壁刻草葉紋，外壁刻長條菊瓣紋。或內壁刻草葉間加篦梳紋，外壁刻長條菊瓣紋一周。青釉刻劃印花盞，外壁刻劃長菊瓣紋一周，內底模印團菊一朵，內壁加印仰菊三朵，空隙處填印纏枝菊葉，花葉紛披連成一周，使器內印花飽滿均勻。

瓶，釉色有青釉、青白釉、青褐釉、醬褐釉、黃釉、黑釉六種。青釉素面小瓶數量較多，器形有盤口短頸，高身圈足的。或盤口長頸，瓜棱腹圈足。或喇叭口長頸，高身圈足。或直口卷唇，短頸橄欖身，臥足。或盤口撇唇，長頸矮足。或花瓣口長頸喇叭足的均有。青釉刻花小瓶，盤口長頸圈足，頸部刻弦紋數道，肩部刻斜綫紋一周，或刻兩層蓮瓣紋，腹下部刻葉脈狀紋。青白釉瓶，喇叭口長頸，瓜棱腹矮圈足。或盤口長頸，頸部突出數道弦紋，鼓腹圈足。或七花瓣口，器肩鏤圓孔四個，底部殘缺。或鳳首直口，尖嘴凸眼，喇叭身平底，瓶身飾弦紋四道。這類鳳首瓶器身很小，通高僅4.3厘米，頗別緻。瓶類裝飾鳳首的極為罕見，此係潮州窰產品。汕頭市博物館收藏有一件完整的作品殊為難得。青褐釉點彩瓶，卷口長頸，橢圓腹圈足，肩部點醬黑釉彩一周。青褐釉刻花點彩瓶，平唇長頸斜肩圈足，頸部輪旋弦紋四道，器肩與器腹各刻劃三綫蓮花瓣一周，然後再在器肩加一圈褐黑色點彩，頗別緻。醬褐釉瓶，直口卷唇，短頸橄欖身，矮圈足。或僅存頸口部分，一種作六花瓣口，長頸，另一種作喇叭口，頸下部雕塑蓮花瓣紋一周。或口沿與頸部殘缺，瓜棱身，瓶身貼附在豆形鏤孔座上。黃釉瓶小口短頸，橄欖身環凹底，素面。黑釉瓶，侈口直頸，筒身圓凹底。

或敞口短頸，圓筒身平底。或盤口長頸，或撇口長頸，橢圓腹圈足。頸部飾數道凹弦紋。

罐，釉色有青釉、青白釉、青褐釉、醬褐釉、醬黑釉六種。器形有大小高矮之分，大罐和高身罐一般為平底，小罐和矮身罐一般為圈足。大罐有敞口卷唇，短頸圓腹四耳（南海奇石窰四耳罐有些在器肩模印有"政和元年"或"政和六年"等北宋年號）。或歛口圓腹肩附兩耳。高身罐直口卷唇短頸，斜肩橄欖身：肩附四耳。或大口折邊，高身肩附兩耳。或小口卷唇橄欖身無耳。小罐又可分小口罐、大口罐、直身罐、四耳罐等。小口罐直口凸唇，短頸圓腹或扁圓腹。或瓜棱腹。或歛口折唇扁圓腹。大口罐和直口罐一般為扁圓腹，或矮身圓筒腹，或瓜棱腹。四耳罐直口短頸，斜肩橢圓腹或瓜棱腹。如細分約有二十多種。這些罐從外形看則有無耳罐、兩耳罐、四耳罐、瓜棱罐、高身罐、矮身罐、小口罐、大口罐、圓身罐、扁圓身罐、蒜頭身罐、橄欖身罐等。罐的裝飾有刻花，刻花點彩，刻花彩繪點彩，彩繪和印花。刻花罐主要是在器腹外壁刻蓮瓣紋，或刻葉脈狀紋，或刻弧形指甲狀紋組成的雲朵和篦齒紋。刻花點彩罐，是在器腹刻仰覆相對蓮瓣紋兩周，肩部塗四點褐色釉彩。刻劃彩繪罐，在器肩刻劃覆蓮瓣紋一周，並加弦紋四道，腹部刻三綫直條紋四組作為間隔，內彩繪花卉圖案。點彩罐，一般是在肩部或頸部也有在腹部點鐵銹色或紅褐色釉彩。點數沒有規定，有點四點或十多點的均有。彩繪罐，主要見於海康窰燒製，器肩有一般彩繪錢紋、卷草紋、方格紋、圓圈紋各一周，或彩繪蓮瓣紋和弧綫紋，或彩繪卷草紋和錢紋各一周。腹部是主題紋飾，較為講究，四、六、八開光的均有，內繪折枝菊花與蓮花相間，或繪折枝菊花與吉祥語相間，如"金玉滿堂"、"長命富貴"、"桃花洞裏"、"藍橋會仙"等。或在八開光內繪折枝菊花與手捧果盆的侍女相間。也有只寫"積善之家，必有餘慶"、"壽比南山，福如東海"等吉祥語，未彩繪花卉襯托⑩。（展品9-11）印花罐，廉江窰燒製較多，紋飾有仿古的回字形雷紋、繩紋、雙綫非字紋和"卍"字紋等，器形均殘破。

盆，敞口折唇平底，或歛口深腹圈足，或敞口平唇外凸，淺腹廣圈足，或敞口淺弧腹平底，或敞口凸唇直身（微外斜）平底。器形大小均有，有不少盆內刻劃很深的篦梳直綫或斜綫紋（有個別刻葉脈形紋）佈滿器壁，凸綫鋒利，其用途當是研擂薯類之用，也可配以擂杵研磨米漿，這類盆一般稱為擂盆，亦有人稱為擂缽，也有人稱為牙盆，各地宋窰均有出土（宋以前未見這類器形），宋以後至今一直延用。此外，有一種歛口平唇外凸平底盆，器内一般施青釉，器外露胎，器内底或内壁彩繪菊葉、蘭草或卷草等紋飾，這類盆南海和順文頭嶺窰燒製數量最多。該窰用這種盆裝燒碗、碟、壺、罐等瓷器(使用時仰覆裝蓋器胚，逐一層叠)，用這類盆代替匣缽(窰址中未發現其它匣缽)，這樣它可節省大量匣缽，又可增加產品數量，但其缺點是這類盆胎質較薄，受壓力差，經高溫焙燒後，容易燒歪變形與盆内裝燒器物黏連在一起，變成廢品。

瓷枕，釉色有青釉、青褐釉、醬黑釉和綠釉四種。紋飾有刻花、刻劃印花、彩繪印花點彩、刻劃彩繪、彩繪五類。刻花枕青釉、綠釉均有。青釉刻花枕為腰形枕，枕面中間微凹，邊沿刻雙綫邊框，枕外腹刻纏枝菊花紋。或枕面及枕腹刻纏枝牡丹紋。或外腹刻菊葉紋。或刻纏枝石榴花。亦有刻蓮葉與蓮花的。綠釉刻花枕為矩形枕，僅存長方殘件，平底，表面刻纏枝牡丹花，間加篦梳紋，枕邊刻單綫長方框。刻劃印花枕，青釉，有如意頭形枕和六角形枕兩種。如意頭形枕，枕面無紋飾，周壁刻雙綫邊框，四壁刻花均極講究，以刻牡丹為主要題材，右壁還加刻鯉魚穿蓮圖案，空隙處模印細小的珍珠地紋，使器壁紋飾飽滿，生動活潑。(圖28)六角形枕，外腹刻荷花蓮葉紋，間加模印珍珠地紋。彩繪印花點彩枕，青褐釉，僅見腰形枕，枕面中間彩繪醬褐色折枝菊花紋，兩側各飾由七個珍珠地圓點組成的花芯紋，枕邊壓印雙綫凹弦紋，並加點彩。刻劃彩繪枕，青褐釉，僅見規形枕，殘存半截，側面為正方形，枕身四周向裏收束，枕外壁彩繪蘭花，枕沿刻三綫長方框。彩繪枕，青褐釉、青釉兩種。青褐釉有腰形枕、杏圓形枕。腰形枕，枕面彩繪菊花紋，腹部彩繪花卉。杏圓枕枕面呈凹弧形，平面作杏圓形，底座呈橢圓形，與枕面相接處用坭漿加固，抹平塗釉，枕面繪醬黑色彩菊花紋。青釉有如意頭形枕，六角形枕，長方形枕三種。如意頭形枕為八純角邊，上寬下窄，中間微凹，枕面邊沿繪卷草紋一周，然後再繪圓圈、方格、連錢與弧綫組合紋作為第二層邊框，中央繪兩朵折枝菊花和一對飛舞蝴蝶，並書寫兩個"心"字，意為心心相印，寓意深刻。六角形枕，枕邊彩繪曲尺紋和卷草紋各一周，枕面中央開光，内繪一朵開放的蓮花，周圍加繪四朵蓮蕊，作為襯托。長方形枕，彩繪弧綫作邊框，枕後壁彩繪卷草，兩邊繪錢紋和弧綫紋，中間開光，内用行書題寫七言詩一首："枕冷襟寒十月霜，小窗閑放小梅香，暗香入被侵人夢，花物依人樂洞房"。這首詩情景融洽，諧和含蓄⑪(展品22)。瓷枕，廣州西村窰和海康窰出土較多，潮州、惠州、廉江、南雄窰也有燒製，但僅見碎片。其中青釉彩繪枕則僅見海康窰燒製。

軍持，青釉、青白釉、醬黑釉、黃褐釉均有。軍持的共同特點是有嘴無耳把。青釉軍持有素面和彩繪兩種。素面的敞口，展唇外撇，大頸圓腹，大圈足(此係西村窰產品)。彩繪的喇叭口，扁圓腹平底。器頸之下用鐵銹色釉料彩繪弦紋一道，器腹彩繪纏枝菊葉一周，口沿點彩七點(南海文頭嶺窰產品)。青白釉軍持，盤口細長頸，扁圓腹圈足，素身(潮州窰產品)。醬黑釉軍持，直口，圓管狀小頸，頸部突出一至四個圓箍，高身橢圓腹，喇叭足，素身(西村窰產品)。黃褐釉軍持，喇叭口扁圓腹，平底，口沿與器頸下半部及器腹上半部露胎，頸部及頸與腹相接處飾凹弦紋兩周，器腹上半部用赭黑色或紅褐色釉料彩繪纏枝菊葉紋一周，頗別緻(文頭嶺窰產品)。軍持是外銷瓷的一個品種，亦是佛家的盛水器，原名是從佛經中翻譯過來的，它是佛教僧侶十八物之一。晉代高僧法顯在他所著的《佛國志》中有"軍持及藻罐棄擲海中"的記載，但至今未見晉代軍持。廣東僅見唐代梅縣水車窰生產軍持，北宋潮州窰、南海文頭嶺窰和廣州西村窰亦有生產。這類產品湖南唐代長沙窰和宋元時期的河北定窰、江西景德鎮窰和福建德化蓋德碗坪崙窰、屈斗宮窰與泉州磁灶窰等也有燒製，但器形和裝飾有所不同。(展品12)。

腰鼓，其共同特點是器身中部呈圓筒形，兩端呈深腹喇叭形，空心，蒙綁鼓皮使用，其長度約50至60厘米左右。這類器形僅見廣州西村窰和南海文頭嶺窰燒製。西村窰燒製的有青釉素身腰鼓，青褐釉彩繪腰鼓(彩繪卷草紋)，醬黑釉腰鼓三種。文頭嶺窰燒製的則僅見青釉彩繪腰鼓(彩繪鐵銹色弦紋與纏枝菊葉紋)，器形新穎，數量極少，出土的可惜均為殘件，難以復原。

香爐，佛教中的焚香用具，釉色有青釉、青白釉、醬黃釉、醬褐釉、醬黑釉和綠釉六種。器形有直身深腹，小圈足爐。有折口寬平沿，深腹平底爐。有敞口撇唇深腹，喇叭座爐。有折口寬沿，深腹圈足爐。有直口深腹，喇叭足爐。有卷唇蓮花瓣腹，圈足爐。有折口寬平唇，短頸鼓腹平底，三S形足爐。有敞口淺腹，斜壁，三尖足(三角形尖足)爐。有敞口卷唇高足爐。有直口卷唇，直腹喇叭足爐。有侈口淺腹喇叭足爐。有寬唇唇，淺圓筒身，或歛口弧腹平底三獸足、六獸足或六花瓣足的均有。香爐的紋飾有刻劃或壓印或刻剔的蓮花瓣、弦紋、鋸齒狀紋、卷草紋、直綫條紋、斜方格紋、斜綫紋。或用鐵銹色釉料在口沿或器外壁點彩，點數沒有規定，有局部點彩或全身點彩的均有。其中蓮花爐數量最多。蓮花是從漢代開始用來裝飾陶瓷的紋飾，南朝至唐宋都很流行。由於蓮花"出污泥而不染"，帶有清淨高潔之意，表示人們心地的虔誠與純潔，所以它在佛教藝術中佔有特殊地位，被奉為"佛門聖花"，因此用蓮花裝飾的香爐一般都很精緻，特別是在腹部刻劃或雕貼的蓮花瓣紋一至四層的均有，刀法生辣，刻出的棱角剛勁有力，立體感很強。

粉盒，盛裝婦女化妝香粉之用，故稱"粉盒"，或盛裝化妝的紅色硃粉，亦稱"砂盒"，器形很小。釉色有青釉、青白釉、白釉、青褐釉、醬黑釉五種。粉盒紋飾有刻花、印花、捏塑刻劃點彩、捏塑四類，此外還有素身粉盒。刻花粉盒圓瓜形，小平底，蓋頂中央有圓紐狀瓜蒂，蓋、身高度各佔二分之一，從蓋頂至盒足周壁刻劃八條弧形紋。或矮身扁平，盒蓋刻劃花卉。或子口直腹，蓋面呈半圓形，盒外壁刻劃半圓圈紋組成的牡丹花朵，間加篦梳紋。或蓋與器腹均刻劃直綫條紋佈滿全身。或刻折枝牡丹，或刻菊瓣紋的均有，蓋頂飾圓形乳狀紐。印花粉盒，子母口，直身，盒蓋與盒身上下對稱，平頂平底，斜肩，周身壓印七條或14條或22條豎弧綫，使盒身呈瓜棱形。或將蓋、身壓印成六棱南瓜形，貼附瓜蒂形組。或直身（高矮身均有），腹下部收歛，平底或假圈足，蓋作半圓形，蓋、腹均壓印五至十四道直綫凹紋，形成瓜棱狀。捏塑刻劃點彩粉盒，小平底或矮圈足，子口帶蓋，蓋面附加捏塑鴛鴦，作游泳狀，首、翅、尾均點褐黑色釉彩，雙翅上加篦梳紋。或盒面飾五組點彩（每組六至七點），或點六點分佈盒面。捏塑類粉盒，是用三件圓形直身平底盒黏連在一起，盒內互不相通，盒蓋亦黏連在一起，捏塑蓮葉蓮花，佈滿盒蓋，並雕貼鯉魚兩條在空隙處作旋轉狀。或在三連盒蓋上只貼附蓮花和蓮葉佈滿蓋面。這是潮州窰產品，這類盒在印尼亦有發現，可見它是當日外銷的一個品種。

狗，玩具，青釉、青褐釉、醬黃釉、黃褐釉均有。狗有兩種，均捏塑而成，一種是高身狗，頭作傾斜狀，翹尾，短身，大耳下垂，有些狗耳及尾部點鐵銹色釉彩。或頭正視作吠狀，或昂首歪頭，卷尾貼耳，均作站立狀。這種高身狗，宋窰中較為常見。另一種是矮身西洋狗，則僅見潮州窰燒製，狗的臉部很短，耳圓而大下垂，身短，各個姿態均不相同，有頭作傾斜狀的，有作跑步狀的，有蹲坐有站立的，有跳躍昂首的，有停步而吠的，雕塑捏造技巧相當高明，造型生動逼真，當年潮州藝人用相同的瓷土，用不同的手法，製作出不同姿態的瓷西洋狗，無疑是為了滿足當年對外貿易的需要。

獸頭類陶瓷，此是石灣窰產品，它是將平底罐坯胎倒覆過來，因材施藝，隨手捏塑刻劃而成。捏塑雖然簡單，但對能夠顯示動物性格特徵的臉部表情，作者毫不拘於細節，而根據需要進行刻劃。如兩眼圓睜，高鼻張口，額飾明珠，口角露出獠牙等，這些都是用誇張的手法進行處理的，使之生動有趣，富有一定的藝術效果，在這點上充分表現了宋代石灣民間藝人，心靈手巧大膽創新的精神。陶塑類石灣窰從唐宋以來一直燒製（唐代主要燒製捏塑雕貼神龍人物高身陶罈等）。從清代宣統年間國內外學者對石灣窰的介紹和研究工作，一直斷斷續續的在進行，可是對石灣美術陶瓷的創始年代，一直是模糊不清的，過去的看法（包括刊物上的介紹）一般均認為石灣窰從明代才開始生產美術陶瓷，直到七十年代和八十年代這種看法一直沒有改變。如《廣東石灣古窰址調查》一文認為"石灣從明代開始生產美術陶瓷"[12]，石灣美術陶瓷廠也認為"石灣美術陶始於明代"[13]。筆者認為這種看法時間偏晚，從現有的考古材料來看，石灣美術陶瓷的創始年代，最遲是唐代，這是無可置疑的。

塑像，有奏樂女像、捧葫蘆女像、捧壺人像、高鼻卷髮西洋人像（圖29）、捧書人像、釋迦牟尼佛像等。其中有四尊完整的釋迦牟尼佛像（"佛"是印度古代梵語"佛陀"的省稱，是佛教徒對得道者的稱呼。"佛像"即得道者的塑像。釋迦牟尼是印度佛教的創始人。中國的佛教是漢代從印度傳進來的），雕塑精緻，神態慈祥，是潮州筆架山窰的代表作。四尊瓷佛都是白釉，釉色白外微泛淺灰或米黃和淺綠色，釉面開細冰裂紋，胎為灰白色，除佛像底部外，通體施釉，像高約三十一厘米左右，頭戴髮髻冠，冠前裝飾一粒白色"明珠"，臉長方微圓，修眉目，眉際有一粒微微凸起的"白毫相"。頭部的髮髻、眉、睛和鬚鬢，描劃醬褐黑色顏料。四佛像均趺坐在四方鈍角座上，外披袈裟式法衣，掩蓋膝部。其中兩尊佛像袈裟的一條長帶，甩在左腕上，座前飾墊布。另兩尊像拱手至腹部，右腕抬至胸前，左腕置於腹部。四尊瓷佛像座上都分別刻有北宋"治平四年"、"熙寧二年"（圖30），"熙寧元年五月"、"熙寧元年六月"（圖31）銘文，並刻有潮州地名，水東中窰（即筆架山中窰）窰名，供奉人和雕塑工匠的姓名（其中一件刻"潮州水東中窰甲，弟子劉扶同妻陳妻十五娘，發心塑釋迦牟尼佛永充供養，為父劉用母李二十娘闔家男女乞保平安，治平四年丁未歲九月卅日題，匠人周明"六十三字。其餘三件亦刻有類似的銘文，這裏從略），五類銘文具備的完整的北宋瓷佛像，在國內僅見此四尊，其學術價值之高可以想見。

軸頂帽，一般均為青釉，是轆轤（即製作圓形器的傳統工具——陶車）的一個關鍵部件，是正八邊形棱軸，平口平

145

底，內底有一圓錐形光滑凹窩，使用時把它固定在轉盤中心，鑲凹窩頂在軸心上，就可以撥動轉盤拉坯。

蕩箍，平面為圓形，直口，淺腹平底，器內施釉，也是陶車旋轉的重要部件，使用時與軸頂帽配套使用，它是套在陶車軸下的一個瓷質圓箍。

壓錘，是製瓷工具，陶質，不施釉，器身平面為圓形，弧底光滑，橫剖面為半月形，實心，其上黏附一個長條圓把柄，便於使用，一般窰址均有出土。其中潮州窰出土的器背刻有"皇祐二年十一月十四日"、"治平□□年三月"、"熙寧五年九月"等北宋年號，這是當時燒窰的絕對年代。

測溫標，青釉、青白釉、醬黃釉、黃褐釉均有。測溫標又名試片或火照，是廣東北宋時期新出現的一種窰具，一般均為三角形，是利用施釉後的廢碗坯胎切成，頂端中間鏤一圓孔，其用途是將測溫標（二、三十個不等），插在裝滿細沙的匣鉢裏，放進接着火膛的窰室前面，燒窰時隨時都可以用長鐵枝鈎出，觀察窰溫和瓷化程度，以便掌握升溫、保溫或止火。測溫標的出現，對掌握大規模燒瓷技術，起着重要作用。這類測溫標宋以後一直沿用。

2．宋代墓葬出土的陶瓷

廣東宋墓分佈範圍很廣，先後在潮州、揭陽、佛山、廣州、南海、珠海、中山、紫金、梅縣、廉江、海康、遂溪、崖縣、新會、深圳、東莞、陽春、化州等地發掘清理了土坑墓石槨墓和磚室墓等約一百多座，隨葬的陶瓷數量不多，每墓一般只有一至五件左右，七件或十多件的也有，但只是個別墓葬而已，出土的陶瓷器形有碗、碟、盒、彩繪瓷罐、彩繪瓷枕、彩繪瓶、三足乳釘爐、生肖俑、陶罎、瓷棺等。其中有紀年墓葬三座，一座是潮州宋代劉景墓，墓碑上刻直行楷書，右側刻"乾道八年二月二十六日銀青光祿大夫開國男劉公"，左側行刻"夫人許氏吳氏潛氏詹氏"，末行刻"正德六年三月二日修"等字樣。劉景為廣東潮陽縣人，於北宋欽宗靖康元年（公元1126年）薦闢為銀青光祿大夫，並賜開國男的爵位，曾任台州、南雄兩州的知事（見《廣東通志》卷六十三）。該墓出土影青暗花瓷碗、黑釉瓷碗和陶盒各一件。影青暗花瓷碗，侈口收腹，小圈足，白胎，器內刻纏枝花卉，製作精細，乃景德鎮宋窰產品。黑釉瓷碗，口微斂，收腹，圈足，灰白胎，素面，上身施半截釉，下身露胎，乃佛山石灣窰產品（原簡報均誤認為潮州窰產品）。陶盒，樺口斂唇，直身平底，上附一圓形平頂蓋，灰白胎，素面無紋，不施釉，蓋內底墨書"五穀龍"三字⑭。

一座是東莞宋代夫婦合葬墓，墓碑刻有一百一十五字，其中有"公行十二生於大宋，官至朝奉大夫，卒於宋之政和年間與恭人羅氏合葬……"最後一行刻"咸豐十年七月吉日重修"。此墓出土有兩件精美的醬黃釉高身陶罎。另一座是南雄縣發現的宋墓，亦出土有兩件高身陶罎，其中一件罎蓋上刻有"紹聖四年十六日鍾博士謹記"等文字（陶罎另有專題文章介紹，這裏描述從略）。

佛山瀾石鼓潁崗宋墓出土的一件南海奇石窰高身人物瓶，是難得的作品，其器肩和器腹下描繪纏枝花卉一周，器腹四開光外描繪蕩漾的海水，四開光內描繪四個人物，亦環壁一周，人物臉部飽滿豐潤，身穿長袍，均席地而坐，動作表情均不相同，有兩眼凝視前方手提酒杯待飲的，有兩手扶地酒意醺醺的，有兩手供起醉臉酣睡的，真是傳神寫照，栩栩如生。這件繪鐵銹色的高身人物瓶，它有一個很大的特點，就是人物的繪製吸收了繪畫的方法，已把繪畫的優點運用到繪瓷上來，因此畫面生動自然，十分逼真，這純然是一種當年民間繪畫的傳統風格（展品29）。在海康縣宋代夫婦合葬墓中出土的一對海康窰彩繪瓷棺也極罕見，瓷棺略作長方形，淡清釉，灰白色胎，質堅硬，棺門在前，有樺套，可以開關，四周棺壁繪赭黃色圖案和寫有文字。男棺棺門竪寫"壽化考黃二公墓"七字，左右壁繪雙綫方框卷草紋內繪鼠、牛、虎、兔、龍、蛇、馬、羊、猴、鷄、狗、豬十二生肖（人身獸臉），中央繪一童子，身穿長袍，雙手捧幡，並繪四爪神龍作騰雲之勢，畫面極為生動。棺頂寫"天門"、"地戶"，棺門前後壁寫"前朱雀"、"後玄武"、"左青龍"、"右白虎"（象徵四方四神）。女棺棺門竪寫"壽化妣劉三孺人墓"八字，器壁繪畫及文字與前者大致相同（展品23）。宋代繪畫近千年來，經歷過歷次的戰亂兵燹，傳世很少，民間繪畫尤其難以見到，而上述出土的彩繪高身瓶和彩繪瓷棺上却保存了三幅出於宋代民間藝人之手的作品，十分難得。

3．地震遺址出土的宋代外銷瓷

海南瓊山海底地震遺址出土的大量宋代對外銷瓷極為重要。海南島明清時期稱為瓊州，據《瓊州府志》、《瓊山縣志》記載：明代萬曆三十三年五月二十八日亥時，瓊山發生過一次大地震，震中在今瓊山、文昌、澄邁、臨高等縣，官署、民房、祠堂、寺廟、牌坊、書院倒塌殆盡，不少地方陸陷村沉。據當地族譜記載，當時沉陷的村莊有一百多處。今瓊山與文昌交界的瓊州海峽，有一處凹進內陸約十六公里，寬約二至八公里的東寨港和演州海，這裏就是昔日陸陷沉海的地方。當海水退潮降至三至五米時，沉入海底的村莊遺址，一般已露出海面，筆者調查了與古代海外貿易有關的舖前灣和新溪角一帶的絕尾溝、西排灣、南排灣、浮水墩、和恭、石見六處遺址。其中範圍最大的是絕尾溝。絕尾溝古稱"西行村"，昔日這裏的面積很大，露出水面的遺址約400×600米，建築物全部都已倒塌。遺址中數以千萬計的宋至明代瓷片遍地皆是，有些地方堆積極厚，且埋藏有完整的宋代瓷器，而且有菊花紋瓦當，獸面紋瓦當，筒瓦，板瓦等宋代建築遺存，說明這裏有宋代遺址，也有明代遺址。遺物以宋代瓷片居多，明代的次之、元代的數量極少，僅偶然可以見到。其餘幾處遺址，也有大量遺物，種類與絕尾溝的大致相同。

上述遺址，發現的遺物種類有碗、碟、罐、盆、盞、壺、壇、瓶、燈、爐、釜等。瓷器的釉色有青白釉、白釉、淡灰釉、黑釉、醬褐釉、黃釉等種。瓷器的紋飾極爲豐富，如宋代瓷碗，有器內底模印菊花瓣，內壁刻劃卷草或菊枝加篦點紋，器外壁刻劃直綫條紋環壁一周。也有器壁接近口沿處只刻劃弦紋一道的。有器內底飾弦紋一道，內壁刻劃卷草與篦點紋相組合，器內壁刻劃四至七綫條紋環壁一周，或外壁接近口沿處飾弦紋一道，其下再飾直綫紋環壁一周。有器內壁接近沿處飾弦紋二道，其下刻劃篦點紋一周，器外壁素面無紋的。有器內刻劃篦紋，器外飾條紋的。有器內刻卷草與篦紋相組合，外壁無紋的。也有器內外均素面無紋的（碗、碟花紋極多，上述所舉的是一式碗的紋飾，碗分十一式，因篇幅關係，其餘紋飾從略）。總的來說，從器形、胎質、釉色、花紋、火候等特徵觀察，這些瓷器有宋代福建同安窰、建窰，元代德化窰，宋代江西景德鎭湖田窰，宋代和元代浙江龍泉窰，宋代廣東潮州窰、廉江窰、遂溪窰、佛山石灣窰和明代惠陽窰等[15]。宋、元、明時期，瓷器是我國對外貿易的主要商品。上述大量外銷瓷的發現，說明今天瓊州海峽舖前灣、新溪角等附近一帶，應該是古代我國對外貿易貨物轉運和商船停泊的一個港口，同時在瓊山、文昌等地亦設有市舶。據趙汝适《諸番志·瓊管條》載，宋代瓊管各縣（按："瓊管"包括瓊山、文昌、澄邁、臨高、樂會五縣），均置市舶，徵收入口稅，徵收方法以船舶之大小爲準，並用丈量。《宋會要·食貨》十七商稅四載："元豐三年（公元1080年）十二月二日，瓊管體量宋初平言，海南稅收，用船之丈尺量納，謂之格納，其法分爲三等……相去十倍。加之客人所來州郡貨物，貴賤不同，自泉、福兩地來者，一色載金銀匹帛，所值或及萬餘貫，自高（廣東高州）、代（廣東化州）來者，唯載米包、瓷器、牛畜之類，所值或不過二、三百貫，其不等如此，而用丈尺概收稅，甚非禮也。以故泉、福客人多方規利，而高、化客人久不至……。今欲立法，使客舶須得就泊瓊、崖、儋、萬四州，不用丈量，根據貨物收稅訖……"可見當時通商港口遍佈海南各州，貿易範圍極廣，稅收方法不用丈量納，有所改進，收入的貨物從泉州、福州、高州、化州等地運來。《諸番志·南海條》又云："省民（按:指高州、化州、遂溪等地）以鹽、鐵、魚、米轉博與番商貿易，泉舶以酒、米、麵、粉、紗、絹、漆器、瓷器爲貨"。可見貨物轉運至海南港口，再以番商貿易，這樣可以增多船舶運輸航次，又可增加市舶收入。《嶺南叢述》云，熙寧年間"番人有居瓊管者，立番民所"[16]，據此記載，海南瓊山、文昌、澄邁、臨高、樂會等地，北宋時期已有番商聚居，從事貿易活動。到了明代，南海諸國商船前來海南貿易者，已絡繹不絕，當時萬州蓮塘港附近，建築有番神廟，香火極旺，來往番舶番商必上岸誠虔祭祀，當時海南島和東海的日本也開始了貿易關係[17]。總的來說，據上述文獻記載，結合現場考察情況分析，當時貿易範圍極廣，通商港口遍及海南各州，宋代瓊山、文昌、澄邁、臨高、樂會等地已設立市舶徵收入口稅。上述遺址大量宋代外銷瓷的出土，亦說明今日瓊山與文昌交界的瓊州海峽舖前灣和新溪角附近一帶，應是古代對外貿易、貨物轉運和商船停舶的一個港口無疑。

4．陵水窖藏、海灘出土的宋代外銷瓷

窖藏出土的宋瓷三百多件，分別於1957年及1972年出土於海南島陵水縣里陵村及陵水縣普軍三十笠生產隊。前者用兩個大陶缸內裝二百多件宋瓷，後者用一個高約八十厘米的四耳大陶罐內裝一百多件宋瓷，分別埋藏在地表下臨時窖藏中[18]。出土的瓷器均屬北宋時期，釉色可分白釉、青釉、黃釉、黑釉和灰釉五種。白釉深處白中微帶淡綠色（即影青色），施釉薄處爲白色，厚處爲影青色，釉面開片和不開片的均有，光澤很強；青釉釉色有青綠色和淺綠色兩種，開片的數量多，不開片的較少，光澤強弱不一；黃釉黃中微帶綠色，施釉厚薄不均，開片和不開片的均有，光澤很強，開片的釉面一般都有剝落現象，不開片的光潤如玉；黑釉黑中微帶黃色，即醬黑色，施釉較厚，釉面有小裂紋，光澤不強；灰釉灰中呈白色，即淡灰色，施釉很厚，開片，光澤僅次於黃釉。

瓷器的器形有碗、盤和船形注水器三種。碗的造形可分爲十一式。有敞口高足卷唇的，有敞口唇微外撇淺圈足的，有敞口圈足，青唇醬黑釉身的（口唇施青釉，器內外均

施醬黑釉,廣州西村窰、潮州窰和惠州窰均有這類產品)。有敞口圈足,白釉薄胎,內壁刻劃卷草紋,外壁刻劃直綫條紋一周的,此乃景德鎮窰產品。有敞口高圈足,器內隆起五條直綫紋環壁一周的,有七花瓣口,矮圈足,外壁刻直綫條紋六條環壁一周的。有敞口圈足,口沿削出六個小缺口,碗內刻弦紋與篦梳組合紋的,此乃潮州筆架山窰產品。有口唇外卷,圈足,碗內飾弦紋一周的。有敞口矮圈足,器內外壁有三分之一灰色釉,其餘爲黃釉的(可能是焙燒時火候不均等原因所造成的)。有白釉薄胎,敞口平底,外形似淺身盅的。盤的造形可分爲五式,有敞口高圈足或敞口矮圈足的,有敞口高圈足,口沿外撇成平邊狀,盤內刻劃弦紋一周的,有敞口矮圈足,器內壁刻弦紋一周,器外壁口沿壓印短條直綫紋十條環壁一周的。或直口凸唇矮圈足,外壁接近口沿處弦紋一周的。船形注水器,青綠釉,灰白胎,器形俯視略作橢圓形,兩面翹起作船形狀,底微凹,器內外均刻卷草紋。此乃龍泉窰典型產品,頗別緻,可惜中央弧形船蓬式提把已殘失。上述兩批窰藏宋瓷,暫且不能全部肯定其窰別,有待進一步的研究。

1978年陵水縣文化館李居禮先生,在該縣城東北十公里的移輦村海灘,發現大量宋代外銷瓷殘片,隨後廣東省博物館派專人進行了調查[19]。遺物散佈在移輦村海灘沙丘表面或埋藏在沙丘中,有幾處地方比較密集,斷續長達一公里許。北宋時期的陶瓷器數量最多,採集到的標本有:定窰白瓷洗,直口斜壁,平底,內壁模印卷草紋,施乳白色釉薄而均匀,僅口沿一周露胎(是芒口覆燒碗)。建窰黑釉盞,黑色粗胎,口沿釉薄處呈醬黃色,外壁施半截釉,釉厚下流呈淚痕,足部露胎,直口斜壁圓窩底,小圈足。龍泉窰刻花碗,灰白胎,施粉青或梅子青釉,器形精巧,足挖得很平整,碗外壁刻蓮瓣紋一周。福建安溪窰和同安窰刻花碗,外壁刻蓮花瓣,碗內刻折枝蓮花。或碗內刻卷草紋間加篦梳紋,或刻纏枝花卉,有些碗外壁刻斜綫條紋一周。江西或福建窰口的影青釉碗也有發現,釉水薄,白色或青白色。此外,還有一些暫時難以確定窰口的青釉碗。宋瓷中也有白釉壺的嘴部殘件,亦有青黃釉瓶和罐等器物。瓶口卷唇長頸,相同的器物在潮州筆架山窰址中發現甚多。罐的式樣較多,器外有些模印花卉紋,耳下貼獸頭裝飾,比較奇特的是一件罐的肩部貼青蛙作裝飾,較爲罕見。此外,在這處遺物地點中,同時還發現有晚唐至五代的青釉罐(雙耳、四耳、六耳罐均有)和青釉碗。在沙灘上還發掘出十多件並排埋在一起的陶罐,大的高50多厘米,並挖掘出不少青釉碗,往往是十件一捆。這些罐、碗與廣東、福建晚唐至五代墓中出土的同類器形基本相同。何紀生認爲:"根據文獻記載和近年來的考古發現,唐宋時期我國東南沿海地區有大量瓷器出口外銷。陶瓷器主要產自廣東、福建、浙江、江西、湖南等地窰口,北方的河北、河南和陝西等地區也有部分貨物運來,這些商品從廣州、泉州等港口裝載上船後,到冬季乘東北風南下,運往東南亞以及印度洋沿岸各地。海南島東海岸是當時航船的必經之路,這些船只也在這裏(海南)停靠和上岸貿易"[20]。這種看法是正確的。不過這批外銷瓷遺留在海灘的原因,也是值得討論的,據報告:"移輦村海灘平直而水淺,外海沒有遮攔,看來不像是一處古代港口……。估計船只由於遇到風暴或其它原因不幸在這裏擱淺,器物搬動倉促,有些可能就遺留在淺海中,以後才被海浪冲上沙堤"。這種解釋看來也是可以的。但沙堤中發現十幾個並排埋在一起的陶罐,並以十件爲一捆的青釉碗,有次序的埋藏在一起,這顯然是人爲的現象,所以筆者估計,船只遇風擱淺後,船上物品曾被海盜所掠奪,這種可能性也是很大的,因爲唐宋時期海南陵水、萬寧、崖縣等地海盜極多,據《太平廣記》載:"唐振州(今崖縣)民陳武振者,家累萬金,爲海中大盜,犀象玳瑁,倉庫數百"[22]。《中西交通史料滙編》亦有談及唐代"盤據在萬安州(即萬寧)的大海盜馮若芳,每年劫取波斯商船二三艘,取物爲己貨,掠人爲奴婢"的記載[22]。陵水與崖縣交界處,近海有個地名叫"軍屯坡"的地方(該地有漢代和唐宋墓葬),顧名思義,"軍屯"即軍隊駐守的地方,距"軍屯坡"約五公里的海灘亦有個叫做"蕃嶺坡"(現屬崖縣)的地名(該地有唐宋阿拉伯墓葬)。過去文獻提到唐代鑑眞和尚曾經在海南見到有"波斯村"。如果把上述情況聯繫起來分析,唐宋海南已有不少阿拉伯商人聚居,而且當時政府曾經派軍駐守在沿海港口一帶,保護外商從事貿易活動。由於海岸綫過長,雖有軍隊保護,但商船經過沿海,被海盜掠劫之事,亦在所難免。上述陵水里陵村和普軍發現的三百多件北宋外銷瓷,分別裝在陶缸和高約八十厘米的大四耳罐中(過去珠海漁民在珠江口的外零汀島附近作業時,打撈起一批唐代青釉外銷瓷碗、碟,也是大小相套分別裝在大四耳罐中),加蓋分別埋藏在地下。據調查發掘所知,這兩處地點均未發現古墓及其它建築遺存。廣東過去已發掘的古墓,亦未發現過類似用缸或四耳大罐裝瓷器隨葬的現象,同時宋墓中隨葬的瓷器,都是寥寥無幾,屈指可數。上述大量宋瓷則埋藏在地下,外表偽裝成一般的墳堆,根據分析,首先這些瓷器的包裝方法,與朱彧《萍州可談》中描述的,北宋廣州商船裝運貨物出口時"貨多陶器,大小相套,無少隙地"的記載是相符的,同時這些瓷器有江西、福建、浙江、廣東窰口的產品，而這些產品又是當年暢銷東南亞等國家的珍貴貨物。據此，這批瓷器埋藏在人烟稀少的偏僻的近海地帶，並不是偶然現象，而正是當年海盜掠奪前往南海諸國商船的歷史贓物。由於當年陸地交通不便，一時難以將贓物全部運走，只好臨時將這批易碎和難以携帶的瓷器先行在附近埋藏起來，隨後又由於種種原因沒有前來挖取，所以才遺留了下來。總的來說，海南島外銷瓷遺物地點，肯定不止上述幾處，有待進一步的調查。

5．西沙羣島採集的外銷瓷

西沙羣島是我國南海諸島的一部分，它是我國古代陶瓷從海上輸出東南亞和西方各國必經之路，地理位置極其重要。1974年和1975年廣東省考古工作人員到這裏考察時，採集到從南朝至清代的陶瓷標本2,138件㉓。其中宋代的620件，元代的157件，明代的577件，清代的658件。宋代瓷器的器形有小口瓶、點彩瓶、點彩罐、四耳小罐、刻花碟、粉盒、凸唇盞、蓮瓣紋碗、凸唇碗、印花盆和執壺等。瓷器釉色有青釉、青白釉、醬色釉和黑釉等種。這些器物主要是廣東、福建、江西和浙江龍泉窰的產品。其中以廣東窰產品數量居多。福建窰次之，江西窰又次之，龍泉窰最少。採集的點彩瓶、點彩罐、瓜棱四耳小罐和青白釉刻花大碗，都是廣州西村窰的典型作品。採集的青白釉小口壺、凸唇碗和瓜棱粉盒，西村窰、潮州窰、惠州窰均有這類產品。採集的青釉小口罐與石灣窰產品基本相同。點彩碟和印花盆亦係廉江窰和南海文頭嶺窰的典型產品。可見這些窰口的瓷器，都是當日暢銷國外的商品。

元代的器形有碗、盤、瓶、罐五類，釉色有青釉和青綠釉兩種。是福建地區和浙江龍泉窰的產品。明代瓷器，其中青花瓷526件，數量最多，主要是江西吉州窰和景德鎮民窰產品，廣東大埔、饒平窰和福建德化窰的也有，但數量極少。此外，還有廣東惠陽仿龍泉青瓷碗和德化窰白瓷盒等產品，製作都很精緻。清代的陶瓷，有景德鎮窰口的白釉瓷和釉上彩繪瓷，也有石灣窰的陶器，數量最多的是青花瓷，絕大部分是福建德化窰的產品，其次是廣東民窰產品，景德鎮民窰產品也有，但數量極少。值得注意的是，有一百一十件青花瓷殘碗，圈足內寫有"成化年製"雙排款，簡報認爲它是清代仿成化的產品，過去江西、福建、廣東等地也發現有古窰燒製這類寫有"成化年製"的青花瓷，但都統統被認爲是後期仿成化的產品，看來國內似乎沒有一處是明代

成化年間的民窰?這是值得今後專題研究的。此外，還值得一提的是，在西沙珊瑚沙中挖出的三件相叠在一起的清初景德鎮青花夔龍紋瓷盤，色澤明亮，完好如新（展品97），這類盤與廣東省博物館收藏的康熙至雍正年間的景德鎮民窰產品完全相同。總的來說，從西沙採集的歷代陶瓷來看，說明我國陶瓷外銷歷史，十分久遠。

三、廣東出土的元代瓷器

1．元代窰址出土的瓷器

元代由於戰亂等原因，民間手工業得不到應有的發展，廣東瓷業相對衰落。這一時期的窰址僅在饒平、遂溪、海康、羅定、佛岡、新豐、高州、深圳、澄邁發現三十四處。其中遂溪和澄邁作過初步複查。遂溪窰分佈在楊柑鄉新埠村舖仔山、坡頭山和甘束村下山井山和溝口山，窰址均露出山坡，係長條形磚砌龍窰，遺物堆積很厚，出土的陶瓷器種類有盤、碗、碟、杯、盞、盞托、鉢、壺、罐、盆、瓶、勺、爐、壇、硯、研船、研輪、爐箅、擂杵、碗模、軸頂帽、蕩箍等。其中有一件碗模，外壁刻有元代"大德六年"（公元1302年）款，係這裏燒窰的絕對年代。瓷器的釉色有青釉、醬黑釉、醬黃釉三種。以青釉居多，有些碗、碟外壁或器內刻劃或壓印蓮花紋、直綫條紋、卷草紋、弦紋或纏枝菊花等紋飾。各類器形，胎質厚重，紋飾和釉色一般都很粗糙，遠比不上宋代潮州窰和廣州西村窰的精美。

澄邁窰分佈在太平鄉碗灶山、山口鄉碗灶墩、紅坭嶺、缸灶墩、深田山和促進山等地㉔，這裏採用龍窰也採用饅頭窰燒瓷。出土的瓷器種類有碗、杯、碟、瓶、壺、盞、盆、權（拜錘）、網墜等。瓷器的胎質作淡灰色，頗細潔。釉色大致可分爲青、灰、醬黑、醬黃、天藍五種。青釉有深淺之分，有青中微泛黃色或青中微泛褐色的，釉面光潤，一般均開片，灰釉有微泛白色（即淡灰色）的，也有深灰色的，釉裏有小裂紋，光澤強弱均有。醬黑釉釉水深淺不一，深處呈黑色，淺處呈黃色，光澤僅次於青釉。醬黃釉一般施釉較薄，有些積釉處呈黃褐色、天藍釉，釉色不甚清澈，釉層厚薄不均，厚處帶藍，薄處帶白，優劣相滲頗不調和。上述釉色以青釉居多，灰釉次之，醬黑釉和醬黃釉又次之，天藍釉最少。該窰的器形除高足杯和瓷瓶繼承了宋代的風格外，其餘的器形與宋代的完全不同，瓷器裝飾花紋簡樸，僅見碗、碟外壁繪有藍黑色的卷草紋等。器物造形一般都很端正，器坯厚薄均勻，曲度規整，可以斷定均爲輪制。上釉技術主要是用

手倒拿圈足,用快速的方法,將器身浸在釉水裏,然後取出,故器內中心與器底足露胎,甚至有部分器物釉藥有下流現象,就是這個原因。器物入窰燒製的方法有兩種,一種是器內中心鋪少許木糠相叠墊燒,另一種是直接相叠,器內沒有任何避黏的介質,故燒成器後,有不少器物互相叠黏連在一起,變成廢品。同時瓷坯進窰煅燒時,沒有採用匣缽裝燒,故燒成器後,有不少器物外表被窰內煙塵所污染,可知該窰在製窰工藝方面,還沒有達到完善的地步。總的來說,澄邁窰址分佈範圍廣,數量多,燒窰時間長,其上限可到元代中晚期,下限(特別是燒青花器的窰址)可能會晚至明末或更晚。

佛山石灣雖然沒有發現元代窰址,但據《石灣霍氏族譜》記載:"霍氏三世祖元山公燒缸瓦窰一座,土名莘崗村,又名文灶,東西俱十六丈七尺,南北俱二丈五尺"(可能是包括部分窰場面積),又說:"霍氏原籍山西,南宋前遷於廣東南雄,宋咸淳九年(公元1273年)再遷於佛山石灣",由此推算,霍氏三世祖原山的時間係在元代。從《石灣霍氏族譜》中的"文灶"圖樣,也可以窺見這座長條形斜坡式龍窰結構,與廣東一般宋代龍窰大致相同。過去佛山石灣和瀾石鼓頡崗等墓葬中,出土過大量元代石灣窰黑釉陶罐等,其中有"至正二年"等年號的黑釉大陶壇,說明石灣陶業在唐宋的基礎上繼續生產。

2. 元代墓葬及遺址出土的陶瓷

元代墓葬有土坑墓、磚室墓、沙灰墓和石槨墓等。隨葬的陶瓷數量不多,每墓一般二至四件不等,最多的只有七件,亦有不少墓葬無陶瓷隨葬。土坑墓以佛山、梅縣爲例。1963年在佛山瀾石鼓頡崗清理了四座元墓[25],均係火葬土坑墓,用陶罐作葬具。火化後的骨灰均裝在直口平底黑釉小陶罐中,然後將小陶罐放入直口鼓腹凹底大黑陶罐內,加蓋用石灰密封後,再放進用麻石鑿成的圓筒形大石盒內,置於土坑中。黑釉陶罐均係石灣窰產品,素面無紋。其中有兩件大罐蓋內分別墨書:"至正二年十二月二十日庚申吉日立";"至正九年己丑歲十一□□□□□□□禮卿義卿生卿安措"等字。這類火葬土坑墓瀾石、石灣一帶數量不少,被推土機推毀的至少有二、三百座之多。

1978年在梅縣畲江清理了一座土坑墓,出土七件青釉瓷,器形有碗、碟、杯三種。碗兩件,灰白胎,敞口卷唇,深腹圈足。底均墨書一個"正"字。碟兩件,敞口淺身,圈足。底部亦墨書一個"正"字。高足杯三件,敞口折唇,深腹,竹節形實心足,底內凹,器身上下各飾弦紋一至兩道,器外壁分成六格,每格模印一朶花卉[26](展品55)。這七件青瓷的共同特點是胎質厚重,其造形、釉色及紋飾與元代龍泉窰產品基本相類似,均係仿龍泉青瓷,窰口待考。

1958年在廣州沙河雙燕崗沙灰墓出土的三件青白釉瓷器也很精美[27],其中蒜頭瓶兩件,長頸直口凸唇,頸部附兩耳(長方耳),耳與耳之間飾弦紋兩道,內貼凸綫卷草紋,器腹貼凸綫折枝梅花一枝。雙耳三獸足香爐一件,腹部也是貼凸綫梅花一枝。相類似的梅花瓶、爐在四川成都、重慶及川東元墓中均有出土。相類似的瓶在南朝鮮新安海底沉船中亦有發現[28],可見這類瓶當日亦係外銷的產品。

1960年東莞縣附城桂子嶺等處基建工地,挖毀一批元代磚室墓葬,出土不少青色晶瑩似玉的龍泉窰青釉碗、洗,當地工人拾獲後均賣給東莞廢品收購站,博物館聞訊後前往購回一批。碗,敞口高身,小圈足,外壁刻凸雕蓮瓣紋,或菊瓣紋。洗,敞口平唇,淺身圈足,內壁模印菊花瓣紋。五十年代在潮州東鳳橫沙堤元代遺址中出土的瓷器,其中亦有龍泉窰青瓷,器形有青釉雙魚大洗和青釉荷葉蓋罐。洗敞口折唇,口沿外張成平唇狀,淺身圈足,器內外及底部均掛釉,內壁刻水波紋,內底貼附鯉魚兩條,作旋轉狀,外壁飾花瓣紋一周(展品53)。荷葉蓋罐,直口短頸,圓腹圈足,器腹壓印竪條狀菊花紋,蓋作荷葉形,蓋沿起伏平緩,圓鈕低平。這些產品製作精細,當年係暢銷國內外的商品。

1957年海康縣附城西湖石槨墓出土的一件海康窰彩繪瓷罐也很精美。據該墓地卷磚記載,死者是一個縣丞,卒於元代至元三年(公元1266年)[29],該罐白地赭花,通高31厘米,斜肩圓腹,下腹內斂,至底處外撇,平底。荷葉形蓋,器腹上部繪雙鳳四喜鵲相對稱,空隙處襯托菊花紋,器腹下部繪菱形四開光,內繪折枝菊花,近底處繪團扇形開光,內飾折枝花卉,三層的主題畫面各以錢紋和卷草紋相隔,構圖嚴謹,互相呼應,主次分明(展品48)。雙鳳四喜鵲紋飾極爲罕見,是當時製瓷藝人創新之作。此外,1983年該地出土的兩件元代海康窰彩繪如意形瓷枕也很別緻。一件枕面施青釉,有冰裂紋,彩繪呈赭褐色,枕邊繪兩道三綫弦紋,中間塡卷草紋,枕面繪一扇開光,內繪一朶初放的蓮花,旁邊繪剛冒出水的帶刺蓮笋,相互襯托。另一件枕面施姜黃釉,枕邊繪弦紋四道,中間塡人字紋或卷草紋等,枕面正中開光內繪一朶怒放的蓮花,周圍襯托四朶蓮芯[30]。

深圳元墓出土的一對彩繪雙耳小瓶,直口凸唇,高身,下腹收斂至底部外撇,頸部與足部塗赭黑色礦物質陶衣,器外壁紋飾分五層,肩部繪覆蓮瓣紋一周,其下繪卷草一道,再下(即器腹中部)飾對稱菱形兩開光,內繪折枝花卉,再下繪三層仰蓮瓣紋,最下一層繪卷草紋。各層均用兩道弦紋作為間隔(展品62)。這類器形及畫風與河北磁州窯、江西吉州窯及廣東南海、廣州、海康等地彩繪瓷風格均有所不同,但很可能是廣東燒製的產品,窯口待考。

3. 珠海出土的元代外銷瓷

1969年,在珠海蚊州島發掘出212件元代外銷瓷。這批瓷器埋藏在該島海灘四十厘米以下的淡黃色細砂層中。細砂層在海水退潮時,高出海面約一米,漲潮時則在海面五十厘米以下的海水中。出土時瓷碗、碟均分類相疊側放,排列六行。遺留有當年包裝瓷器已腐朽的草木灰痕。

出土的瓷器,其中瓷碗85件,瓷碟127件。碗碟的口沿可分為葵瓣口和圓形口兩種,以前者居多。碗均敞口圈足,碟為敞口淺腹矮圈足。這批瓷器胎質和釉色都比較粗糙,均屬浙江龍泉窯東區產品。瓷質的釉色有青、黃、灰三種。胎質可分灰、灰白、磚紅、淡黃四種。瓷器有紋飾的佔85%,素面無紋的佔15%。全部紋飾可歸納為模印刻劃輪旋組合、模印輪旋組合、模印刻劃組合、輪旋刻劃組合、模印、輪旋、刻劃七類。模印刻劃輪旋組合,主要是在器內壁模印折枝花卉或花瓣一周,有個別器內底兼飾輪旋弦紋和模印花卉,器外壁近口沿處飾輪旋弦紋二至四道,其下再刻直綫條紋一周(圖22)。模印輪旋組合,器內底飾輪旋弦紋一道,弦紋內模印花卉,外壁素面無紋,也有器內壁模印折枝花卉一道或花瓣一周,器外壁近口沿處飾輪旋弦紋二至四道,器內印花較淺,釉藥較厚,隱約可見。模印、刻劃組合,器內壁平均刻劃六格,格內模印花卉,即六格花卉紋。(圖33)輪旋、刻劃組合,器內壁或內底刻劃卷草紋,綫條熟練,但深淺不一,器外壁近口沿處飾輪旋紋三至四道,其下刻劃蓮花瓣一周(圖35),或在器內壁近口沿處飾輪旋紋一道,其下刻水波紋和菊花瓣一周,外壁飾雙綫輪旋弦紋和刻劃直綫條紋一周。(圖36)模印,器內壁模印菊花瓣或花卉一周,外壁素面無紋。(圖38)輪旋,主要是在器外壁近口沿處,飾輪旋紋二至五道,器內無紋。刻劃,器外壁刻劃雙綫直綫條紋一周,器內無紋飾[31]。(圖34、37)

上述紋飾以模印刻劃兼用和模印輪旋兼用數量最多,模印、刻劃、輪旋兼用和模印次之,輪旋和刻劃兼用數量最少。元代龍泉窯瓷器銷路極廣,在日本、朝鮮、菲律賓、印尼、馬來西亞、印度、巴基斯坦甚至伊拉克等國家都有發現[32]。特別是1976年朝鮮新安海底發現的我國元代沉船,已打撈出的瓷器共一萬多件,其中元代龍泉窯青瓷和景德鎮青白瓷數量最多,可見昔日龍泉窯青瓷在國際市場上,佔有相當重要的地位。

四、廣東出土的明代瓷器

1. 廣東窯址出土的瓷器

A. 廣東明代仿龍泉青瓷

龍泉窯屬南方青瓷系統,在宋代民窯諸系中興起雖然較晚,但由於它的產品釉色青翠,晶瑩似玉,深受國內外人士的喜愛,銷路極廣。所以隨後江西、福建、湖南、雲南、廣東等地均有仿製。廣東元代瓷業比較衰落,到了明代又有了空前的發展,大量燒製民用青白瓷、黑瓷、青花瓷、仿龍泉青瓷及仿製南北各地名窯產品等。據調查所知,其中仿龍泉青瓷範圍最廣,窯址分佈在大埔、興寧、五華、龍川、河源、澄海、惠來、平遠、陸豐、惠州、惠陽、博羅、中山、番禺、高州、化州、遂溪等十八個縣市,約50多處。1960年在惠陽新庵發掘了四處仿龍泉窯址(其中有兩座完整的窯灶),出土遺物4,900多件[33]。這裏主要是根據上述調查、發掘材料,綜述廣東仿龍泉青瓷特點。

各窯採集的瓷器,歸納起來有碗、碟、盤、罐、瓶、杯、盞、爐、盆、鉢、器蓋等。此外還有捏塑的瓷牛。碗有三種不同的形式。第一種,青釉、灰釉、白釉、白陶衣均有,器形大小不一,青釉碗數量最多,約佔80%以上,均敞口圈足,器內外均施釉,底部露胎。灰釉、白釉和白陶衣碗外壁一般均素面,但也有只刻劃一、兩種弦紋、直綫紋或菊花瓣紋的。青釉碗紋飾比較複雜,其中有弦紋水波組合紋、菊瓣紋、直綫條紋、水波紋、卷草紋、斜綫條紋、弦紋直綫條組合紋、弦紋卷草菊瓣組合紋、水波弦紋組合紋、弦紋水波直綫條紋組合等,如細分有三十五種之多(圖39-73)。有不少碗內中心刻印"福"、"祿"、"壽"、"富"、"仰"、"青"、"寧"、"誠"、"信"、"金"、"用"、"積"、"溪"、"晴"、"翕"等文字,並有梵文中的"卍"字紋。第二種,青釉撇口高足,器內外均施釉,足底露胎,其特點是器身與器足的高度基本相等。這類碗僅見龍川、澄海、惠州、惠東和惠陽窯燒製。器外壁刻劃弦紋、菊花瓣組合紋,也有素面無紋的,完整器不易採得(圖75)。第三種,青釉、深腹直口圈足,器內外壁施釉,外壁飾弦紋之道(圖74)。盤,青釉、灰釉、白陶衣均有,以青釉為主,可分敞口圈足、瓣口圈足、歙口圈足、菱口圈足等。它們的共同特點是矮身,器內外均施釉,圈足或底部露胎,紋飾

151

一般均刻劃在器內壁或內底。有少數刻在外壁。紋飾有直綫條紋、弦紋、長條菊花瓣、谷粒紋與弦紋組合(圖76,77)、卷草與條紋組合、弦紋、短條直綫紋與菱形紋組合等。有些盤內中心刻印有"福"、"壽"等吉祥文字或印簡單的團形花卉。但大多數盤均素面無紋。碟,敞口圈足,外形與盤大致相似,惟碟身較淺,器形較大,一般均素面,但也有個別碟內中心刻印"福"字或印簡單的折枝團形花卉紋。盞,係點燃豆油用的燈盞,青釉灰釉均有,使用時一般置於燈座上,敞口平底,器內外均施釉,底部露胎,口徑一般約在十厘米左右。罐,青釉、白釉均有,直口鼓腹,短頸矮身圈足,器腹刻劃弦紋卷草菊花瓣組合紋,或刻劃弦紋與直綫條紋組合,也有素面無紋的。器蓋剖面作弓形狀,蓋頂有圓椎形鈕,蓋內榫口凸起如環狀(圖78)。這類罐僅澄海、惠東、大埔等窑口燒製。但大埔產品一般均無紋飾。瓶,青釉,小口長頸雙耳,斜肩,瓶身修長,喇叭足。素面無紋,這類產品,數量不多,均係殘件,僅見大埔窑與惠陽窑燒製。杯,青釉,造形有兩種。一種是敞口平底,另一種敞口圈足,均無紋飾。缽,青釉,撇口斜腹平底或斂口直身矮圈足,器形較大,一般器外施釉,器內壁刻劃很深的斜綫或長條箆梳紋,凸綫鋒利,其用途是擂薯類之用,亦可配以擂杵研磨米漿。盆,青釉,灰釉均有,斂口直身平底,無紋飾,均爲碎片,瓷牛,牛背有一牧童盤足而座,這類產品極少,僅見惠陽白馬窑燒製(展品79)。香爐,青釉,有兩種形式,第一種,撇口深腹矮圈足,器外壁刻劃直綫條紋和蓮花瓣等紋飾(展品50)。第二種,斂口直身,深腹平底,三獸足或三蹄足的均有。器內外均施釉,足底露胎。器外壁刻弦紋箆紋與八卦組合紋,或刻劃弦紋與八卦紋等。八卦紋是《周易》中的八種基本圖形,是用"—"和"- -"符號組成,以"—"爲陽,以"- -"爲陰。名稱是乾(☰)、坤(☷)、震(☳)、巽(☴)、坎(☵)、離(☲)、艮(☶)、兑(☱)。〈易傳〉認爲八卦象徵天、地、雷、風、水、火、山、澤八種自然現象。有人認爲八卦紋"是我國明代嘉靖皇帝好黃老之道,而相應反映到瓷器上的,在嘉靖以後才流行"並據此作爲斷代的依據㉞,這種看法當誤。八卦紋是元、明、清時期的瓷器特別是香爐和鼎類中常見的一種紋飾。元代龍泉窑也曾生產八卦紋瓷器,並大量外銷,1977年南朝鮮新安海域發現的一艘元代中國沉船,已打撈了一萬多件中國外銷瓷,其中亦有元代龍泉窑八卦紋三足香爐。這類產品過去在日本鳥取縣也有出土㉟。最近在廣東省圖書館基建工地亦出土有宋代青釉三足龍泉八卦紋香爐。可見八卦紋瓷器並不是明代嘉靖以後才流行。

廣東燒製的仿龍泉青瓷,製作精緻,深受國外人士的喜愛,行銷不少國家和地區,其產品過去在東南亞的菲律賓、馬來西亞、新加坡、印尼以及中東和日本均有發現。1985年香港考古學會在香港大嶼山竹篙灣發掘出二千多件明代青花瓷、五彩和青瓷等碎片,其中亦有仿龍泉青瓷㊵,該地是否昔日貿易港口或商船臨時停泊之地?這個問題有待進一步的研究。1957年廣東省文管會與中山大學歷史系聯合組成的文物普查團,在海南島海口、瓊山、文昌、萬寧、陵水、三亞、臨高、通什、澄邁等地均採集到不少以惠陽窑爲代表的仿龍泉青瓷碎片。在廣州、英德、深圳、東莞、博羅等地亦有發現。說明這類仿龍泉產品,它既內銷本省及香港,同時也遠銷東南亞各國,甚至到達了中東和日本。

B. 廣東窑址出土的明代青花瓷

青花瓷是一種釉下彩繪,它是用氧化鈷作呈色劑,用毛筆在白色的器物坯胎上進行山水、花鳥、人物等紋樣描繪,或在坯胎上兼寫吉祥語或詩詞等,然後施一層透明的白釉或影青釉,入窑經1,250至1,300℃左右的高溫,在還原氣氛中一次燒成。"青花瓷"實際上是白地藍花瓷的代名詞,它是實用與美術相結合的作品,從問世開始,就深受國內外人士的喜愛樂用,明清以來曾大量傾銷東南亞和世界許多國家和地區。爲了適應國際市場的需要,廣東也曾經大量燒製這類瓷器,據近年來初步調查所知,燒青花瓷的窑址分佈在本省饒平、惠來、揭陽、博羅、惠東、海豐、廉江、羅定、始興、高州、興寧、大埔、平遠、五華、新豐、澄邁十五個縣。其中揭陽、博羅、澄邁、饒平和大埔窑的調查材,曾經在有關刊物上作過報導,其它窑口具體年代及分期,有待進一步的複查發掘研究。從已報導的材料來看,初步有十一處窑址定爲明代中晚期,茲分述如下。

饒平縣明代青花瓷窑,分佈在該縣九村鎮鄭屋坷、頂竹坪、三斗坑、老窑坷和鐵寮坑五處地點,範圍很大,堆積很厚,據初步分析研究,其時代的上限是嘉靖年間,下限已到清代㊱。其中嘉靖至明末的產品,胎質潔白,器物用匣缽裝燒,用細沙墊燒,沙足。青花花紋主要繪於器物內底,和外壁。內沿下,底和近足處多數畫一道弦紋圈。器形主要有碗、盤、碟數種。碗,有內底和外壁均繪天官人物,捧笏配以童子、靈芝或仙鶴的。有內底畫折枝花或靈芝,外壁畫童子六人。或外壁繪雙獅滾球或繪雙龍的均有。或內底繪折枝花、靈芝、蘭草、仙鶴或荷花鷺鷥,外壁繪纏枝花卉、荷花鷺鷥。或折枝花鳥,或雙魚水藻。亦有內底寫一個"福"字,外壁寫"蓬萊松柏枝枝秀，方丈芙蓉朶朶鮮，壽山不老年年茂，福海無窮歲歲堅"詩句的。盤，內底繪鳳鳥，襯托雲朶、山石、靈芝、蘭草，近口沿處內外壁均飾花葉和絲帶。碟，內底繪仕女、天官人物、折枝花鳥、旋紋花朶，或在蘭色花朶內繪白兔。

大埔縣明代晚期青花瓷窯，分佈在高陂區陶溪上、陶溪下、井背山和湖寮區板坑四處㊲。這裏的青花瓷產品僅見碗、碟兩類。紋飾主要繪在碗、碟外壁，有弦紋、折枝花、纏枝花和單片草葉紋等，其中折枝花有折枝葵、折枝草葉和藤狀枝葉三種，多數以三枝或四枝平均分佈在器物外壁。折枝草葉紋的裝飾比較特殊。參差裝飾，密而不亂。弦紋主要裝飾在器物的口沿，外壁近足處以及內底。單片葉紋飾較少見。主要裝飾在外壁弦紋之間。有些碗、碟內底寫青花文字，有行書和楷書，主要是寫"正"、"元"、"豐"、"立"、"福"等吉祥文字。

揭陽縣明代晚期青花瓷窯，分佈在河婆鎮嶺下山(現屬揭西縣管轄)㊳。這處窯址的產品種類有碗、碟、杯、瓶和器蓋等。器外壁一般描繪簡單的折枝花卉或纏枝菊葉，或描繪簡單的山水風景。有不少碗、碟內底或外底寫有單字青花文字，如"福"、"祿"、"壽"、"中"、"上"、"正"、"和"、"士"、"信"、"佳"、"玉"、"仁"、"魁"、"元"等。這處窯址範圍很大，堆積很厚，燒窯時間很長，其時代的下限會到清代。

博羅縣明代中晚期青花瓷窯，分佈在角洞水庫、角洞山一帶。這處窯址的青花瓷產品，種類有碗、碟、杯、瓶等。器壁紋飾一般彩繪卷草、弦紋、纏枝或折枝花卉，有些碟內中心寫"雨香齋"三字，底部圈足內豎寫兩排"大明成化年制"款。上述窯址出土的青花瓷極為重要，其中裝飾吉祥語詩句、人物、山水、花鳥及寫"成化年製"款的青花瓷，過去汕頭舊海灘和西沙羣島以及東南亞等地均有類似或相同的瓷器發現。值得一提的是故宮博物院已故韓槐準先生，過去在東南亞發現不少明代"沙足青花器"，六十年代初期韓先生兩次前來廣東考察，曾詢及沙足青花的窯口問題，筆者茫然未能奉告，深感是件憾事。如今饒平、大埔窯口均發現有這類沙足青花(即用細沙墊燒的青花瓷器)，經與韓先生送給廣東省博物館的標本對比，其中有些與明嘉靖鳳鳥紋青花盤極為相似。近年來在福建安溪和江西樂平明代青花窯址中亦發現有沙足青花器㊴。福建、江西均與廣東毗鄰，明清以來三省均大量生產青花瓷，器物風格，關係密切，青花瓷器形與紋飾有不少雷同或相似之處，其產品當日均係以外銷為主，這是毫無疑問的。至於東南亞發現的沙足青花器的窯口問題，估計三省的產品均有，至於更具體的窯口，則有待今後對比研究後，才能得出更準確更圓滿的答案了。

2．廣東明代墓葬出土的陶瓷

廣東明代墓葬各地一般均有發現，大致有土坑墓、石墩墓、灰沙墓和磚室墓四種。其中隨葬的陶瓷器數量極少。有些墓葬則未見陶瓷器隨葬。1963年在佛山瀾石鼓頴崗清理了四座土坑火葬墓㊶。火化後的骨骸裝在直口圓腹凹底黑釉陶罐中，然後將陶罐放入平底直口黑釉陶盆內，接着再用相同的陶盆作蓋，用石灰將口唇密封後，放進小土坑墓中。或將火化後的骨骸裝在歛口直身，凹底高身小白陶罐中，加蓋後再放入直口圓腹凹底黑釉大陶罐內(即大小罐相套)，再加蓋密封。或在相套的罐頭再複蓋一件平底直口凸唇黑釉陶盆。上述陶罐均係佛山石灣窯產品，黑釉大陶罐器肩和器蓋飾附加堆水波紋。其中有三件罐蓋內寫有墨書，一件是："大吉歲次戊申嘉靖二十七年十二月二十五吉日"；一件是："盧江名大羅村氏莫庚子生潤正月十四日卯時壽原四十四歲天順七年十月初九日世中(終)至成化五年廿(十)二月十二日號"；另一件是："成化壬寅年正月初八□□□"。這類火葬墓數量很多，僅瀾石鼓頴崗一帶被當地磚瓦廠推土機推毀的，估計至少有六、七百座之多。

近年來深圳南頭至沙井沿海一帶明墓出土的瓷器也很重要。據楊耀林先生介紹，這裏的明墓葬品，每墓一般均有一罐、一碗、一碟，或兩罐、一碗、一杯出土，此外還有銅錢和裝飾品等隨葬。明代早期以仿龍泉青瓷為多，白瓷次之，青花極少。中晚期則以青花器為主。正式發掘的明墓有三十餘座。出土的瓷器，連同採集的共三百多件，其中碗近二百件，杯一百多件，碟二十餘件。其中青花瓷題材廣泛，內容豐富，有天空的飛鳥、神龍、浮雲煙雨，有地上的田園山水、花卉草木、奔馬醒獅、飛禽走獸，有水中的風帆漁人、魚螺海藻，此外還有佛教的"卍"字紋和梵文裝飾，亦有道教的八掛紋和吉祥語，人物方面，既有唐人形像，也有番人畫像。釉彩方面，有濃有淡，層次分明。畫風方面有粗有細，寫意傳神。明代帶年款的瓷器很少，僅見三件青花瓷杯，一件器底寫"宣德年造"，外壁繪四條對稱而形態不同的鯉魚戲水圖。另一件器底寫"成化年制"(寫在雙道青花圈內，行書)。還有一件在底部寫"大明正德"草書。有明確年代而又有瓷器陪葬的明墓，僅見兩座。一座是西鄉"天順元年"(公元1457年)墓，出土兩件外壁刻劃水波紋的青瓷碗，係惠東白馬山仿龍泉窯產品。另一座是大亞灣"正德四年"（公元1509年）武略將軍徐勛墓，出土兩件精製的青花瓷碗，內繪纏枝牡丹，外繪八寶圖案、躍魚和纏枝花卉，另一件外繪卷雲龍紋。此外，有一件雲彩奔馬碗與"萬曆通寶"共出，與銅錢共出的瓷器數量不少，但較難斷定其絕對年代，一般明墓都有宋代年號銅錢出土[41]。

東莞明代沙灰墓和磚室墓較多，其中莞城近郊桂子嶺、下海山竹頭嶺和石龍火車站附近的低矮山崗一帶，明墓極為密集，均係墓羣，1960年至1964年由於基建、築堤及建築公路等，在這些地方開山挖土，平整土地，被挖毀的明墓估計至少有七、八百座之多，隨葬的瓷器絕大部分是青花瓷，每墓一般均有兩罐、一碗一碟，或兩碗兩罐，或一碗一杯，或兩罐兩小瓶，或兩罐四小瓶，或只有兩罐。碗有青花碗、仿龍泉窰青釉碗或白釉碗。青花碗外壁繪鳳鳥花卉，或繪纏枝花卉，圈足內繪雙綫圓圈內寫"大明年造"四字，或外壁繪雲朶奔馬圖案。青花杯、碟繪卷草紋或寫意花卉。杯，亦有龍泉窰高足杯。青花小瓶有兩種，一種撇口圓腹圈足，施影青釉，口沿掛鐵銹色釉，器腹繪纏枝花卉，高僅六厘米左右，這類小瓶的紋飾與造形與博羅角洞明代窰址出土的同類產品基本相同，可能就是角洞窰的產品。另一種小瓶，喇叭口圓筒身，平底，外壁繪山水風景，這類小瓶與揭西婆河嶺下山明代青花窰出土的同類器形亦基本相同。出土的大青花罐，有一定的東莞地方特色，採集的標本約100多件，其特點是胎質厚重，有白地藍花和藍地白花兩類，青花顏色深淺不一，有藍中帶灰的，也有深藍或淡藍的。器形有短頸直口圓腹圈足的（是用兩個相同的大碗坯胎，口唇與口唇仰覆用胎漿黏連，然後挖去一方圈足內的底部，作為罐的口沿）。或直口高身橢圓腹，或直口扁圓腹，或直口圓肩下腹收歛，均圈足。青花紋飾繪在罐的腹部，分上下兩層，器腹中間繪雙綫弦紋作為間隔，上下腹均繪纏枝菊花（菊花有細長花瓣，團菊短花瓣和寫意花瓣），或繪菊花圈草組合，或繪寫意花卉。這類青花罐至今僅見東莞縣有所出土，它與福建、江西以及本省已發現的明代青花瓷窰產品完全不同，應該是東莞本地燒製的，但其窰至今尚未發現。東莞明墓正式發掘的只有五座，其中有明確記年的三座，一座是"正統元年"（公元1436年），一座是"正德二年"（公元1507年），另一座是"萬曆二十四年"（公元1596年），這三座明墓均出土有上述東莞青花罐，可見這類青花瓷罐的生產，其時間至少延續了一百六十多年。此外有三件帶蓋青花瓷罐，係景德鎮民窰產品（據東莞縣博物館鍾創堅先生介紹，出土時該罐與萬曆年間的墓誌共出，墓誌已丢失），其特點是其中一對器蓋繪弦紋、雜寶、蝴蝶和花卉，外壁紋飾分四層，第一層是頸部，飾綬帶，其上下加飾弦紋，第二層是肩部，飾四開光，內繪折枝花卉，其下飾弦紋兩道，第三層是器腹周壁，飾蘭草花鳥，第四層是近圈足處，飾卷草一周。另一件器蓋繪花卉，頸部繪短條直綫紋一周，器肩四開光內繪折枝花，器腹六開光內各繪柵欄人物或月亮人物和花卉圖案，頗別緻。這類青花罐與廣東省博物館庫藏萬曆青花罐及景德鎮民窰出土的萬曆青花罐基本相同。

1954年在廣州小北清理的兩座磚室墓，其中有一座出土五件帶蓋青花小瓷罎[42]較為重要。其特點是地色普遍作微藍色，但部分因水和礦物質滲蝕而略呈米黃色，青花作暗藍色。器外壁紋飾大致可分為兩種。第一種是肩部上下各飾弦紋兩周。中間夾着十七組白描多層蓮花形連貫紋樣。腹部繞纏枝牡丹花四組，每組有開滿的主花一朶，半開的輔花兩朶，葉作三出雞爪形，分佈在枝葉上。器腹外壁下部繪十一組"斗"字卷雲紋，其下再飾雙綫弦紋。第二種外壁紋飾與上述第一種大致相同，器腹牡丹花葉形式雖仍四組，但每組作一螺旋形枝，枝盡處作滿開的牡丹花一朶，無輔花。器蓋紋飾與器肩紋飾相同，其中有一件蓋面有五組近似文字的花紋。據發掘者初步認定其中有"宋己酉"三字，認為"宋己"二字是楷書，"酉"字是草書，另兩個似花紋亦似文字的形體。最後根據"宋己酉"的年款和共同陪葬的"熙寧元寶"、"元豐通寶"等北宋銅錢，初步推測上述青花瓷的年代屬北宋時期。並認為這一發現極其重要，它給"宋代已有青花瓷"之說提供了寶貴的實物資料。當時發掘者（黃文寬先生等人）對這批材料的處理是比較慎重的，因為覺得"宋青花"的發現太突然了，還未放心報導，1955年初故宫陳萬里先生到廣州時，曾請他鑑定，陳先生認為是"早期青花"，後來發掘者認為既然是早期青花，蓋上又有宋代年款，同時還有宋錢作為旁證，所以寫了《廣州小北宋墓簡報》一文，在《文物參考資料》（以下簡稱《文參》）1955年10期發表。隨後傳楊發表了《關於廣州古墓青花瓷罎時代問題的商權》《文參》（1956年6期），玉志敏發表了《廣州小北古墓的青花瓷罎不是宋器》（《文參》1956年10期）、黃文寬發表了《廣州小北宋墓簡報補充說明》（《文參》1957年1期）、麥英豪、黎金、區澤聯名發表了《我們對推論廣州小北古墓及出土青花瓷罎年代問題的意見》（《文參》1957年5期）、楊有潤發表了《談廣州小北宋墓的爭論》（《文參》1957年5期）。上述文章討論的主題是該墓的斷代問題，着重在青花瓷罎的年代上，從器形、釉色、胎質、花紋的比較及紋飾的演變規律，說明這五件青花瓷罎的年代，不可能是宋代,並一致肯定是明代作品,同時指出"宋己酉"不是文字,而是折枝花的誤解。並從墓葬結構進行了排比分析,認為該墓是屬明代墓葬。我認為上述討論,得出的結論是正確的。理由是纏枝牡丹是明代青花瓷中常見的紋飾,纏枝上作出三鷄爪形的葉,正統、弘治、正德、嘉靖年間的青花瓷也常有這類葉形,器外壁下部飾"斗"字卷雲紋的青花瓷在景德鎮民窰中"成化"、"弘治"、"正德"年間的青花罐(罎)、瓶上亦較為常見,類似廣州出土的青花瓷罎,在景德鎮市新平公社"正德十二年"墓亦有出土[43]。總的來說,在刊物上開展學術討論,各抒己見,有助於對問題的統一認識。

3. 汕頭出土的明代青花瓷器

1971年在汕頭金砂海灘集中出土64件明代青花瓷器,沒有其它遺物伴隨出土,據分析,這批瓷器與上述珠海出土的瓷器均係外銷的一種商品,因當年貨船沉沒而被海水沖擊至沙層中所遺留下來的[44]。這批瓷器器形有碗、杯、碟、罐。其中碗有高身矮身之分,均敞口圈足。器表裝飾可分六種。第一種是器外壁近口沿處飾弦紋一道。器外壁直書青花文字:"□□□□枝枝秀,美芙蓉朵朵鮮,壽山不老年年茂,福海無窮歲歲□"。青花藍中帶灰,其中五個字藍釉散開,難以辨認。第二種是器內底繪雙綫長方框,內寫有"聖報佔中三元"六字,外壁寫三個"喜"字。第三種是器內底繪雙綫長方框,內寫"大明成化年制"六字青花款,青花藍中帶灰,器內口沿和器腹,器外口沿與器足繪雙綫或單綫弦紋,外壁寫三個"喜"字,其下繪簡單花卉各一枝。第四種是器內底繪折枝菊花三朵,口沿內外壁和內腹繪雙綫弦紋一道,足部繪單綫弦紋一周,圈足內繪雙綫弦紋。第五種是器內底繪獅子戲球圖,頗別緻,口沿內外壁繪雙綫弦紋一周,圈足繪雙綫弦紋,器外底繪單綫圓圈,內寫"大明成化年制"六字青花款。第六種是碗內底繪博古圖案。青花瓷杯,紋飾有兩種,第一種是器壁內外近口沿處和器內底與器足均繪雙綫弦紋一周,器外底繪圓圈一道,內寫"大明成化年制"六字青花款。第二種是器外壁近口沿處繪雙綫弦紋一道,下繪花鳥山水或花鳥山水人物一周,再下佈雙綫弦紋一道。青花瓷碟的紋飾也可分為兩種,第一種是器壁內繪花蝶,近口沿處繪弦紋一周。器外底繪圓圈一道,內寫"大明成化年制"六字青花款。第二種是器內繪魚藻圖案,器內壁近口沿處繪單綫弦紋一周。圈足內寫"大明成化年制"六字青花款。帶蓋青花瓷罐僅一件,器外壁描繪花卉,近口沿處與器腹下繪弦紋一周,器足繪弦紋二道,器蓋

外壁繪折枝花卉和弦紋。汕頭出土的這批青花瓷器,從其胎質、釉色和裝飾來看,均屬一般的民窰產品,其窰口有江西的、福建的,也有廣東的。一般來說,白地釉色帶灰,青花顏色泛灰,胎質較厚和較粗糙的都是廣東窰的產品,但也有些青花瓷燒製較好,與江西景德鎮和福建德化民窰的產品極為相似,所以這批青花瓷的具體窰別,還有待進一步的對比研究。

上述青花瓷器雖有不少"大明成化年制"款,但過去北京故宮專家認為它是萬曆仿成化的作品,據此,筆者曾經初步將這批青花瓷定為"萬曆年間的產品"[44],最近有人懷疑這批青花瓷是清代仿成化的作品,在學術上有不同意見這是正常現象,但筆者認為現在在論據未足之前,將其年代暫時定為"萬曆"還是可以的。

五、廣東出土的清代陶瓷

1. 窰址出土的清代青花瓷器

據普查材料統計,清代窰址分佈在潮州、普寧、澄海、揭西、東莞、惠東、連平、佛山、三水、中山、陽春、湛江、吳川、海康、廉江、高要、始興、仁化、連縣、翁源、化州、高州、信宜、龍川、興寧、大埔、平遠、豐順、五華和香港新界,共三十個縣市和特區,約275處。其中有10多個縣和特區燒製清代青花瓷,青花瓷是這一時期暢銷的商品,它既內銷本省各地,也外銷東南亞等國家。這裏根據已發表過的材料,先行扼要分述饒平、大埔窰址出土的清代青花瓷。

饒平縣青花瓷窰分佈在三斗坑、老河坷、下坪埔、鐵寮坑、鄭屋坷、項竹坪、公婆和半崋坡等地[45]。這些窰址出土的青花瓷器與明代後期產品相比,它既有繼承關係,也有不同之處。器物入窰仍是逐件裝入匣缽內,底足墊沙,器形較大,青花淺淡明亮,不如前期渾厚凝重。較早的花紋比較工整,後期趨向草率,逐漸演變為寫意。器形有碗、碟、杯、盤、匙、小瓶等。碗,有高身和淺身之分,高身碗外壁紋飾有松鼠葡萄、團鶴、纏枝牡丹、菊花、山水。或外壁四面開光,或在纏枝花卉中間寫"馬"字。也有在外壁一側繪山水,另一側寫"壽無窮界,祿如東海"字句。或在外壁繪雙鳳鳥夾結帶寶書,或繪雲龍火珠和五獅滾球。或外壁繪纏枝牡丹,近底繪一圈柵紋,內底飾折枝花,口沿下繪卷草紋。或外壁繪潦草的纏枝花卉,近底一周飾藍地白綫魚鱗紋。或外壁繪山水、屋舍、釣翁漁舟。或是山石樹木和馬羣。或外壁一側繪城牆、門樓,附城河、小船,另一側寫"閣中帝子今何

在,檻外長江空自流"詩句。或內底繪螺旋紋,內外壁分兩排。每排六至八格,裏面交錯填靈芝和牽牛花。或內外壁均繪過牆龍和雲朵。有不少碗內底紋飾與外壁紋飾相同,亦有少量碗內底畫"卍"字紋。圈足內多數寫有商號或窰場等名稱,各窰都有三、五種以上,有些款在幾處窰址中均有,如"永玉"、"仁玉"、"正玉"、"元玉"、"美玉"、"文玉"、"珍玉"、"仁利"、"生利"、"玉利"、"三利"、"文利"、"引利"、"順興"、"永興"、"三合"、"利和"、"怡和"、"雙和"等。淺碗和碟內外壁紋飾有獅子、蘭草、山水花卉亦有繪靈芝和牽牛花的,但筆法較為潦草。杯,內底繪梅花,外壁繪蘭草蜂蝶或纏枝菊花,圈足內畫"卍"字紋,或寫"福"字款。或外壁繪山水紋。盤,內底繪雲龍。或繪山石梅蘭,或繪花卉蘭草魚藻。也有盤內繪過牆龍或繪蟹紋的均有。瓶,外壁繪纏枝花卉。

大埔縣青花瓷窰,主要分佈在與高陂相鄰的光德和桃源兩個區,在平原等區也有發現,計有廖尾坷、九社上窰、窰地、上坪上窰、上坪下窰、井欄面、圓子墩、青子地、老路崗、老君石、石角、青坑、庵格子、九社上窰、茅坪坑、乾廠、沙梨崗、塘子、水口、火燒斗、吳仔祭、圴仔頭等二十多處[47]。器形有碗、碟、盤、杯、爐、器蓋、器座等。青花紋飾大致可分為山水、花卉樹木、人物、動物、宗教圖案和文字六類。山水類紋飾有山水漁舟、水棚漁舟、山水樹木房屋、山水城牆樓閣等。花卉樹木類紋飾有牡丹、柳樹、壽桃、葵斗、纏枝菊、折枝菊、蘭草、團菊、桃花、梧桐葉、石榴、佛手、草葉、竹葉花卉、蘭草花卉、荷花、蘭花鴛鴦、菊瓣海螺等。動物紋飾有蝴蝶、獅子繡球、鳳鳥、團鶴、羊、飛鳥、魚藻蝌蚪、三爪雲龍、夔龍、蟹紋、仙鶴等。人物類僅見高士隱坐於山石樹木中一種。宗教類文飾有道教的八卦紋和佛教的"卍"字紋。文字類有商號、吉祥語、詩詞及記年款識等,主要寫在碗、碟內底或圈足內,計有"玉"、"魁"、"尚"、"福"、"寶"、"佳器"、"口冠世祿"、"梧桐葉子口□"、"黃和"、"黃玉"、"元和"、"上玉"、"清合"、"榮和"、"和興"、"金玉"、"王玉"、"明泉"、"得利"、"合玉"、"順玉"、"和"、"合"、"元"、"元興"、"如玉"、"合元"、"佳"、"中紅"、"蘭玉"、"公玉"、"永興"、"雅"、"賦"、"喜"、"文武佳器"、"金玉滿堂"、"忠悌孝信"、"年至□□七八"、"梧桐葉落"、"雲台山下高士臥"、"檻外長江空自流"、"老泉一日家宴,令兒女作冷香語"、"東坡曰:泉在石中流出冷,風從花裏過來香"、"小妹曰:叫月子規喉舌冷,宿花蝴蝶夢魂香"、"老泉曰:爾等不若也",以及"太平年制"、"太平年己未口"、"太平年庚申口"等。

由於窰址尚未發掘,上述青花瓷籠統定為清代是可以的,其中寫有"太平年製"、"太平年己未口"、"太平年庚申

口"的青花瓷,其年代就更具體了。中國歷史上從三國至宋遼時期,曾經先後出現過七個"太平"的年號,這些"太平"年號時間過早,與本窰產品無關,但與清代咸豐至同治年間出現的"太平天國",應該是關係密切,當年太平軍曾經在嘉應州梅縣、大埔等地活動過很長的時間,筆者認為青花瓷中所寫的"太平年製",意即太平天國時期製造的。"太平天國"共建立十三年(公元1851—1863年)。歷史上各個朝代一直用干支記年,太平天國時期民間同樣用干支記年(辛亥至癸亥),按此推算"太平年己未口"應該是公元1859年(即清代咸豐九年);"太平年庚申口"應該是公元1860年(即清代咸豐十年)。明清以來大埔、饒平青花產品主要通過昔日潮州港口,大量傾銷東南亞各國,貿易額逐年增加,據《潮州志》記載,同治十年對外貿易額是3,889,459兩,至光緒二十六年增至11,912,478兩。對外貿易之繁盛,可以想見。近年來印尼出土了不少饒平和大埔明清青花瓷[64],證實了這裏的產品曾經大量外銷,這是歷史事實。

2. 清代墓葬出土的陶瓷器

清代墓葬大致有土坑墓和沙灰磚室墓兩種,隨葬的陶瓷器數量不多,每墓一般二至四件不等,器形有碗、碟、杯、罐等,有個別墓葬隨葬六、七件或隨葬200多件的均有。各地由於基建工程取土等原因,被推毀的清代墓葬,數量極多,無法統計。這裏以深圳、東莞、大埔為代表,分述如下。

據介紹,深圳清代墓葬出土的瓷器數量不少,絕大部分是推土機推出的,共採得各類瓷器二百七十多件,其中碗類最多,杯類次之,碟類最少。青花瓷的胎質和紋飾前後期區別明顯,前後胎質細膩,花紋題材有梅、蘭、菊、竹、神龍、荷花、百壽圖和吉祥語。蛇口和南頭出土的杯、碟,其中有"十里杏花香"的題款,同時還有八卦紋的圖案作裝飾。後期青花其胎質、釉色和花紋一般都比較粗糙,紋飾以條紋和田園山水為主,其次是蓮荷紋。碗、碟器形多作侈口斜腹,絕大部分是香港新界大埔窰的產品。大鵬咸豐三年一品夫人劉太君林夫人墓出土的七件碗,亦有一定的代表性,敞口、斜腹、矮圈足,底不施釉,器內有一圈疊燒痕跡,外壁繪寫意青花蓮荷圖案。大鵬核電站工地,道光十一年福建水師提督劉起龍墓,出土的兩件青花碗則較為精美,器內青圈點彩,外繪牡丹、竹石[48],可能是福建窰口的產品。

東莞清代墓葬出土的青花瓷器,數量亦不少,筆者最近在東莞縣博物館看到的藏品,均屬江西景德鎮窰的產

品，製作精細，釉色晶瑩，花紋講究，寫意傳神。從器形和紋飾來看，大致有清初和道光、咸豐、同治年間的作品。全部均係帶蓋青花罐(有些蓋已散失)，其共同特點是一般均直口短頸，斜肩鼓腹，下身收斂，平底或假圈足。清初蓋罐，器蓋與器腹繪局部連環如意圖案，內加繪牡丹、菊葉和花卉，頸部繪菊花紋。近底處繪弦紋，其上繪半截蓮花，再上則繪斜方雜寶紋。蓋項飾坐獅鈕(展品95)。或器蓋和器身均繪纏枝花卉，佈滿器壁，器頸和接近底部則繪花瓣一周。道光年間的青花罐，紋飾有三種。第一種是器外壁上腹一側繪五個人物(其中一個是身穿長袍的紳士，另四個侍男侍女分佈其後及兩旁)，均站立在湖邊高處的柵欄內，觀賞湖中仕女划船(湖中繪兩小船，一前一後，前三人後四人一船)，柵欄兩旁點綴松柏及高掛綬帶，迎風招展。第二種是器蓋與器頸繪折枝花卉，器外繪雲龍紋，雲朵密集，滿佈器壁，肩部飾四鋪首。第三種是器身繪雙鳳花卉圖案，器蓋繪纏枝花。咸豐年間的青花罐。器頸飾折枝花，器肩繪連環回字形雷紋，外壁繪纏枝花葉，均佈滿器壁。或頸部繪折枝花，器腹繪雙龍戲珠圖，近底處飾海水波浪紋。同治年間的青花罐，器蓋邊沿、器肩和足部施鐵綉色釉料，器蓋飾人物花草、器頸和器身繪花卉圖案。或在器腹寫一至二個雙喜大字，並加繪纏枝花卉。

開平咸豐四年墓出土的一件青花瓷大蓋罐，製作也很精緻，出土時內裝火化後的骨灰。蓋內墨書死者的生卒年月等七十四字。其中寫明死者"生於乾隆己亥年"(即乾隆四十四年，公元1779年)、"終於咸豐甲寅年"(即咸豐四年，公元1854年)，蓋面繪火焰紋、雲紋及波浪紋，器腹繪雙龍戲珠圖案，並加繪火焰、雲朵襯托，器壁下端繪弧綫紋和變形波浪紋。這件罐的胎質、器形、釉色和繪畫風格與東莞縣出土的道光青花雙龍戲珠罐，基本相同，故應屬道光年間景德鎮民窰產品(展品96)。

1962年在大埔縣發掘了清初的將領(總兵官)吳六奇墓，出土200多件陶俑等[49]，形式多樣，內容豐富，亦係這一時期的代表作。陶俑大致可分為三組，第一組是陰森恐怖的官府俑(包括成羣的武士俑、衙差俑、傳令俑、吏役俑等，一個個神氣十足的在公堂枱桌前兩旁站立着(展品104)；第二組是前呼後擁坐轎出巡的情況，捏塑有造型別緻的官轎、轎夫和開路的儀仗隊陶俑等(展品105)；第三組是內庭生活的一瞥，周圍站立的都是他的妻妾和僕人，有男侍俑、女侍俑、舞樂俑和象棋盤、象棋子、搖賭盒、骰子、天九牌(賭具)。此外還有衣箱、袍冠、木架床、衣架、香爐、燭台、酒壺、酒杯、糧倉和炊具等。其中男侍俑頭戴瓜皮式帽，身內穿窄袖口袍，外加短袖寬口對襟掛，穿靴。女侍俑頭梳單層平髻或雙層高髻，上身內穿掛，外穿描金或帶紅硃彩的對襟長氅，兩手持果盆或宮扇等物(展品106)。各類俑的造型均極傳神，生動逼真，把吳六奇生前的威武和豪華淫逸的生活情景，塑造得淋漓盡致。《清史列傳》和《潮州志》等均有吳六奇的傳記，蒲松齡的著名小說《聊齋志異》中亦有他的故事。

結語

1. 廣東五代陶瓷僅見廣州番禺石馬村南漢墓和增城五代墓中有所出土，數量不多，這一時期的遺址則至今尚未被發現，有待今後的努力，才能填補。1957年發現的南海官窰文頭嶺窰址，曾經有人認為是"五代南漢劉氏的官窰"，主要論據是該窰的"碗是敞口圈足，釉有到脚或短釉露胎，具有廣東五代時期瓷器的作風"並"估計窰的時代當與皇帝崗窰址的年代相差不遠"，認為"皇帝崗窰址的年代要比劉氏建立南漢封建割據政權稍早，可能是晚唐的"，因為"廣州西村皇帝崗一帶在南漢時期為劉氏的御花園，發現皇帝崗之初，尚有用磚砌的池塘殘迹，窰址孤立地隆起和其外表有這麼厚的坭土封蓋着，顯然在南漢時已被利用作池邊的假山，南漢建立政權後，可能把皇帝崗的瓷窰廢了，到附近選擇地點繼續燒瓷，供給朝廷使用，南海官窰的得名和所有劃黑花青瓷比皇帝崗的精美就是這個原因[51]。筆者認為上述推測論據不足，難以成立。並認為文頭嶺窰址的年代定為宋代比較可靠，理由是(1)、敞口圈足碗、施釉到足或短釉露胎(即施半截釉)的，這類碗在南海奇石北宋窰址中屢見不鮮，奇石窰瓷器其中有些四耳罐等刻印有"政和元年"、"政和六年"等北宋年號，這是燒窰的絕對年代。文頭嶺窰址有不少碗、碟、盆等器形與奇石窰的同類產品基本相似，釉色和胎質也基本相同。此外石馬村南漢劉晟墓出土的青釉夾耳罐、六耳罐等典型的五代南漢器物，却未見於該窰燒製，故其年代定為宋代是可以的。(2)、認為皇帝崗窰址的年代要比劉氏南漢割據政權稍早的看法，現在也是不能成立了。皇帝崗窰址過去定為晚唐、五代[52]，實屬偏早，現在考古界比較一致的看法是"北宋"。(3)、所謂文頭嶺窰址"所有劃黑花青瓷比皇帝崗窰精美"的說法，也是不確切的。文頭嶺窰雖然有一些碎片和最近出土的一些彩繪軍持、腰鼓和彩繪壺等殘件比較精緻，但碗、碟、盆、罐等彩繪瓷和青釉瓷器約90%以上的其胎質、釉色和紋飾都很粗糙，遠比不上皇帝崗、潮州窰和惠州窰的精美。這些粗瓷絕不可能供給南漢朝廷使用。(4)、有人認爲官窰文頭嶺窰屬五代是沒有問題的,其主要依據是"官窰"一名照例是皇帝撥款建造的才能稱做"官窰",並說"在廣東建立皇朝的有南越和南漢,南越在西漢初年當無官窰之設,能設官窰的只有南漢劉氏"。這種說法似乎有一定道理,但南海"官窰"過去是指公社的地名(範圍很大),現在是鎮名即"官窰鎮",文頭嶺窰址距官窰鎮約有十里之遙,其窰址所燒製的陶瓷,未見五代南漢典型器物,缺乏考古材料,所以該窰年代,五代之說,暫時亦難以成立。

2. 北宋一百六十多年中,由於社會經濟的發展,北方人口的大量南遷,陶瓷的大量對外輸出和燒瓷技術的巨大進步,陶瓷業遠遠超越了唐代,器形種類與釉色品種成倍增加,並正式出現了白瓷、青白瓷、青瓷和黑瓷等新品種,造型豐富多樣,雖是同一類器物也有多種多樣不同製作手法,器物胎質普遍轉薄,造型輕巧。宋代瓷器突破了唐代的舊規,瓷塑類出現了釋迦牟尼佛像、奏樂女像、捧書人像、騎馬人像、獸頭類陶塑、人身禽獸臉的十二生肖以及專供外銷的高鼻卷髮瓷西洋人頭像及西洋狗等。碗碟瓶罐等生活用瓷亦出現了印花、刻花、剔花、彩繪、點彩、印花刻劃組合、刻劃彩繪組合、刻劃點彩組合等紋飾,其主要題材有自然界中的牡丹、蓮花、纏枝菊花、團菊、菊瓣、折枝花、卷草、梅花、蘭花、竹葉、石榴、蕉葉和古代的回字形雷紋、連錢紋、方格紋、繩紋、圓圈紋、雙綫非字紋、箆紋、水波紋、水葉紋、弦紋、菱紋、魚鱗紋、直綫紋、斜綫紋、斜方格紋、卷草箆梳組合紋以及梵文中的"卍"字紋、象徵愛情的鴛鴦、鯉魚穿蓮、飛舞蝴蝶、士大夫豪飲的醉態、侍女、吉祥語及七言絕詩等,均被列爲瓷器的裝飾題材。值得注意的是廣州、潮州、惠州、南海、海康、遂溪、廉江等窰口有不少紋飾和器形與耀州窰、磁州窰、定窰、景德鎮窰等窰口的紋飾與器形都有相同或相類似之處,說明早在北宋時期,廣東有不少窰口在製瓷技術上,曾經受到上述名窰的影響,取其之長補己之短,爲適應外銷需要,善於模仿創新。

3. 關於廣東仿龍泉窰的年代問題,曾經有過幾種推論,一種認爲是"南宋以後"[53],一種認爲"或許是宋代",一種認爲"不出宋明"[54],亦有人認爲是"元代",澳門賈梅士博物院則將這類產品定爲"宋代"[55],二十五年前筆者對這類仿龍泉窰的年代也作過推論,認爲是"明代或稍早一些"[56],現在看法仍然沒有改變,理由是(1)、這類窰址中至今尚未發現有絕對年代可考的實物,同時出土的器物沒有宋代風格。(2)、從胎質、釉色、紋飾特點看,它與元明時期龍泉窰產品有很多相似之處。(3)、再從器形來看,青釉三足八卦紋香爐,平底刻花敞口盤,撇唇歛口圈足盤和菱口盤,這些器形雖具有元代風格,但明初或明代中晚期尚有生產,值得注意的是,生產數量最多的碗類則沒有元代遺風,具有廣東地方特色,應屬明代產品。出土的高足碗,這類器形元明兩代極爲流行,當時浙江龍泉、福建德化,河南鈞州,河北磁州以及江西景德鎮等窰均有生產,造形大致相似,但工藝則有所不同,元代高足碗的碗身與足部一般是用膠結的瓷泥黏壓上去的,接口擠出的瓷泥刮平後常有裂痕。而明代高足碗的碗身與足部係用釉藥黏貼的,接口平整光滑。而本窰產品亦係平整光滑,看不出駁口裂痕,故應屬明代產品無疑。(4)、1961年在東莞附城基建工地明代永樂二年墓墳土中,曾經發現過惠陽仿龍泉窰瓷碎片,近年來深圳西鄉明代"天順元年"(公元1457年)墓亦出土有兩件惠東白馬山窰仿龍泉劃花青瓷碗[57]。1980年在海南島瓊山明代萬曆三十三年大地震陸陷沉海的遺址中也發現有這類仿龍泉青釉劃花瓷片[58],1982年在大埔百侯中學明代嘉靖庚子年(公元1540年)墓中亦出土有大埔仿龍泉釉碗、碟、杯等器物[59]。由於外銷原因,近年來在日本界環壕都市遺址出土的遺物中亦有廣東地區仿龍泉青釉劃花碗,伴隨出土的還有明代青花瓷和日本"天正十三年(公元1585年)木簡銘記[60],天正十三年相當於中國明代萬曆十三年。在日本馬場屋敷遺址上層出土的大量明代青瓷、白瓷和青花瓷,其中亦有廣東仿龍泉窰青瓷,伴隨出土的還有日本"寬永通寶"(公元1636年鑄)銅錢[61]。1636年相當於中國明代崇禎九年。上述資料的發現極爲重要,它可以幫助印證廣東仿龍泉青瓷窰址的年代上限最遲是明代永樂二年,下限則可到明代崇禎年間。但其中大埔、龍川、澄海窰出土青釉八卦紋三足香爐,刻花大碟和青釉弦紋卷草組合紋蓋罐,故其年代可能會稍早一些,或許會到元代晚期。惠陽窰有些碗內中心刻印有"清"字,故有個別窰址的下限或許會到清初[50],至於更具體更準確的分期,則有待今後進一步的發掘研究。

4. 廣東是祖國南方重要門戶,早在漢代廣州已成爲我國官方與南洋諸國通商的重要港口。唐宋時期廣東與東南亞、印度和阿拉伯等一些國家貿易往來極爲頻繁,當時廣州已成爲中國國際貿易的重要都會,陶瓷則已成爲一宗重要商品投入國際市場。據《新唐書》載,我國與西方交通的海路,是從廣州經南海西沙羣島、越南東海、印尼、馬六甲海峽到印度西南的故臨,再西行到波斯灣的幼發拉底河口,復傍波斯灣的西海岸,到亞丁附近[62]。又據《蒲壽庚考》載,關於阿拉伯商人來華的航綫,多自波斯灣經印度洋,繞馬來半島以抵達廣州、廣州之外嶺南之高州,江南之揚州,福建之泉州,亦為自唐以來阿拉伯商人通商之地⑬。可見上述海路溝通了中國與東南亞、印度和阿拉伯等各國人民的文化交流和貿易往來。據《宋史·三佛齊》載,從廣州沿着海沿綫到汕頭的潮州和海南島瓊山、文昌、澄邁、臨高、樂會、陵水、崖縣等地,也是當日對外貿易的港口和交通點。這些地方在中外南海貿易史上,具有十分重要的作用。宋以後廣東海路交通路綫,仍以南洋及西洋諸國為主。上述汕頭、珠海、台山、瓊山、陵水和西沙羣島宋至明清陶瓷遺物地點,均屬當日對外貿易港口或海路航綫必經之地,其遺物絕大部分均係當日商船觸礁沉沒後所遺留下來的。發現的窰口計有宋代的廣東西村窰、潮州窰、廉江窰、遂溪窰、佛山石灣窰、南海奇石窰、文頭嶺窰;福建同安窰、安溪窰、建陽窰、德化窰;浙江龍泉窰;江西景德鎮湖田窰。元代的福建泉州地區窰、浙江龍泉窰。明代的江西吉州窰、景德鎮民窰、廣東惠陽窰、大埔窰、饒平窰、福建德化窰、浙江龍泉窰。清代的江西景德鎮窰、廣東饒平窰、大埔窰、佛山石灣窰、福建德化窰等。這些窰口燒製的各類瓷器,均係當日暢銷海外的商品。可見一千多年來我國的陶瓷不但經由陸地"絲綢之路"遠銷世界各國,同時還通過海上"陶瓷之路"源源不斷地輸出海外諸國。據宋朱彧《萍州可談》、趙汝适《諸蕃志》、《宋史·食貨志》、元周達觀《眞臘風土記》、汪大淵《島夷志略》、明費信《星槎勝覽》、鞏珍《西洋番國志》、《明史·食貨志》等文獻記載,宋至明代我國陶瓷由東南海路運銷東南亞、印度洋沿岸、西亞、北非五、六十個國家和地區,有不少是標明廣州、潮州、瓊州、泉州、溫州等港口輸出的。廣東窰口的產品過去在菲律賓、印尼、馬來西亞、泰國、巴基斯坦以及阿拉伯的一些國家和日本等地均有出土。特別是西村窰產品,極受國外人士的重視和喜愛,據林業強《海外遺留西村窰系標本著錄表》統計,海外有數十個單位和學者收藏廣東西村窰產品⑮。宋代廣東西村窰瓷器外銷數量之多,產品之精,工藝欣賞價值之高,由此可以想見。

5. 從現有的考古材料來看,廣東製瓷業鼎盛時期是北宋,其次是明清兩代,南宋和元代則比較蕭條,其原因是從南宋至元代,中國出口商品的主要港口,已從廣州轉移到泉州,所以這一時期福建泉州地區的陶瓷大量外銷,廣東陶瓷出口量相對大量減少。此外南宋高宗腐敗無能,無法抵抗金兵的入侵,處在戰亂時期的廣東。社會秩序極不穩定,同時元代亦由於貴族的殘酷統治,除了官營手工業較為發達之外,民間陶瓷工業得不到應有的發展,所以廣東南宋和元代陶瓷業的蕭條,是與當時的社會歷史背景分不開的。

6. 上述窰址和墓葬以及古外銷瓷遺物地點,出土的本省各個窰口的陶瓷,正在逐個填補廣東五代至明清陶瓷發展史的空白。但深入的調查研究則有待今後進一步的開展。

註釋

① 五代南漢建都廣州,它的勢力範圍包括現在的廣東及湖南南部的汝城、宜章、蘭山、郴縣、桂東、永興、耒陽;廣西的南寧、西林、樂業、巴山、融安、尤勝、興安、桂林、賀縣、梧州、東興、合浦以及海南島等地(詳見《中國歷史地圖集》第五冊,中國地圖學社出版1975年)。
② 商承祚《廣州番禺石馬村南漢墓發掘簡報》,《考古》1964年6期;麥英豪《關於廣州石馬村南漢墓的年代與墓主問題》,《考古》1975年1期。
③ 見上引麥英豪文章。
④ 周世榮《石渚長沙窰出土的瓷器及其有關問題的研究》,《中國古代窰址調查發掘報告集》文物出版社1984年10月。
⑤ 蕭湘《長沙銅官窰》,《中國陶瓷全集·長沙銅官窰》上海人民美術出版社1985年。
⑥ 主要參考廣州市文物管理委員會《廣州西村古窰址》文物出版社1958年;廣東省博物館《潮州筆架山宋代窰址發掘報告》文物出版社1981年;廣州市文物管理委員會、香港中文大學文物館《廣州西村窰》香港中文大學中國文化研究所中國考古藝術中心出版1987年;廣東省文物管理委員會《佛山專區的幾處古窰址調查簡報》,《文物》1959年12期;曾廣億、吳定賢《廣東惠州北宋窰址清理簡報》,《文物》1977年8期;曾廣億《廣東古窰出土陶瓷及有關問題探討》,《廣東陶瓷》1981年2期;陳智亮《廣東石灣古窰址調查》,《考古》1987年;黃玉質、楊少祥《廣東潮州筆架山宋代瓷窰》,《考古學集刊》1982年第二集;曾廣億《廣東唐宋陶瓷工藝特點》,《廣東唐宋窰址出土陶瓷》香港大學馮平山博物館出版1985年。
⑦ 陝西省考古研究所《陝西銅川耀州窰》科學出版社出版1965年。
⑧⑨ 林業強《北宋廣東窰》,《亞洲海運陶瓷遺物》牛津大學出版社(英文版)1985年。
⑩⑪ 鄧杰昌《廣東海康地區陶瓷》香港大學亞洲研究中心古陶瓷研討會論文1986年。
⑫ 陳智亮《廣東石灣古窰址調查》,《考古》1978年3期。
⑬ 詳見1982年佛山石灣美術陶瓷廠美術陶瓷陳列館前言說明。

⑭廣東省博物館彭如策《廣東潮州北宋劉𤩽墓》,《考古》1963年9期。

⑮㉜曾廣億《略論廣東發現的唐宋元明外銷瓷》、《古陶瓷研究》1982年第一輯。

⑯《嶺南叢述》卷五十七番商條。

⑰《瓊州府志》卷十九上。

⑱曾廣億《廣東陵水、順德、揭西出土的宋代瓷器、漁獵工具和元代鈔版》,《考古》1980年1期。

⑲⑳何紀生、李居禮《陵水縣移輋村海灘發現唐宋時代陶瓷器》《文博通訊》(廣東)1979年第8期。

㉑《太平廣記》卷二百八十六。

㉒張星烺《中西交通史料滙編》第三册,古代中國與阿拉伯之交通。

㉓廣東省博物館《廣東省西沙羣島文物調查簡報》、《文物》1974年10期;廣東省博物館等《廣東省西沙羣島第二次文物調查簡報》、《文物》1976年9期;廣東省博物館、海南行政區文化局《廣東省西沙羣島北礁發現的古代陶瓷》、《文物資料叢刊》1982年6期。

㉔曾廣億《海南島古瓷窰調查記》,《考古》1963年6期;曾廣億《廣東博羅、揭陽、澄邁古瓷窰調查》、《文物》1965年2期。

㉕㊵曾廣億《佛山鼓顙崗宋元明墓記略》,《考古》1964年10期。

㉖古運泉《廣東梅縣古墓葬、古窰址調查、發掘簡報》,《考古》1987年3期。

㉗黎金《廣州沙河雙燕崗發現元墓》,《考古》1960年4期。

㉘㉟《國際シンポジクム 新安海底引楊げ文物報告書》中日新聞社1983年。

㉙宋良壁《介紹一件元代釉裏褐鳳鳥紋蓋罐》,《考古》1983年1期。

㉚鄧杰昌《廣東海康縣出土兩件彩繪枕》,《考古》1986年4期。

㉛㊹曾廣億《廣東珠海、汕頭出土的元明瓷器》、《文物》1976年10期。

㉝廣東省文物管理委員會、華南師範學院歷史系《廣東惠陽新庵三村古瓷窰發掘》,《考古》1964年4期。

㉞㊲㊼(59)楊少祥《廣東大埔古瓷器生產初探》,《廣東文博》1986年1、2期合刊本。

㊱㊻何紀生、彭如策、邱立誠《廣東饒平九村青花瓷窰調查記》、《中國古代窰址調查發掘報告》文物出版社1984年。

㊳曾廣億《廣東博羅、揭陽、澄邁古瓷窰調查》,《文物》1965年2期。

㊴安溪縣文化館《福建安溪古窰址調查》,《文物》1977年7期;陳柏泉《江西樂平明代青花窰址調查》,《文物》1973年3期。

㊶㊽(57)楊耀林《深圳出土的明清瓷器》中國古陶瓷學術討論會論文1985年。

㊷廣州市文物管理委員會《廣州小北宋墓簡報》,《文物參考資料》1955年10期。

㊸黃雲鵬《景德鎮明代紀年墓出土的民間青花瓷》,《江西歷史文物》1983年2期。

㊺此係香港中文大學文物館林業強先生向筆者提供的材料(實物現存香港考古學會)。

㊾楊豪《清初吳六奇墓及其殉葬遺物》,《文物》1982年2期。

㊿曾廣億《廣東明代仿龍泉青瓷初探》,《東方文化》第2期香港大學亞洲研究中心刊行1985年。

(51)(54)廣東省文物管理委員會《佛山專區的幾處古窰址調查簡報》,《文物》1959年12期。

(52)廣州市文物管理委員會《廣州西村古窰址》文物出版社1958年;陳萬里《中國青瓷史略》上海人民出版社1956年。

(53)陳萬里《中國青瓷史略》上海人民出版社1956年。

(55)1985年12月筆者應邀訪問澳門時,曾經到澳門賈梅士博物院參觀,該院陳列柜中有10多件惠陽仿龍泉釉劃花碗,其年代被標明是"宋代"。

(56)曾廣億《廣東惠陽白馬山古瓷窰調查記》,《考古》1962年8期。

(58)曾廣億、古運泉《海南島明代地震遺址調查記要》1981年(未刊稿)。

(60)森村健一《界環壕都市遺迹出土の陶磁器の組成と機能分擔》、《貿易陶磁研究》日本貿易陶瓷研究會出版1984年4期。

(61)川上貞雄《新潟縣馬場屋敷遺址出土の陶磁》、《貿易陶磁研究》日本貿易陶磁研究會出版1984年4期。

(62)《新唐書》卷四十三(下)。

(63)《蒲壽庚考》第一章第33頁。

(64)此係1987年12月印尼耶加達馬立克博物館館長(印尼陶瓷學會會長),蘇瑪拉艾地亞文夫人(Mrs. Sumarah Adhyatman)到廣州考察時,在參觀了饒平、大埔明清青花窰產品後告訴筆者的。

(65)林業強《海外遺留西村窰系標本著錄表》,《廣州西村窰》香港中文大學中國考古藝術中心出版1987年,第75至85頁。

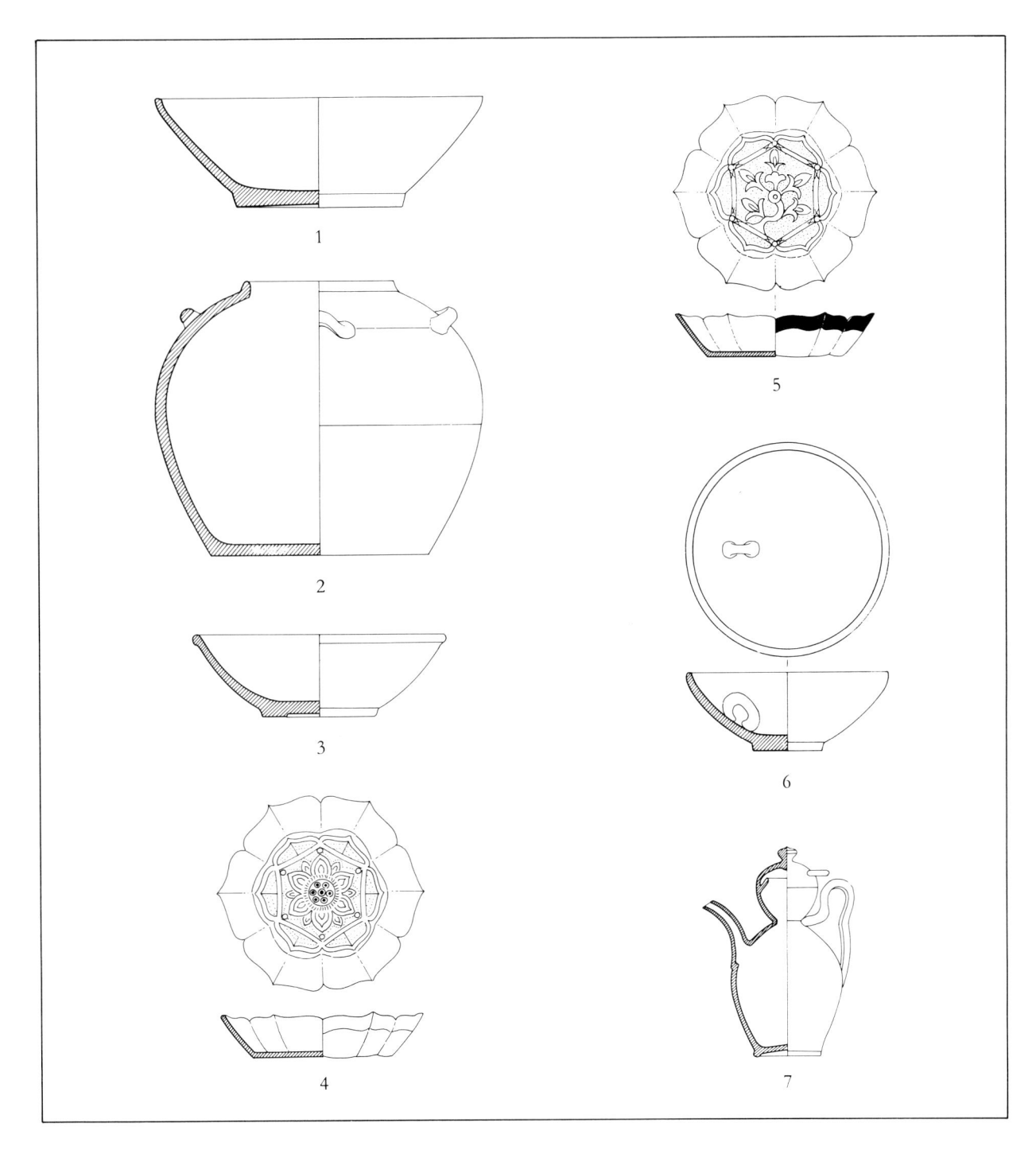

增城五代墓中出土器物

1. 晚唐定窑白釉瓷碗
2. 晚唐四耳陶罐
3. 五代青釉碗
4. 五代铜官窑菱形六瓣口印花碟
5. 同上
6. 五代铜官窑灯盏
7. 五代铜官窑葫芦执壶

Ceramics Found from a Tomb of the Five Dynasties in Zengcheng:

1. White glazed bowl, Ding ware, late Tang.
2. Pottery jar with four looped handles, late Tang.
3. Green glazed bowl, Five Dynasties.
4,5. Dish with moulded pattern and bracket-lobed rim, Tong'guan ware, Five Dynasties.
6. Oil lamp, Tong'guan ware, Five Dynasties.
7. Gourd-shaped ewer, Tong'guang ware, Five Dynasties.

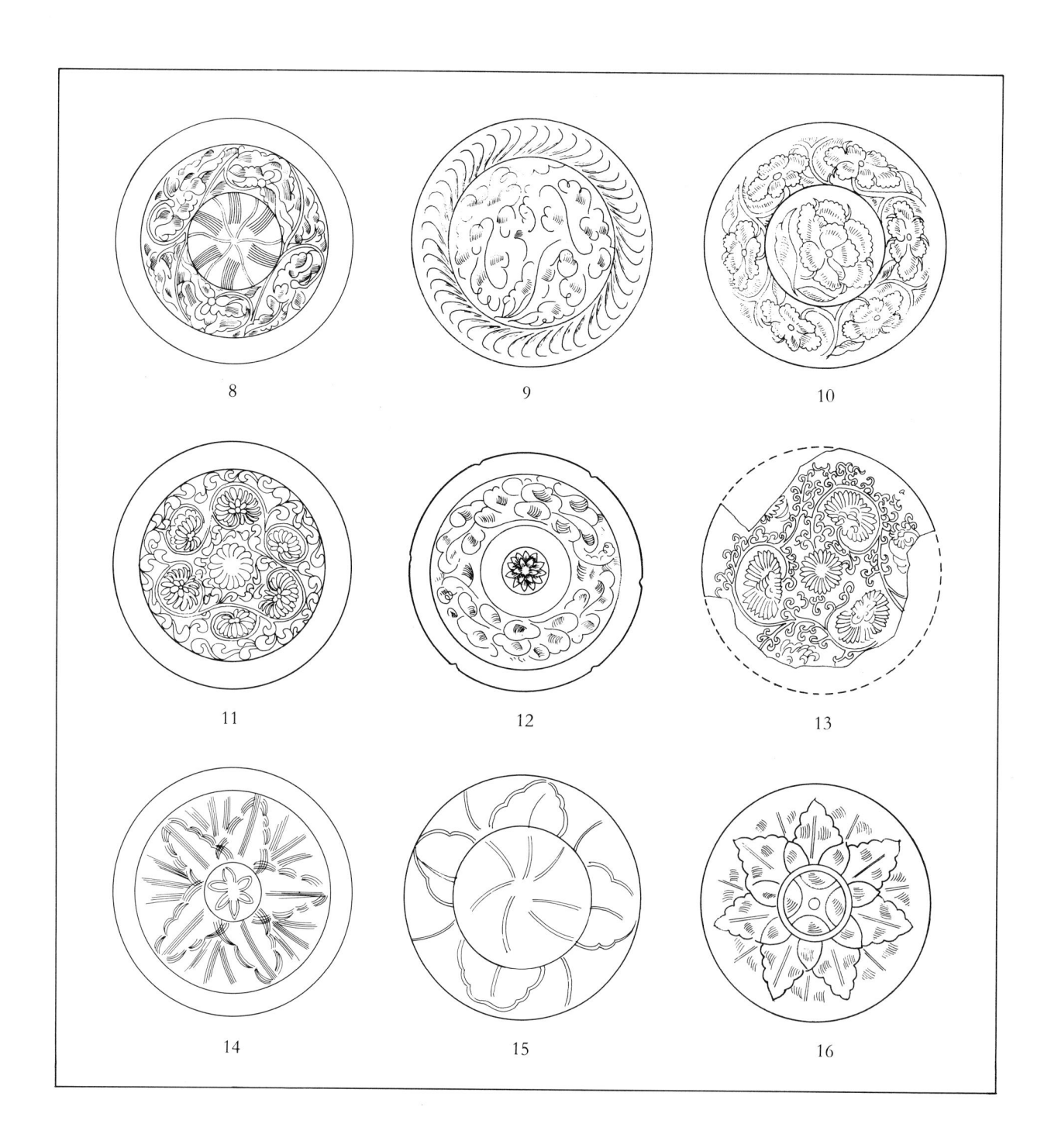

圖 8　北宋惠州窰刻花碗內紋飾
圖 9、10　北宋廣州西村窰刻花碗內紋飾
圖11　北宋惠州窰印花碗內紋飾
圖12　北宋惠州窰刻花劃印花碗內紋飾
圖13　北宋廣州西村窰刻劃印花碗內紋飾
圖14　北宋惠州窰刻花碟內紋飾
圖15　北宋潮州窰刻花碟內紋飾
圖16　北宋廣州西村窰刻花碟內紋飾

Decorative Designs, Northern Song:

8. Bowl, carved, Huizhou ware.
9,10. Bowl, incised, Xicun ware.
11. Bowl, moulded, Huizhou ware.
12. Bowl, impressed, carved and incised, Huizhou ware.
13. Bowl, impressed, carved and incised, Xicun ware.
14. Dish, carved, Huizhou ware.
15. Dish, carved, Huizhou ware.
16. Dish, carved, Xicun ware.

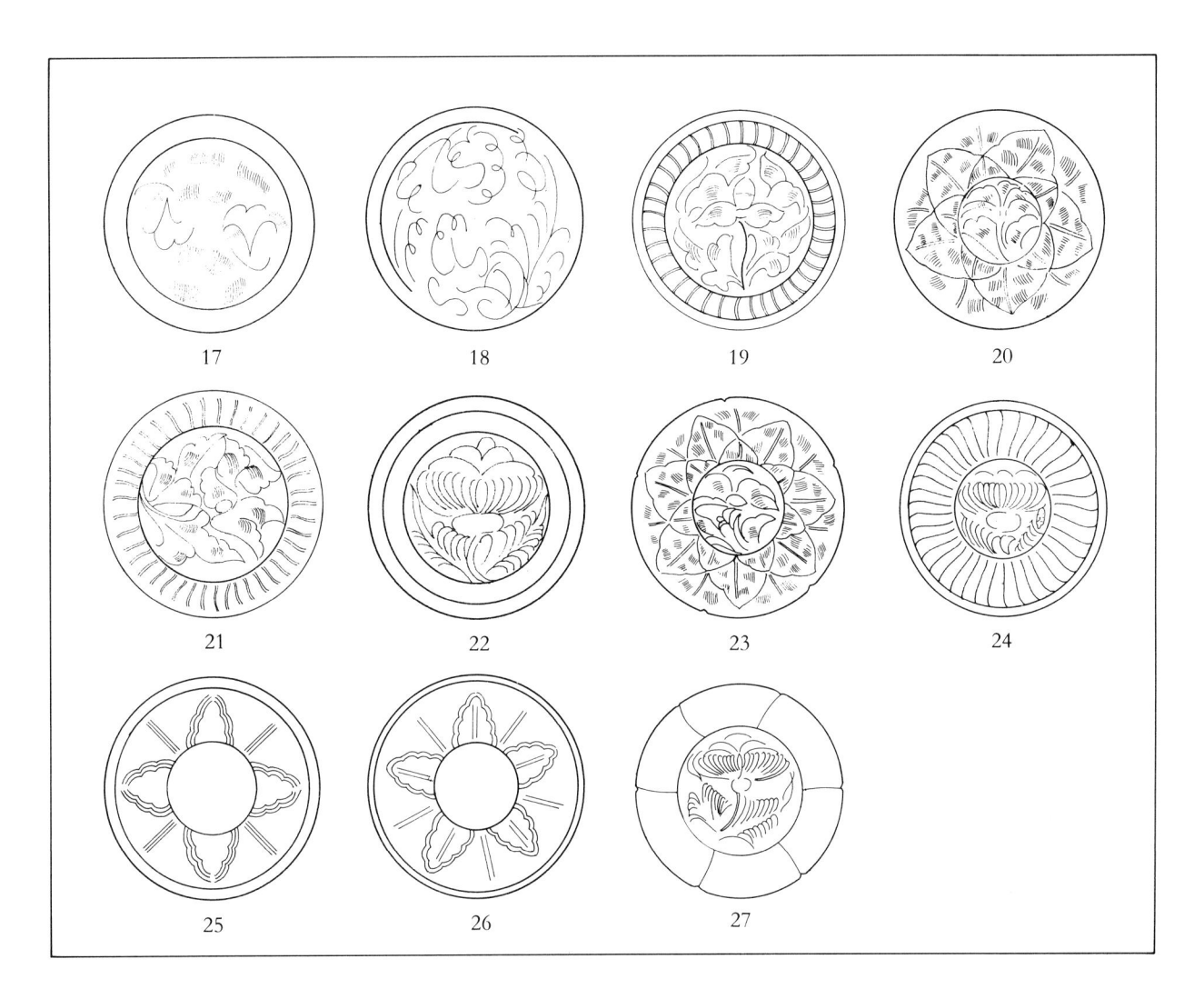

圖17、18　北宋潮州窰刻花碟內紋飾
圖19、20、21、22、23、24、27　北宋廣州西村窰刻花碟內紋飾
圖25、26　北宋惠州窰刻花碟內紋飾
圖28　北宋廣州西村窰刻劃印花瓷枕紋飾

17,18. Dish, carved, Chaozhou ware.
19-24,27. Dishes, carved, Xicun ware.
28. Pillow, carved incised and impressed, Xicun ware.

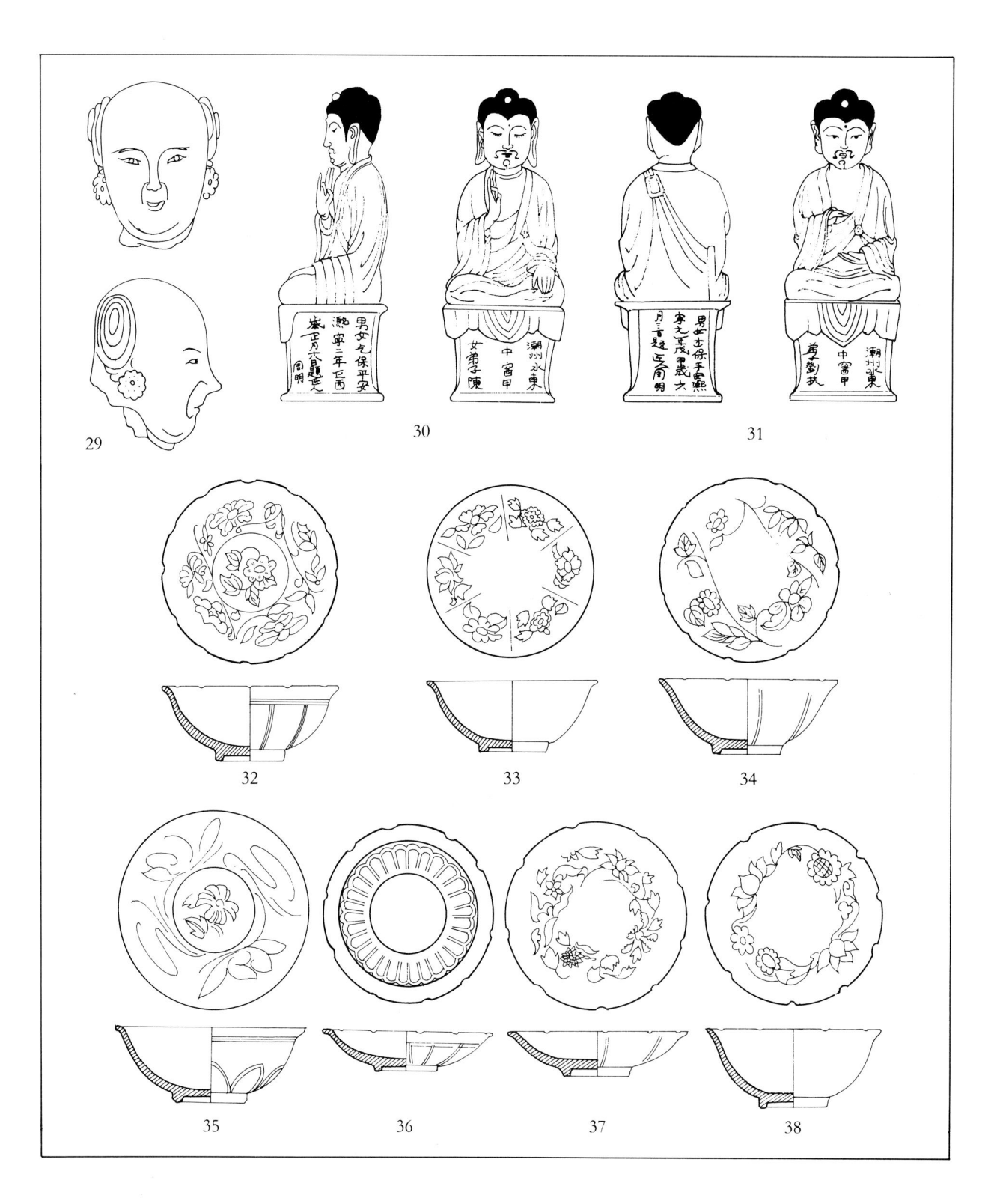

圖29　北宋潮州窰西洋人頭像（正、側圖、殘）
圖30　北宋潮州窰"熙寧二年"瓷佛像（正、側面圖）
圖31　北宋潮州窰"熙寧元年"瓷佛像（正、背面圖）
圖32-38　珠海出土的元代浙江龍泉窰瓷碗

29. Figure of Westerner, Chaozhou ware, Northern Song.
30. Buddhist figure with inscription datable to AD1069.
31. Buddhist figure with inscription datable to AD1068.
32-38. Longquan celadon bowls, found in Zhuhai, Yuan dynasty.

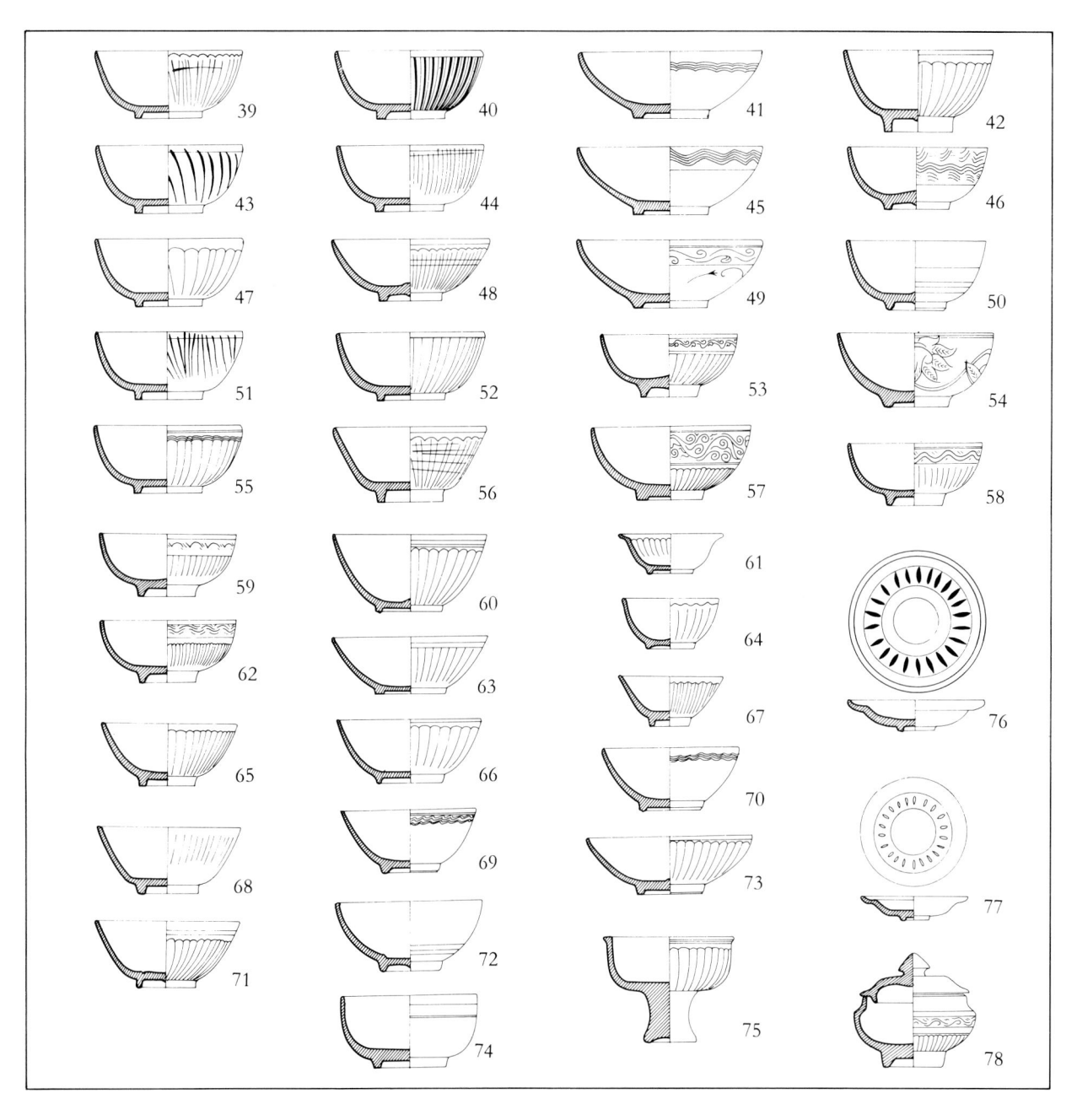

圖39、40、41、43、47、49、51、52、55、56、57、70、72　惠州明代仿龍泉青瓷碗

圖42、64、69　中山明代仿龍泉青瓷碗

圖44、45、46、48、50、54、62、65、68　惠東明代仿龍泉青瓷碗

圖53、58、59　大埔明代仿龍泉青瓷碗

圖60、61　龍川明代仿龍泉青瓷碗

圖67、73　澄海明代仿龍泉青瓷碗

圖66、63、71　河源明代仿龍泉青瓷碗

圖74　惠州明代仿龍泉青瓷碗

圖75　惠東明代仿龍泉高足碗

圖76、77　惠東明代仿龍泉青瓷盤

圖78　澄海明代仿龍泉青瓷罐

39, 40, 41, 43, 47, 49, 51, 52, 55, 56, 57, 70, 72.
Bowls, Huizhou ware.
42, 64, 69. Bowls, Zhongshan ware.
44, 45, 46, 48, 50, 54, 62, 65, 68.
Bowls, Huidong ware.
53, 58, 59. Bowls, Dapu ware.
60, 61. Bowls, Longquan ware.
67, 73. Bowls, Chenghai ware.
63, 66, 71. Bowls, Heyuan ware.
74. Bowl, Huizhou ware.
75. B Stem-bowl, Huidong ware.
76, 77. Dishes, Huidong ware.
78. Covered jar, Chenghai ware.

165

Five Dynasties to Qing Ceramics Found in Guangdong
Zeng Guangyi
(English Abstract)

This paper attempts to summarize the ceramic finds in Guangdong from the Five Dynasties to the Qing dynasties. Kiln site finds as well as artifacts unearthed from tombs and hoards are discussed.

I. Five Dynasties period.
Two tombs of this period had been discovered in Guangdong. One was the tomb of Liu Cheng, the third emperor of Nan Han and dated to AD958. From this tomb nearly two hundred ceramic pieces were found (Exhibits 1-5). The green glazed ware from this tomb provides important clue for the identification of Guangdong products of this period. The other tomb was found in Zengcheng. The ceramic finds include an assortment of different type of wares. The white glazed ones were probably of the Ding type fired in Quyang, Hebei, while the moulded dishes and ewer were from Changsha, Hunan (Figs. 4-6).

II. Song Dynasty.
1. Kiln site finds:
More than six hundred kiln sites of this period were located throughout the province. The most common products were green and dark brown wares, including daily utensils, objects for the scholar's desk, musical instruments, weaving tools, fishing implements, cooking utensils, funerary objects, kiln furniture, potter's tools and decorative items. The major type-forms are: bowls (Figs. 8-13), dishes (Figs. 14-27), large dishes, ewers, cups, tea bowls, bottles, jars (Exhibits 9-11), basins, pillows (Fig. 28, exhibit 22), *kendis* (Exhibit 12), waist drums, tripod censers, covered boxes, toys, figurines, tools for the potter and kiln furnitures.

2. Tomb finds:
About one hundred earth pit, stone and brick chamber tombs of the Song period were discovered in Guangdong. The ceramic finds include bowls, dishes, boxes, painted jars, pillows, censers, figures of the zodiac, funerary urns and coffins. Of these tombs, a few were dated, providing dating criteria for similar types, especially pottery urns. Brown painted wares of this period are of exceptionally quality. The painted vase from Lanshi, Foshan and the painted coffin from Haikang are excellent examples of this group (Exhibits 23, 29).

3. Submerged village site:
According to historical records, in the 33rd year of Wanli (AD1605) a severe earthquake occurred in Chongshan, Hainan Island. As a result some district in this area was submerged. A great mass of ceramics of the Song and Yuan periods were found in this site, which is easily accessible during low tide, and most of the finds were common export items from the coastal kilns in Jiangxi, Fujian and Guangdong. The site was probably a sea port for the anchorage of sea-going vessels.

4. Hoards:
Two hoards of ceramic finds were discovered in Linshui, Hainan Island. The finds were buried inside three large pottery jars and dated from the Northern Song period. Most of the pieces were local products, but there were also some coming from the Longquan complex in Zhejiang, as well as from other unidentified kilns in south China. A great quantity of export wares of the Song period was also found in a beach/sand bar site in Linshui. All these finds must have some relationship with the export trade in the Song period.

5. Export wares found in the Paracels:
More than six hundred pieces of Song ceramics were found in the Paracels together with specimens of the Yuan to the Qing periods. The majority of the pieces were from Guangdong kilns, but wares of the Fujian, Jiangxi and Longquan were also represented.

III. Yuan Dynasty
1. Kiln site finds:
Among the 34 kiln sites of this period, Suiqi and Chengmai have been investigated. Both sites produces coarse wares for the local market, and the latter continued production well into the late Ming period. Apart from these a few black glazed urns of the Yuan period have been discovered in Shiwan and Lanshi near Foshan city.

2. Tomb site finds:
Tomb site ceramic finds of the Yuan dynasty include pottery urns for cremated human ash and provincial copies of the Longquan celadons (Exhibit 55). Some *qingbai* ewers and Longquan celadon dishes and bowls were also found in Guangzhou, Dong'guan and Chaozhou (Exhibit 53). All of them were popular products for both local and overseas markets. The most unique finds of this period were the painted vases and pillows of the Haikang kiln (Exhibit 48). The pair of brown painted vases from Shenzhen were also very unusual specimens with a totally different painting style (Exhibit 62). They were probably fired in Guangdong, but the exact kiln site has still to be located.

3. Export wares found in Zhuhai:
In 1969 a large hoard of Longquan celadon bowls

and dishes was found in Wenzhoudu, Zhuhai. These open forms have either plain or foliated mouth rims and moulded in the interior with floral patterns combined with incised borders (Figs. 22, 33-38). All of them were common export items for overseas market.

IV. Ming Dynasty
1. Kiln site finds:
A. Local imitations of Longquan celadons:

More than 50 locations have been noted for the production of imitation Longquan celadon wares in Guangdong, and four sites in Xin'an, Huiyang were excavated. These Guangdong copies (Figs. 39-79) are characterized by an olive green glaze with either plain or incised/impressed overlapping petals on the exterior. The interior is impressed with a character in the centre. Open forms such as bowls and dishes prevail, but there are also basins, deep bowls, jars and censers.

B. Blue and whites:

Blue and white porcelain has been produced in Guangdong since the 16th century in the Jiajing reign. Kiln sites producing underglaze blue wares were located in more than 15 counties and among them, Boluo, Jieyang, Chengmai, Raoping and Dapu have been reported upon. Some of the Ming products were fired inside individual saggars resting on a layer of fine sand. Therefore sandy adhesions appear on the base. Similar sandy base types were also fired in Fujian and Jiangxi. Further studies on these wares will throw new light on the so-called "Swatow" wares so commonly found in the Southeast Asian countries.

2. Tomb site finds:
Very few funerary objects were found in Ming tombs in Guangdong. Black or dark brown glazed urns were used to hold cremated ash in earth pit tombs in the Foshan area, some of these urns were dated by ink inscriptions on the interior of the covers. Imitation Longquan celadon wares and white wares were found in early Ming tombs, whereas blue and whites appears after the mid. Ming period.

3. Blue and whites found in Shantao:
A hoard of more than sixty pieces of blue and white ware was found in the Jinsha beach in Shantao in 1971. There were dishes, bowls, jars and plates. Some of them bear a six-character "Chenghua" mark in blue and white on the base. There has been some debate on the dating of this group. The present author tends to put them within the Wanli reign in the late Ming.

V. Qing Dynasty
1. Kiln site finds:
The main product of the Qing kilns in Guangdong was underglaze blue ware. The major centres were Raoping and Dapu, producing popular blue and white wares for both the domestic and overseas markets in the Southeast Asian countries. The whole group can be roughly dated to the Qing period and there are a few with "Taiping" reign marks, corresponding to the "Taiping rebellion" period (c. 1859-60).

2. Tomb site finds:
Blue and whites are the major finds from Qing tombs in Guangdong. The earlier ones are as a rule better finished and painted than the later ones. Type forms include dishes, bowls and large covered jars (Exhibits 95, 95). From the early Qing tomb of Wu Liuqi three groups of pottery figures were found (Exhibits 104-106). They are valuable illustrations of the daily life of the early Qing officials.

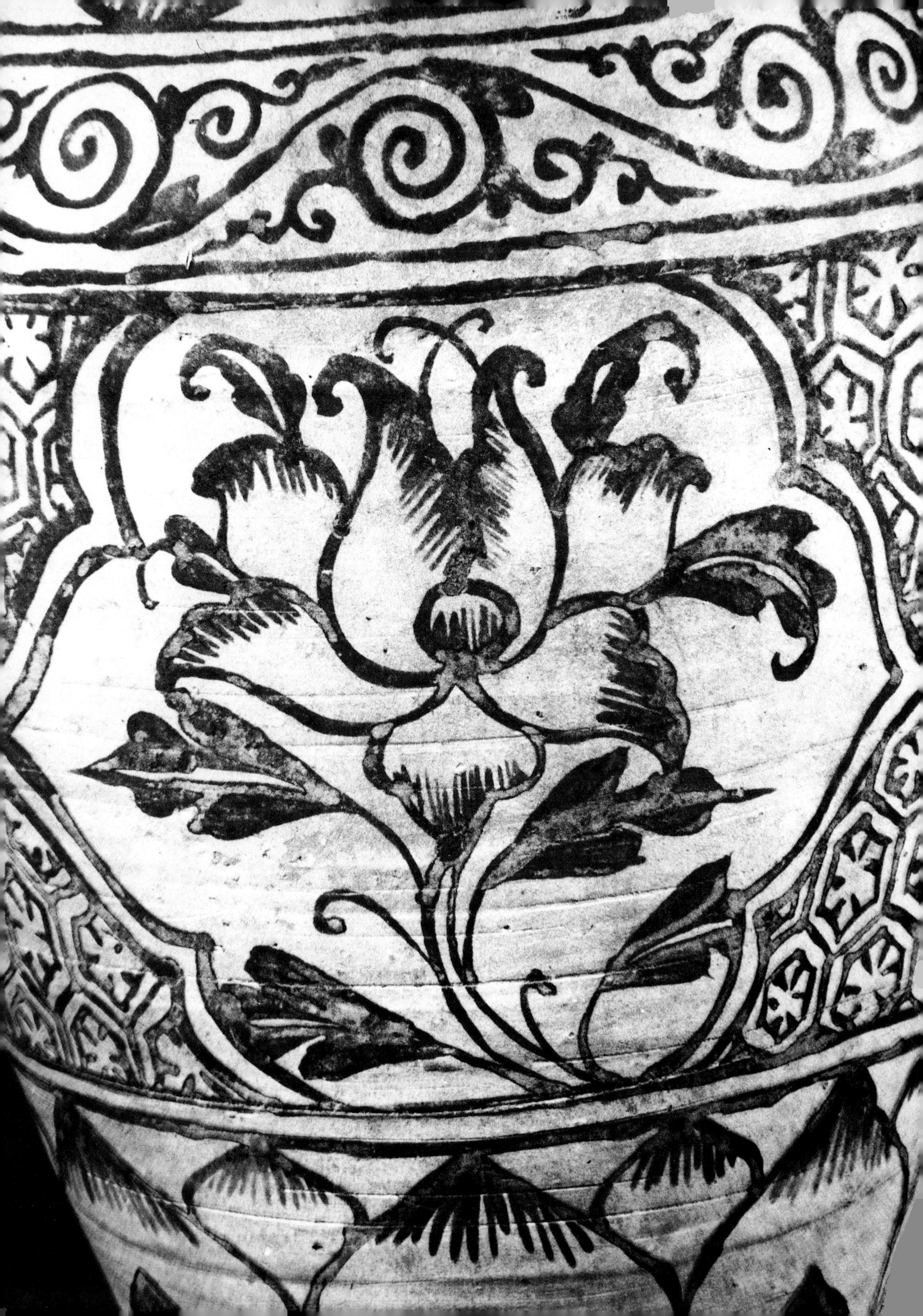

廣東瓷器與國內外瓷窰的關係

楊少祥

廣東位於我國南部，古代爲越人居住之地，它與全國一樣，新石器時代已有陶器生產，周代已出現了釉陶器，唐宋以後便進入了大量生產瓷器的階段。秦統一嶺南後，由於民族遷徙和海外交通發展，廣東陶瓷的生產技術、瓷器造型、花紋受到內地瓷窰的影響，並與國外某些瓷窰瓷器有一定的聯繫，本文僅就唐宋以來廣東瓷器與國內外瓷窰的關係，作一些初步的探討。

一、外地瓷器對廣東瓷窰的影響

從出土和傳世的廣東瓷器看，唐代以後，對廣東瓷器影響較大的外省瓷窰有越窰、定窰、磁州窰、耀州窰、龍泉窰、官窰、鈞窰、哥窰、汝窰、建窰和景德鎮窰等。

唐代，越窰對廣東瓷器影響較大。越窰是指浙江省上虞、餘姚、紹興一帶窰場，這裏唐代爲越州地，當時通常以所在州名命名瓷窰，故稱越窰。它自東漢時期已生產青瓷器，經晉、南北朝至唐代，瓷器生產有了更大規模發展，所生產的青瓷器，代表了當時青瓷的最高水平。唐代陸羽在《茶經》中已有"盌，越州上"，"越瓷類玉"等記載。廣東青瓷器，早就受到越窰的影響，在晉、南朝墓中出土的雞首壺、耳杯托盤、盆、唾壺、碗、盤等造形，已與越窰產品很相似，至唐代早、中期，廣東墓中出土的多足硯、碗等，亦與越窰生產品相接近。唐代晚期，受越窰影響的有梅縣市水車窰、潮州市北郊窰上埠窰。這兩處窰址，主要生產罐、壺、碗、盤、碟、杯、水注、盆、爐、研輪、研槽、器蓋等生活用品。瓷器胎呈青灰色，釉作青灰或青綠色，部分罐、壺器物體形修長豐滿，腹部壓凹直綫，壺嘴作多角形，碗、盤口作葵瓣形，足作壁形或圈足等，都是唐代中、晚期越窰產品常見的作風，其中出土的短頸、鼓腹、底有三蹄足爐，與越窰產品更爲接近，[1]可見二窰深受越窰的影響（圖1）。

宋代，對廣東窰場影響較大的主要是景德鎮窰和磁州窰。景德鎮窰是宋代重要的窰場之一，以燒制青白瓷爲主，因釉色介於青白之間，故一般習慣稱爲"影青瓷"。它的產品，在浙江、湖南、湖北、安徽、河南、陝西、四川以至吉林、內蒙都有出土，但與之關係密切的，主要是福建和兩廣地區窰場，形成了一個龐大的青白系。《中國陶瓷史》中，將廣東筆架山窰列入了這一系統。[2]其實，廣東與之有關的窰場，遠不止潮州筆架山窰一個，從出土文物看，廣東宋代不少窰場都有燒造與青白釉瓷相近的產品，在出土的瓷器中可以看出，碗、瓜棱形壺等瓷器造形，都與江西景德鎮青白釉瓷作風相似。生產盒子，是景德鎮宋窰的一大特點，不僅產量多，而且有專門從事生產的作坊，在廣東宋代窰場中，如潮州筆架山窰和廣州西村窰，亦大量生產盒子，這亦說明了在產品上，他們也有一定的共同點。他們之間的不同，只不過是瓷器製造工藝的粗細，和各地因製瓷原料不同，而使胎和釉色不盡相同而已。廣東青白釉瓷器釉多帶灰色，就是釉藥含鐵較多的緣故。磁州窰位於河北省磁縣，是宋代著名的民間窰場，產品極爲豐富，有白釉、黑釉、白釉劃花、白釉綠斑、白釉釉下黑彩、白釉釉下褐彩、白釉釉下醬彩劃花、白釉釉下黑彩劃花、珍珠地劃花、綠釉釉下黑彩、白釉紅綠彩、低溫鉛釉三彩等十多個品種，其中白釉釉下黑彩是其主要的裝飾方法，白釉釉下褐彩也是其突出的產品。它的影響，主要在河南、山東和山西省，形成了北方最大的民間窰體系。南宋以後，安徽、江西部分窰場，和廣東廣州西村窰、南海縣和順鎮文頭嶺窰、以及海康、遂溪縣窰，也受到不同程度的影響。廣州西村窰、南海和順鎮文頭嶺窰受磁州窰系瓷器影響的，除了如意形瓷枕、長方形瓷枕、腰形瓷枕等造形與磁州窰相似外，在彩繪技術上，仿磁州窰系的主要是白釉釉下黑彩瓷器。這種瓷器彩繪紋飾，在廣州西村窰和南海和順鎮文頭嶺窰中，多裝飾在碗、碟內底，紋樣主要是雲紋和花卉紋，雖然是仿磁州窰系釉下黑彩瓷器，但紋飾簡單草率。不似磁州窰瓷器紋飾那樣眞切生動，紋樣也遠不及磁州窰豐富，而且花紋色彩也不如磁州窰系產品那樣黑，而多呈醬黑色。仿磁州窰系白釉釉下褐彩瓷器，廣東目前所見，南海和順鎮文頭嶺窰有小量生產，品種是軍持、壺和鼓，紋飾僅見有卷草紋。（展品12）仿制產區主要在雷州半島的海康、遂溪兩縣。海康縣窰址衆多，主要分佈在南渡河沿岸的紀家、楊家、客路等鎮，已發現窰址六十餘處，其中十多處有仿磁州窰的釉下褐彩瓷器生產。遂溪縣與海康縣相鄰，窰址主要分佈在沿海地帶的楊甘、下元、港門、界炮、黃略、民樂等鎮，其中楊甘鎮下山井、白銀村、新埠、松樹園、大屋村窰，港門鎮黎東、坑口、洋仔村窰，界炮鎮犀牛地窰，黃略鎮蔴雷村窰，以及民樂鎮新灣村窰，都有釉下褐彩瓷器生產。兩地產品品種主要有罐、碗、缽、枕、棺等，其中罐和枕造形與磁州窰系瓷器相似或相同，花紋則與磁州窰系有較大的差別，它不像磁州窰瓷器那樣，以大朶的牡丹花作爲瓷器的外壁裝飾，而較多地採用多層裝飾法，一般瓷罐都有幾組紋飾。罐類腹部開窗或分格，畫纏枝菊、折枝菊、團菊仕女，肩部和腹下畫錢紋、卷草紋、蓮瓣紋、弦紋和水波紋是其彩繪的特點。有的瓷器外壁並寫有"仙會藍橋"、"長壽富貴"、"桃花洞裏"、（展品10、11）"金玉滿堂"、"積善之家必有餘興"、"旣醉以酒,旣飽以德"、"枕冷襟寒十月霜,小窗閑放早梅芳。暗香入被侵人夢,花物依人樂洞房"等吉祥文字和詩句。碗、碟、缽類則多在外壁畫卷草紋,口沿上施點彩或在內底畫大朵的折枝花卉。這些紋飾,筆法洗練流暢,活潑奔放,具有濃厚的水墨畫特點。從海康縣墓葬中出土有"至元三年"銘紋買地券,(展品48)"洪武通寶"銅錢(展品67),和遂溪縣窯址中出土有"大德九年"銘文碗模看,元明時期,海康、遂溪縣褐色釉下彩繪瓷器還有生產,只不過是元代瓷器更臻於繁縟完美,而明代則較為簡單而已。關於海康、遂溪縣這些釉下褐彩瓷器的年代,有二種看法,一種認為是宋代產品,一種認為是元代產品,從釉下褐彩瓷器的共存物,花紋、造型、墓葬型制等分析,筆者認為,海康、遂溪縣釉下褐彩瓷器的年代,並不是單一的,在宋至明三個朝代中均有生產,理由有如下幾點:

(1)在器物造形上,海康發現的口寬,腹微鼓,器形近似筒狀無耳罐,與宋代當陽峪窯剔花瓷罐相似,③短頸、敞口、平底,腹下收縮明顯的無耳罐與磁州窯系宋代陶罐相似,④瓷枕枕面作如意頭形,亦與磁州窯同類器物相同,⑤說明了這些瓷器具有宋代的作風。

(2)在花紋上,不少瓷器花紋較簡單粗獷,有的僅見在罐外壁畫簡單的長條形菊瓣紋,與共存有"至元三年"買地券的元代罐(展品48)相比,花紋沒有那麼繁縟細膩,罐肩部畫鳳鳥、喜鵲、纏枝菊組合紋,腹部採用兩層開光的裝飾方法也無發現,其中仕女團菊罐(展品9)中所畫的仕女像,頭部兩邊雙髻與潮州筆架山宋窯出土的女頭俑髮式相同,⑥說明了瓷器在花紋裝飾上有宋代的特點,而與元代有一定的區別。

(3)出土的完好瓷器,多出自墓葬中,埋葬時,罐外有用磚疊砌的圓形外槨,墓磚以海康蟹坡M11為例,磚長29,寬19,厚4厘米或長26,寬23,厚3厘米,與過去廣東發現的宋代墓磚大小相接近,而與海康縣發現的元墓為磚石結構,明墓用弓形大磚兩邊對合砌成墓室的作法有明顯的區別。

(4)由於瓷罐在墓葬中多作為裝骨灰使用,不少出土時有銅錢共存,以海康縣的釉下褐彩瓷器墓葬為例,在七座墓葬中,共出土銅錢35枚,除了一座明墓出土有兩枚明"洪武通寶"銅錢外,其餘六座墓中,發現的都是宋代以前的錢幣,最晚的是北宋晚期宋徽宗趙佶政和年間(公元1111年—1118年)鑄造的"政和通寶",1986年在海康公益窯發掘中,在器物堆積第二層也發現有一枚相當於南宋早期的金國"金隆元寶"銅錢,這些銅錢為研究海康釉下褐彩瓷的年代提供了重要的資料。雖然古代有後期沿用前代錢幣的習慣,元代也可能使用宋代銅錢作為隨葬品埋入地下,這在個別元墓中出土都是宋代銅錢不足為奇,但在數座墓中和公益窯堆積中出土的都是南宋早期以前的銅錢,那就不是偶然的事情了。因為宋代歷代皇帝都鑄造錢幣,海康、遂溪雖地處我國邊陲,在南宋統治下長達一百多年中並非沒有南宋錢幣流通,現海康縣博物館已徵集到出土的南宋建炎、紹興、開禧、嘉定淳佑五個年號銅錢三十多枚,如果釉下褐彩瓷器都是元代產品,那就不可能在埋有彩繪瓷罐的數座墓中只發現有南宋早期以前的銅錢,而沒有後期的錢幣。綜合上述幾點,可以認為雷州半島地區仿磁州窯系釉下褐彩瓷器的生產時間,大致始於南宋早期,那些花紋粗獷,具有宋代特點的釉下褐色彩繪瓷器,都應是宋代產品,這時期應是此地區釉下褐彩瓷器生產的早期階段。海康出土的元代釉下褐彩瓷罐(展品48),伴有"至元三年"墓誌出土,罐肩部畫飛鳳,喜鵲、纏枝菊組合紋和帶狀錢紋,腹中部作棱花形四開光,內畫一朵折枝菊,腹下部上端劃帶狀卷草紋,下端畫弧形四開光,內畫折枝菊。花紋繁縟精細,飛鳳、喜鵲纏枝菊組合紋構圖嚴謹不亂,繪畫比較嚴謹,比宋瓷花紋繪畫粗獷大大前進了一步,反映了這時期釉下褐彩瓷器生產進入了繁盛時期。明墓有二件釉下褐繪瓷罐伴有"洪武通寶"銅錢出土,瓷罐體形矮小紋飾簡單,僅見在腹部和肩部畫卷草紋,(展品67)瓷器發現數量也少,這時期應是仿釉下褐彩瓷器的衰落期(圖2)。

除了上述瓷窯外,宋代廣東部分窯場還受到耀州窯、定窯和龍泉窯的影響。耀州窯創燒於唐代,以陝西省銅川市黃堡鎮為代表,它以刻花犀利灑脫而聞名於世,並兼燒印花青瓷器,當時它的製瓷技術對河南省影響較大,涉及到臨汝、宜陽、寶豐、新安城關、禹縣均台、內鄉大窯店等窯場,嶺南地區的廣西永福窯和廣州西村窯也受到一定影響。西村窯產品極豐富,有瓶、壺、碗、爐、狗、杯、盒、盤、枕、盞等,釉色有青白釉、青釉、黑釉等,花紋有刻花和彩繪等。仿耀州窯產品主要是印花瓷器,一般是內底印一朵團菊;外壁印纏枝菊花。由於紋樣與耀州窯完全相同,所以《中國陶瓷史》中說:"西村窯青釉標本之中有印花纏枝菊小碗,除釉色不同外,看不出與耀州窯有甚麼區別",認為"有可能是使用耀州窯印模",或"原版印花模不敷應用,以複製或翻刻製出印模,以滿足燒造大量外銷瓷的需要……"。⑦定窯的燒造地點,位於河北省曲陽縣澗磁村及東西燕山村,是宋代著名瓷窯之一,它始燒於唐而盛於宋,產品以燒造白瓷為主,兼燒黑釉、醬釉、綠釉瓷器。瓷器裝飾方法有刻花、劃花和印花三種,以工整雅素的印花瓷器獨步一時,爲同時印花瓷器之冠,此外瓷器的覆燒工藝,也是其主要特點之一。廣東受定窰影響的窰址,是梅縣市瑤上南宋窰。產品有碗、盤、盞、盅、碟、壺等,釉色有青綠、青白和醬褐色三種,其中青綠和醬褐色釉瓷器製作較爲粗糙,仿定窰的青白釉印花較爲精巧,它胎骨細薄,花紋細膩,在碗、碟內壁刻劃或印蓮花篦梳紋,牡丹飛鳳紋和荷花飛鳳紋,印花圖案布局均稱規整,刻花瓷器紋飾流暢奔放,與定窰印花瓷器布局嚴謹、綫條清晰,密而不亂,花紋以牡丹、蓮花、游魚圖案爲多見,刻劃花瓷盛行劃花與篦紋相結合等裝飾方法基本相同。在裝燒工藝上,瑤上窰採用墊圈組合,取代廣東宋代常見的圓筒形和漏斗形匣鉢,將瓷器倒置覆燒的作法,也與定窰相同。龍泉窰位於浙江省龍泉縣,瓷器以釉色見長,它胎骨厚重,釉層較厚,以翠青、米黃、淡黃、淡紫爲多見,以梅子青、粉青爲最佳。廣東仿造這種瓷器,宋代僅見有潮州南郊竹園墩窰,器物也僅見雙魚洗一種,這種雙魚洗盤口,圈足,內底模印有凸出的雙魚,仿造得唯妙唯肖,幾可亂眞,僅在胎上稍有區別,可見當時該窰仿製龍泉窰產品極其成功。

明代,廣東仿龍泉窰瓷器有了新的發展,在惠東縣白馬山、大埔縣三河鎮餘鯉村、興寧縣滑壙坳等地窰址均有發現,(展品71,72)產品有罐、瓶、爐、盤、碗等,釉色多作青綠色,其中瓶、罐造型與同時期青白釉瓷相同。碗外壁多劃菊瓣紋、水波紋,內底多印"壽"、"福"、"寧"等吉祥文字。盤作盤口,弧壁,圈足。爐作直口,直壁,外壁刻劃纏枝花或八卦紋,都與龍泉窰產品較爲接近。從清康熙十二年《肇慶府志》物產記載,陶器"出陽春、新興,皆閩人效龍泉爲之,然不能精也"看,在清代,廣東境內仿龍泉窰瓷器還有生產,可惜沒有調查,情況不詳。除龍泉窰外,明清時期對廣東窰場影響較大的還有景德鎮燒製的青花瓷器。廣東明清時期生產青花瓷器的地點,主要集中在粵東地區,尤以大埔和饒平縣最爲顯著,品種主要是碗、碟、盤、杯等生活用品。瓷器紋飾題材可分爲山水、花卉、動物和文字四類,都是人們生活中熟悉的事物,民間工匠在創作的過程中,以圖案化裝飾在瓷器上,具有濃厚的民間色彩。其中嬰戲圖、折枝牡丹、佛手花、海螺彩帶、仙鶴等許多紋飾,以及青花發色等,都與江西景德鎮窰相同,用細沙墊燒器的作法,也見於江西東平窰中,馮先銘先生就曾指出,饒平縣"器物造形、紋飾、鈷料以及款識與景德鎮毫無二致"。[8]可見當時景德鎮窰對廣東青花瓷器影響極深。福建與廣東粵東地區相鄰,生產的青花瓷器也和廣東青花瓷器相接近,如福建安溪縣吉山沙坑窰、福昌窰發現的明鳳鳥紋碗,德化縣屈斗宮窰出土的雲龍紋碗、盤,在廣東饒平九村窰瓷器中也有相同的發現。[9]

明清時期佛山石灣窰比較特殊,除了仿製宋代官窰、汝窰、哥窰、定窰典型產品外,宋代著名的福建窰鷓鴣斑瓷、磁州窰白釉釉下褐彩瓷,和龍泉窰青瓷亦有仿造,但最成功的是仿鈞窰瓷器,這種仿鈞窰瓷器,世人稱爲"廣鈞,有的外國學者稱爲"佛山鈞"或"軟鈞"因其胎坯用陶泥製造,胎骨含沙,日本人又稱爲"沙鈞"。由於石灣窰仿製鈞窰的蟹爪紋、玫瑰紫、黑彩翠毛等釉色都極其成功,故有的鑒藏家認爲,鈞窰色釉是石灣窰的典型色釉,可見當時石灣仿製鈞窰瓷器有着豐富的經驗。但由於石灣窰和鈞窰瓷器燒成氣氛和胎釉成份不盡相同,仿製的鈞瓷也有不足之處,如梅子青釉難得純粹無瑕而多帶黃色,青釉中所帶的紅斑不如鈞瓷透徹流麗,在平滑釉上出現紅斑的現象也無仿造。

從上述外省瓷器對廣東瓷器的影響不難看出,唐代以後,在不同的歷史時期中,由於各種原因,廣東部分窰場瓷器,都受到了外省瓷器的影響,它們不但在瓷器造形、釉色、花紋上加以仿造,而且某些先進的燒造方法也加以效仿。有的瓷窰產品,如龍泉窰和磁州窰瓷器,從宋代至明清都有仿製,時間沿續了數百年,不少瓷窰產品並仿製得極其成功,如廣州西村窰仿耀州窰印花瓷,梅縣瑤上窰仿定窰瓷、潮州南郊竹園墩窰仿龍泉窰等,都達到了較高的水平,特別是明清石灣窰,有選澤地仿造與本地陶器胎釉厚實相似的官窰、哥窰、龍泉窰、均窰等名窰瓷器,使仿製品更爲精妙。但是較多的窰場瓷器,既有本地的作風,又有外省瓷器的特點,如海康、遂溪縣宋元窰釉下褐色彩繪瓷器,雖造形和繪畫釉色仿磁州窰系產品,但紋樣却不似磁州窰瓷器那樣,以大朶牡丹花,折枝花作爲器物外壁裝飾,而主要是採用在器物腹部開窗或分格,畫折枝菊花紋、蓮花紋、纏枝卷草紋和錢紋等作爲裝飾;宋代潮州窰、廣州西村窰等生產的青白釉瓷器,造形刻花等雖與外地瓷器類同,但釉色却多呈灰色。這些都與當地源料、燒造方法、生活習慣,和工匠接觸的事物不同有關,是當地因素和外來因素相結合的結果,當然也與燒製技術水平有密切的關係。

二、廣東瓷器受外省瓷器影響的原因

廣東瓷器受外省瓷器影響的原因是多方面的,從歷史背景和地理環境看,不同窰場應有所差別,主要有如下

幾點:

一是與客家人的遷移密切相關。客家人過去稱為"流人",後來稱為"客家人",有流散和客居外地的意思,他們起源於華北黃土平原的河南省,早在公元三一一年已渡過長江,到達江西和安徽,至唐代中葉以後,由於統治者的荒淫腐敗,導致了安史之亂,平定後,宮廷為了籌集軍餉,又加強了對人民的搾取,增設了繁多的賦稅,加上土地兼併嚴重,人民不斷喪失土地,民不聊生,連綿不斷的農民起義,又使河南、浙東、湖北、安徽等地戰火紛飛,導致了人民大量逃亡,出現了客家人的第二次大遷移。從《唐會要》記載:"寶應元年四月敕:近日百姓逃散,至於戶口,十不存半",⑩可知當時逃亡人數相當大。北宋以後,迫於外患,宋室南渡,國勢日弱,而上昏下佞,只知偷安,不思禦侮,以至元兵南下,又迫使客家人進行了第三次大遷移。由於當時廣東東部、北部、東北部和南部的韶州、惠州、潮州、嘉應州、雷州等地較為安定,逐有一部分客家人遷到了這些地點。《雷州伏波廟記》記載:"自漢末至五代、中原避亂之人多家於此,今衣冠禮樂蓋斑然"。⑪《崇正同人系譜》記載"世居渤海,散居中州,其後隨王朝入閩,而又於粵之潮嘉等處"。⑫梅縣各地相傳其祖先從河南遷來,海康縣不少人相傳其先輩自宋遷入,以及《太平環宇記》記載,太平興國五年至端拱二年(公元980—998年),梅州客戶367戶,而至相距百年左右的《元豐九域誌》記載,梅州客戶達6548戶,客戶人類激增近十八倍,都說明了唐宋時期,外地居民大量遷入這些地區的事實。明代嘉靖以後,江西景德鎮瓷器生產激增,御器廠一般只燒造部限瓷器,而欽限瓷器,則採用官搭民燒的方法,使民窯受到極大的損害。《江西大志、陶書》中就有"欽限瓷器,官窯每分派散窯,其能成器者,受囑而擇之,不能成器者,責以必辦,不能辦,則官窯懸高價市之,民窯之所以困也"的記載。而且當時京城派出監製瓷器的太監和當地官吏勾結,對百姓進行百般勒索,一到地方"凡百供應役使與無名之徵,歲該銀幾萬兩,奏帶參隨供奉,又該幾萬兩,至於燒造太監應辦物料與供應役使之人,歲該銀二萬七千兩"⑬這些開支,均落在當地人民身上,大大加重了人民的負擔。加上嘉靖以後,景德鎮災荒、瘟疫、兵災時有發生,如嘉靖十九年,"浮(梁)景德鎮民以陶業,聚傭萬餘人,會大水食絕,遂肆擄掠,村鎮為墟"。⑭嘉靖二十年"辛酉,初,江西樂平縣民黨傭工於浮梁,歲飢食,浮梁民負其傭值,盡遣逐之,遂行劫奪"。⑮隆慶五年,正值兵災、減災之後,朝廷又強迫燒制御器十萬件,引起"地方工匠等鳴告"。⑯萬曆年間,"陶戶既當大疫,又復增稅,財務勝涌,米鹽阻絕,亡命鼓譟,幾成大亂"等。⑰使當地民不聊生,一方面引起了強烈反抗,另一方面也迫使部分工匠流散遷移。大埔和饒平縣與江西相鄰,向來是客家人流入廣東的聚居地,這時期應有一部分陶瓷工匠流入了這些地區,這與饒平九村窯工傳說他們製造青花瓷器技術,來自江西景德鎮是一致的。一九八二年我們在饒平九村老窯坷窯調查時,還發現有一座清代末期窯工供奉其來自江西祖師的小廟。正是這些歷代流入廣東的客民和工匠,帶來了各地的製瓷技術,使廣東窯場出現了與外地相似的瓷器。所以,位處當時客家人聚居地的梅縣市水車窯、瑤上窯,潮州市北郊窯上埔窯、南郊竹園墩窯,海康、遂溪縣宋元窯,明代仿龍泉釉的大埔縣餘鯉村窯、惠東縣的馬山窯、興寧縣滑壙坳窯,和大埔、饒平縣青花瓷窯,出現仿外省瓷器,都應與此有密切關係。

二是與海外交通的發展,瓷器從海路大量輸出相關。中國瓷器的外銷,早在唐代已有不少數量,至宋代,由於朝廷在海外貿易中獲利甚厚,頗助國用,所以對海外貿易十分重視,採取了許多鼓勵海外貿易的政策和措施,如派遣使節齎敕書金帛往南海諸國招引商舶,對能招誘舶舟,抽解物貨到一定數量者補官有差,每年十月蕃舶歸時,舉行慰勞送別宴會等"以來遠人,通遠物",大大促進了海外貿易的發展。當時政府規定,我國與南海諸國進行貿易的商品是:以我國的金、銀、鉛、錫雜色帛,瓷器等,購買外國的香藥、犀角、象牙、珊瑚、琥珀、珠璣、鑌鐵、玳瑁、車渠、水精、蕃布、烏楠、蘇木等物,⑱瓷器成了我國主要的外銷商品。南宋後,由於銅錢大量外流,國內錢幣越來越少,造成了錢荒,嘉定十四年,又規定了凡購買外貿,以絹、綿綺、瓷漆之屬博易,不得用金銀銅錢,⑲這就更大大地促進了我國瓷器的對外輸出。當時廣州是我國對外貿易繁盛的商港之一,最早設立了市舶司,專門管理對外貿易,商舶往來不斷,國內不少窯場產品由廣州港大量運銷國外。其中耀州窯和磁州窯瓷器便是當時頗受國外歡迎的商品,在巴基斯坦卡拉奇,埃及福斯特等地都有發現。西村窯位於廣州市西部南海和順鎮文頭嶺窯與廣州相鄰,從窯址地處貿易港所在地,能廣泛接觸到各地窯場產品,其產品又主要以外銷為主看,窯內出現仿耀州窯和磁州窯瓷器,顯然與海外貿易有密切相關。

三是各地工匠的相互往來。廣東與外地窯工的相互往來,從文獻上看,主要在明清時期。福建《上杭縣誌》記載:《佛坑有碗窯二廠……除本地市場銷集外,亦有銷潮、梅各屬者,西路上逕廠主近年聘粵省工師,極意改良仿造描花各項……"⑳和康熙十二年《肇慶府志》記載:陶器出陽春、新興,皆閩人效龍泉爲之,然不能精也"等,㉑都證明了這一事實。當時各地製瓷工匠在相互往來中,都帶去了本地的製瓷技術,給對方窯場以一定的影響。明清時期,廣東粵東地區瓷器燒造技術和瓷器花紋等,與福建瓷器有一定的聯繫,正是此原因。

明清時期,佛山石灣窯仿製各大名窯產品的原因,有兩種說法,一是認爲,當元兵佔領鈞州時,那裏的窯工直接逃到了廣東,石灣的許多陶工或是宋、元時期官窯和鈞器製造者的直接後裔。㉒佛山父老亦有關於元代鈞窯工人曾在佛山設窯的傳說,謂當時石灣村有封姓人,傭於該窯場,後該窯他遷,此封姓二人於是在本村集資設窯,燒造鈞器,現封姓子孫猶存於石灣,多居於石灣四街。㉓張維持先生在《廣東石灣陶器》一書中,則認爲鈞窯本身是金元時代的產物,石灣之所以仿鈞瓷較多,是因爲當時的一般風尚,這些仿製品,不見得就出自原地陶工之手。㉔我們認爲,張維持先生這種說法較爲合適。因佛山石灣窯宋代主要是生產青釉、醬釉瓷器,元代產品沒有見到,但根據元代蔣祈《陶記》記載可知,當時"江、河、川、廣,器尚青白",並無其他瓷器生產,目前所見的石灣窯仿各地名窯瓷器,亦都是明清時期產品,所以元代石灣窯是否已有鈞瓷生產還難於確定,也就很難確立元代有鈞窯二人在石灣設窯,仿造鈞瓷的論點。石灣窯之所以大量仿製宋元各名窯瓷器,從其不僅仿製鈞窯瓷器,而且還廣泛仿製龍泉窯、官窯、汝窯、哥窯、建窯等宋元名窯瓷器,而這些名窯瓷器,在當時國內許多窯場都有仿造,如鈞瓷,除石灣窯仿製外,在鈞州附近和黃河以北地區許多地方窯場都有生產,官窯、哥窯、汝窯等瓷器,在景德鎮窯亦有仿造者,明清時期宋元各名窯瓷器,確已普遍受到人們的喜愛和珍貴,形成了崇尚的風氣,刺激着各地窯場紛紛加以仿造。佛山石灣窯仿製各大名窯瓷器,應基於這一原因。

三、廣東彩繪瓷器與東南亞窯的關係

唐宋以來,中國製瓷技術隨着中外貿易和海外交通的發展,得到了廣泛的傳播,不僅對相鄰的朝鮮、日本、越南、泰國等地產生了顯著影響,而且影響至西亞、非洲、歐洲等許多國家,出現了許多仿製中國瓷器的窯場。受廣東彩繪瓷器影響的東南亞地區窯址,通過瓷器的造形、裝飾方法、花紋繪畫風格等對比分析,主要是越南窯和泰國窯。

越南彩繪瓷器,始見於十一至十二世紀,即我國北宋晚期至元代初期,產品有青釉褐彩四葉罐、青釉褐彩劃折枝花蓮瓣盆等,瓷罐的裝飾法是腹部分爲四格,格內畫草率的草葉紋。這類罐、盆和花紋,目前在廣東窯場和出土瓷器中還沒見到,與廣東瓷器裝飾相似的,是十三世紀末至十五世紀中期產品。瓷器的罐類裝飾方法,是在罐口沿和肩部局部施醬褐色釉,腹部不施釉處畫褐色卷草紋,或肩部畫卷草紋,腹部下端畫重瓣蓮瓣紋;碗、碟類則在口沿畫卷草紋,內底畫折枝菊。㉕這些裝飾方法,在廣東褐色彩繪瓷中,都能找到其踪跡,如廣東南海縣窯就曾發現有口至頸部和腹下部施醬褐色釉,在不施釉的肩和腹部之間畫卷草紋瓷壺(展品12)。用折枝菊花紋、卷草紋和蓮瓣紋作爲裝飾,是廣東西南部海康等地窯場最常見的紋樣,在碗、碟口沿上畫卷草紋,內底畫折枝花的裝飾方法,在海康西園窯瓷器中就有發現,而且越南瓷碟中所畫的折枝菊花,畫法與海康窯瓷器菊花亦頗爲接近,此外在越南窯青瓷中,碗外壁施醬釉,內壁施青白釉的作法,㉖在海康窯中也有發現。(圖3,4)以上越南瓷器與廣東瓷器的共同點,表明了他們之間有着一定的聯繫。星加坡陶瓷學會出版的《越南陶瓷》一書中,有三件十五世紀的褐色彩繪瓷器,一件是無耳罐,頸部和底部施釉,不施釉的肩部畫重瓣蓮瓣紋,腹部畫折枝牡丹紋;一件是四耳小口罐,口、頸和肩上部施釉,肩下部和腹下部畫卷草紋,腹部畫折枝牡丹紋;另一件是壺,形狀近似瓶,長頸上畫卷草紋和蓮瓣紋,腹部畫折枝牡丹紋。㉗同類風格瓷器,在廣東深圳(展品62)和湛江(圖68)均有發現,如在裝飾花紋上,越南這三件瓷器所畫的蓮瓣紋,與深圳出土的四耳瓶畫法完全相同,牡丹花紋畫法也較接近。湛江發現的瓷瓶,與書中的彩繪壺更爲相似,不但所畫的蓮瓣紋、卷草紋,牡丹紋基本一致,器物造型也基本相同(圖5,6),可以說是同一窯場的產品。如果上述三件瓷器能確定是越南產品,說明越南和廣東瓷器有着密切的關係。但是《越南陶瓷》一書中,這三件彩繪瓷器除無耳罐註明出自印尼西里伯斯島外,其餘二件說明中無明確的出土地點,在越南考古瓷料中,也未見有這類瓷器確切窯口的報導。廣東目前雖然還不能認定這類瓷器產於何處窯場,但出土有此類風格瓷器,這就不能排除這類瓷器產自廣東或中國南部的可能性了。

泰國速古台窯和宋加祿窯彩繪瓷器,國外學者多與我國磁州窯作比較,自海康發現大量窯址和出土了大批彩繪瓷器後,經過對比,筆者認爲,泰國瓷器與廣東海康瓷器也有一定的關係。海康窯彩繪瓷器,從宋至明代都有生產,泰國速古台窯和宋加祿窯彩繪瓷器的年代在十三至十五世

紀,即在我國元代至明代中晚期,雖然由於兩地瓷窯生產時間有一定的距離,各地風俗習慣亦不盡相同,在瓷器的品種、造型、紋飾上都會形成一定的差異,但在泰國二窯瓷器中,還是能找到海康窯彩繪瓷器的特點。如在器物造型上,泰國某些罐類與海康窯產品存在着相似之處;在裝飾方法上,罐類腹部用短直綫分格,格內畫花卉,是海康窯裝飾的一大特點,北方磁州窯系器中並無發現,但在泰國陶瓷中,却有不少罐和盒類採用這種裝飾方法;在花紋上,以折枝菊花作爲裝飾,在磁州窯較少見,但却是海康窯罐、碗、盤類的主要紋飾之一,在泰國速古台窯碗類內底亦有發現,而且菊花採用意筆畫法,奔放飄逸,亦比較接近,此外,在泰國瓷罐、盒類中,腹部分格內常見畫方格紋,在海康窯一些罐肩部紋飾上也有發現。㉘(圖7)。

越南和泰國彩繪瓷器,與廣東彩繪瓷器類似的原因,從當時的歷史背景和廣東的地理位置看,可能與我國古代沿海人民移居國外,我國窯工受聘到國外傳授技術,和當時瓷器大量輸出有密切的關係。宋代以後,我國人民由於生活窮困、戰亂頻繁、或隨海舶經商等原因,曾不斷移居國外,在古代文獻中,如鄭思肖《心史》記載,宋亡以後"諸文武臣流離海外,或仕佔城,或婿交趾,或別流遠國";《宋史陳宜中傳》記載,"至元十九年,大軍伐佔城,宜中走暹,後設於暹"。《眞臘風土記》記載"唐人之爲水手者……往往逃逸於彼""餘鄉人薛氏,居蕃三十五年矣"。《島夷志略》龍牙門條記載"男女兼中國人居之",勾欄山條記載"軍士征闍婆,遭風於山下……有病卒百餘人不能去者,遂留山中,今唐人與蕃人叢雜居之"。《明史》三佛齊條記載"有梁道明者,廣東南海縣人,久居其國,閩粵軍民泛海從之者數千家"。《瀛涯勝覽》爪哇條記載"……蓋因中國人之來所創居遂名新村,至今村主廣東人也,約千餘家"。《海語》記載"華人流寓者,始從本姓,一再傳亦忘矣"等,都記錄了古代我國人民大量遷居國外的事實。廣東是我國華僑最多的省份,人員遍布世界各地,泰國和越南與廣東鄰近,來往貿易頻繁,遷入人數尤爲顯著,據說,漢唐時期已有兩廣居民移入泰國北部,㉙康熙年間,有雷州人莫玖率領一批華人遷入越南,定居在越南南部河仙一帶開墾,後來又不斷有華人成羣結隊流入越南,在該地建立了許多村舍,㉚形成了越南華僑以廣東人居多,越南和泰國某些地名與兩廣相同的局面。㉛廣東流寓國外的華僑雖然成份複雜,但主要是破產農民,漁民和手工業者,如果在流寓國外的手工業者中,包含有陶瓷工匠,那麼,這些陶瓷工匠就必然會帶去家鄉的製瓷技術,給移居國瓷器帶來一定的影響,使之出現與我國相似的瓷器。此外,泰國和越南在古代也曾聘請中國陶瓷工匠前往傳授製瓷技術,據說十五世紀時,越南曾聘請中國技師教與製瓷,1936年倫敦舉辦的中國藝術展覽,展品中有一件青花天球瓶,腹部橫書"大和八年匠人南策州裴氏戲筆"銘文,就是明景泰元年(公元1450年)中國製瓷技師在越南燒造的。元大德四年(公元1300年)暹羅國王敢木丁到中國謁見元成宗回國時,亦曾帶回一批中國陶瓷工匠。㉜這些受聘國外的陶瓷工匠,帶去的製瓷技術,亦會直接影響聘請國瓷器的風格。

瓷器是中國古代對外貿易的大宗商品,廣東窯場因濱臨南海,地處貿易港所在地,所產瓷器曾得到大量輸出,東南亞各國就是其陶瓷貿易的重要市場。泰國和越南位於中西交通必經之地,古代越南稱爲占城,泰國元代爲暹和羅斛地,暹和羅斛合併後才稱爲暹羅。宋代以後,他們雖然已有陶瓷生產,但還不斷進口中國瓷器,這可在《宋史·食貨志》互市舶條:"開寶四年(公元971年)置市舶司於廣州……凡大食、古邏、闍婆、占城、渤泥、麻逸、三佛齊諸番,並通貿易,以金、繒錢、鉛錫、雜色帛、瓷器市香藥、犀象……等物。"元《島夷志略》占城條:"貨用青磁花碗……燒珠之屬",靈山條"貿易之貨,用粗碗、燒珠鐵條之屬",羅斛條"貨用青器、花印布……"蘇門傍條"貿易之貨,用白糖……大小水埕之屬"。明《星槎勝覽》暹羅國條:"貨用青白瓷器……燒珠之屬"。《瀛涯勝覽》占城國條:"其買賣交易,使用七成淡金,或銀,中國青瓷盤碗等品,紵絲綾絹燒珠等物"等記載,以及泰國和越南現發現和保存有不少中國瓷器中得到證實。㉝這些外銷到越南和泰國的中國瓷器,有不少就是廣東窯場產品,三杉隆敏先生在《海上絲綢之路》一書中,就曾談到在泰國"但如蒐集到的是碎片,那裏面將混雜着福建、廣東等處民窯的粗劣青花,與越州窯青瓷,極爲相似"。㉞衆所周知,廣州港自古是對外貿易的大港,宋代以後,設立有市舶司,專門管理對外貿易,明代更與泰國關係密切,廣州市舶司專門管理中泰貿易。除廣州港外,雷州港和海南島諸港也是當時廣東地區的重要港口。據記載,宋熙寧年間,(公元1068年至1085年)海南島神應港是番舶所聚之地,㉟當時瓊山、澄邁、臨高、文昌、樂會皆有市舶,以船舶大小徵稅。㊱元至元三十年,(公元1293年)海南還設有市舶司,㊲管理貿易事宜,與之貿易的是何國商舶,宋元時期沒有記載,據清代記載,主要是東南亞地區的暹羅、越南、星架坡、柬埔寨等國商人,海南島是古代水路前往東南亞地區的必經之地,相信宋元時期與之貿易的國家,與清代亦不會相差太遠。雷州港位於古雷州府,即今之海康縣。它三面距海,北負高凉,有平田沃壤之利,且風帆順易,船隻不但南出瓊崖、東通閩浙,㊳而且外國商舶也常至此貿易,宋寧宗嘉定年間,雷州知州鄭公明,趙伯東就曾因使用銅錢博易番貨而遭到放罷。㊴廣東西南部的海康、逐溪、廉江縣窰址數以百計,採用龍窰生產的大量瓷器,單在本地是無法完全銷售的,這時期,也可能有一部分瓷器通過海南、雷州港與番商博易而運銷國外,使越南和泰國瓷器受到一定的影響。

　　縱觀我國褐色釉下彩繪瓷器,最早生產的是河北、山西、山東、河南磁州窰系瓷窰,南宋時南方江西和廣東部分窰場也受到了影響,稍後東南亞地區越南、泰國窰場中,亦出現了這類彩繪瓷器,而越南、泰國的彩繪瓷器,又與廣東等地同類產品有一定相似之外,那麼,當時磁州窰彩繪瓷器,是否通過我國南方窰場傳播到東南亞地區,又是如何傳播的,是一個值得研究的問題。

註釋

① 參見《太宰府展》福岡縣立明東出土的瓷鍑。
② 參看《中國陶瓷史》271頁,文物出版社1982年版。
③ 參看《中國陶瓷史》圖版25,文物出版社1982年版。
④ 參看曹克家、王書文《宋代民間陶瓷紋樣》上海人民美術出版社1960年版。
⑤ 陳萬里《陶枕》上海朝花美術出版社1954年版。
⑥ 廣東省博物館《潮州筆架山宋代窰址發掘報告》文物出版社1981年版。
⑦ 《中國陶瓷》259頁,文物出版社1982年版;
⑧ 《中國古代窰址調查發掘報告集》項,文物出版社1984年版;
⑨ 何紀生等《廣東饒平九村青花窰調查記》,中國古代窰址調查發掘報告集,文物出版社1984年版。
⑩ 《唐會要》卷八五。
⑪ 《海康縣志》卷八。
⑫ 引自羅香林《客家研究導論》第46頁。
⑬ 《明臣奏議》卷一六,唐龍:《停差燒造太監疏》。
⑭ 《明世宗實錄》卷二四〇。
⑮ 《明世宗實錄》卷二五〇。
⑯ 《浮梁縣誌》陶政。
⑰ 《明神宗實錄》卷三四五。
⑱ 《宋史》卷一八六,食貨志至市舶法。
⑲ 《宋史》卷一八五,食貨志香附。
⑳ 《上杭縣志》卷九,物產。
㉑ 《肇慶府志》卷二十二,物產。
㉒㉓㉔ 參看張維持《廣東石灣陶器》。
㉕ 見香港東方陶瓷學會1979年版。《東南亞瓷與中國出口瓷》圖版161、162、176、177、178、228。
㉖ 同上,圖版170。
㉗ 星架坡東南亞陶瓷學會《越南陶瓷》圖126至128,1982年版。
㉘ 參見狄．李察士《泰國瓷器》南澳大利亞美術館,1977年版,魏禮澤《東南亞陶瓷藝術》星架坡東南亞陶瓷學會,1971年版。
㉙㉛ 參看高事恒《南洋論》南洋經濟研究所出版。
㉚ 《簡明廣東史》355頁,廣東人民出版社1987年版。
㉜ 參見葉文程、丁炯淳《明代我國瓷器銷行東南亞的考察》,景德鎮陶瓷中國古陶研究專輯第一輯,1983年版。
㉝㉞ 參見三杉隆敏《海上的絲綢之路》第二章,引自中國古陶瓷、古外銷瓷《中國古外銷陶瓷研究資料》第三輯。
㉟ 《嶺南叢述》卷十。
㊱ 趙汝适《諸番志》瓊州條。
㊲ 楊德春《海南島古代簡史》61頁。
㊳ 參看《讀史方輿記要》
㊴ 《宋會要輯稿》職官。

圖 1
A: 梅縣市水車窰生產的碗碟
B: 梅縣市出土的三足爐

圖 2
A: 宋褐色彩繪罐，同出銅錢有"太平通寶"一枚，"紹聖元寶"一枚，"聖宋元寶"一枚，"元平通寶"一枚。
B: 宋褐色彩繪罐，同出銅錢有"太平通寶"五枚，"皇宋通寶"一枚，"熙寧通寶"一枚。
C: 元褐色彩繪罐，同出土有"至元三年"買地券。
D: 明褐色彩繪罐，同出土有"洪武通寶"銅錢。

Fig. 1
A. Bowls and dish from Shuiche kiln, Meixian.
B. Tripod censer from Meixian City.

Fig. 2
A. Brown painted jar containing Song coins of the reigns of "Taiping", "Shaosheng", "Shengsong", and "Yuanfeng".
B. Brown painted jar containing Song coins of the reigns of "Taiping", "Huangsong" and "Xining".
C. Brown painted jar, found together with a tomb tablet datable to the 3rd year of Zhiyuan of the Yuan dynasty.
D. Brown painted jar found together with "Hongwu" coins of the Ming dynasty.

圖 3
A: 越南瓷繪畫的折枝菊(選自《東南亞瓷與中國出口瓷》)
B: 泰國速古窯瓷繪畫的折枝菊紋(選自《泰國陶瓷》)
C: 海康瓷器繪畫的折枝菊紋。

圖 4
A: 海康縣公盆窯生產的醬釉碗
B: 越南生產的醬釉碗(選自《東南亞瓷與中國出口瓷》)

Fig. 3
A. Chrysanthemun spray in Vietnamese ceramics.
(After *Southeast Asian and Chinese Trade Pottery.*)
B. Chrysanthemun spray in Sukhothai ceramics of Thailand.
(After *Thai Ceramics*)
C. Chrysanthemun spray found on ceramics from Haikang.

Fig. 4
A. Brown glazed bowl from Gongyi kiln, Haikang County.
B. Brown glazed bowl from Vietnam.
(After *Southeast Asian and Chinese Trade Pottery.*)

5A

5B

5C

圖 5
A、B、越南陶罐（選自《越南陶瓷》）
C：深圳南頭出土的陶瓶

Fig. 5
A. Brown painted jars Vietnam.
(After *Vietnamese Ceramics*)
B. Vase with brown painting from Nantao, Shenzhen.

圖 6
A: 越南陶壺（選自《越南陶瓷》）
B: 湛江出土的陶瓶

圖 7
A: 泰國宋加祿窯瓷罐（選自東南亞陶瓷藝術》）
B: 海康出土的瓷罐
C: 海康瓷器繪畫的方格紋。

Fig. 6
A. Kendi from Vietnam.
(After *Vietnamese Ceramics*)
B. Vase, unearthed in Zhanjiang.

Fig. 7
A. Swankhalok jar, from Thailand.
(After *Southeast Asian and Chinese Trade Pottery*.)
B. Jar from Haikang.
C. Square pattern found on painted ceramics from Haikang.

Guangdong Ceramics and their Relationships with Other Chinese and Foreign Wares

Yang Shaoxiang

(English Abstract)

1. Relationships with other Chinese wares:

a. Yueyao:

The influence of Yueyao in Guangdong ceramics was first seen in the finds from the Jin to the Southern Dynasties tombs in Guangdong. The Yueyao features are more prominent in the inkslabs and bowls from the Tang tombs, as well as in the kiln wasters from the Shuiche and Shangfou kilns in Guangdong (Fig. 1).

b. Jingdezhen:

Apart from Chaozhou kiln site, the Xicun kiln and a great many sites in Guangdong produced *qingbai* wares after the Jingdezhen tradition. The standard types of bowl, lobed ewers and covered boxes were made in massive quantity, but the quality varied and was generally coarser than the Jiangxi ones, and the glaze is invariably greyish in tone due to the higher iron content.

c. Cizhou ware:

Cizhou wares are well-known for their rich varieties in decorative techniques. Two of these are found in Guangdong, namely painting in black and brown. The former technique was employed by the potters of the Wentouling kiln in Nanhai and the Xicun kiln in Guangzhou, but the painting was normally much simplified and sketchily executed on the interior of bowls and dishes. Pillows were also produced in these two sites after the Cizhou standard forms. A small quantity of brown painted wares, such as *kendis*, ewers and waist drums were also made in Wentouling, but the main centre of production of this type of ware was located in the two counties of Haikang and Suiqi in the Leizhou Peninsula. The jars and pillows share common forms with Cizhou, but the painting was done in a very different style. They were not boldly executed, but arranged in bands with panels, and sometimes with inscriptions or auspicious phrases as decorative elements. Judging from datable specimens, the brown painted tradition in Leizhou started some time in the early part of the Southern Song and continued well into the early Ming in the Hongwu Reign. (Fig. 2)

d. Northern celadon:

Two of the kiln sites in the Lingnan area show distinctive features of the Yaozhou yao (Northern celadon tradition) in Shaanxí province in northern China, namely the Yongfu kiln in Guangxi and the Xicun kiln in Guangzhou. The green glazed bowl with impressed design of chrysanthemun medallion and floral scrolls from Xicun duplicates exactly the prototypes found in Yaozhou.

e. Dingyao:

This type of delicate white ware was imitated in the Yaoshang kiln of the Southern Song period in Meixian City. The well arranged designs of birds and flowers were finely incised or moulded on white glazed bowls or dishes, which were fired upside-down as in Dingyao in ringed saggars instead of the usual cylindrical or conical saggars popular in Guangdong.

f. Longquan celadon:

The typical Longquan celadon dish with sprigged double-fish was imitated in the Zhuyuandun kiln in the Southern suburb, Chaozhou. Both the glaze and potting are identical to the Zhejiang ones, the only difference is the body texture and colour. Longquan celadons were also imitated by the Guangdong potters in the Ming dynasty. Kiln sites producing these type of copies were mainly located in Huidong, Dapu and Xingning. The glaze is usually olive green. The bowls are incised on the outside with petals or waves with the interior impressed with a single character.

g. Other wares:

In eastern Guangdong, especially in Dapu and Raoping, blue and white porcelain wares were produced in the Ming and Qing periods, sharing the same tradition with Fujian and Jiangxi. In Shiwan, Jun type ware was produced in massive quantity during the Ming and Qing periods, but the body was never so high fired, and invariably tempered with sand, hence the terms "Soft Jun" and "Sandy Jun".

2. Causes for the interaction

a. The migration of the Hakkas:

The migrations of the Hakka people throughout the centuries had contributed immensely to the interaction and influence of ceramic technology between Guangdong and other provincial centres for ceramics. The most significant was the great migration occurred in the late Song. Moreover in the middle Ming, in the 16th century, because of harsh tax, combined with unreasonable conscript labour and famine, a great many potters left Jingdezhen. Some of them must have migrated to the northern part of Guangdong, especially to Dapu and Raoping, bringing with them the technique of producing blue and white and celadon wares.

b. The development of overseas trade:

Since Tang times, a great deal of ceramics had been exported to overseas countries. During the Song period, this trade expanded further under the direct management and promotion of the government. Special policies and institutions were enforced to encourage export trade. Envois were sent to the South Seas and a special Maritime Trade Commissioner was established in Guangzhou to manage and supervise the trading activities.

c. The mobility of the potters:

According to documentary evidences, potters often moved from one place to another. The technique of making ceramics thus also traveled with these artisans. It was recorded that Guangdong artisans were employed by the ceramic factories in Shanghang, Fujian and imitation Longquan celadon wares were made by Fujian craftsmen working in Zhaoqing, Guangdong. This type of technical exchange brought forth a common style in most of the ceramic wares in these coastal provinces during the Ming and Qing periods. However, in view of recent research, the old belief that Shiwan pottery was started by Junyao potters migrated to Guangdong should be eschewed, as so far no reliable specimens of Shiwan ware datable to the Yuan exists.

3. The relationship with Southeast Asian wares

a. Vietnamese ceramics:

The brown painted wares of Vietnamese ceramics of the late 13th to 15th centuries show a very similar style to the painted pieces from Nanhaixian and Haikang kilns. The jars or pots are glazed brown along the neck and shoulder, below which are brown paintings of classical scroll (Fig. 12) or overlapping lotus petals done on the unglazed biscuit. The open forms, such as bowls and dishes are painted with classical scroll on the mouthrim, enclosing a chrysanthemun spray in the centre. The latter type was found in the Xiyuan kiln in Haikang. There is also another type of bowls with outside wall glazed in brown, but the interior in *qingbai*. This is found both in Vietnam and Haikang. (Fig. 3, 4) Finally there is a group of brown painted wares which are found both in Vietnam and Guangdong (Exhibit 62, Fig. 6B). The brown painting is finely executed and is done on an unglazed buff biscuit. Most of the pieces found in Southeast Asian sites have been attributed to a Vietnamese provenance, but so far no definite kiln site in Vietnam has been located. Identical pieces have been unearthed in Shenzhen and Zhanjiang, Guangdong. Thus it is not impossible that the whole group was fired in Guangdong or South China.

b. Thai ceramics:

Students of ceramics have long since been trying to trace the origin of Sukhotai and Sawankholok wares of the 13th to 15th centuries to the Cizhou wares of north China. However, in light of recent discovery, a closer affinity can be found in the Haikang wares from Guangdong. The brown paintings on the pots are arranged in a very similar style of rectangular panels separated by short straight lines with floral (normally chrysanthemun) sprays as the main decorative motif. Sometimes the panels are filled up with net pattern. The same type of spray is also found in the interior of bowls and dishes. (Fig. 7). None of these features are found in the Cizhou pieces.

c. Causes for the interaction:

The influence of Guangdong ceramics on the Southeast Asian wares can best be understood from a historical perspective. Over the centuries a multitude of Chinese from south China migrated to the overseas countries. Among these overseas Chinese, there were farmers, fishermen and craftsmen. In the last category, there must have been some potters. Moreover there is enough historical evidence to support that Chinese potters were recruited by Thai or Vietnamese potteries. The colossal export ceramics trade also brought forth a direct impact of the Chinese ceramic styles on the local wares of Southeast Asian countries.

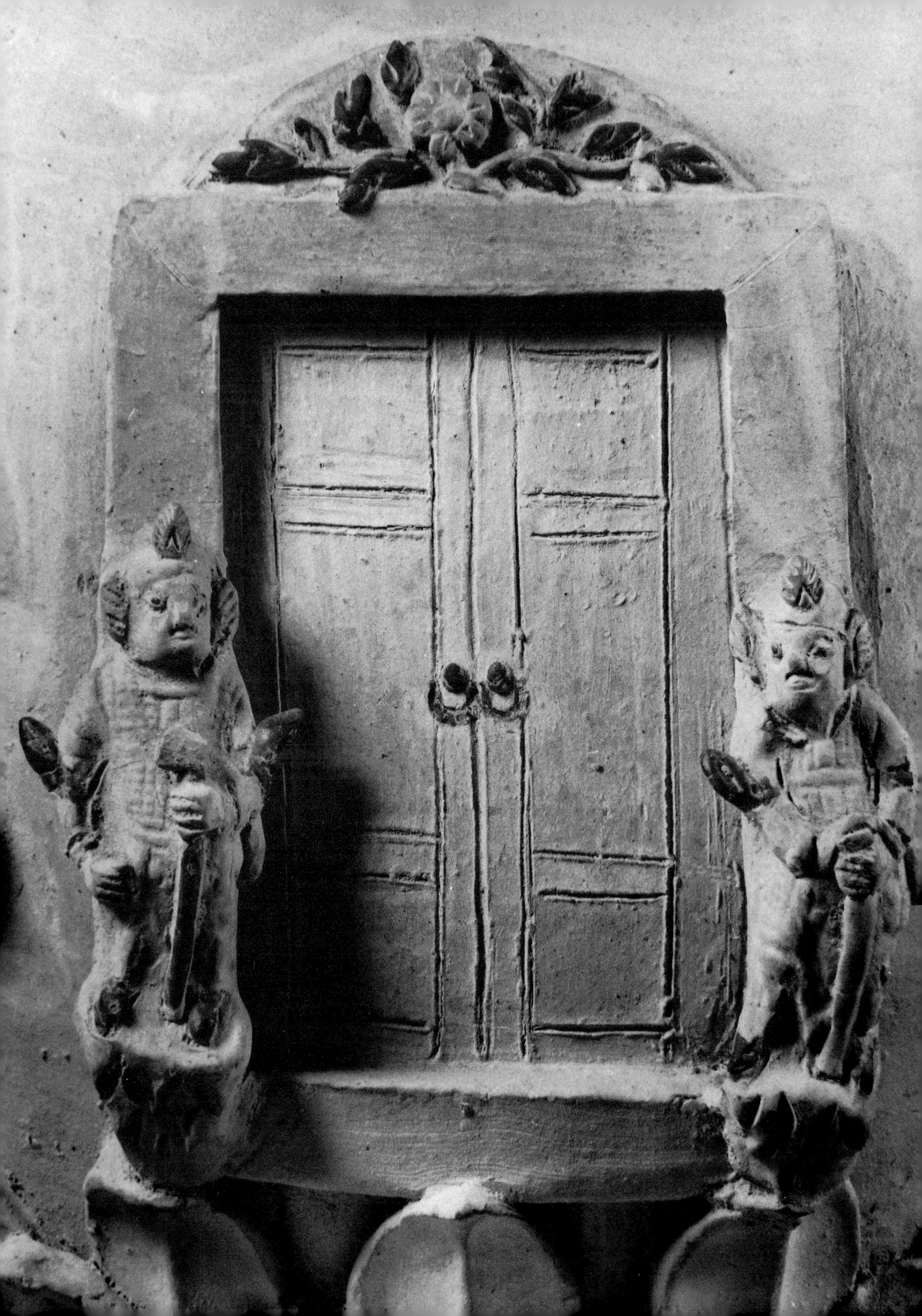

淺析廣東古代陶罈

朱非素

廣東境內各地出土的宋元明時期的各類陶罈(罐)，形制多樣，花紋別具一格，有鮮明的時代特徵。器類有堆塑人物罈、多角罐、釉陶罈和瓷罈等。其中堆塑人物的圖象相當複雜，題材之廣泛包括宗教活動、佛像、樂舞伎、蟠龍、虎、飛鳥神獸、十二生肖俑等；用堆塑、模印堆貼、劃刻、雕刻等表現技法使其形象栩栩如生，爲研究廣東造型藝術史提供了不可多得的實物資料。絕大多數陶罈和罐從火葬墓中出土，火葬作爲一種同佛教信仰有密切關聯的葬俗，曾在廣東流行了六百多年。本文僅就火葬習俗、宋元明代各類陶罈的形制特點、陶罈的造型藝術給予人們的啓示等問題，提出一些粗淺的認識。

一、

古籍中有關火葬的記載，遠在先秦已出現，《墨子·節葬下》卷六談到："秦之西有儀渠之國者，其親戚死，聚柴薪而焚之，燻上，謂之登遐，然後成爲孝子，此上以爲政，下以爲俗"。儀渠國在陝西之西，春秋戰國時是戎國之地。漢以後的史籍亦記載有火葬，《後漢書·南蠻西南夷列傳》卷八十六："冉駹者，武帝所開。元鼎六年，以爲汶山郡。……其山有六夷七羌九氐，各有部落。其王侯頗知文書，而法嚴重。貴婦人，黨母族。死則燒其屍"。漢置汶山郡地望位於現在四川省茂縣以北。《南史卷七十八夷貊上·海南諸國》記載："林邑國，本漢日南郡象林縣，古越裳界也。……其國俗，居處爲閣，名曰干蘭。……死者焚之中野，謂之火葬"。古林邑國在越南南部。上述史料証明了古代少數民族地區，包括古代百粵都曾流行火葬習俗。《新五代史·高祖皇后李氏傳》記載乾祐三年三月，李太后得重病，"謂帝曰：'我死，焚其骨送范陽佛寺，無使我爲虜地鬼也！'遂卒。帝與皇后、宮人、宦者、東西班皆被發徒跣，扶舁其柩至賜地，焚其骨，穿地而葬焉"。上述這條材料說明，到了五代十國時期，皇族死後亦有用火葬的，遺囑中指定送骨灰進范陽佛寺保存，無疑的，此舉已同信仰佛教有關。

西漢晚期佛教從印度傳入中國後，開始信仰佛教的只是少數西域商人、僧人和當時的皇族。至西晉以前，外來的佛教，經歷了二百多年的傳播、中外交流，兩晉南北朝時，佛教開始興盛，建佛寺、造佛像已很盛行。有名的廣州光孝寺建於東晉，曲江縣南華寺、清遠縣峽山古寺、廣州六榕寺分別始建於南朝梁天監三年(504年)、梁武帝普通元年(520年)和梁大同三年(537年)。由於上層權貴的提倡並身體力行，到了隋唐，佛教盛行達到了新的高峯，佛教中國化有了進一步的發展。廣東境內唐宋時期從城市到鄉村建了許多佛寺，如潮州開元寺、潮陽靈山寺、梅縣靈光寺、新興龍山國恩寺均始建於唐代，乳源雲門寺建於後唐，廣州海幢寺建於南漢。而保留下來的三十多座宋塔，正是佛教在廣東盛行的產物。

用火葬處理死者的方法，五代時已在皇族中提倡，到了宋代，民間紛紛效法僧人死後用火葬。僧人死後用火葬的做法，源於印度國中民間所流行的殯葬習俗，而隨佛教傳入中國的。唐玄奘著《大唐西域記》卷三中談到印度民間葬俗："送終殯葬，其儀有三：一曰火葬，積薪焚燎；二曰水葬：沈流漂散；三曰野葬，棄林飼獸"。有關宋元明時期各地盛行火葬一事，《宋史·禮二十八》記："紹興二十七年(1157年)監登聞鼓院范同言；'今民俗有所謂火化者，生則奉養之具唯恐不至，死則燔藝而棄捐之，何獨厚於生而薄於死乎？……'"。又說："河東地狹人衆，雖至親之喪，悉皆焚棄"。當時城鎮附近的寺院裏因專設焚人亭而得利。

火葬雖在各地流行，但到了宋代，朝廷認爲是事關風化之舉，必須禁止。《東都事略》卷三記述北宋初年太祖下詔書禁止火葬。詔曰："王者設棺槨之品，建封樹之制，所以厚人倫而一風化也。……(火葬)自今宜禁止"。《宋史·禮二十八》；"紹興二十八年，戶部侍郎榮嶷言：'此因臣僚陳請禁火葬，令州郡置荒閑之地，使貧民得以收葬，誠爲善政'"。《明史·禮十四》記載洪武五年，"諭禮部曰：'古者掩骼埋胔之令，近世犯元俗，死者或以火焚，而投其骨於水。傷恩敗俗，莫此爲甚，其禁止之。若貧無地者，所在官司擇寬閑地爲義塚，俾之葬埋'"。"犯元俗"反映了明代初年仍因襲元代火葬習俗。爲保証朝廷禁止火葬的禁令能有效地實施，在大明律的禮律、刑律中寫明懲治的條例。到了清代，大清律例規定除允許僧尼和夷人死後用火葬外，民喪不准火化，否則將嚴拿盡法懲治。從此，死者用火葬的作法逐漸衰落。火葬在廣東流行時期，約爲宋元明之際，明代已近尾聲。考古發現也証明了這一點，只見清代二次葬陶甕，不見火葬後盛骨灰的陶罈。而土葬仍是當時佔主導地位的埋葬習俗。

二、

廣東全省各地出土的陶罈爲數不少，但多數出土情況不明，進行科學發掘所得的資料有限。現將陶罈與墓葬形制相關的問題作初步分析。

(一)小型土坑墓：以正式發掘的8座宋代墓葬爲例，

地表設有三合土棺形塚，墳前嵌墓碑，設祭台，墓塚之下是方形、圓形、長方形的豎穴土坑，以後者居多。單人葬的坑內置一件陶罎，兩件盛骨灰陶罎並排放置的為合葬墓。隨葬品中最常見是銅錢，其次是稻谷。墓例有廣州市河南簡家岡"維皇宋咸淳二年歲次丙寅十二月"下葬的簡公墓。地表墳面用灰沙板築而成，如土棺形，前寬且稍高，後稍狭且低，墓塚下面築三合土基座，墳頭前面豎墓碑，刻上墓主人姓名和下葬年月。碑之下有一直徑48厘米，坑深92厘米的圓形土坑，埋一件大陶罎，內盛骨灰①（圖一：1）。又如佛山市瀾石皷頟崗M1宋墓，地表墳面已遭毀壞，墓室平面為長方形，長1.5、寬1、深2.1米。墓底經過夯打，用三塊長方形灰磚在墓底排成十字形，正中置一件帶蓋附加堆紋釉陶罎，蓋用石灰密封，內置裝有骨灰和銅錢的黑釉小陶罐。周圍放置六個內盛稻谷的黑釉小陶罐。②

元代火葬墓的形制仍為長方形豎穴土坑墓，火化後盛骨灰的陶罎形制和器具同前期相比出現了差異。以佛山瀾石皷頟崗的M6元代墓為例，骨灰盛在素面黑釉小陶罐中，小罐套在大罐裏，用石灰密封罐口，再放在用麻石鑿成的大石盒中，石盒底部鑿一圓孔③。

明代火葬墓均為平面呈長方形的土坑墓，骨灰放入黑釉陶罐中，外面套一個釉陶罐或陶盆。如瀾石皷頟崗M9，將骨灰裝在小型直身素面陶罐中，外套一件黑釉大罐，用灰漿密封蓋口，在蓋上再覆一件黑釉陶盆，也有不用套罐的④。

（二）小型磚室墓：少數骨灰罎在長方形小型磚室墓中出土。1957年12月在陽江縣郊區出土的一件塔形蓋陶罎，內盛骨灰，置磚室墓中。1972年東莞市篁村鎮白泥坑發現的一座北宋墓，為方形雙室券頂磚室墓，東西兩墓室各出土兩件堆塑陶罎，內盛少量稻谷隨葬，可見堆塑陶罎的用途亦有例外的。

三、

廣東宋元明時期的各類陶罎，其共同特點是它們都是隨葬時用的明器，或盛骨灰或裝稻谷，可能還盛水或酒。因其造型和功能的獨特，引起考古學家的注目，其中又以宋代堆塑人物罎的造型最為巧妙。

（一）堆塑人物罎

器形整體高且修長，器蓋製成亭閣式、塔形、塔剎形。器蓋和器身上堆塑佛像、比丘、供養人、飛鳥、神獸、樂舞伎及蓮花裝飾等。此類題材及造型藝術，宋代達到高峯，元明兩代少見，到了清代完全消失。

為研究廣東宋代出現堆塑人物罎的前因，必須尋源探索。堆塑人物罎在中國出現的歷史時期，最早是東漢，浙江嘉興九里滙東漢墓出土了堆塑罐⑥，又稱五管瓶，無蓋，口沿中間是一盤口葫蘆形大管，四周緊貼敵口的小管，罐肩部貼塑動物。三國時在五管之間堆塑有動物如鸞鳳、瑞獸和盤坐在蓮花座上的佛像及人像，有的將五管塑造成人形，或中間一管改塑成樓閣式建築⑦。西晉時期，五管瓶消失，代之而起的是塑有亭台樓閣、樂舞、飛禽走獸的谷倉罐。因受佛教藝術的影響，東晉時罐上貼塑坐佛的形象更常見。南朝時墓磚和青瓷碗上已有浮雕和刻劃蓮瓣紋。曲江縣南朝墓就曾出土一件青瓷蓮花碗。羅定縣羅鏡龍日鄉M1南朝墓出土一件青瓷豆，豆盤外壁刻劃蓮瓣紋。青瓷器上模印堆貼人像花紋是六朝早期青瓷器上裝飾的手法之一，影響是深遠的。這時期的堆塑人物罐，或稱魂罎，或稱谷倉罐，只不過是墓中的陪葬品之一，尚未發現在火葬墓中出土。因為具有濃厚佛教色彩的火葬習俗，當時還不流行。

佛教盛行時期的盛唐至唐末，中原地區常見下大上小似塔的塔形罐在墓中出土，中部器身作罐形，圓腹，平底，上部是一個高聳的圓錐形蓋，模印堆貼葉紋、佛像、人物及花卉，下部是高大的底座，承托罐身，部分罐身飾蓮瓣紋。迄今為止廣東境內唐窰和唐墓出土文物中不見堆塑罐，所見多數是富有唐瓷特點的渾圓飽滿，造型簡練，施青釉素面無紋的青瓷罐。關於廣東堆塑罎出現年代的上限，目前有三種意見，多數學者認為上限在唐末五代，另一種意見是唐末宋初，第三種意見上限定在北宋，筆者亦然。

現從器物的形制、模印堆貼人物的服飾、花紋、亭閣、樓閣建築結構的特點以及每件陶罎器身普遍出現的附加堆紋，進行排比歸類，分六式敘述。

Ⅰ式器身修長，卷圓唇，小口，短頸，廣肩，深腹，器身最大徑在肩部，肩向下斜收為平底，下加高圈足，足上有四個對稱的圓孔。器表施醬黃釉，大部分已剝落。肩部堆塑蟠龍和人物，腹部模貼蓮瓣或雕鏤花紋。肩以下連接三周附加堆紋，作水平凸出如魚鰭狀，製作時外緣用手指輕按，使其呈不明顯的小波浪紋。器蓋上塑亭閣式或樓閣式建築。1976年南海縣官窰鎮出土一件堆塑罎，無蓋，殘高55、口徑11.8厘米。肩部堆塑蟠龍，龍身至龍尾均勻地縮小，鋸齒形的背鰭和尾鰭相連，組成肩部最高一組花紋。龍咀尖長，與唐代龍相比，開口不大，露利齒，龍舌短小，鼻生在口吻和眼之間，龍角分叉，頰部已生出一周刺狀物，全身施鱗，僅腿部無鱗，三爪。六條泥柱承托龍身，這是一條典型的宋代龍。緊靠蟠龍的第二組堆塑是前後高矮兩排共31人和四尊護法獅子。其中道士5人，頭戴冠，身穿對襟大袖寬身袍服，肩披如意狀披巾，腰繫帶下垂，吹豎笛。僧人26人，光頭，著交領大袖寬身僧衣，手執鈸。前後兩排5-7人為一演奏組，樂器有一只豎笛，兩件細腰鼓，其餘是鈸。反映了宗教活動時演奏音樂的場景。器肩以下是三周附加堆紋。腹部模印堆貼一周13個蓮瓣，蓮瓣內用印模製出一組纏枝牡丹紋，凸起的陽文，猶如一幅白描花卉小品，花形與宋代汝窰瓷器同類花紋近似（圖式：1，2，3，4）。另一件是1983年陽春縣馬水鄉石菉汶涌出土（展品28號）。從罎的肩部至圈足，可分為四組花紋，之間用附加紋帶間隔。第一組也是一條蟠龍環繞，由15個貼塑的供養人承托龍身，缺龍首，僅見舞動的四腳及腳上的三爪，背鰭、尾鰭相連呈鋸齒形。第二組是一周圍欄，雕鏤卷葉紋。第三組是纏枝花葉紋，現部分花葉剝落，清楚地看到用刀刻後遺留在器胎上的刻痕。第四組花紋在束腰形的高圈足上飾蕉葉紋鏤孔。雕鏤手法嫻熟，刀鋒犀利，花紋線條顯得流暢舒展。卷葉紋和纏枝花葉紋是宋代瓷器中最常見的紋飾。該件陶罎的器蓋很獨特，外有一周圍欄，雕鏤出宋代建築版門和窗櫺上常見的毬紋格眼裝飾。中央堆塑一座平面呈四方形的樓閣兩層，具備宋代小型建築平面多為方形的特點，歇山頂。四根角柱有柱側腳，上部稍內收，柱頭上承櫨斗，櫨斗上出單栱，直接承托四角屋檐，屋角起翹，屋內無柱。樓閣的一面有門和障日版，其他三面為直櫺窗、四葉紋窗，反映了廣東宋代小型樓閣建築講究采光和通風，其造型給人以玲瓏輕巧的感覺，很是別緻和富有地方特色。

II式器身修長，比I式小型。圓唇卷沿，小口，短頸，廣肩，深腹，從肩部向下漸收，下接高圈足，有2-4個圓形鏤孔。肩部塑一周上飾鋸齒紋的泥條，似簡化了的蟠龍。常用橢圓形模印泥餅堆貼在肩部，上連泥條或鏤孔圍欄。模印的題材有護法獅子、武士、供養人、樂伎等。同I式罎相比，堆塑較簡化，從肩至腹部有3-5周附加堆紋，製作時用手向上（肩部）按其外緣，使之呈大波浪狀。器蓋多數製成塔利形，有相輪寶珠。施醬黃釉已剝落。1964年佛山瀾石鼓顙崗M14出土的1號堆塑罎，通高43、口徑9.5厘米⑧。肩部塑一周圍欄，上沿作鋸齒紋，有六個橢圓形鏤孔，孔與孔之間模貼供養人、武士各3人。供養人頭戴幞巾，身穿圓領寬身袍服，腰繫革帶，腳踏尖靴，雙手執一供物，側身趨前。武士面有美髯，頭戴幞巾，身著披髆、胸甲、身甲、腳穿尖靴，作持立狀。二者均身穿宋代流行的服飾和頭飾。器身有三周波浪狀附加堆紋，器蓋為塔利形（圖叁：1、2、3）。1986年中山市古鶴鎮出土一件堆塑罎，通高46，口徑10厘米。最引人注意的是罎口覆蓋青瓷碗，碗的形制特點是敞口，斜壁，小圈足，碗外壁刻蓮瓣紋兩層，是宋瓷中最為普遍的紋飾（圖肆）。II式陶罎在全省各地均有出土，常見罎內盛骨灰和隨葬"開元通寶"。

III式與I、II式陶罎不同之處是不見口沿附近的蟠龍，圓唇稍外卷，小口，短頸，廣肩，深腹下斜收成平底，加高圈足，足上穿四個鏤孔。肩部堆塑動物和人像，腹部不見貼塑。以東莞市篁村鎮白泥坑北宋墓東室出土的2號陶罎為例（展品26），出土時罎內盛稻谷，器肩不設圍欄，上排模塑四尊護法獅子和堆塑四丹鳳。丹鳳頭頂有高冠，圓眼，鉤喙，後曳長尾，展雙翅作振飛狀。下排為三人一組的樂舞形象，一人雙手擊鈸，左右各一舞伎，頭梳宋代流行的高髻，上著廣袖衫，下著長裙，裙束至腰間，肩披長帛，和着節拍起舞，披帛隨風飄動，栩栩如生。早在唐代，敦煌的樂舞壁畫中已反映了當時與宗教藝術互相渗透的樂舞形象，該罎上貼塑舞伎是北宋時廣東舞蹈藝人表現的豐富多彩的舞姿之一，是研究舞蹈藝術史不可多得的資料。

IV式圓唇或方唇不外卷，口稍斂，頸稍長，削肩，鼓腹，平底，接高圈足，足無鏤孔，肩部有四個對稱的橫耳，不見蟠龍，緊靠口沿附一周圍欄，上無鏤孔，貼塑一周人像。腹部最大徑下移至中部。附加堆紋與前三式有較大的區別，同是波浪紋，用手向上按的邊緣部分緊貼器身，器身上的附加堆紋作等距離的排列，之間刻劃水波紋。器蓋製成塔利狀或樓閣式塔。1955年博羅縣出土一件陶罎（編號甲2371），通高68、口徑11厘米。灰胎，醬黃色釉，釉層已剝落。從整體觀察，猶如一座七級浮屠。肩至腹部有四道附加堆紋，貼模坐佛42尊，造像的手法簡練、粗糙，穿交領廣袖寬身袍，結跏趺坐在蓮花座上。近口沿附一周圍欄，貼塑20尊佛像。如此之多的坐佛，可能包含千佛塔之意。罎蓋為樓閣式，分四層，平面近圓形，圓形塔心，每層有平座和欄板，之間是迴廊，下三層四面有壺門，壺門之間是四尊坐佛，最高一層是方形亭閣，懸山式屋頂，角柱上承柱頭枋，插入柱的單栱承托前檐，屋角起翹。看得出單體建築結構由於功能的要求，變得靈活多樣，而柱身的加高正是宋代木構建築中柱子的新變化（圖伍）。東莞市篁村白泥坑北宋墓西室出土的兩件陶罎歸於IV式，西1號陶罎，通高55、口徑12厘米，器蓋作塔利形。方唇，小口，頸稍長，削肩，附近一周圍欄,上貼塑坐像10尊,坐像之間是1-2棵樹,肩附四橫耳,最大腹徑在肩以下。墓碑上記載:"公行十二,生於大宋,官至朝奉大夫,卒於宋之政和年間,與恭人羅氏合葬於邑之治南五里……"。墓碑是清代咸豐十年七月重修時由西室墓主人封德清第二十六世孫所立。叙述了封德清卒於北宋政和年間,與其妻羅氏合葬,顯然封公其妻死在前,因此西室陶罈比東室隨葬的陶罈年代要晚一些,形制特點有較明顯的差別,不過均屬北宋晚期的陶罈(圖陸)。

Ⅴ式目前僅見此一件,全身堆塑人物和龍虎,五十年代初在廣州郊區出土(編號000006)⑨。通高30.2、口徑9.5-10厘米,胎灰質硬,施黃綠釉不到底。器身修長,圓唇,侈口,長頸,削肩,深腹,平底。以肩部突出的平座爲界,分上下兩層堆塑。平座上堆人物7人(一人殘缺)和一座靈牌及供桌。兩人雙手拍細腰鼓,一人敲架子鼓,一人吹豎笛,一人吹橫笛,一人雙手舉之胸前作吟唱狀,供桌上置靈牌和供品。人物的服飾很有趣,身穿寬袖廣身袍服,頭戴牛耳腳幞頭。這種形狀幞頭是宋代優伶人的常服。宋代陳暘樂書記載:"優伶常舞大曲……"此罈堆塑了優伶舞大曲場面,大曲是歌舞節目,殘缺的一人可能是舞蹈者。平座下層腹部堆塑青龍白虎,均爲三爪,龍的形象爲典型的宋代龍,尾部和龍身均勻相連,龍角如鹿角分叉生在額角部,龍咀長形合口,龍鼻在口吻和眼之間。與龍相對的虎,長形頭和咀,無角。龍虎造型手法簡練生動(圖柒)。

Ⅵ式龍虎罈(展品63號),1976年揭陽縣新亨鎮碩和石交椅山出土,內盛骨灰。從器身和堆塑的手法分析,有別於上述五式陶罈。圓唇,小口,短頸,溜肩,鼓腹,腹下部近直,漸收成平底,足徑大於口徑,罈的整體造型顯得肥矮厚重。堆塑花紋和人像題材從下至上可分三個層次,近底部是三層盛開的蓮瓣,清瘦,規整。第二層塑祥雲朵朵,青龍白虎在空中飛騰。龍的形象是四爪,鋸齒形的背鰭和尾鰭,鹿形角,細長頸,這是元代龍的特點,身上剔刻出龍鱗,虎的形象是短臉,長髮向後飄灑,虎身上繪條紋。第三層是腳踏祥雲的十二時辰俑。十二屬相之說源於東漢,中原地區隋墓中已出現十二屬相俑。廣東到宋代和元代墓中才出現石刻的和線刻在長方磚上的時辰俑,但爲數不多⑩。該陶罈正面塑一版門,門額上端雕一朵菊花,這類版門結構是北方宋金時期單體建築上常見的,門前兩旁塑武士,頭戴盔,額上有纓,雙側有掩耳(壓耳帽),著圓袖緊身窄袖甲衣,長不過膝,披膊不過肘,穿的是輕甲,著靴,手握長劍和斧,甲冑式樣因襲宋制。這種火葬陶罈約在南宋至元代流行。四川省西昌市三坡曾發現過一座火葬墓,是大理政權宣宗段智

興盛德二年下葬,正是南宋孝宗淳熙四年(1177年),外罐器腹堆塑兩層蓮瓣,內罐肩部貼塑十二生肖動物像,器腹模貼頭戴硬腳幞頭,衣著圓領大袖寬身袍,雙手執笏的人物像⑪。它同揭陽出土的陶罈形制雖有差別,但具有相同的時代風格,如清瘦的蓮瓣紋、十二生肖、人像雙手執笏的做法是一致的,不過從龍的形象和罈的形制考察,揭陽縣出土的龍虎罈應屬元代。

堆塑人物罈是陶罈中數量最多,形制多樣的一類器物,Ⅰ式罈在珠江三角洲地區較多見,Ⅱ、Ⅲ、Ⅳ式罈全省各地均出土,雷州半島較少見。從中山市古鶴鎮出土的Ⅱ式陶罈口上覆蓋蓮瓣青瓷碗的特徵推斷,Ⅱ式罈年代下限可能到北宋晚期。而Ⅵ式罈則有鮮明的元代風格。

(二)多角罐(罈),也有稱多咀罐、牛角罐的。器形特點爲小口,高身,平底,器肩有四橫耳,器身作寶塔狀,分爲五層。其特點是從器肩到腹部附錐形角,部分罐的近底部線刻蓮瓣紋。中山市小欖鎮郊區出土過一件多角罐,內盛骨灰。連縣城郊宋墓出土一件多角罐,通高45.5、口徑8.5厘米。蓋頂塑一個人,頭戴斗笠,手執棍棒,蹼踞其上(圖捌)。佛山瀾石石墟M9出土的多角罐內盛稻谷⑫。1981年封開縣封川鎮山頭兒出土了兩件陶罐(編號甲4221、4222),據說出土時兩罐並排放置。一件多角罐,通高32.5、口徑9厘米。胎灰色,施醬綠釉,已剝落。平唇,口微歛,斜頸稍高,削肩深腹,矮圈足。器身作罐形,錐狀角的尖黏貼在罐壁上(圖玖:1)。另一件罐身飾三周波浪形附加堆紋(圖玖:2),通高31.5、口徑9.5厘米。口沿外周附圍欄,蓋作塔利形。多角罐在南方流行的時間,福建省出土唐墓已見塔式多咀谷倉⑬。湖南省考古學者稱之謂牛角罈的出現在晚唐五代之際至北宋中晚期墓葬中⑭。廣東多角罐的出現,可能同湖南境內牛角罈的流行有關,出現時間上限約在北宋中晚期,因材料不足,下限的年代還不清楚,元明時期已消失。總之多角罐流行的時間比較短暫。

(三)**釉陶罈**

在珠江三角洲地區火葬墓中有較多出土。形制爲方唇,大口,短頸,圓肩,鼓腹,平底內凹。器蓋蓋鈕作螺形,蓋上飾兩周、肩飾一周附加堆紋,並以蓋鈕爲中心用泥條作瓦脊狀放射排列,可能寓意爲一座房子,內盛骨灰和隨葬銅錢若干枚⑮⑯⑰。廣州河南簡象岡M1:4號釉陶罈有確鑿年代,該墓墓碑右行刻小字"維皇宋咸淳二年歲次丙寅十二月"。M4墓中埋着內盛骨灰的釉陶罈,墓碑上遺留

"維皇宋"三字,與M1釉陶罈形制相似,說明這類陶罈是南宋晚期咸淳(1265-1274年)期間的遺物⑱(圖拾)。陶罈器表施黃釉色釉或醬黑釉(展品27)。另外也有作套罐用的,如佛山皷顙崗M1,為一小型土坑墓,大型釉陶罈是小型骨灰罐外面的套罐。這種用套罐盛骨灰埋葬的作法,到元代和明代都曾流行過(圖拾壹:1、2、3)。明代釉陶罈的器蓋及肩部的附加堆紋已減為1-3周,不見泥條作瓦脊狀排列⑲。附加堆紋的作法已不見Ⅰ式堆塑罈的水平凸出作小波浪形,也不見Ⅱ、Ⅲ式堆塑罈的大波浪形,而是一條寬約1-2厘米泥條黏在蓋或肩部,用手指均勻地下按成繩索狀。從元代開始流行在陶罈蓋背面用毛筆書寫死者生死年月日或下葬日期⑳(圖拾貳)。

(四)瓷罈

器胎灰白,燒成溫度高,青釉釉色晶瑩潤澤,不易剝落。形制特點是器蓋作成亭閣形,肩腹之間附一周鏤孔圍欄。方唇,小口,削肩,斜腹近直,平底,腹部飾繩索狀附加堆紋。器形較矮小,同堆塑人物罈有較大的差別,多數罈內盛骨灰,部分是墓中隨葬的明器。1975年12月在海康縣白沙鎮水尾村馮村坡發掘了一座元代墓(M3),墓碑上書:"潁川郡君李氏墓",左側書:"大元至正□年八月十二日□□",是一座石槨蓋板磚室墓,在墓室和石槨之間,放置兩件瓷罈隨葬。1號瓷罈蓋作亭閣式,屋頂為四角攢尖頂,正面設門,三面設花形漏窗。腹部附一周圍欄,圍欄的上沿敞開,鏤刻出直櫺窗和花形漏窗。而宋代堆塑罈上圍欄上沿是直的。兩周繩索狀附加堆紋,通高35.4、口徑7.3厘米(圖拾叁:1)。M3:2瓷罈為覆缽形蓋,方唇,小口,削肩,深腹,平底,只在蓋和肩部飾附加堆紋。通高20.8、口徑6.2厘米,均施青釉已剝落(圖拾叁:2)。1960年在廣西省合浦縣郊區(原屬廣東管轄)在深約1米的土層中出土了兩件瓷罈㉑。其中一件器表施泛青色的青釉,色透明,釉層結合緊密,無開片。器蓋為亭閣形,歇山式頂,四面牆多刻直條作門窗,蓋沿有一周圍欄。器身口沿為方唇,侈口,圓肩,斜腹,平底,肩下附一周上沿部位敞口向下斜收的圍欄,上開四個長方孔,並用赭彩繪出門框,附近書寫紀年銘文:"正德元年八月"(1506年)(圖拾肆)筆者根據上述兩件有年代可考的瓷罈作為標準器,認為《廣東出土的古代陶罈續介》㉒一文中提到的Ⅱ式陶罈,如圖版捌:5,應是元代瓷罈;圖版捌:6瓷罈形制與明代正德元年的瓷罈完全一致。該類瓷罈在雷州半島元、明時期的墓裏有較多發現,到了清代已消失。

綜上所述,廣東古代陶罈流行的年代,反映了火葬習俗在廣東的興衰。而堆塑罈的造型藝術,較真實地模擬着當時宗教活動的情景和社會生活一角。從罈的器蓋上堆塑的亭閣和樓閣,觀察到了宋代的單體建築繼承了廣州東漢時期屋角起翹的做法㉓,使樓閣顯得玲瓏輕巧,利於采光和通風。在亭閣建築結構上還可見到宋代《營造法式》上談到的障日版(牙頭護縫造)、毯紋格眼等。堆塑人像中反映了當時佛、道、樂舞伎、武士、平民的形象。很顯然,這些人像、樓閣是研究嶺南地區宋代至元代服飾、樂舞、單體建築時珍貴的實物資料。

注釋

①、⑱廣州市文物管理委員會:《廣州河南簡家岡宋元墓發掘簡報》,《文物》1957年第6期。

②、③、④、⑳曾廣億:《廣東佛山皷顙崗宋元明墓記略》,《考古》1964年第10期。

⑤、⑧、⑮、⑯、⑰、㉑、㉒廣東省文物管理委員會:《廣東出土的古代陶罈續介》,《考古》1965年第6期。

⑥姚仲源:《浙江漢、六朝古墓概述》,《中國考古學會第三次年會論文集》,1985年,文物出版社。

⑦衢州市文管會:《浙江衢州市三國墓》,《文物》1984年第8期。

⑨曾廣億:《廣東出土的古代陶罈》,《考古》1962年第2期。

⑩廣東省博物館:《廣東紫金縣宋墓出土石雕》,《考古》1984年第6期。

⑪黃承宗:《四川西昌三坡火葬墓調查記》,《考古》1983年第3期。

⑫、⑲廣東省文物管理委員會:《廣東佛山市郊瀾石唐至明墓發掘記》,《考古》1965年第6期。

⑬福建省博物館:《建國以來福建考古工作的主要收穫》,《文物考古工作三十年》,1979年,文物出版社。

⑭周世榮:《湖南出土盤口瓶、罐形瓶、牛角罈的研究》,《考古》1987年第7期。

㉓劉敦楨主編:《中國古代建築史》,71頁,1980年中國建築工業出版社。

Ⅰ

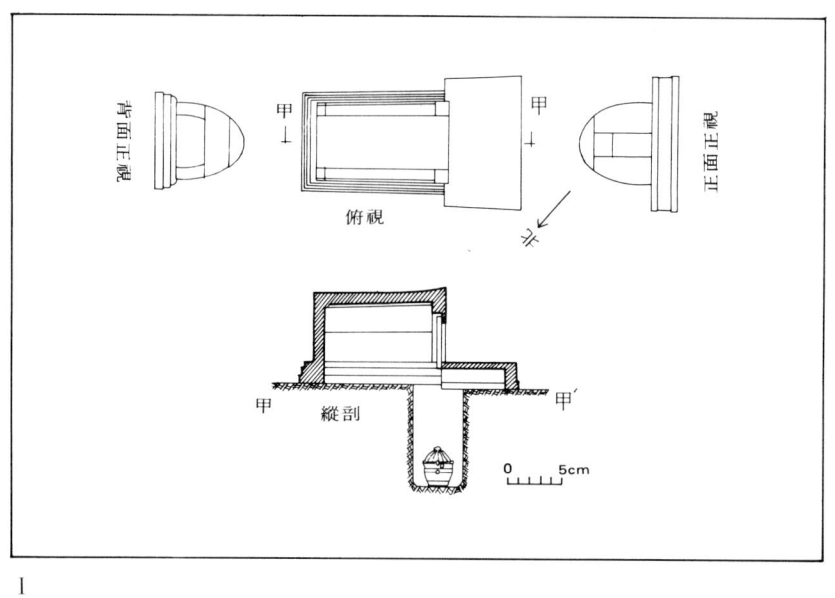

Ⅱ、1

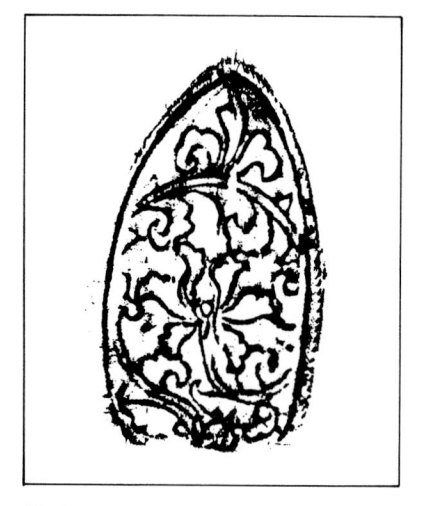

Ⅱ、2   Ⅱ、3   Ⅱ、4

圖壹：廣州市河南簡家崗 M 1 俯視剖面圖
圖貳：1　Ⅰ式堆塑人物罐（南海縣官窰鎮出土）
圖貳：2　花紋拓片
圖貳：3，4 Ⅰ式堆塑人物罐的細部（南海縣官窰鎮出土）

Fig. I
Plan and section of tomb M1 at Jianjia'gang, Henan, Guangzhou City.

Fig. II
Urn with applique figures from Guanyaozhen, Nanhai.
2. rubbing of detail 3,4. details

188

Ⅲ、1 　　　　　　　　　　　Ⅲ、2 　　　　　　　　　　　Ⅲ、3

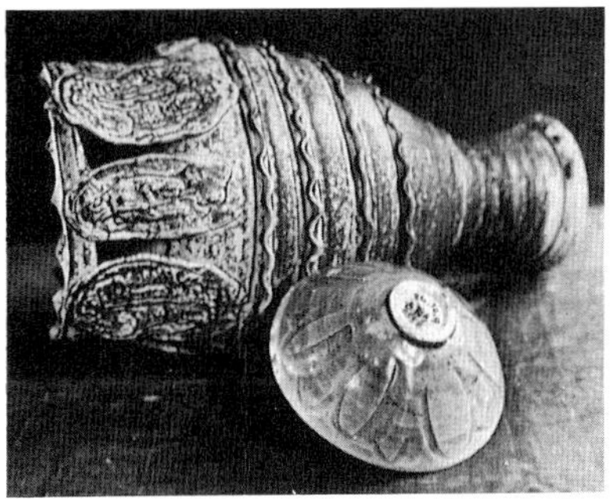

Ⅳ

Ⅴ 　　　　　　　　　　　　Ⅵ

Fig. III
Urn with applique figures, from Gusang'gang, Lanshi, Foshan.
2. rubbing of dedicative figure 3. rubbing of warrior

Fig. IV
Urn with applique figures, from Guhezhen, Zhongshan City.

Fig. V
Type IV urn with applique figures, from Bolo County.

Fig. VI
Type IV urn with applique figures, from west chamber of the N. Song tomb at Bainikeng, Huangcun, Dong'guan City.

圖叄：1　Ⅱ式堆塑人物罈
　　　　（佛山瀾石鼓颸崗 M14出土）
圖叄：2　供養人拓片
圖肆：3　武士拓片
圖伍：Ⅳ式堆塑人物罈（博羅縣出土）
圖陸：Ⅳ式堆塑人物罈（東莞市篁村白泥坑北宋墓出土）

189

Ⅶ 　　　　　　　　　　　Ⅷ 　　　　　　　　　　　Ⅸ、1

Ⅸ、2 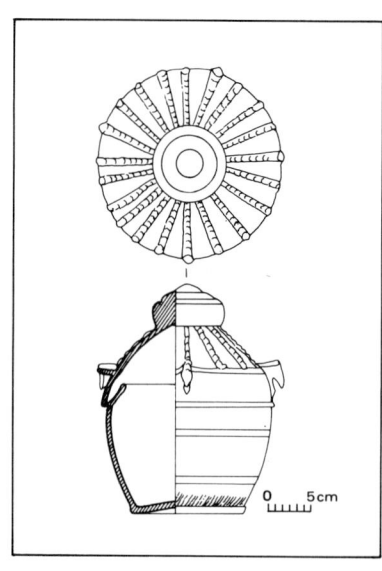　　　　　　　　　　Ⅹ

圖柒：　Ⅴ式堆塑人物罐（廣州市郊區出土）
圖捌：　多角罐（連縣城郊出土）
圖玖：1　多角罐（封開縣封川鎮山頭兒出土，編號甲(4221)）
圖玖：2　陶罐（封開縣封川鎮山頭兒出土，編號甲(4222)）
圖拾：　釉陶罈（廣州市河南簡家岡 M1：4）

Fig. VII
Type V urn with applique figures, from suburb, Guangzhou City.

Fig. VIII
Urn with projections, from suburb Lianxian City.

Fig. IX
1. Urn with projections, from Shantao'er, Fengchuanzheng, Fengkai County, No. A4221.
2. Pottery urn, from Shantao'er, Fengchuanzheng, Fengkai County, No. A4222.

Fig. X
Glazed urn, from tomb M1.4 Jianjia'gang, Henan, Guangzhou City.

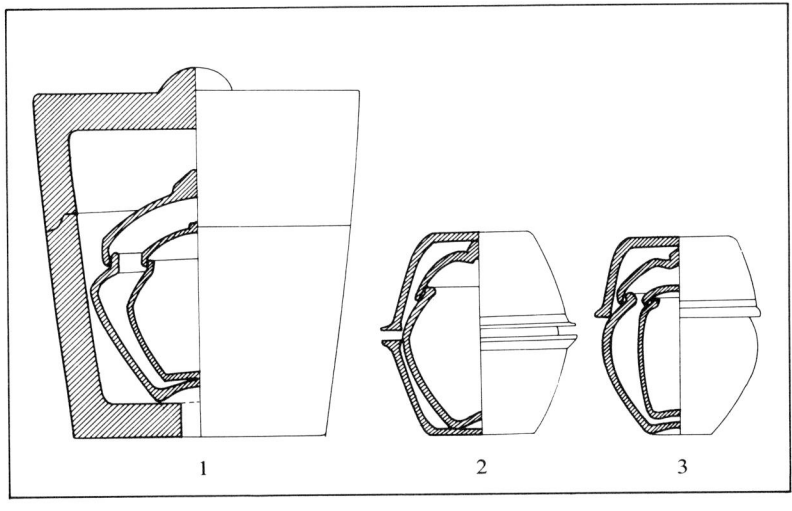

ⅩⅠ

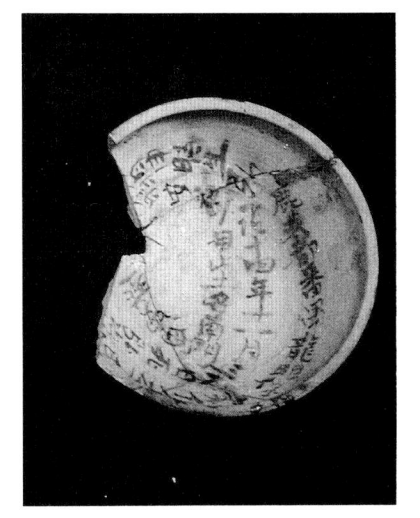

ⅩⅡ

ⅩⅢ、1   ⅩⅢ、2   ⅩⅣ

圖拾壹：套罐和大石盒
1，盛骨灰陶罈和大石盒（元代，佛山瀾石鼓顙崗 M 6 出土）
2，套罐（明代成化十八年，鼓顙崗 M11出土）
3，套罐（明代嘉靖二十七年，鼓顙崗 M 9 出土）
圖拾貳：釉陶罈蓋內書寫文字
圖拾叁：1　瓷罈（元代，海康縣的沙鎮馮村坡 M 3：1）
圖拾叁：2　瓷罈（元代，海康縣的沙鎮馮村坡 M 3：2）
圖拾肆：瓷罈（明代，廣西省合浦縣郊區出土）

Fig. XI
Large stone box and casing jar urns.
1. Large stone box with pottery urn for cremated ash, from tomb M11 at Gusang'gang, Lanshi, Foshan, Yuan dynasty.
2. Casing urns, from M11, Gusang'gang, 18th year Chenghua, Ming dynasty (AD1482).
3. Casing urns, from M9, Gusang'gang, 27th year Jiajing, Ming dynasty (AD1548).

Fig. XII
Cover of a glazed urn with inscription.

Fig. XIII
Porcelain urns
1. from tomb M3:1, Fengcunpo, Baishazhen, Haikang County, Yuan dynasty.
2. from tomb M3:2, Fengcunpo, Baishazhen, Haikang County, Yuan dynasty.

Fig. XIV
Porcelain urn, from suburb, Hepu County, Guangxi Province.

Studies on Ancient Pottery Urns of Guangdong

Zhu Feisu

(English Abstract)

This paper attempts to study the different types of funerary urns of the Song to Ming periods found in Guangdong. The majority of them were discovered from cremation burials and were used mainaly as ash containers. The practice of cremation started very early in China. Historical evidences show that cremation was already practiced in Pre-Qin times, and continued into the Han. Following the introduction of Buddhism into China, cremation was widely popular after the Han dynasty, especially among the monks. In the Five Dynasties period, the nobles encouraged the custom, and in early Northern Song cremation was the normal way of burial, even among the commoners. The practice continued well into mid. Ming in spite of repeated prohibition since Song times. It was only in the Qing period that cremation was completely prohibited.

Most of the urns were found from small scale rectangular earth pit tombs with above ground structure (Fig. I). More rarely the urns were placed inside tomb chambers made of brick. The followings are the main groups:

1. Urns with applique decoration:

This group is characterized by elaborate applique decoration of figures, animals and birds, lotus petals or architectural structures on the cover and shoulder, and can be subdivided into six types.

Type I:

Slender body, with elaborate applique figures and "pastry" bands, four diametric holes near foot, normally covered with a flaky glaze. The flower motif can be compared to the incised peony pattern found on Northern celadons and the architectural style points to a Song date. (Fig. II and exhibit 28)

Type II:

Slightly smaller than type I, shoulder with oval blocks supporting a solid border or openwork structure. The blocks are always impressed with designs of votive figures, lions, warriors or musicians (Fig. III). One urn of this type was found together with a celadon bowl of typical Song period. (Fig. IV)

Type III:

Without dragon band or openwork structure near mouthrim. A fine specimen of this type was found in Dong'guan City (Exhibit 26).

Type IV:

With cover in the form of a pavillion, the body becomes more globular, with the widest diameter in the midway. High foot without any perforation, incised wavy bands in between the "pastry" bands. (Figs. V). The piece illustrated in Fig. VI was found from the tomb of Feng Deqing, who died in the Zhenghe reign of late Northern Song.

Type V:

The only specimen of this type is the one found in Guangzhou city (Fig. VII). The slender body has a flat base. The yellowish green glaze stops near the foot.

Type VI:

This type is different in style from the above (Exhibit 63). The main theme of decoration is dragon and tiger, supplemented by the zodiac figures and lotus petals. By comparison with finds of known date, this type can be dated to the Yuan dynasty.

2. Urns with horn-shaped projections:

With small mouth topped by a cover, the body is in the form of a tiered pagoda with horn-shaped projections on each layer. (Fig. VIII). One piece of this type was found together with another with "pastry" bands in Fengkai County (Fig. XI). All of them dated from the middle to late Song and existed probably over a very brief period.

3. Glazed urns:

Pot shaped, with "pastry" bands on shoulder and cover, radial "rafter" design luted on the top of the cover, flat base slightly concave. One piece excavated in Guangzhou is datable to the Xianchun reign (AD1265-1274) of late Southern Song (Fig. X). Some of them are glazed in yellow or dark brown (Exhibit 27) and still some others were used in sets of two or three of different sizes, with the smaller ones encased in the larger ones (Fig. XI). In some specimens ink inscriptions appear on the interior of the cover (Fig. XII). This last group of encasing type started in the Yuan and continued into the Ming dynasty.

4. Porcelain/stoneware urns:

High fired stoneware/porcelain urns, with pale green glaze well fused to the biscuit. The cover is usually in the form of a pavillion enclosed by an openwork fence-structure around the shoulder. A typical piece of this type is datable to the Zhizheng reign of the Yuan dynasty (Fig. XIII.1), while another one unearthed in Hepu, Guangxi was inscribed with a Zhengde date (AD1506) of the Ming (Fig. XIV).

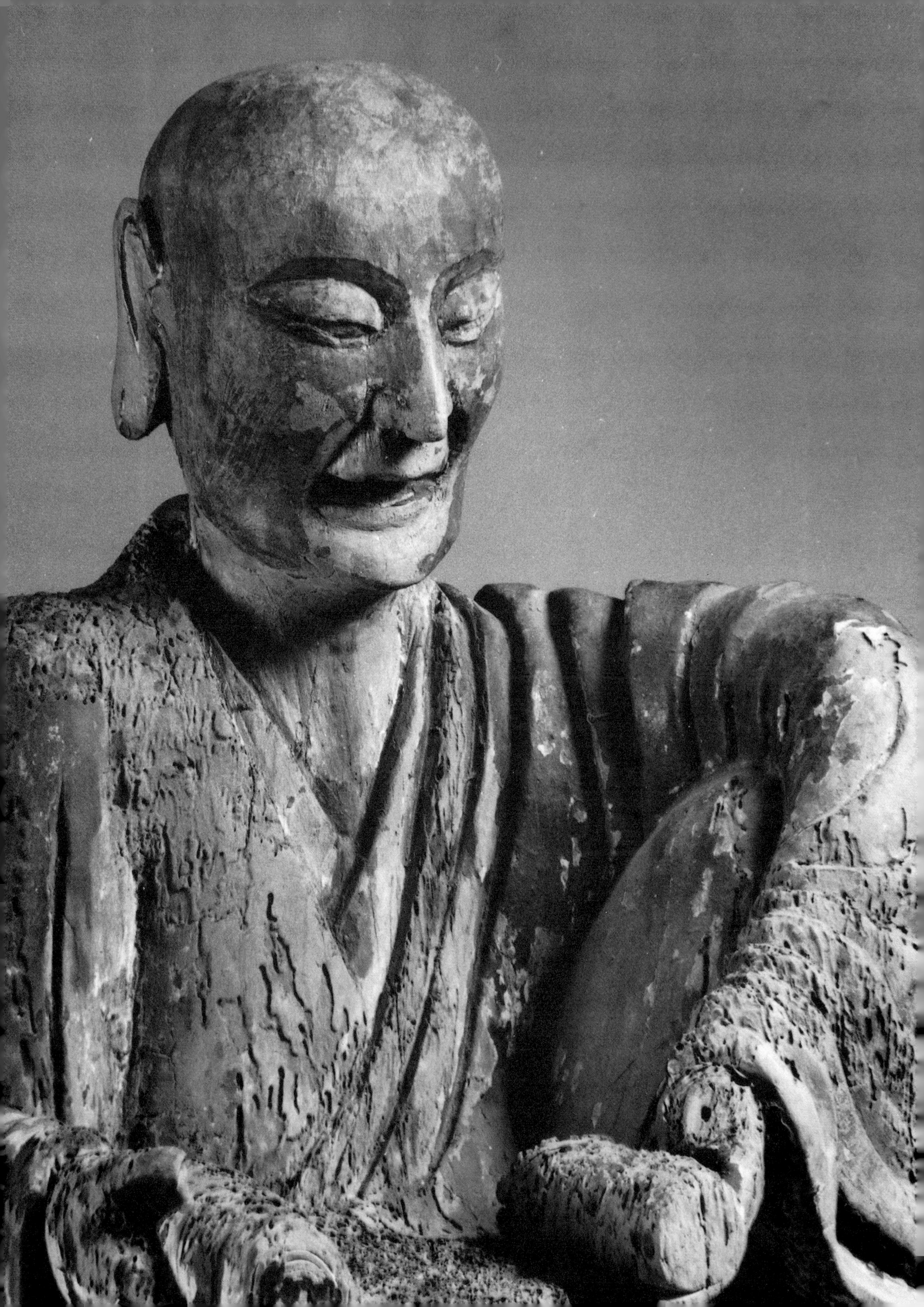

淺談南華寺木雕像座銘文

黃玉質

曲江縣南華寺保存的宋代三百六十尊木雕羅漢像中(展品47),有二百八十九尊在座上刻有銘文,其中九十八尊的銘文被鑿去或磨滅,三十四尊僅剩下部分銘文,完整的只有一百五十七尊。在木雕像座銘題記中,雖沒有直接記錄社會政治經濟活動,但仍在一定程度上反映了當時廣州的情況,尤為可貴的是提供了有關對外貿易的一些綫索。

座銘所記施像人,標明身份的有:軍人("郡武軍")1人,官眷(已故"都知兵馬使"之妻)1人,僧人7人,外貿商人頭領("綱首")2人。在銘文中標明捐造者的籍貫有廣州98人,連州(今廣東省連縣),17人,衢州(今浙江省衢縣)3人,泉州(今福建省泉州市)15人,潮州(今廣東省潮州市)3人。身份、籍貫、住址均不明的21人,這些未表明身份的人應屬市民階層,可能多數是商人及其眷屬。在短短的幾年之內,他們使用大量的進口貴重木材(檀香在當時是蕃貨),完成了規模如此巨大,工藝如此精緻的五百羅漢雕造工程,捐贈人又多以市民為主,這就反映了當時廣州城市經濟發達的情況。

座銘還記錄了從事施造羅漢像抄募工作的,如刻有"會首楊仁喜抄到"的羅漢像就有6尊(圖1)。"會首"意味着日常經濟生活以及宗教活動中已經存在經紀、把頭,組織"殘會"之類的中人。這是當時廣州社會行業分工相當複雜,經濟活動非常廣泛頻繁的反映。

外地人客居廣州的,以泉州籍的居多,這不僅說明廣州的商業繁盛,而且與對外貿易也有關係。宋代泉州、衢州商業已相當發達,但北宋對外貿易最主要的口岸是廣州。宋置市舶司以廣州為最早,時在太祖開寶四年(公元九九二年),稍後是杭州和明州①。泉州置市舶司是哲宗元祐二年(公元一〇八七年)②,仁宗朝尚未置司。神宗元豐三年(公元一〇八〇年)還規定:"請非廣州市舶司,輒發南蕃綱舶船,……以違制論"③。機構設置和制度規定表明,廣州的地位較之諸口岸更為重要。從對外貿易情況看,也是如此。清梁廷枏《粵海關志》卷三引北宋神宗熙寧十年(公元一〇七七年)統計材料:"三州市舶司所收乳香三十五萬四千四佰四十九斤,其內明州所收惟四千七佰三十九斤,杭州所收惟六佰三十七斤,而廣州所收者則有三十四萬八千六佰七十三斤"④。當時外地商業城市有不少人到廣州經商,施造羅漢像的泉州人就有一半以上是攜眷南來的,有的開店舖,有的則是在廣州市舶司登記的外貿商人。

與對外貿易有關的第二個情況是,有的施像人在姓名之前加上"大宋國"字樣(圖2)。"大宋國"、"大明國"之類,本來是當時同中國有通貢關係的國家對中國的稱呼。日本人伊東忠太,鎌倉芳太郎《南海古陶瓷》一書所載琉球南海諸國交涉史料,有明宣宗宣德九年(公元1434年)琉球國中山王致邏羅國的咨文和明憲宗成化十七年(公元1481年)滿剌加國致琉球國王的回咨,都稱中國為"大明國"⑤。自稱"大宋國"、"大明國"之類的中國人,很可能是經常與外國人接觸的外貿商人及其眷屬,才習慣於此種稱謂的。

尤為值得注意的是,捨造羅漢像的人中有兩個是"廣州綱首"〔雕像題名樊密的有6尊(圖3),題名陳德安的有8尊之多(圖4)〕。"綱首"為何?史籍只載各目,未作解釋。《萍州可談》卷二云:"甲令,海舶大者數百人,小者百餘人,以巨商為綱首,副綱首。雜事,市舶司給宋記,許用笞其徒,有死亡者籍其財"⑥。日本藤田豐八據此認為是操縱海舶之技術者。因此種綱首,為結伴商旅之長,故又言此種海舶為綱船⑦。這種解釋是不夠全面和準確的。

"綱"在宋代為運輸貨物的名稱,如"花石綱"、"鹽綱"、"糧綱"之類。官府運輸還規定每一綱由若干艘船或若干重量的貨物組成,運費也有規定⑧。

海舶綱首的由來,有其特殊的原因。宋代對蕃貨的貿易之利極為重視,故管理甚嚴,北宋尤甚。不僅蕃貨入口有"抽解"(徵收實物稅)與"和買"(政府統購全部或部分貨物)的規定,"商人出海外蕃國貿易者",也規定必須到市舶司"請給官券","違者沒入其寶貨"⑨。申請給券要有"本土有物力戶三人委保"⑩。這種官券的發給,當然只能以船為單位,即一船為一綱。同時由於當時海上交通不便,又因外國不論船大小一律按船索取"獻送"。故商旅出海都要結伴使用較大的船隻⑪。大者數百人,小者百餘人,這樣多的商人,當然只能由其中資本最雄厚的巨商領頭申請給券,此人即成為船的綱首。這些巨商可能多數本人有船,但也不一定是船主才能擔任綱首,《宋會要》關於互市舶方面的記載中即另有"船戶"、"船主"的名目⑫。這種綱首由於經常同市舶司打交道,逐漸成為一種特殊人物,作為蕃商旅中固定的頭領,只有他們才有資格出面辦理出海手續,每次出海只有他們出面組織。綱首不僅有中國人,也有外國人。

後來,宋政府還依靠綱首招引外國商船來華貿易,規定:"諸市舶綱首能把誘舶船,抽解物貨,累價及五萬貫,十萬貫補助以上者,補官有差."南宋高宗紹興六年(公元1136年),即有泉州綱首蔡景芳與大食蕃客蒲囉辛同時補官承信郎專例⑬。請路市舶司"每年於遣發蕃舶之際,宴設諸國蕃商",也得請綱首一同赴宴⑭。此外,還有三佛齊詹卑國主托南蕃綱首帶信給廣東市舶官之事⑮。

當時此種海商頭領身份甚高,見主官也習慣施主客專禮。仁宗時,廣州有海商大戶樊氏見南海縣主簿蘇緘,因直登大堂就坐而被杖,樊氏告到州官去,主簿老爺竟被官召責⑯。不知此樊氏與刻銘的綱首樊密有否關係?

這些事實,說明宋代作爲外貿商人頭領的綱首,是有錢有勢的。無怪樊、陳兩人拿來冠於姓名之前,作爲銜頭。而綱首之能成爲煊赫一時的身份,又反過來證明當時廣州對外貿易的繁榮。

外貿商人之所以踴躍捐款於宗教活動,不僅有其本身的原因,也有其社會原因。

宋皇朝由於重視蕃貨貿易之利,很注意同海外貿易交往。太宗"雍熙中,遣內侍八人,齎勅書金帛,分四路招致海南諸蕃"⑰。仁宗時,對外交往還發展到由皇室出面進行宗教性活動。明道二年(公元1033年),就曾以大宗皇帝和皇太后名義,遣僧至摩伽陀國(在今印度)爲超荐太宗皇帝而建塔一座⑱。作爲當時主要通商口岸的廣州的外貿商人們,不能不受這類活動的影響。

海商們本身爲求神佛保佑,大發"洋"財,也要進行此類活動。《萍州可談》卷二云:"商人重蕃僧,云度海危難禱之,則見於空中,無不獲濟。至廣州飯僧設供,謂之羅漢齋"⑲。這是他們熱心捐造羅漢像的又一原因。

此外,施像目的見於座銘的還有:"爲四恩三友"的,"追荐先亡""早超世界"的,保自身和家人"安吉"的,"乞兒子一名"的,還有出家僧人俗緣不斷爲在堂母親而捨羅漢的,也可見一時的風習。

座銘中,"都武軍",不見於《宋史·兵志》,應爲地方駐軍的泛稱,而非專有的名號。"都知兵馬使"亦不見於《宋史·職官志》。宋代軍制:"百人爲都""五都爲營,五營爲軍,十軍爲廂"⑳。"每都有軍使,副兵馬使,都頭,副都頭,十將,將,虞侯、承局、押官"㉑。都知兵馬使應即爲統轄一都的軍使。

座銘所記廣州施主的住地,作第幾"廂"第幾"界"(或"屆"),"廂"又有"左""右"之分(圖5)。鄧爾雅認爲當是保甲區域"㉒。這種解釋不符合歷史事實。宋始行保甲法於神宗熙寧三年(公元1070年)㉓。仁宗時尚無保甲組織,此其一;宋代保甲之法:十家爲一保,五十家爲一大保,十大保爲一都保㉔,亦無"廂"、"界"之類的名目,此其二。座銘中之"廂"、"界"又有不少明言"住房"或"住址",此"廂"亦顯然不是軍制之"廂"。看來,"廂"是城廂,應當是指城區,"左"、"右"即城之東西。"界"("屆")即街也。北宋時廣州城範圍不會很大,區街有可能是以次序編名的。廣州至今尚有名爲第幾"約"的街道,可資參證。

座銘中還刻有廣州佛寺的名稱三個:法性寺、寶光寺和開元寺。

法性寺,即現今光孝寺,在廣州市區光孝路,1961年公布爲全國重點文物保護單位。據寺志記載:"唐太宗貞觀十九年(公元645年)改制止王園寺爲乾明法性寺","宋太祖建隆三年(公元962年)改法性寺爲乾明禪院",以後再未用法性之名㉕。按建隆三年廣州爲南漢興王府,南漢是與宋敵對的,宋太祖怎能在此給此寺改名?現據南華寺木雕像座銘,則慶曆年間仍名法性。南宋方信儒《南海百詠》詩題也作法性寺,並引《圖經》云:"本乾明 法性二寺,後併爲一。"又云"劉氏爲乾亨寺,後復舊名,今爲報恩光孝寺"㉖。據此,座銘可正寺志之誤。

寶光寺,已廢。道光《廣東通志》謂即大通寺,五代南漢時爲列布廣州四方的二十八寺之一,原址在廣州市郊河南大通滘。《南海百詠》南七寺詩首句即出:"井軫南官煥'寶光'",另有單詠大通寺之詩。大通之名係宋徽宗政和六年(公元1116年)所改,曰大通慈應禪㉗。"大通煙雨"爲宋、元時八景之一㉘。但近人黃佛頤輯《廣州城坊志》引化《廣州府志》,則謂寶光寺原址在城西舊南海縣署,即崇報寺。"迺市舶司始創啓元,以爲蕃舶祈福之所。宋大觀中,賈故捨財重修,市舶司請於朝"賜額崇報寺,毀於明洪武二年(公元1369年)㉙。

開元寺,久廢,原址已不可考㉚(圖6)。《光孝寺》載:現存光孝寺內南漢大寶十年(公元968年)建造的東鐵塔,"原址在開元寺。宋端平間本寺住持僧紹喜移歸光孝,建殿覆上。"據塔銘,此塔是用南漢皇帝(劉鋹)名又勅有司鑄造的,目的是"保龍躬有慶,祈風歷無疆……"。建造僧的職銜有"內殿大僧錄","內供奉講經首座"等,且列名四僧均封"教中大法師,金紫光祿大夫,檢梭工部尚書"㉛,可見此寺當時之顯赫。

南華寺北宋木雕像座銘題記中的許多材料,或者可以印證文獻的記載,從而窺見當日廣州社會面貌的一鱗半爪,或者補正文獻記載的遺誤,具有一定的歷史價值。

註釋:
① 《宋史》卷一八六食貨志市舶法條,四部備要本第二十九冊。
② 同上。原文云:"元祐三年……乃置密州板橋市舶司。而前一年亦置市舶司於泉州"。
③ 蘇軾:《東坡奏議》卷八,四部備要本《東坡全集》第十一冊。
④ 轉引張星烺編:《中西交通史料匯篇》第三冊第五八頁,一九三〇年北京輔仁大學版。
⑤ 伊東忠太、鐮倉芳太郎:《南海古陶瓷》文學第一部分第十、二十八頁,昭和十六年(公元1941年)東京寶雲舍版。
⑥ 同4。第二六一頁。
⑦ 何健民譯:《中國南海古代交通叢考》第三〇六頁,一九三六年商務印書館版。
⑧ 《宋史》卷一七五食貨志漕運條,卷一八六食貨志至市舶法條,四部備要本第二十七、二十九冊。
⑨ 《宋史》卷一八六食貨志至市舶法條,四部備要本第二十九冊。
⑩ 蘇軾《東坡奏議》卷八、四部備2要本《東坡全集》第十一冊。
⑪ 轉引張星烺編《中西交通史料匯篇》第二六一頁。
⑫ 何健民譯《中國南海古代交通叢考》第三一八、三二七頁轉引。
⑬ 《宋史》卷一八五食貨志香條,四部備要本第二十九冊。"蒲囉辛"原作"囉辛",據藤田豐八引《宋會要》改正。
⑭ 何健民譯《中國南海古代交通叢考》第三二四頁引《宋會要》
⑮ 據戴裔煊《宋代三佛齊重修廣州天觀碑記考釋》一文註十二引《宋會要輯稿》,見《學術研究》一九六二年第二期第六十五頁。
⑯ 道光《廣東通誌》卷二三七宦績錄蘇緘傳,商務印書館影印同治重刊本第四一五五頁。
⑰ 《宋史》卷一八六食貨志至市舶法條,四部備要本第二十九冊。
⑱ 《河北第一博物院半月刊》第十三期第一版,一九三二年三月版。
⑲ 轉引張星烺編:《中西交通史料滙篇》第二六二頁。
⑳ 《宋史》卷一九五兵志訓練之制條,四部備要本第三十一冊。
㉑ 《宋史》卷一八九兵志廂兵條,四部備要本第三十冊。
㉒ 鄧爾雅:《曹溪南華寺宋刻五百羅漢記》,《國立中山大學文史學研究所月刊》第一卷第三期第七頁,一九三三年三月版。
㉓ 《宋史》卷十五神宗紀、四部備要本第三冊。
㉔ 《宋史》卷一九二兵志保甲條,四部備要本第三十冊。
㉕ 《光孝寺志》卷二,一九三五年廣東省立編印局排印本。
㉖ 宋方信孺:《南海百詠》,學海堂光緒重刊本。
㉗ 道光《廣東通志》卷二二九古蹟略,商務印書館影印同治重刊本第四〇一六至四〇一七頁。
㉘ 清仇池百輯:《羊城古鈔》卷首,嘉慶刊本。
㉙ 黃佛頤輯:《廣州城坊志》卷三第六二至六三頁,廣東叢書第三集。
㉚ 道光《廣東通誌》謂元妙觀即唐開元寺,但該處在宋真宗大中祥符年間(公元1008-1016年)已改為天慶觀,而天慶觀至神宗元豐二年(公元1079年)重修立碑時沒有再改,是則仁宗朝之開元寺應在另一地點,此寺起碼存在到南宋理宗端平年間(公元1234-1236年)光孝寺僧搬走東鐵塔之前。
㉛ 《光孝寺誌》卷三,一九三五年廣東省立編印局排印本。

On the Wooden Lohan Inscriptions Found in Nanhua Temple

Huang Yuzhi
(English Abstract)

Of the 360 wooden lohans preserved in the Nanhua Temple in Qujiang (Exhibit 47), 289 pieces carry inscriptions on their pedestals. About half of these inscriptions are intact, the rest being fragmentary. This article attempts to study the social, political, and trading activities in Guangzhou in the Song times as reflected by the contents of these inscriptions.

1. Donors

Most of the statues were inscribed with the details of the donors. Their status includes: soldier (1), spouse of soldier (1), monk (7), trade leader (2), and their hometowns: Guangzhou (98), Lianzhou (17), Chuzhou (Zhejiang, 3), Quanzhou (Fujian, 15), Chaozhou (3). Twenty-one of the donors were unidentified, who were probably ordinary civilians or merchants and their spouses. The fact that such a massive quantity of lohan figures were finished in a few years with imported sandalwood, and sponsored by the common folks, indicates that the trade as well as the economical situation in Guangzhou must have been very prosperous.

2. Social organizations

The following terms are discussed:

a. "*huishou*" – middleman or agent for trading or religious activities (Fig. 1).
b. "*Da Song guo*" – the Great Song Country, a foreign term adapted by merchants and their spouses (Fig. 2).
c. "*Gangshou*" – trade leader, (Figs. 3, 4).
d. "*Duwujun*" – local garrison troop.
e. "*xiang, jie*" – city district and street, (Fig. 5).

3. Temples

a. Faxing temple, better known as the Guangxiao temple, situated in the Guangxaio street in Guangzhou.
b. Baoguang temple, in the Southern Bank of Guangzhou.
c. Kaiyuan temple, no longer extant. One of the iron pagoda now preserved in the Guangxiao temple was from this temple.

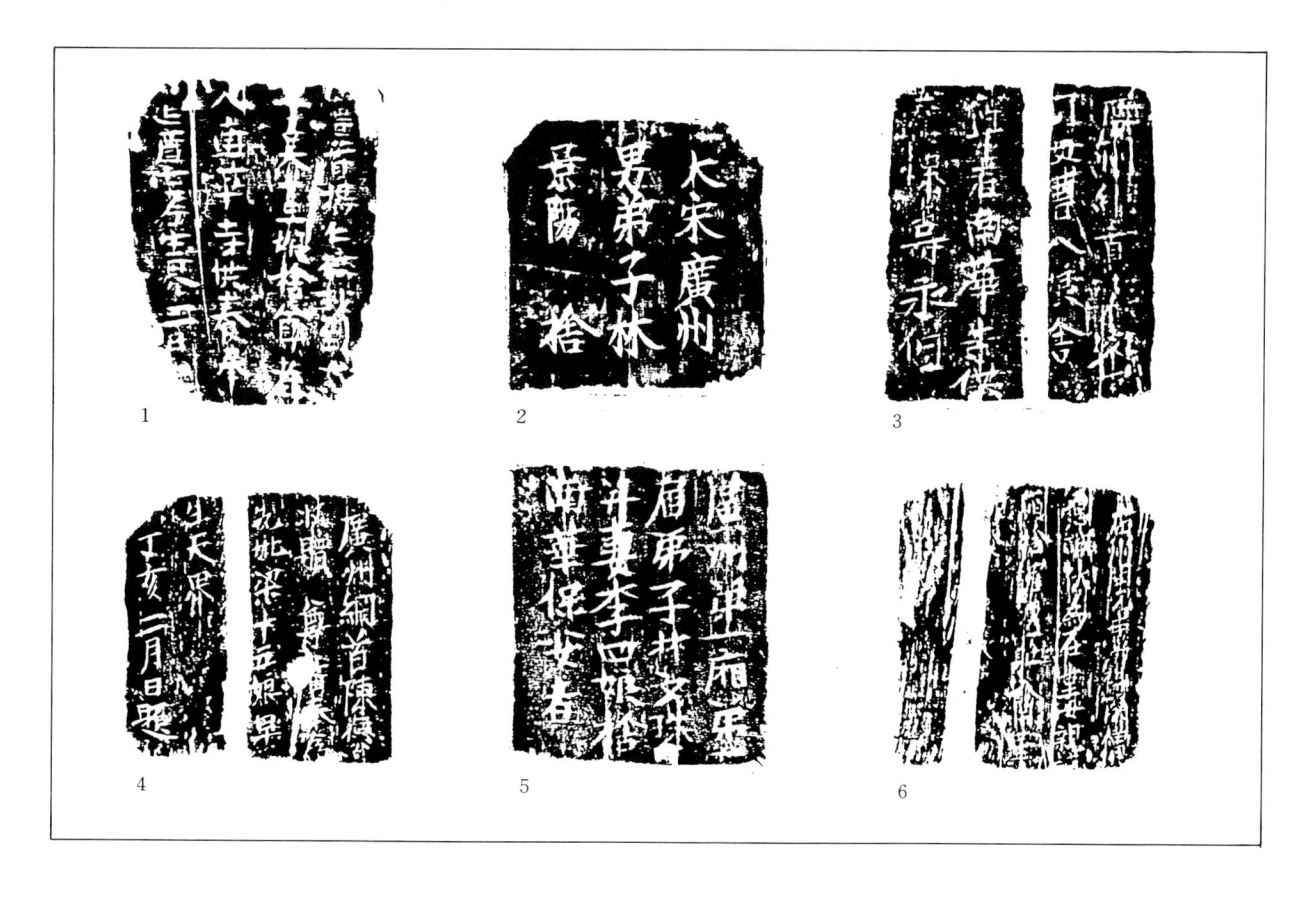

出身……史黃春……地方……

廣東地方兼管屯田鹽法湖廣道監察御史前選授內翰林國史院……

東內翰林弘文院讀書庶吉士眷年姪楊鍾岳頓首拜書册

進士出身中憲大夫都察院右僉都御史□弟羅萬傑頓首拜篆額

……當朝……間吾之潮郡有當錫吳少師公其人者……

……朝為且勁力征剿屢建異績

……勤思無……在師三……何以加焉今日者臺……

……不予動容嗟嘆……凡我東……人士無不推為鞠躬……

[illegible]

潮州展品小識

饒宗頤

　　此次廣東省博物館與中大文物館合辦南漢至清文物展覽，展品中潮汕地區出土文物佔相當份量，循覽之餘，頓引起鄉梓之思。雖諸位專家論著說明，周詳精闢，已無遺蘊，然涉及史蹟方面，尚有不少可以補充者，爰不揣固陋，略舉數事，以供談助：

1．南漢宮硯

　　廣州東郊石馬村南漢墓出乾和十六年磚，有瓷器多件。（展品1-5）王漁洋《池北偶談》記其"故友陸漢東卿孝廉有小硯，是南漢劉鋹宮中物，有鋹宮人離非女子篆銘"。陸卿，饒平人，原名漾波。余家舊藏有其《廻風草堂集》與《吳越百吟》合爲一册，清初刻本，陸卿與漁洋以詩交往。漁洋深惜是硯，漢東歿後不知流落何許。）此次展品有宋硯二（展品44，45），聯想及此，因附記之。

2．王大寶銅鏡（展品39）

　　鏡在大寶墓出土，有銘文云："臨安府承父陸家眞煉銅照子"，大寶於宋高宗建炎二年（1128）廷試第二。時宋室南渡，初建都於錢塘，此鏡必在浙所得者，當是臨安府鏡匠所造。大寶《宋史》有傳，又明潮州知府王源亦爲其撰傳。曩年見《王氏族譜》，載其建炎二年龍飛榜，主司本擬爲第一，時車駕駐揚州，偶次名李易爲揚州人，遂取易，以之居二，故其詩有云："對策丹墀中上游，天顏撫諭逐龍頭"之句。潮州府城大街有坊曰"榜眼"，即爲大寶置者，文革時已毀去矣。大寶封開國男，食邑海陽登瀛三百戶，乾道六年四月十三日卒，御葬於登瀛神前山，登瀛領有今之龜湖。郭春震嘉靖《潮州志》"登瀛都，統龜湖、山洋、曲灣三村"。

　　此次展品又有揭陽漁湖、及黃岐山出土之宋代銅鏡（展品40），則必爲當地鑄造、潮劇《荔枝記》演陳三（泉州陳伯卿）磨鏡故事，宋鏡形狀，可於展品觀之。

3．桃坑劉氏與筆架山窰

　　廣東潮州宋墓有紀年者以1958年發掘乾道八年之劉景墓最受人注目，彭如策有文記之（見《考古》1963年9期）。本刊曾廣憶《陶瓷》一長文引《廣東通志》卷六十三稱："劉景爲廣東潮陽縣人"。按景乃劉允之子。嘉靖《潮志》七人物志："劉允字厚中，海陽人。子昉，龍圖閣學士，景，舉賢良方正。孫汶、渭、滋、漁、少集，皆繩繩繼美"。吳穎順治《潮志》，科名部：

"海陽劉允，默子，紹聖四年第三甲

海陽劉昉，允子，宣和六年第三甲……

海陽劉少集，昉孫，乾道八年第四甲……"。

　　往年曾見鈔本《桃坑劉氏族譜》："劉景海陽人、賜爵開國男、食邑三百戶，劉漁，景次子，蔭官食邑三百戶"。昉與景俱爲劉允之子。《夷堅志》卷十四"開源宮主"條記其事云："劉允，潮州海陽人。……（臨絕前）呼二子昉、景。……潮人陳安國嘗敍其事。昉後更名旦，……知潭州，景嘗知台州。又同書廬陵人張敦夢醫條，記其僑寓潮州，與提學劉景事。據上諸記載，劉景爲劉允之子，當是海陽人。宋初潮州領海陽、潮陽二縣。《宋史》地理志："宣和三年，新置揭陽縣，紹興二年，省揭陽潮陽併入海陽"。故劉景當爲海陽人。作潮陽者非是。據《劉氏族譜》，劉氏族居韓山（筆架山）後之東湖，其地亦稱桃坑，劉氏蔚爲盛族。允子昉、景，昉子四人，景子九人，皆一時顯仕。

　　潮窰所以集中於筆架山，以其附近白嶺出產磁土之故，北宋有治平四年（1064）款佛像銘云："潮州水東中窰甲弟子劉扶……爲父劉用……造，匠人周明"。潮州城內開元寺之"靜樂禪院"政和四年（1114）鐘款云"白瓷窰住弟子劉滿……捨錢……祈平安"。白瓷窰爲地名，在筆架山，劉扶、劉滿疑皆劉允、劉景之族人，筆架山窰所在地，爲桃坑劉氏聚族之區，故有劉姓多人製造供養。倘以劉景作潮陽人看待，則顯違事實。惜《桃坑劉氏族譜》抄本，經亂久佚不可復問，茲就記憶所及參以舊作《潮州宋瓷小記》補述於此。

4．關於吳六奇與郝尙久

　　諸展品以大埔湖寮墟出土吳六奇墓誌銘（輔助圖片五）最有史料價值。其殉葬遺物已見楊豪簡述（《文物》1982，第2期）墓誌銘之額泐刻康熙六年七月十四日諭祭‧銘辭出楊旬瑛手筆，旬瑛福建人，進士，任廣東巡按御史。（《廣東通志》四十三職官表三十四）書丹者楊鍾岳，澄海人，著有《摹華堂文集》，梁佩蘭選閱，並爲撰序，康熙壬申刻本。篆額者羅萬傑，揭陽人。甲申後祝髮入山，著有《瞻六堂集》，余家舊藏爲乾隆乙酉餘軒刊本，前沈德潛序。稱其人格可與熊魚山、方密之、金道隱比倫。其次女嫁吳六奇之子啟鎮,故稱爲姻弟。六奇有子十一人,皆與當時權貴結爲姻親,如啟師即聘海澄公黃梧之女;又有女適潮州鎮總兵劉伯祿。伯祿遼陽廣寧人,順治十年以都督同知任潮鎮總兵。

誌銘記六奇征討功績、如鍾凌秀、張文斌等征撫之事,可參吳穎順治《潮志》兵事部:鍾凌秀之變、張文斌之變諸條。六奇歸附清在己丑之冬,即順治六年(1649)時清兵南下。《清史稿》尚可喜傳云:七年正月,尚可喜克韶州,下英德、清遠、從化諸縣,明將吳六奇等迎降。二月師陳廣州……復招潮州守將郝尚久,惠州守將黃應傑,皆以其城降"六奇與尚久同時降清。繼而尚久殺車任重,九年,結寨金山頂。此墓誌云:"潮將郝尚久據潮以叛,請藩統師至討"。尚久以順治十年三月,正式叛清奉永曆正朔,自稱新泰侯。王昶撰陸振芬傳亦稱自新泰侯。吳穎志"郝尚久之變"條所記亦同。(乾隆潮志作"新泰伯",誤)《清史稿》耿繼茂傳:"(順治)十年,潮州總兵郝尚久據城叛,繼茂與靖南將軍喀喀木、總兵吳六奇合軍討之,圍城逾月。城將王立功爲內應,樹雲梯以登。尚久入井死,餘賊盡殲,潮州及饒平、揭陽、澄海、普寧諸縣悉平"。是役六奇與有功焉,故墓誌特表之。

六奇早年與查伊璜之事,見《觚賸》、《聊齋誌異》、《香祖筆記》,已近小說家言。此墓誌記其一家子女及姻親關係,足爲地方志徵獻之助,故略爲考證以供參考。

郝尚久事蹟,明季《潮州忠逸傳》爲立專傳,余弱冠於溪東關帝廢廟搜得尚久於辛卯(順治八年)所立之碑記,自署籍貫古汴守潮州等處總兵宮,蓋與六奇同降清後所建者。此碑省州縣志均不載,全文收入拙作《固庵文錄》中。

Notes on Finds from Chaozhou

Jao Tsung-i
(English Abstract)

In this exhibition of "*Archaeological Finds from the Five Dynasties to the Qing Periods in Guangdong*", a fairly high per centage of the exhibits were from the Chaozhou and Shantao regions. This brief essay attempts to bring out the historical significance of these finds and to supplement the scholarly essays written by the Guangdong experts.

1. Southern Han inkstone

Quite a number of ceramic artifacts have been discovered from the dated tomb of Southern Han in Shimacun, Guangzhou. Wang Shizhen in his *Chibei Ao' tan* mentioned that his friend Lu Handong once had a small inkstone with an inscription in seal script of a court lady of the palace of Liu Zhang. Lu was a native of Raoping and after his death, this inkstone was lost. Two collections of Lu's works, *Huifeng caotang ji* and *Wujiu baiyin* had been published.

2. Bronze mirror from the tomb of Wang Dabao

From the tomb of Wang Dabao a bronze mirror with an inscription was found (Exhibit 39). The inscription is a shopmark of the Lu family of Lin'an Prefecture. Wang attended the imperial examination in the 2nd year of Jianyan (AD1128) when the Southern Song capital was at Qiantang. This mirror was very probably acquired when Wang was in Zhejiang. There was a biography of Wang in the *Songshi* (Dynastic history of the Song). Wang Dabao was conferred a title of Dynasty-founding Baron and given 300 households in Haiyang and Dengying as fief. He died on the 13th day, 4th moon, 6th year Qiandao (AD1170) and was buried in Shenqianshan, Dengying. The other two Song mirrors (exhibits 40) found in Yuhu and Huangqishan, Jieyang were probably cast locally.

3. The Liu family or Taokeng and the Bijiashan kiln site

In 1958 the tomb of Liu Jing, which can be dated to the 8th year of Qiandao (AD1172), was excavated in Chaozhou. In the reports, the authors, quoting the *Guangdong tongzhi* (Gazetteer of guangdong) mentioned that Liu Jing was a native of Chaoyang. However, according to the Jiajing version of the *Chaozhou zhi*, and a genealogy of the Lu family of Taokeng, Liu Jing was the second son of Liu Yu, from Haiyang. In early Song, both Chaoyang and Haiyang was under the jurisdiction of Chaozhou. The Liu family, living in Donghu at the back of Hanshan (Bijiashan), was a most powerful and prosperous clan in Chaozhou. Inscriptions found on ceramic statutes and bronze temple bells carry names of the Liu family.

4. Wu Liuqi and Hao Shangjiu

Of all the exhibits, the rubbing of the stone tablet from the tomb of Wu Liuqi in Huliaoxu, Dapu (supp. illustration 5) is probably the most valuable historical document. The upper portion of the tablet was inscribed with the imperial eulogy written by the Kangxi emperor and the main text composed by Yang Xunying, a native of Fujian and a Regional Inspector of Guangdong. The inscription was copied by Yang Zhongyue, a native of Chenghai, and Luo Wanjie, a native of Jieyang wrote the title in seal script.

The text records the military expeditions and battles that Wu Liuqi took part, especially the battle against the Ming loyalist Hao Shangjiu in the 10th year, Shenzhi (AD1653). Apart from these, the tablet also supplies valuable information on the relationship between Wu and Zha Yiheng.

大金貞祐寶券貳拾貫元至

貳貫

壹貫

主要參考書目

1. 羅香林，《香港新發現南明永曆四年所造大砲考》，《大學生活》，1957年第2卷第9期。
2. 麥英豪，《廣州發現南漢鉛錢》，《考古通訊》，1958年4期。
3. 饒宗頤，《九龍與宋季史料》，香港，1959。
4. 羅香林等，《香港前代史，1842年前香港及其對外交通》，香港，1959。
5. 饒宗頤，《九龍與宋季史料補遺》，《香港大學中文學會年刊》，1960。
6. 簡又文，《宋皇台紀念集》，香港，1960。
7. 林曦，《廣東揭陽明墓發現"蔡伯喈"戲曲抄本》，《文物》，1961年1期。
8. 許舒，《石壁出土遺物初步報告》，《香港考古學會會刊》，第2卷，1962。
9. 子稚，《潮安王大寶墓》，《羊城晚報》，1962年6月1日。
10. 曾廣億，《廣東惠陽白馬山古瓷窰調查記》，《考古》，1962年8期。
11. 廣東省文管會等，《廣東惠陽新菴三村古瓷窰發掘簡報》，《考古》，1964年4期。
12. 商承祚，《廣州石馬村南漢墓葬清理簡報》，《考古》1964年6期。
13. 廣東省文管會，《廣東出土的古代陶罈續介》，《考古》，1965年6期。
14. 古列治，《明末火炮》，《香港皇家亞洲學會刊》，第7卷，1967。
15. 屈志仁，《石壁出土宋錢及陶瓷》，《香港考古學會會刊》，第1卷，1968。
16. 屈志仁，《石壁出土蓋罐一對》，《香港皇家亞洲學會刊》，第9卷，1969。
17. 屈志仁，《香港出土宋瓷簡報》，《香港皇家亞洲學會刊》，第十一卷，1971。
18. 蔣順洪，《香港大埔碗窰陶業初探》，香港，1973。
19. 曾廣億，《廣東珠海、汕頭出土的元明瓷器》、《文物》，1974年10期。
20. 屈志仁，《香港發現之暹羅陶及其有關問題》，(未刊稿)，1974。
21. 霍羅仕，《糧船灣洲沙咀，I》，《香港考古學會會刊》，第5卷，1974。
22. 何清顯等，《糧船灣洲沙咀，II》，《香港考古學會會刊》，第5卷，1974。
23. 麥英豪，《關於廣州石馬村南漢墓的年代與墓主問題》，《考古》，1975年1期。
24. 廣東省博物館，《西沙文物——中國南海諸島之一西沙羣島調查》，北京，文物出版社，1975年。
25. 霍羅仕，《沙洲》，《香港考古學會會刊》，第5卷，1976。
26. 廣東省博物館等，《廣東省西沙羣島第二次文物調查簡報》，《文物》，1976年9期。
27. 何紀生，《東沙羣島發現的古代銅錢》，《文物》，1976年9期。
28. 霍羅仕，《稔樹灣》，《香港考古學會會刊》，第7卷，1979。
29. 曾廣億，《廣東陵水、順德、揭陽出土的宋代瓷器、漁獵工具和元代鈔版》，《考古》，1980年1期。
30. 科大衞，《祖墓出土陶罈》，《香港皇家亞洲學會會刊》，第21卷，1981。
31. 古運泉，《廣東高要縣發現明初銅鐵銃》，《文物》，1981年4期。
32. 楊豪，《清初吳六奇墓及其殉葬遺物》，《文物》，1982年2期。
33. 曹騰騑，《廣東揭陽出土明抄戲曲蔡伯喈略談》，《文物》，1982年11期。
34. 曹騰騑等，《廣東海康元墓出土陰綫刻磚》，《考古學集刊》，第2集，1982年。
35. 蕭國健，《清代香港之海防與古壘》，香港，1982。
36. 蕭國健，《族譜與香港地方史研究》，香港，1982。
37. 周月齡，《略論香港大埔碗窰村的青花》，(未刊稿)，香港，1982。
38. 葉祖康，《活的歷史——保護香港的歷史建築》，香港，1982。
39. 宋艮壁，《介紹一件元代釉裏褐鳳鳥紋蓋罐》，《文物》，1983年1期。
40. 曾廣億等，《廣東瓷器》，上海，上海人民美術出版社，1983年。
41. 饒宗頤，《港、九前代考古雜錄》，《新亞學術集刊，中國藝術專號》，1983。

42. 吳毓璘,《新安縣志——香港地區地方誌》,香港,1983。
43. 廣東省博物館,《廣東陽春縣發現南漢錢範》,《考古》,1984年4期。
44. 廣東省博物館,《廣東紫金縣宋墓出土石雕》,《考古》,1984年6期。
45. 金馬倫,《赤臘角深灣村——唐代作坊遺址》,《香港考古學會會刊》,第10卷,1984。
46. 黃玉質,《記曲江南華寺北宋木雕羅漢像》,《嶺南文史》,1985年1期。
47. 林天蔚,《香港前代史論集》,台北,1985。
48. 蕭國健,《香港離島史蹟志》,香港,1985。
49. 許舒,《大嶼山竹篙灣考古遺址》,《香港考古學會會刊》,第11卷,1986。
50. 高維法,《香港發現的窖藏宋錢》,《香港考古學會會刊》,第11卷,1986。
51. 蕭國健,《清初遷海前後香港之社會變遷》,台北,1986。
52. 科大衛等,《香港碑銘彙編》,香港,1986。
53. 楊揚,《古粵瓷枕》,《羊城晚報》,1987年6月23日。
54. 宋艮壁,《廣東南雄出土一批宋代銀鋌》,《文物資料叢刊》,第10輯,1987年。
55. 林業強,《大埔碗窰——香港十九至二十世紀窰址》,《東亞藝術風格,亞洲美術考古論叢》,倫敦,卷14,1987。
56. 秦維廉,《大嶼山竹篙灣明代貿易遺址》,《香港考古學會會刊》,第12卷,1988。
57. 白爾德,《香港文物誌》,香港,1988。
58. 林業強,《香港大嶼山竹篙灣出土十五世紀晚期至十六世紀初青花瓷》,《香港考古學會會刊》,第12卷,1988。

Selected Bibliography:

1. Luo Xianglin, "On the Newly Discovered Southern Ming Iron Cannon", *Daxue Shenghuo*, Vol. II, No. 9, 1957.
2. Mai Yinghao, "Southern Han Lead Coins Discovered in Guangzhou", *Kaogu tongxun*, 1958:4.
3. Rao Zongyi, *Kowloon in Historical Records of Sung Dynasty*, Hong Kong, 1959.
4. Luo Xianglin, et al, *Hong Kong and Its External Communications before 1842*, Hong Kong, 1959.
5. Rao Zongyi, "A Supplement to 'Kowloon in Historical Records of the Song Dynasty'", *Journal of the Chinese Society, University of Hong Kong*, 1960.
6. Jian Youwen, *Sung Wong Tai, A Commemorative Volume*, Hong Kong, 1960.
7. Lin Xi, "Manuscript of Cai Bojie Script Discovered in a Ming Tomb in Jieyang, Guangdong", *Wenwu*, 1961:1.
8. Hayes, James W., "Preliminary Report on the Finds at Shek Pik", *Journal of the Hong Kong Branch of the Royal Asiatic Society*, Vol. II, 1962.
9. Zizhi, "The Wang Dabao Tomb in Chao'an", *Yangcheng wanbao*, 1:6:1962.
10. Zeng Guangyi, 'Investigations of Ancient Kiln Sites in Baimashan, Huiyang, Guangdong", *Kaogu*, 1962:8.
11. CPAM, Guangdong, "Brief Excavation Reports of Ancient Kiln Sites at Sancun, Xin'an, Huiyang, Guangdong", *Kaogu*, 1964:4.
12. Shang Chengzhuo, "Brief Report on the Southern Han Tomb in Shimacun, Guangzhou", *Kaogu*, 1964:6.
13. CPAM, Guangdong, "More Ancient Pottery Urns from Guangdong", *Kaogu*, 1965:6.
14. Goodrich, L. Carrington, "A Cannon from the End of the Ming Period", *Journal of the Hong Kong Branch of the Royal Asiatic Society*, Vol. 7, 1967.
15. Watt, James C.Y., "Finds of Sung Coins and Porcelain at Shek Pik, Lantau Island, 1962", *Journal of the Hong Kong Archaeological Society*, Vol. 1, 1968.
16. Watt, James C.Y., "A Pair of Pottery Covered Jars Found at Shek Pik, Lantau Island", *Journal of the Hong Kong Branch of the Royal Asiatic Society*, Vol. 9, 1969.
17. Watt, James C.Y., "A Brief Report on Sung-type Pottery Finds in Hong Kong", *Journal of the Hong Kong Branch of the Royal Asiatic Society*, Vol. 11, 1971.
18. Tjio Soen-hong, *Preliminary Study of the Ceramic Industry of Wanyao at Dapu*, Hong Kong, 1973.
19. Zeng Guangyi, "Yuan and Ming Porcelain Discovered in Zhuhai and Shantao, Guangdong", *Wenwu*, 1974:10.
20. Watt, James C.Y., "*Thai Ceramics Discovered in Hong Kong and Some Related Problems*", Unpublished paper, Hong Kong, 1974.
21. Frost, R.J., "Sha Tsui, High Island - Part I", *Journal of the Hong Kong Archaeological Society*, Vol. V, 1974.
22. Ho Ching Hin, et al, "Sha Tsui, High Island, Part II", *Journal of the Hong Kong Archaeological Society*, Vol. V, 1974.
23. Mai Yinghao, "The Date and Identity of the Southern Han Tomb in Shimacun, Guangzhou", *Kaogu*, 1975:1.
24. Guangdong Provincial Museum, *Xisha Wenwu - Investigations on the Paracel Islands, South China Sea*, Beijing, 1975.
25. Frost, R.J., "Sha Chau", *Journal of the Hong Kong Archaeological Society*, Vol. V, 1976.
26. Guangdong Provincial Museum, et al, "Second Cultural Relics Investigations on the Paracel Islands, Guangdong", *Wenwu*, 1976:9.
27. He Jisheng, "Ancient copper coins discovered in the Donsha Islands", *Wenwu*, 1976:9.
28. Frost, R.J., "Nim Shu Wan", *Journal of the Hong Kong Archaeological Society*, Vol. VII, 1979.
29. Zeng Guangyi, "Song Porcelain, Hunting and Fishing Tools and Yuan Block for Papernotes Unearthed in Lingshui, Shunde, and Jieyang, Guangdong", *Kaogu*, 1980:1.
30. Faure, David, "Funeral Pots from an Ancestral Grave", *Journal of the Hong Kong Branch of the Royal Asiatic Society*, Vol. 21, 1981.
31. Gu Yunquan, "Early Ming Brass and Iron Cannons Discovered in Gaoyao County, Guangdong", *Wenwu*, 1981:4.
32. Yang Hao, "The Early Qing Tomb of Wu Liuqi and Its Funerary Objects", *Wenwu*, 1982:2.
33. Cao Tengfei, "Some Notes on the Cai Bojie Drama Script Unearthed in Jieyang, Guangdong", *Wenwu*, 1982:11.
34. Cao Tengfei, "Bricks with Incised Designs from a Yuan Tomb in Haikang, Guangdong", *Kaoguxue jikan*, No.2, 1982.
35. Xiao Guojian, *Ch'ing Fortifications in Hong Kong*, Hong Kong, 1982.
36. Xiao Guojian, et al, *Studies on Chinese Genealogies and the History of the Hong Kong Region*, Hong Kong, 1982.
37. Zhou Yueling, *On the Blue and White Kiln Site in Wanyao Village at Dapu, Hong Kong*, Unpublished thesis, Qinan University, 1982.
38. Yip, C.H., *History around Us, Preserving our Historic Buildings*, Hong Kong, 1982.
39. Song Liangbi, "A Covered Jar with Underglaze Brown Phoenixes Design", *Wenwu*, 1983:1.
40. Zeng Guangyi, et al, *Guangdong ciqi*, Shanghai, 1983.
41. Rao Zongyi, "Miscellaneous Archaeological and Historical Notes on the History of Hong Kong and Kowloon", *New Asia Academic Bulletin, Special Issue on Chinese Art*, Vol. IV, 1983.

42. Ng, Peter Y.L., *New Peace County, A Chinese Gazetteer of the Hong Kong Region*, Hong Kong, 1983.
43. Guangdong Provincial Museum, "Southern Han Coin Moulds Discovered in Yangchun County, Guangdong", *Kaogu*, 1984:4.
44. Guangdong Provincial Museum, "Stone Sculptures Unearthed in a Song Tomb in Zijin County, Guangdong", *Kaogu*, 1984:6.
45. Cameron H., et al, "Shan Wan Tsuen, Chek Lap Kok, (A Tang Dynasty Industrial Site)", *Journal of the Hong Kong Archaeological Society*, Vol. X, 1984.
46. Huang Yuzhi, "Wooden Lohan Figures in the Nanhua Temple in Qujiang", *Lingnan wenshi*, 1985:1.
47. Lin Tianwei, et al, *A Collection of Papers on the History of Hong Kong*, Taibei, 1985.
48. Xiao Guojian, *Some Hong Kong Outlying Islands in History*, Hong Kong, 1985.
49. Hayes, James, "Archaeological Site at Penny's Bay, Lantau", *Journal of the Hong Kong Archaeological Society*, Vol. XI, 1986.
50. Crawford, James, R., "Southern Sung Coin Hoards from Hong Kong", *Journal of the Hong Kong Archaeological Society*, Vol XI, 1986.
51. Xiao Guojian, *The Social Change in Hong Kong before and after the Compulsory Evacuation in Early Qing*, Taibei, 1986.
52. Faure, David, et al, *Historical Inscriptions of Hong Kong*, Hong Kong, 1986.
53. Yang Yang, "Ancient Ceramic Pillows from Guangdong", *Yangcheng wanbao*, 23:6:1987.
54. Song Liangbi, "A Group of Silver Ingots Unearthed in Nanxiong, Guangdong", *Wenwu ziliao congkan*, Vol. 10, 1987.
55. Lam, Peter Y.K., "Dapu Wanyao: a 19th-20th Century Kiln Site in Hong Kong", *Style in East Asian Tradition, Colloquies on Art and Archaeology in Asia*, No. 14, London, 1987.
56. Meacham, William, "A Ming Trading Site at Penny's Bay, Lantau", *Journal of the Hong Kong Archaeological Society*, Vol. 12, 1988.
57. Bard, Solomon, *In Search of the Past: A Guide to the Antiquities of Hong Kong*, Hong Kong, 1988.
58. Lam, Peter Y.K., "Late 15th to Early 16th Century Blue and White Porcelain from Penny's Bay, Lantau, Hong Kong", *Journal of the Hong Kong Archaeological Society*, vol. 12, 1988.

展品說明:
（粵方）:楊少祥、邱立誠
（港方）:林業強
編輯:林業強
設計:梁超權
繪圖:黃鳳好、陳紅冰
照片:楊少祥
攝影:葉立中、梁超權
暗室:葉立中、關子鴻
校對:陳步遠、鄒少貞

Credits:
Descriptive Entries:
(Guangdong) Yang Shaoxiang, Qiu Licheng
(Hong Kong) Peter Y.K. Lam
Editor and Translation: Peter Y.K. Lam
Design: Leung Chiu-kuen
Line Drawings: Huang Fenghao, Chen Hongbing
Rubbings: Yang Shaoxiang
Photography: Sidney L.C. Yip, Leung Chiu-kuen
Darkroom: Sidney L.C. Yip, Kwan Tze-hung
Proofreading: Vivian P.Y. Chan, Chou Siu-ching